Migration, Homeland, and Belonging in Eurasia

Migration, Homeland, and Belonging in Eurasia

Edited by Cynthia J. Buckley
and Blair A. Ruble
with Erin Trouth Hofmann

Woodrow Wilson Center Press
Washington, D.C.

The Johns Hopkins University Press
Baltimore

EDITORIAL OFFICES
Woodrow Wilson Center Press
One Woodrow Wilson Plaza
1300 Pennsylvania Avenue, N.W.
Washington, D.C. 20004-3027
Telephone: 202-691-4029
www.wilsoncenter.org

ORDER FROM
The Johns Hopkins University Press
Hampden Station
P.O. Box 50370
Baltimore, Maryland 21211
Telephone: 1-800-537-5487
www.press.jhu.edu/books/

Printed in the United States of America on acid-free paper ∞

2 4 6 8 9 7 5 3 1

Library of Congress Cataloging-in-Publication Data

Migration, homeland, and belonging in Eurasia / edited by Cynthia J. Buckley and Blair A. Ruble with Erin Trouth Hofmann.
p. cm.
Includes index.
ISBN 978-0-8018-9075-8 (hardcover : alk. paper)
1. Former Soviet Republics—Emigration and immigration. 2. Nationalism—Former Soviet Republics. 3. Soviet Union—Emigration and immigration. 4. Forced migration—Soviet Union. 5. Minorities—Soviet Union. 6. Russia (Federation)—Emigration and immigration—Government policy. 7. Migration, Internal—Russia (Federation)—Siberia. 8. Crimean Tatars. 9. Russian Germans. 10. Jews, Russian. I. Buckley, Cynthia J. II. Ruble, Blair A., 1949– III. Hofmann, Erin Trouth.
JV8181.M55 2008
325.47—dc22

2008015571

The Woodrow Wilson International Center for Scholars, established by Congress in 1968 and headquartered in Washington, D.C., is the living, national memorial to President Wilson.

The Center is a nonpartisan institution of advanced research, supported by public and private funds, engaged in the study of national and world affairs. The Center establishes and maintains a neutral forum for free, open, and informed dialogue.

The Center's mission is to commemorate the ideals and concerns of Woodrow Wilson by providing a link between the world of ideas and the world of policy, by bringing a broad spectrum of individuals together to discuss important public policy issues, by serving to bridge cultures and viewpoints, and by seeking to find common ground.

Conclusions or opinions expressed in Center publications and programs are those of the authors and speakers and do not necessarily reflect the views of the Center staff, fellows, trustees, advisory groups, or any individuals or organizations that provide financial support to the Center.

The Center is the publisher of *The Wilson Quarterly* and home of Woodrow Wilson Center Press, *dialogue* radio and television, and the monthly newsletter "Centerpoint." For more information about the Center's activities and publications, please visit us on the web at www.wilsoncenter.org.

Contents

Tables and Figures

Tables

Figures

Acknowledgments

This volume is the product of two workshops on immigration, forced migrants, and refugees in Eurasia hosted by the Kennan Institute of the Woodrow Wilson International Center for Scholars in Washington. The workshops, held in March 2004 and January 2005, brought together an interdisciplinary group of scholars to discuss the causes and consequences of migration in Eurasia, both past and present. The workshops allowed scholars from different backgrounds to share their diverse research and discover common themes related to population movements in the former Soviet Union.

The Kennan Institute has sponsored sixteen similar topic-specific working groups and workshops since 1996. Each group has been designed to bring together scholars engaged in a related area of research from varying perspectives. These multidisciplinary, multinational, and multigenerational sessions have explored such topics as civil society, social capital, and development in Eurasia (1996–98); urban civic cultural and democratic transitions (1997–2000); regional Russia (1998–99); rural Russia (1998–2000); Russia's and Ukraine's experience of economic and political transformation (1999–2001); marketization and democratization in Russia (2000–1); the role of women in postcommunist transitions (2001–2); integrating Russia into Europe (2001–3); multicultural legacies in Russia and Ukraine (2002–3); contemporary and historical perspectives on conflict in the former Soviet Union (2002–3); Russia and the world (2005); diverse cultures in contemporary society (2005–6); state and society relations in transnational societies (2005–6); religion in post-Soviet societies (2005–6); civil society and democracy in Ukraine (2006–7); and international development assistance in the post-Soviet space (2007–8). These forums enable researchers to present their research, share ideas, and develop common themes and policy insights within their projects. Research discussed at the first workshop meeting becomes the basis for the plan of a book, with participants returning home to write original papers on the new topics before convening once again for a final manuscript review.[1]

This format challenges each participant to prepare new work that is substantially different from what he or she has published before. It produces a collective voice that rises above the sum of its individual parts. This process thus achieves two important goals. First, it produces a publication of lasting value. Second, it encourages the formation of a thematic "invisible college" that takes on a life of its own as the group disperses.

Funding for the workshops on immigration, forced migrants, and refugees in Eurasia was provided by the U.S. Department of State Program for Research and Training on Eastern Europe and the Independent States of the Former Soviet Union (the Title VIII Program), and the Kennan Institute's George F. Kennan Fund. Kennan Institute staff members Margaret Paxson, Erin Trouth Hofmann, and Markian Dobczansky, and Woodrow Wilson Center Comparative Urban Studies Program staff members Lisa Hanley and Mejgan Massoumi were involved in making the workshops a success. The Institute for Innovation, Creativity, and Capital at the University of Texas, Austin, provided support during the editorial stages of work on the manuscript.

We are very grateful to the funders of the workshop, the staff members who were involved in the project, and all the participants in the migration workshops for making this volume possible.

1. Five books have appeared as a result of the work done at these workshops (all published by Woodrow Wilson Center Press and Johns Hopkins University Press): Blair A. Ruble, Jodi Koehn, and Nancy Popson, eds., *Fragmented Space in the Russian Federation* (2001); David O'Brien and Stephen Wegren, eds., *Rural Reform in Post-Soviet Russia* (2002); Kathleen Kuehnast and Carol Nechemias, eds., *Post-Soviet Women Encountering Transition: Nation Building, Economic Survival, and Civic Activism* (2004); Dominique Arel and Blair A. Ruble, eds., *Rebounding Identities: The Politics of Identity in Russia and Ukraine* (2006); and Douglas W. Blum, ed., *Russia and Globalization: Identity, Security, and Society in an Era of Change* (2008).

Migration, Homeland, and Belonging in Eurasia

Introduction: New Approaches to Migration and Belonging in Eurasia

Cynthia J. Buckley

> Home is a name, a word, it is a strong one; stronger than magician ever spoke, or spirit ever answered to, in the strongest conjuration.
>
> —Charles Dickens

National and international migrations are pervasive processes. Though forms of mobility are diverse, migration is a historically persistent phenomenon, systematically patterned by historical, social, and political contexts.[1] Population movements across the globe are tied to the simultaneous and conflicting processes of global homogenization and regional reification, raising new issues in the conceptualization of citizenship, belonging, and place. The complexity and diversity of contemporary human migration flows challenge standard approaches to the study of how states develop policy agendas, exert control over their borders, and govern their populations.

Mass movements have broadened the possibilities for identity construction and exposed myriad complications concerning the process of migrant integration and acceptance. At the same time, the structural contexts of migration decisionmaking are changing. Increasingly complex visa regimes, employment permits, and guest worker programs add to the administrative challenges that migrants must navigate, while expansions in global communication and improvements in travel expand the array of possible destinations. These structural changes may increase both access to and the importance of social networks for facilitating migration, for overcoming barriers, and for accessing information. Often, network ties link back to migrant perceptions of belonging, influencing identity construction and conceptualizations of home. They can also serve to reinforce ties to communities of origin for some migrants or to assist the integration and assimilation into communities of destination for others. Challenges to migrant assimilation and acceptance, whether in terms of access to legal standing, citizenship, or social inclusion, are growing across destination states in North America, Europe, and Eurasia. In what continues to be a world in motion, the processes of economic integration, social and cultural acceptance, citizenship, and homeland remain contentious.

This collection of essays focuses upon migration experiences within Eurasia, highlighting the unique ways political concerns, historical experience, community identities, and economic context shape migration processes and perceptions of belonging. The contributors to this volume seek to integrate the Eurasian experience into global discussions of migration systems and processes, providing a richer theoretical understanding of migration processes in the region, while offering case studies to extend and challenge present approaches to migration. The volume reflects a series of workshops held at the Kennan Institute of the Woodrow Wilson International Center for Scholars in Washington, supported by the U.S. State Department, which brought together scholars from a variety of disciplines and backgrounds for extended conversations concerning historical and contemporary migration processes in Eurasia. By incorporating disciplinary orientations from political science, anthropology, geography, sociology, urban planning, and history, these workshop discussions and debates reflected two central tendencies in many Eurasian migration studies to date: ethnic determinism and state control.[2]

Ethnicity and Approaches to Migration in Eurasia

First, ethnicity (and, to varying extents, language) has long been viewed as the critical marker of belonging and legitimacy, either in terms of citizenship or claims to regional authority and autonomy across much of Eurasia. These approaches, often linked to primordialist conceptualizations of ethnicity, draw support from the unique Leninist nationality legacy of the Soviet era, the recent revival of titular language requirements for citizenship in regions such as the Baltic countries, and current ethnic hostilities and conflict in Central Asia and the Caucasus. In broader studies of migration processes, the operation of migrants' ethnic identities is well developed, whether at their place of origin or destination—through social networks, connections to a unique structural status (e.g., citizenship), access to information (language), an ability to integrate socially and economically into destination societies, and perceptions of social exclusion.[3]

With some notable exceptions, approaches to migration in Eurasia tend to emphasize ethnic identity itself as the main motivator of migration, in some cases hampering examinations of the interwoven relationships between ethnicity and socioeconomic factors.[4] This lessens the potential linkages to classical economic approaches to migration, which focus on the economic returns from migration, or to neoclassical approaches, which incorporate family strategies and risk management. Even more problematic, ethnic approaches can sometimes hide the complex composition of migration flows, veiling the potential importance of factors such as age, health, gender, class, and family status. Focusing on ethnicity alone as a static identity minimizes the importance of individual characteristics and their relationship to agency, serving as a barrier to engagement with active areas of inquiry within the migration literature such as migrant selectivity, health, transnationalism, and particularly gender.[5]

Theorizing the role of ethnicity in migration is challenging. Ethnic identity is often a consideration in the development of restrictive entrance requirements for immigrants, and it can be an overt or hidden category in structural factors encouraging exits from migrant-sending regions. Related issues of language, religion, or other cultural practices linked to ethnicity can serve to assist migrants in settling into migrant-receiving cultures similar to their own or into enclaves of co-ethnics. Ethnic groups may find it beneficial to maintain their original traditions and behaviors in host societies, becoming model minorities reaping high rates of economic advancement.[6] At the same time, ethnicity, and its related cultural practices, can provide a powerful barrier to integration, either culturally or economically, precluding assimilation into host societies even into the second and third generations.[7]

Ethnicity is linked closely to dual labor market theory, which extends classical and neoclassical approaches to migration. This approach posits that barriers to economic integration stem from the relegation of migrants to secondary labor markets. Thus, migrants—faced with dangerous, dirty, and demeaning labor that native workers will not undertake—seldom break into the primary labor market, and their labor market choices are not directly related to wage fluctuations and employment trends in the primary labor market. Ethnic migrants, whether Tajiks in Moscow, Algerians in Paris, or Guatemalans in Houston, find their ethnic identities reinforced and defined for their host society by their marginal economic position. As Brettell and Sargent contend, migrants occupy "multiple subject positions, some they define and others defined for them."[8] The persistent power of ethnicity as a marker of identity and difference among migrants, and as an important enabling or disabling factor in migration processes, highlights the concrete, complex nature of ethnicity as a defining identity. Far from the globalized economy, where place is conceptual and identity is constructed by choice, ethnicity remains remarkably resonant.

What can the migration experiences of Eurasia add to discussions of ethnicity, migration, and incorporation? Eurasia's unique legacy of Soviet-era Russification and simultaneous support for ethnic-language schooling, ethnic classification, and autonomous ethnic homelands across the USSR introduce conflicting historical influences, adding complexity to the negotiation and maintenance of identity. The Eurasian experience both supports and challenges traditional approaches to assimilation, which view migrant adaptation and integration as increasing generation by generation.[9] The persistent salience of ethnicity as a marker of individual identity within the Soviet context tended to limit the extent to which minority groups could hope to, or wish to, assimilate into majority cultures while maintaining their ethnic identity.[10] Educational policies stressing native-language instruction and political structures reifying ideas of ethnic homelands reinforced the primacy of ethnic identity. Rather than generating a multicultural society where identities were equal and rights were uniform, there were often ethnic hierarchies, which sometimes (especially in families of mixed marriages) motivated ethnic reidentification.[11]

In the post-Soviet period, overlapping political and social perceptions regarding ethnicity, nationality, and homeland have percolated, leading to contested ideas of linkages between ethnic identity, residence, language, and rights to citizenship, particularly in the Baltic states.[12] The dissolution of the Soviet Union and the creation of fifteen new successor states enabled citizens to "vote with their feet" by moving to the regions that best suited to their interests, reflecting complex and deeply embedded ties to place, real or imagined. Language and ethnicity alone are not always the whole story.

As Pilkington reports, ethnic Russians repatriated to the Russian Federation were seen as culturally different by local Russians, but their perceived otherness was mediated by the resonance of primordial approaches to ethnicity in Russia.[13] Approaches to ethnicity in Eurasia, whether in the media or academic literature, have seldom questioned the permanence of ethnicity and may prove valuable in reassessments of ethnicity and migration. Though today's diverse, large-scale global mobility may identify all individuals as potential migrants who could utilize formal and informal resources to select destinations, the evidence from Eurasia can help illuminate the persistence of shared identity and how ethnicity is linked to perceptions of homeland in justifying residence socially and politically.

The Interventionist State in Eurasian Migration

Approaches to migration within Eurasia are also marked by a conscious focus on the power of the state to manage migration, thus running the risk of failing to engage with growing literatures investigating the limits of individual states in controlling migration processes.[14] Far from calling into question the authoritarian nature of rule in the Russian Empire or Soviet Union, researching these regimes' policy formation processes and conflicting interests vis-à-vis migration policy provides a dynamic opportunity to view such highly centralized states in action. Thus, a careful examination of the effect of migration control techniques (using registration documents, work permits, and exit visas) can provide insight into the validity of official records concerning population, uncover the unanticipated consequences of state intervention, and delineate the characteristics that enable individuals and groups to circumvent state policies directing migration and population settlement.

Throughout history, mass deportations and restrictive internal migration policies have trammeled the life chances of communities and individuals within Eurasia, evincing extraordinarily costly state interventions in migration processes implemented with a unique disregard for human rights. To more fully understand these deportations and policies, scholars need to explain the economic and social factors within targeted communities and the larger social context that enabled or challenged their implementation. For instance, what happened over time within the ethnic enclaves created by deported communities? Insightful work by Hill and Gaddy highlights the massive long-term economic costs of maintaining the Siberian settlements grown by the Gulag system of the Soviet era, raising questions about the unintended consequences of other state interventions in migration processes.[15]

By focusing on the state as the main actor of influence (and official registration statistics as the main source of information), scholars of migration in Eurasia sometimes miss valuable opportunities to incorporate their studies into the active debates on the limits of state intervention, the estimation of unregistered migration across the globe, and the standard economic theories underpinning many analyses of migration.[16] Soviet-era migration studies, by centering on the scientific management of population, tended to develop in parallel to rather than in conversation with approaches focusing on microlevel decisionmaking and agency. Within global migration studies, theoretical approaches that stress macro forces, such as world systems theory, have rarely engaged directly with analyses of migration trends in socialist economies or the so-called second world. World systems theory's globally integrated approach emphasizes the importance of colonial linkages and capitalist market penetration as key factors in developing the structures that encourage migration from the periphery to the core; thus, it has rarely been used in analyses of authoritarian states such as the Soviet Union, which instead have focused on the internal practices that sought to scientifically manage the labor resources within a state's boundaries.

Authoritarian state management, whether successful or unsuccessful, has often been an important characteristic of migration in Eurasia. Attempts to control urbanization through the use of residency permits were well known during the Soviet period and can be traced back to limits on migration to Saint Petersburg and Moscow in the seventeenth century.[17] Restrictions on the mobility of rural residents, which were embedded in the social structure of Imperial Russia, also survived throughout the Soviet era.[18] Outmigration was tightly controlled in both the Imperial and Soviet periods, and forced migration was employed to quell dissent or punish specific, typically ethnic, populations viewed as threatening state security or challenging state authority.[19] State interventions also encouraged migration with ideological and financial incentives, particularly to target areas designated as strategically or economically important. The Virgin Lands campaign to encourage migration to northern Kazakhstan during the Khrushchev era stands out for both the strong ideological framing used to motivate migration and the large number of migrants resettled.[20] As in other countries, Soviet attempts to control migration had unanticipated and costly consequences, while often failing to achieve their goals.[21]

Focusing on the role of the state in migration decisionmaking tends to obfuscate the importance of undocumented or irregular migration in Eurasia, by framing population movements as processes effectively controlled, directed, and counted. With respect to Russia, there is overwhelming evidence for widespread irregular and undocumented migration during the Imperial, Soviet, and post-Soviet periods. As Gatrell documents, Imperial administrators were woefully unable to manage the massive movements of refugees and displaced persons into and within Russia as a result of World War I, leading to claims of lawlessness, disease, and danger.[22] Later, as the Soviet system matured, persistent labor shortages in some regions of the Soviet Union prompted the use of either officially organized or undocumented seasonal labor brigades. Such seasonal migrants often came from the southern tier of the USSR and provided both valuable labor resources to labor-short areas such as western Siberia and important earning opportunities for men from the Caucasus and Central Asia.[23]

Managing migration became nearly impossible in the post-Soviet period. Migration across Eurasia was made possible by open visa regimes among many of the newly independent states and spurred by opportunities for citizenship in Russia, Germany, and Israel; attempts to unify families within new national boundaries; and the severe but varied economic dislocation associated with the dissolution of the Soviet Union. The resulting increase in migration occurred while political and institutional restructuring constrained states' capacities to monitor, let alone manage, vast migration flows. This diminished state ability to measure migration and increasing international contacts have encouraged the emergence of such countries as Ukraine and Russia as important new transit points for "irregular" migrants and human trafficking both within and outside the former Soviet Union.[24] In Russia, growing numbers of unregistered arrivals and departures have raised both internal and international economic and military security concerns.[25] Undocumented migration, estimated in the tens of millions, calls into question the ability of states to "manage migration." Moreover, undocumented migration highlights the need to explain the factors that push individuals and groups to migrate, pull them toward destinations or transit points, and encourage their desires to migrate—as well as the need to elucidate the mechanisms that enable them to realize their migration choices.

The ability of states to intervene effectively in migration processes, particularly in migrant-receiving countries, is a vibrant area of discussion and debate in the migration literature. Stephen Castles, in his assessment of the return of guest worker programs throughout Europe, points out that many states continue to seek methods for importing labor rather than allowing in immigrants.[26] Not only have such programs failed historically, but their very adoption comes only at significant costs in democratic ideals and adherence to fundamental human rights. In an earlier examination of state policies toward international migration, Massey attributes variations in state immigration policy to five key factors in receiving states: the intensity of labor demand, the existence of democratic institutions, constitutionalism, an independent judiciary, and immigration tradition.[27] This framework provides an important initial model for understanding the institutional relations that make possible the extremely restrictive immigration policies of the Gulf states in comparison with the ongoing conflicts over immigration policy in North America and Western Europe. In an era of universal human rights, democratic states with independent judiciaries, particularly those backed by clear constitutional assurances, provide immigrants with avenues to gain political inclusion and to claim their rights. Particularly in states with high labor demands and a tradition of immigrant inclusion, restrictive immigration policies are incompatible with the attitudes and institutions associated with democratic societies. The conflicting goals of maintaining authority over entry and maintaining rights-based ideologies leads many developed countries to a contentious and volatile crossroads of vacillation between restrictive and inclusive immigration policies.[28]

The resurgence of interest in migrants' remittances and the role of diasporas in economic development in recent years highlight the importance of migrant-sending states' interests, raising a different set of policy concerns. How can sending states best harness the development potential of remittances? How can diaspora populations help or hinder international relations? How can sending states maintain cultural and economic linkages with migrants? There is still substantial academic debate over the economic benefits for sending countries of either temporary out-migration or remittance receipts.[29] Migrant remittances do represent a large and unrestricted capital flow to sending states, unfettered by the limitations of international aid and without the credit liability of development loans. Numerous national and private development organizations participate in and sponsor a wide variety of remittance initiatives across migrant-sending regions, including small-scale investment and community banking programs and entrepreneurship development,[30] but a consensus on how to extract the maximum development benefits from remittances remains elusive. The processes that encourage social, political, and cultural ties to diaspora populations and maintain psychological ties to home are also important areas of theoretical and policy interest, representing diverse approaches and orientations.[31]

In both migrant-sending and -receiving states, what can Eurasia's experiences bring to discussions of state intervention in migration processes?

The Eurasian region provides a uniquely valuable opportunity to examine the forces shaping the newly independent states' policies during their incorporation into global capitalism, potentially adding to our understanding of world systems approaches. Likewise, the continuing importance of Soviet-era networks and migration patterns gives researchers important opportunities to examine the influence of postimperial linkages in spurring migration and maintaining inequalities across Eurasia. Historically, the region offers numerous, blatant examples of extreme state-based migration interventions, providing useful test cases for the importance of institutional context, state capacity requirements for implementation, and the short- and long-term economic costs of such policies. Recent moves across the region—rhetorical and otherwise—toward democratization, judicial independence, constitutionalism, and inclusion in international protocols for human rights may combine with high labor demand to encourage open migration policies in receiving nations, such as Russia. Conversely, the powerful historical legacy of intervention, control, and approaches to identity and belonging based on ethnicity may prove more effective in steering states' migration policies toward restrictive approaches.

Migrant-sending states in Eurasia, beset by the dislocations of their economic transition, are particularly vulnerable to fluctuations in migration policy in receiving regions. Because Eurasia's southern tier, particularly Tajikistan and the southern Caucasus, remains heavily reliant on migrants' remittances for survival, its experiences can provide insights into the potential development effect of remittances in extremely poor nations.[32] The rapid growth of this region's commercial banking sector may facilitate sending remittances, but underdeveloped investment opportunities and extreme deprivation may combine to minimize remittances' development potential. Remittance flows within the region also highlight the complex implications of large financial flows, with press reports of billions being sent from receiving countries often used to excite anti-immigrant sentiments and encourage migration restrictions in destination states.[33]

New Directions: Decisionmaking, Sociopolitical Inclusion, and Perceptions of Belonging

The contributors to this volume have brought a wide variety of unique and valuable insights to the study of how factors of ethnicity and state intervention influence migration in Eurasia, bringing the region's migration experience into conversation with migration theory, and providing important cases that extend and expand these theories. Through in-depth discussions and several rounds of revisions, the authors of the chapters that follow have collectively sought to integrate three central queries into their individual chapters. First, how can we best reflect the factors involved in the process of migration decisionmaking, and the various levels of influence on decisionmaking? Second, how can ideas of sociopolitical belonging and exclusion be incorporated into the analyses of the push and pull factors faced by migrants? And third, in spite of regional shifts to market relations and increasing globalizing ties, how have ideas of "home" remained salient, and how do ideas of home and homeland influence migration movements? By collectively considering these three questions, the contributors to this volume have made an effort to avoid the marginalizing influences of a focus on ethnicity and the state and to bring their case studies of migration in Eurasia into closer dialogue with current discussions and debates on migration.

Across Eurasia, both migrant-sending and -receiving states are actively engaged in projects to shape perceptions of belonging and construct definitions of home. Structurally limiting migration choices is a pattern with strong historical roots in the region. The replacement of Russia's relatively open in-migration and repatriation policies of the early 1990s with increasing restrictions on migrants and heightened visa enforcement harkens back to familiar state strategies. In-migration is gaining political potency in an era of rising concerns over national identity and population. As with the debates raging across countries such as France and the United States, in-migration is framed as threatening to the economy, security, and culture of the Russian Federation. Calls to decrease in-migration—and especially to combat irregular (or unregistered) migration—are being well received in destination states, drowning out concerns about labor supply, health, and overall demographic change. Conversely, in Russia, some political figures and academics have highlighted the economic and demographic benefits of in-migration, basing their arguments on empirical analyses. Such arguments typically face political and popular ridicule, because calls to send migrants—particularly ethnic minority migrants—home (wherever that might be) are widely welcomed in many destination states.

In contrast, migrant-sending nations—such as Tajikistan, Armenia, and Georgia—struggle to balance their economic dependence on migrants' remittances with concerns about population loss, household disruption, an increasingly powerful illegal migration "industry," and out-migration's possible long-term negative effects on the development of their internal labor market. The responsibilities and rights of citizens working abroad—such as tax liability, health care, and pensions—are at best unclear and at worst unenforceable. The extension of rights to citizens working abroad, often without registration, is problematic and typically often left to nongovernmental or intergovernmental organizations. Sending nations are increasingly concerned with how to more effectively monitor out-migration and remittance flows. However, as noted above, the possibilities of harnessing remittance flows for domestic economic development are challenged by underdeveloped financial markets, high poverty rates, and limited investment opportunities. Though labor migration provides a viable opportunity to support families at home, the ability of remittances to generate local development remains unclear and offers a valuable case for testing assumptions about remittances and development.

The question "Where is home?" is important for both migrant-sending and migrant-receiving societies in Eurasia. In the early 1990s, throughout the former Soviet Union, many considered the possibility of large-scale migration flows based upon ethnic identity.[34] In the extreme, such approaches incorporated little or no regard to issues of length of residency, economic context, degree of assimilation, or location-specific capital accumulation. Nonetheless, ethnic identity in Eurasia has consistently operated as a key vector for the construction of economic opportunity, social networks, and collective experience, often serving as a category for state interventions into settlement and migration policies. Ethnicity within the Eurasian migration system—inextricably linked to the construction and maintenance of personal and collective memory, and reified by current and historical state interventions—is important in ideas of belonging, conceptions of home, and state attempts to formalize structural constraints on mobility. In considering migration processes in this area of the world, the importance of home is central but far from simple, as the chapters of this book illustrate.

Bringing the Eurasian Experience into Current Migration Debates

The essays developed by the contributors to this volume all focus on issues of ethnicity, state intervention in migration processes, and memories or perceptions of home. To bring these case studies into greater dialogue with contemporary approaches to migration theory, the contributors focus discussion on four areas in the migration literature: how macrolevel influences affect individual decisionmaking; the conflicting interests of state actors in addressing migration (economic needs vs. cultural maintenance); understanding the decisionmaking processes of nonmovers; and the economic, cultural, political, and emotional salience of memories of home. These areas of inquiry inform analyses of the Eurasian experience and situate the case studies within broader themes in the study of migration in other regions of the globe. By incorporating perspectives and approaches from the world systems approach, classical and neoclassical economic perspectives, human capital approaches, and network analyses, the case studies seek to bring the Eurasian case into broader comparative perspective.

A first important issue, then, is how societies seek to strike a balance between the state's macrolevel motivations to control or manage migration and the typically microlevel migration choices made by individuals, families, and social networks. To what extent can states effectively set the contours of microlevel choices? Macrolevel policy has been actively utilized to influence migration throughout the history of the Eurasian region. Examining the motivations and mechanisms of macrolevel interventions in Eurasia, and their effects on actual migration flows, leads to insights into the multilayered contextual effects of migration decisionmaking, while providing a more nuanced understanding of how potential migrants estimate the costs and benefits of a move and the central importance of networks for pooling resources to counter contextual restrictions.

Conflicts between economic—or perhaps even demographic—pragmatism and national concerns over the preservation of cultural identity and security are a second important issue. This conflict can be found across many migrant-receiving states historically and today. In-migration is a powerful engine for economic advancement, as immigrants spur economic growth and add to public revenue. With many developed economies experiencing very low fertility and rapid population aging, the addition of young, often healthy, immigrants can maintain a robust labor supply, keep dependency ratios low, and perhaps even raise fertility. Yet the benefits from immigration are now, as in the past, under scrutiny in countries around the globe—often framed in terms of the cultural costs of immigration. Targeting immigrants as a threat to national identity or cultural heritage is a far from novel approach, but in the contemporary Eurasian context affords interesting insight. The framing of immigrants and refugees reflects historical patterns. In addition to challenging national ethnic, linguistic, and religious identities, immigrants can be framed as threats to national security, as potential enemy combatants, or as sources of disease and corruption. Russia provides an important test case for the continued salience of cultural concerns during a period of intense demographic decline.

A third, and often overlooked, issue is the systematic evaluation of nonmovers. In situations when migration is economically justified and openly encouraged, what ties bind specific actors or groups to a particular place? Are nonmovers employing a different calculus when estimating the costs and benefits of migration? Do nonmovers differ from migrants in their susceptibility to familial or community-level influences? How can we best model, compare, and understand their reluctance to move? The detailed case studies in this volume indicate that choosing to stay in a location is often a carefully calibrated and conscious choice, influenced by institutional settings and state policies. Such case studies can add to our understanding of migrant selectivity.

This volume's case studies also add to our understanding of a fourth important issue for migrants: perceptions of *home.* Is home a psychological construct, an emotional memory, or a physical place? How important are cultural, religious, economic, political, and geographic characteristics in determining what and where home might be? How long do perceptions of home persist? Inherent in the discussion of home are the concepts of belonging and of commitment to place, issues central to understanding migrant assimilation during displacement. Eurasia provides historical and contemporary examples of denying groups the right to consider themselves at home, the "construction" of officially defined "homes" for minority ethnic groups, and the removal of groups from their self-professed homes. Most recently, the rise of sustainable, multiethnic, and active transnational communities in cities such as Kyiv may mean that greater links to the global economy, as well as improvements in communication technology, information access, and transportation in the region, may give rise to more familiar forms of transnationalism; but it is still too early to judge.[35] The survival of ideas of home in individual and communal memory can further our ability to theorize the negotiation of transnationalism and better explain the strength of commitment to place—even a place that is unseen.

Plan of the Book

The chapters that follow are presented in three thematic groupings. In the first part of the book, the vast scale of migration and the active role of the state in managing migration in Eurasia serve to illustrate the importance of the region for contemporary studies of international migration. The second part highlights the historical continuity of debate and disagreement over issues of migration in Eurasia generally, and in Russia specifically. Historical concerns regarding ethnic minorities, security concerns over immigration, and debates over the balance between economic need and the desire for cultural hegemony are remarkably consistent across the region. Continuing the theme of belonging, the third part provides insight into the experience of displacement, the challenges of cultural maintenance, and new constructions of home based on long-held identities. The repatriation of Soviet-era deportees and the repudiation of migration restrictions have expanded opportunities among long-displaced populations. Case studies from across the region highlight the complex interactions of economic opportunity with the perceptions of home and belonging as individuals and families evaluate such opportunities.

Part I portrays trends in post-Soviet migration ranging from the macro level of the post-Soviet space to the micro level of the cities of the Irkutsk Oblast. In chapters 1 and 2, Timothy Heleniak and Andrei Korobkov, respectively, provide detailed overviews of current trends in population mobility within the former Soviet Union and in the Russian Federation. Heleniak's overview of migration in the post-Soviet space establishes the empirical contours of migration in the region, illustrating the size and diversity of population movements within and between the fifteen successor states. Utilizing an extensive review of official migration statistics, he examines how migration is used both as a strategy for economic adaptation and as a means of cultural reassertion or identity maintenance. The difficult balance between cultural and economic migration motivations are further developed in chapter 2 by Korobkov, highlighting the strategic use of economic and cultural framing of migration within Russia by political actors. Contrasting the potential demographic contribution of migration in mediating Russia's dire population trends with rising concerns over issues of security, public order, and the ethnic and linguistic identity of Russia, he examines ties between the migration movements within the region and other global international migration systems.

In chapter 3, Andrew Robarts brings the experience of migration within the Eurasian space into clear comparative perspective. He contends that the region is now best understood as one of the major global migration systems, inextricably linked with global migration processes but containing its own internal patterns. He emphasizes that the region as a whole, particularly the

Russian Federation, continues to suffer from the conceptual, legal, and policy orientations of its Soviet past. Resonating with the key arguments raised later in the book (in chapter 5), he delves into the long-standing conflicting interests of the Russian state to both participate in the global economy and maintain tight control over its borders and population composition. The resulting conflict generates a myriad of poorly coordinated and contradictory migration policies, preventing Russia from enjoying the potential benefits of migration or protecting its cultural identity and providing secure borders. Faced with a declining labor force and continued concerns regarding Russia's standing in the international economy, the Russian government should be highly motivated to resolve its contradictory approaches to migration. However, compromise and cooperation with proponents of tight border controls and limited ethnic and religious diversity will be critical if the state is to successfully negotiate these persistently conflicting interests.

In chapter 4, Seema Iyer examines the contemporary implications of Soviet economic strategies that encouraged industrial development in the Far North and Siberia. Employing ideological and economic incentives, the Soviet state actively encouraged migration to remote cities. Focusing on Irkutsk, deep within the Soviet "Frostbelt," she discusses the continued attraction of the city for its residents and for those residing in nearby settlements. Using *propiska* (residency registration) records, she examines the age and sex correlates of migration decisionmaking, finding that in spite of the hardships associated with living in the Frostbelt, the city continues to be perceived as an attractive destination for migrants and a desirable place of residence by inhabitants. The rescinding of restrictions on mobility has not led to out-migration, in spite of the economic and environmental costs of remaining in Irkutsk. The viability of other areas as potential destinations, the importance of local ties, social networks, and the stability of what is known all help to maintain the attraction of Irkutsk, particularly among those who call it home.

The historical roots of current migration paths are provided in part II of the book, which examines three unique cases in which state policies have sought to shape migration patterns. Across the cases, ethnic identity plays a significant role in the construction and enforcement of migration policy. In chapter 5, Eric Lohr investigates the issue of Jewish emigration in Imperial Russia, providing insight into both an unquestioningly interventionist state asserting its right to determine who can enter and exit the country, and also a much more complex and conflicted state seeking to balance the needs of its economy with thinly disguised xenophobia—resonating with the Russian Federation's contemporary approaches described by Korobkov and Robarts.

In chapter 6, Bruce Adams discusses migration and repatriation, providing a telling example of the continued role of the state in issues of migration well into the Soviet period. Foreshadowing issues related to the tenacity of ethnic identity among diaspora communities, Adams highlights the role of international relations in facilitating population movement and the importance of ethnically based claims to citizenship. In chapter 7, Otto Pohl continues on the theme of homeland and ethnic identity in his examination of those he refers to as "special settlers." Viewing the fates of internally displaced and ethnically deported people through the lens of social capital, Pohl illustrates ethnic communities' perseverance in exile, families' resilience in overcoming the hardships of forced migration, and groups' commitments to maintaining cultural identity, finally seeking return to their "home."

Part III offers insight into migration in cases where home is less known, more abstract, or perhaps only imagined. Three investigations of diaspora populations within Eurasia—the Crimean Tatars, Kazakhs, and Germans—offer insight into ideas of belonging, remembrance, and ownership. How do such factors influence the motivations for return migration among individuals and families that are generations removed from any direct experience with the location anointed as home? In chapter 8, Idil Izmirli provides poignant information on the repatriation of the Crimean Tatars to Crimea, vividly portraying the struggles of returnees and accentuating the potential gulf between perceptions of a remembered homeland and the contemporary reality found at a never-before-seen destination.

Ethnic Kazakhs returning to Kazakhstan are examined in chapter 9, by Alexander Diener, who highlights the hardening of the Kazakh space. He delineates both the historical demise of nomadic lifestyles and the establishment of the Republic of Kazakhstan as critical elements in the construction of an ethnic Kazakh home. In explaining how returning to the Republic of Kazakhstan solidifies identity, he returns to an examination of the economic and ethnic motivations for migration raised in chapter 1 by Heleniak. The Kazakh case is especially interesting because appeals to diaspora groups may be as closely tied to ideas of solidifying a titular ethnic majority in a multiethnic state as to the desire to welcome co-ethnics to a meaningful historical homeland.

In chapter 10, Ruth Mandel continues the exploration of diasporas in Kazakhstan, but in examining the out-migration of the German diaspora from Kazakhstan (and the Russian Federation). Her examination highlights the difficult ethnic legacies and adaptation challenges following the collapse of the USSR, while highlighting the ways internal Eurasian migration networks reach out beyond the region. By analyzing diaspora communities from an economically advanced country, Mandel sheds light on the questions of ethnic versus economic motivations raised by Diener and Heleniak. For her, the fact that ethnic Germans perceive "no viable future in Russia or Kazakhstan" is a central motivating factor in their choosing to migrate, rather than perceptions of Germany as their home or homeland. Interestingly, she finds that members of the diaspora community often maintain close ties with friends and family in their communities of origin in Russia and Kazakhstan, calling into question precisely where their emotional home may be located.

Finding Home

This volume raises important and engaging questions concerning what home is believed to be, and how such beliefs are constructed and by whom. In the conclusion, Blair Ruble highlights the consistent conflict regarding migration in Eurasia from a comparative perspective, focusing on issues of cultural protection, fears of outsiders, the need for economic growth, and uniform approaches to citizenship rights and responsibilities.

The migration experiences discussed in this volume add to our understanding of the pervasive importance of ethnicity, the role of the state, and the persistence of memory in understanding population movements. These forces interact with the economic factors, integration opportunities, and social networks that currently dominate theoretical approaches to the study of migration. The migration experiences within Eurasia offer unique and valuable opportunities to reconsider the ways identity, structural interventions, and perceptions influence individual-level migration decisionmaking, while also providing clear insight into the conflicting economic and cultural interests of governments addressing an increasingly mobile, and in some cases immobile, world.

In their research examining the portrayal of the roles states play in international migration, Massey and his colleagues emphasize the importance of considering the four basic "facts" of the migration process: structural factors promoting migration at the place of origin (push factors), structural factors enticing migrants at the place of destination (pull factors), the goals and aspirations of actors (desire), and the socioeconomic resources and networks enabling migration (resources).[36] Though focused geographically on Eurasia, the chapters in this volume provide insight into an exceptionally wide array of push factors, ranging from relative economic hardships to ethnic hostilities to the costly and systematic deportations of particular ethnic groups. Push factors in Eurasia have historically been marked by strong and costly structural interventions forcing groups of migrants from specific locations, as with the Volga Germans, Crimean Tatars, and Meskhetian Turks, or restricting the movement of others, as with the Jews in the Imperial period. Perceptions of ethnicity and belonging have continued to play a role in the post-Soviet period, whether pushing the Russian-language population out of the Baltics or ethnic Germans from Kazakhstan. Further exploration of the ways macrolevel push issues interact with and possibly amplify classical microeconomic factors such as unemployment, wage differentials, and perceptions of social mobility can improve our understanding of the multiple layers of push factors at places of origin and open opportunities to systematically study patterns of reinforcement and contradiction.

The Eurasian migration experience also affords unique insight into issues related to the attractiveness of destinations. The establishment of titular republics both reinforced ethnic identity and sought to make specific regions more attractive to particular ethnic groups. Subnational economic interventions, such as subsidized housing and higher wages, pulled migrants to Siberian cities such as Irkutsk, while far harsher regimes of forced migration pulled thousands into prisoner settlements throughout Siberia. Many scholars have emphasized the importance of shared culture, religion, and language in pulling migrants to specific regions or communities across Eurasia. The return movements of ethnic minorities, often marginalized at their place of exile, and the movement of Jews and Germans to Israel and Germany in the post-Soviet period, are often used to reinforce such approaches. Yet relative economic opportunities, perceptions of social mobility, environmental factors, perceptions of social benefits, and political rights are critical in activating ethnic pulls to destinations. Low birthrates, a rapidly growing retirement-age population, and positive economic growth translate into increasing demand for labor in many regions of Eurasia. Those implementing state-based efforts to attract migrants of shared ethnicity or culture, such as the Russian Federation and Kazakhstan, would do well to consider the social, economic, and political factors underlying ethnic pulls to a perceived homeland.

Diverse push and pull factors set the context for migration decision-making. To clearly assess mobility in Eurasia, it is critical that there be additional emphasis on how actors conceptualize their migration options and determine the costs and benefits of migration—especially as emerging markets for labor and housing across the region facilitate mobility. Such approaches can add to our understanding of migrant selectivity and immobility. Market development enables greater emphasis to be placed on economic issues, but political and economic instability, limited channels for information, and the persistent importance of social networks and location-specific resources during the transition may decrease mobility. The experiences within Eurasia give us a valuable opportunity to explore what happens after state-based interventions to pull migrants to individual locations (or push them out of other regions) end. Is there an enduring effect? What types of actors adapt most quickly? Examining how actors, individually and collectively, consider their migration choices in changing administrative contexts can add significant insight to our understanding of the legacy of state intervention in migration decisionmaking and the individual and collective influences of culture over time.

An individual's ability to act on the desire to migrate (or remain at the place of origin) relies heavily on social networks linking places of destination and origin for information, access, and support. Regional networks, *zemlakchestvo,* have always played a significant role in paving the path for migration, particularly among rural-to-urban migrants in Eurasia. Whether based on global economic ties, imperial legacies, region, ethnicity, family, clan, or other factors, social networks lessen the costs of migration, direct migration flows, and decrease the uncertainty involved in relocation. In turn, these networks strongly influence the generation of migration expectations within a population, determining the development of migration desires and in turn enabling migration. In most cases, networks mitigate the effects of state- or market-based barriers to migration by providing the means of circumvention. Thus, the exploration of the networks underlying migration movements within Eurasia is a promising area worthy of additional research. The unique and tragic experiences of deported communities in the former Soviet Union, in particular, provide important case studies in network maintenance in exile and the influence of such networks on migration desires. And even more important, the long-term experiences of these groups provide the possibility for studying the establishment and success of networks at the places of destination as these communities seek to reestablish their collective idea of home.

What interpersonal networks and social linkages underpin the identification of home? How is the desire for home manifested and kept alive?

What factors push peoples from their homes, and pull them back or to new homes? Are such processes best considered at the individual, familial, or community level? How long does the idea of home survive in individual or communal memory, and how important are cultural, religious, economic, political, and geographical characteristics in determining what and where home is, or how often it is reconfigured? Saskia Sassen contends that "migrations are acts of settlement and of habitation in a world where the divide between origin and destination is not longer a divide of Otherness, a world in which borders no longer separate human realities."[37] Geographic ties may no longer bind individuals, families, or social groups to specific locations, making ideas of belonging and home more challenging. In addition to integrating the Eurasian experience into global discussions of pulls, pushes, desires, and networks involved in migration processes, the examples highlighted in this volume provide valuable insight into the continued importance of home—as a memory, as a concept, as a significant set of relations. These examples can assist in the critical evaluation of theories of globalization, transnationalism, and international mobility by providing promising avenues for assessing ethnic persistence and the enduring question of belonging. They provide interesting points of departure for future research on movement throughout the emerging Eurasian migration system, highlighting the need for a larger comparative perspective and for engagement with broader migration theory.

Notes

1. S. Sassen, *Guests and Aliens* (New York: New Press, 1999).

2. This is, of course, a broad generalization of the broader literature. Excellent economic investigations of migration during the Soviet period have been conducted, in spite of severe data limitations. See B. Mitchneck and D. Plane, "Migration and the Quasi-Labor Market in Russia," *International Regional Science Review* 18, no. 3 (1995): 267–88; and Ira N. Gang and Robert C. Stuart, *Russian Cities in Transition: The Impact of Market Forces in the 1990s,* IZA Discussion Paper 1151 (Bonn: IZA, 2004), http://ftp.iza.org/dp1151.pdf.

3. See R. Waldinger, ed., *Strangers at the Gates: New Immigrants in Urban America* (Berkeley: University of California Press, 2001); and S. Castles and A. Davidson, *Citizenship and Migration: Globalization and the Politics of Belonging* (London: Routledge, 2001).

4. For a notable exception, see R. Brubaker, "Citizenship Struggles in Soviet Successor States," *International Migration Review* 26, no. 2 (1992): 269–91.

5. M. Boyd and E. Grieco, "Women and Migration: Incorporating Gender into International Migration Theory," Migration Information Service, 2003, http://www

.migrationinformation.org/Feature/display.cfm?id=106. See also B. R. Chiswick, "Are Migrants Favorably Selected? An Economic Analysis," IZA Working Paper 131, 2000, ftp://repec.iza.org/RePEc/Discussionpaper/dp131.pdf.

6. S. Lee, *Unraveling the "Model Minority" Stereotypes: Listening to Asian American Youth* (New York: Teachers College Press, 1996).

7. M. Zhou, "Segmented Assimilation: Issues, Controversies, and Recent Research on the New Second Generation," *International Migration Review* 31, no. 4 (1997): 975–1008.

8. C. Brettell and C. Sargent, "Identity and Citizenship: Anthropological Perspectives, *American Behavioral Scientist* 50, no. 3 (2006): 3–8; the quotation is on 4.

9. R. Alba and V. Nee, "Rethinking Assimilation Theory for a New Era of Immigrants," *International Migration Review* 31, no. 4 (1997): 826–74.

10. Y. Slezkine, "The USSR as a Communal Apartment, or How a Socialist State Promoted Ethnic Particularism," *Slavic Review* 53, no. 2 (1994): 414–52.

11. B. Anderson and B. Silver, "Some Factors in the Linguistic and Ethnic Russification of Soviet Nationalities: Is Everyone Becoming Russian?" in *The Nationality Factor in Soviet Politics and Society,* ed. Lubomyr Hajda and Mark Beissinger (Boulder, Colo.: Westview Press, 1990), 95–130.

12. R. Brubaker, "Nationhood and the National Question in the Soviet Union and Post-Soviet Eurasia: An Institutionalist Account," *Theory and Society* 23 (1994): 47–78.

13. H. Pilkington, *Migration, Displacement and Identity in Post-Soviet Russia* (New York: Routledge, 1998).

14. V. I. Perevendenstzev, "Ob upravlenii migratsiei natseleniia," *Migratsiia naseleniia RSFSR: Sbornik statei* (Moscow: Statistika. 1973).

15. F. Hill and C. Gaddy, *The Siberian Curse: How Communist Planners Left Russia Out in the Cold* (Washington, D.C.: Brookings Institution Press, 2003).

16. G. Borjas, "Economic Theory and International Migration," *International Migration Review* 23, no. 3, Special Silver Anniversary Issue: International Migration—An Assessment for the 90s (1989): 457–85.

17. C. Buckley, "The Myth of Managed Migration," *Slavic Review* 54, no. 4 (1995): 896–916.

18. V. Danilov, *Rural Russia under the New Regime* (Bloomington: Indiana University Press, 1988).

19. P. Polian, *Against Their Will: The History and Geography of Forced Migrations in the USSR* (Budapest: Central European University Press, 2004).

20. M. Pohl, "Planeta Sta Iazakov': Etnicheskiet otnosheniia I sovetskaia identichnost's nat tselene," *Acta Eurasica / Vestnik Evrazii* 1, no. 24 (2004): 5–33.

21. D. Massey, J. Durand, and N. Malone, *Beyond Smoke and Mirrors* (New York: Russell Sage Foundation, 2002).

22. P. Gatrell, *A Whole Empire Walking: Refugees in Russia during the First World War* (Bloomington: Indiana University Press, 1999).

23. M. Shabanova. *Sezonnaia i postoiannaia migratsiia naseleniia u sel'skom raione* (Novosibirsk: Nauka, 1991).

24. B. Ruble, O. Malynovs'ka, et al., *Netraditsiini immigratsi v Kievi* (Kyiv: Stiloc, 2003).

25. I. Ivakhniouk, "Illegal Migration: Russia," *European Security* 13, nos. 1–2 (2003): 35–53.

26. S. Castles, "Guest Workers in Europe: A Resurrection?" *International Migration Review* 40, no. 4 (2006): 741–66.

27. D. Massey, "Internal Migration at the Dawn of the Twenty-first Century: The Role of the State," *Population and Development Review* 25, no. 2 (1999): 302–22.

28. See W. Cornelius and M. Rosenblum, "Immigration and Politics," *Annual Review of Political Science,* 2006, 99–119.

29. D. Kapur, *Remittances the New Development Mantra,* G-24 Working Paper 29 (New York: United Nations Conference on Trade and Development, 2004); H. Oleson, "Migration, Return, and Development: An Institutional Perspective," *International Migration* 40, no. 5 (2004): 125–50.

30. See D. Ratha, "Workers' Remittances: An Important and Stable Source of External Development Finance," in *Remittances: Development Impact and Future Prospects,* ed. S. M. Maimbo and D. Ratha (Washington, D.C.: World Bank, 2005); and J. E. Taylor, "The New Economics of Labour Migration and the Role of Remittances in the Migration Process," *International Migration* 37, no. 1 (1999): 63.

31. J. Brazeil and A. Mannur, eds., *Theorizing Diaspora* (New York: Blackwell, 2003).

32. See A. Mansoor and B. Quillin, *Migration and Remittances: Eastern Europe and the Former Soviet Union* (Washington, D.C.: World Bank, 2007). See also S. Olimova and I. Bosc, *Labour Migration in Tajikistan* (Dushanbe: International Organization for Migration, 2003.

33. On the enormity of financial flows from Russia, see V. Tishkov, Z. Zayinchkovskaya, and G. Vitkovskaya, "Migration in the Countries of the Former Soviet Union," paper prepared for the Policy Analysis and Research Program of the Global Commission on International Migration, Global Commission on International Migration, 2005, http://www.gcim.org/attachements/RS3.pdf. On debates over immigration into Russia, see L. Grafova, "Grigory Yavlinsky: Our State Does Not Need People, Despite the Low Birthrate," *Nezavesimaya gazeta,* July 29, 2002, http://www.eng.yabloko.ru/Publ/2002/papers/ng-290702.htm; and A. Vishnevsky, "*Replacement Migration: Is It a Solution for Russia?*" United Nations Population Division Working Paper UN/POP/PRA/2000/14 (New York: United Nations, 2000).

34. J. Dunlop, "Will a Large-Scale Migration of Russians to the Russian Republic Take Place over the Current Decade?" *International Migration Review* 27, no. 3 (1993): 605–29.

35. B. Ruble, *Creating Diversity Capital: Transnational Migrants in Montreal, Washington, and Kyiv* (Washington and Baltimore: Woodrow Wilson Center Press and Johns Hopkins University Press, 2005).

36. D. Massey, J. Arango, G. Hugo, A. Pellegrino, and J. Taylor, "An Evaluation of International Migration Theory: The North American Case," *Population and Development* Review 20, no. 4 (December 1994): 699–751; D. S. Massey, J. Arango, G. Hugo, A. Kouaouci, A. Pellegrino, and J. E. Taylor, *Worlds in Motion: Understanding International Migration at the End of the Millennium* (Oxford: Clarendon Press, 2002.

37. Sassen, *Guests and Aliens,* 6.

Part I

Trends in Post-Soviet Migration

Migration is a complex and contentious phenomenon in today's world. It raises a large number of questions that are both academically intriguing and politically salient: What factors lead people to migrate? How do migrants affect their host societies? What role can and should states play in managing migration? Because migrants are a heterogeneous group—originating in many different societies, motivated by a variety of factors, and settling in diverse host countries—the answers to these and other questions about migration are neither easy nor straightforward.

Part I of this volume consists of contributions by Timothy Heleniak, Andrei Korobkov, Andrew Robarts, and Seema Iyer that draw attention to three major issues in migration studies: the reasons for migration, the integration of local migration flows into larger global systems of migration, and the state regulation of migration. The question of why people migrate is probably the most widely researched issue in migration theory, and there are dozens of theories to explain why some people move and not others, how they calculate the costs and benefits of migration, and where they choose to go. Many theories are based on economic calculations, which treat migration as a type of investment. For example, individuals may invest time and money in a move in the hopes of earning higher wages in the future,[1] or families in unstable or underdeveloped economies may choose to diversify their income sources by sending one or more members to work abroad.[2] Other scholars, particularly those writing about the former Soviet Union, argue that a fear of discrimination and a desire to live in one's national homeland can be a motivation for migration among ethnic minority groups.[3]

Although the decision to migrate is made by individuals, families, and communities, migration can also be understood at the global level. People tend to follow established paths of migration, as evidenced by the large flows of Mexicans to and from the United States, the large proportion of Turks among migrants to Germany, and the popularity of Russia as a destination for migrants in post-Soviet countries. Explanations for the existence of these paths include the influence of community networks in migrants' choice of destination[4] and the existence of world economic systems.[5]

In looking at migration at the levels of individual decisionmaking and global systems, the role of the state in regulating migration should not be forgotten. Vast flows of illegal migration throughout the world demonstrate that states have a limited ability to counteract strong economic and other incentives to migration through regulation. Nevertheless, all states do regulate migration in some way or another, and state regulations play an important role in shaping the migration experience by determining how easily migrants can cross borders, what types of jobs they can obtain, and how easily they can send money to their home countries. In countries with large inflows or outflows of migration, these issues tend to become extremely contentious politically.

In chapter 1, Heleniak illustrates the tremendous scale and scope of population movements in Eurasia since the collapse of the Soviet Union. He notes that in the Soviet period, the state created significant disincentives against migration. International migration was generally prohibited, while the tightly regulated labor and housing markets, along with the *propiska* (registration) system, limited internal migration. When these systems of regulation collapsed with the Soviet Union, migration within Eurasia increased dramatically. Migrants, Heleniak demonstrates, are influenced by a wide variety of political and economic considerations.

According to Korobkov in chapter 2, the considerations that motivate Eurasian migrants have been changing over time. He categorizes migration to and from Russia from 1991 through 2006 into five separate periods. These five periods highlight the substantial variation in migration policies, the size and composition of migration flows, and the motivations for migration that have characterized Eurasian migration since the collapse of the Soviet Union. Korobkov's five stages demonstrate two major trends. First, Russia has gone from a country of emigration to a country of immigration. Second, migration in the region has gone from being primarily ethnically and politically motivated to being primarily economically motivated.

Heleniak's and Korobkov's chapters point to the development of Eurasia as a "normal" global migration system. The collapse of the Soviet Union and the end of repressive Soviet policies triggered large-scale migration of a type not typical of other migration systems. Particularly notable—and worrying to many observers at the time—was the migration of ethnic Russians and other groups to the states and regions identified as their ethnic homelands. Though ethnically motivated migration has been significant, it is now being overtaken by migration that appears to be driven by the more familiar factors of economics, demographics, and social networks.

In chapter 3, Robarts examines the political implications of the Eurasian migration system for Russia. As the political center of the former Soviet Union and the region's strongest economy, Russia has been the most attractive destination for migrants throughout Eurasia but has faced tremendous difficulty in developing an effective migration regime. Russia, as Robarts describes it, is in a similar position to many European and North American states. Though economic and demographic considerations have led some Russian policymakers to push for policies that would facilitate legal immigration, national security concerns and anti-Islamic bias have led many others to support a hostile migration regime. Social and political support for a more secure migration regime is strong, but such a regime would be extremely difficult to implement, and increasing restrictions on migration are more likely to increase the exploitation of migrants (described in chapter 2) than to substantially decrease migration flows.

In chapter 4, Iyer focuses on the issue of internal migration within the Russian Federation, demonstrating the complex consequences of state regulation of migration. Soviet planners encouraged internal migration to remote regions, creating urban centers in previously uninhabited regions of the Far North and Far East. Iyer's analysis of migration in the Irkutsk region demonstrates that the creation of this region's cities had important consequences for Russian society. These cities remain attractive to many residents, and they even attract intraregional migrants, in spite of growing concerns among post-Soviet policymakers over the economic viability of these far-flung urban centers.

Any attempt to understand the Eurasian migration system must be tempered by the fact that migration, throughout the world, is very difficult to measure. A significant number of international migrants either enter their host country illegally or are living and working without official documents. This is particularly true in the societies of Eurasia, where—in comparison with other major destination countries, such as the United States, Germany, and France—the rule of law is weak and the unofficial economy is large. Undocumented migrants are difficult to count and are not included in official statistics on migration, forcing researchers to resort to unofficial estimates to gauge the true scope of migration.

Historically, the Soviet Union constituted a region of very limited migration, and migration theory has not been informed by data from that part of the world. However, since the collapse of the Soviet Union, Eurasia has become one of the world's major migration systems, and Russia and Ukraine are now home to the second- and fourth-largest populations of migrants in the world. Analyses of migration in Eurasia can add insight into questions of how migration works and how we measure and understand it. Any attempt to understand Eurasian migration, however, must be tempered with a knowledge of the limitations of the available data. As Heleniak explains, the post-Soviet states have faced more challenges in collecting migration data than most other countries. Statistics from the region are compromised by porous borders and visa-free travel between most states belonging to the Commonwealth of Independent States, corruption and the weakness of the rule of law, and—in some cases—by the manipulation of official data for political reasons. Nevertheless, by combining official data and unofficial estimates, we can draw conclusions about general trends of migration in the region, even if we cannot precisely quantify its magnitude.

Notes

1. Barry R. Chiswick, "Are Immigrants Favorably Self-Selected? An Economic Analysis," in *Migration Theory: Talking across Disciplines,* ed. Caroline B. Brettell and James F. Hollifield (New York: Routledge, 2000), 62–64.

2. Douglas S. Massey, Joaquin Arango, Graeme Hugo, Ali Kouaouci, Adela Pellegrino, and J. Edward Taylor, *Worlds in Motion: Understanding International Migration at the End of the Millennium* (Oxford: Clarendon Press, 1998), 21–22.

3. John Dunlop, "Will a Large-Scale Migration of Russians to the Russian Repub-

lic Take Place over the Current Decade?" *International Migration Review* 20, no. 4 (Fall 1993): 605–29.

4. Douglas S. Massey et al., "An Evaluation of International Migration Theory: The North American Case," *Population and Development Review* 20, no. 4 (December 1994): 699–751.

5. Nadje Al-Ali and Khalid Koser, *New Approaches to Migration: Transnational Communities and Transformations of Home* (New York: Routledge, 2002).

1

An Overview of Migration in the Post-Soviet Space

Timothy Heleniak

On January 12, 1989, the Soviet Union conducted what would turn out to be its final population census. That census enumerated 285 million persons spread across the fifteen then-union republics ranging from 147 million in Russia to 1.6 million in Estonia. Since that date, the Soviet Union has split up into fifteen independent states.[1] The successor states have, to widely varying degrees, instituted the tenets of market economies by privatizing large segments of their economies, liberalizing prices and foreign trade, and generally withdrawing the state from economic planning and decisionmaking. Many of the countries have adopted nominally liberal democratic structures, while others have become autocratic dictatorships. Most of the countries have liberalized society by allowing freedom of speech and movement, including the right to emigrate. The countries, again in varying degrees, have opened up to the outside world by allowing increased foreign trade, travel, and communication, and have taken up membership in international organizations. These changes in the societies and economies of the fifteen successor states have combined to greatly alter the spatial distribution of the population of these countries in the decade and a half since the last Soviet population census. This chapter provides a broad overview of the migration movements that have taken place during the initial post-Soviet period.

The chapter begins with a summary of relevant migration theories and how well they apply to the post-Soviet migration reality. This is followed by an overview of migration and population changes across the post-Soviet space and includes a discussion of the availability and veracity of migration statistics in the Soviet successor states. The next section covers changes in the ethnic composition of the states of the former Soviet Union (FSU) and what role migration played in these changes. Following this is an analysis of the causes of migration across the FSU that attempts to disaggregate political and ethnic factors on the one hand and economic factors on the other. The final section examines the factors that might influence future migration movements across the region.

Migration Theory and Post-Soviet Migration

One of the major questions regarding post-Soviet migration was whether the patterns and trends that took place were what was expected according to established migration theory. Thus, before a review and analysis of the data on post-Soviet migration patterns, a brief review of major migration theories and how they might predict migration across the post-Soviet space is presented here. Migration is just one strategy of adaptation that people employ in response to changing circumstances. Migration theory posits that potential migrants calculate a cost/benefit equation comparing incomes in their current location versus that in potential destinations, and, if the difference outweighs the costs of moving, that the person moves. Wages in potential destinations are discounted by possible spells of unemployment. In addition, various noneconomic, quality-of-life measures are factored into a potential migrants' decisionmaking calculus.

Neoclassical economics states that it is differentials in wages among regions, or countries, that causes people to move from low-wage, high-unemployment regions to high-wage, low-unemployment regions. Extensions of neoclassical theory called "the new economics of migration" use households, families, or other groups of related people as their unit of analysis.[2] These units operate collectively to maximize income and minimize risk and often send one or a few family members to other parts of the country, usually a larger city, or abroad in order to increase overall family income while others remain behind earning lower but more stable incomes.

There was certainly migration during the Tsarist and Soviet periods; however, there were always a number of obstacles that prevented migration. During the Soviet period, migration became increasingly regulated, as evinced by the *propiska* (residency registration form) system introduced in 1932. As discussed below, the ability of the FSU successor states to control migration is much less than that of the Soviet Union. Another intervening obstacle was and remains distance. Gravity models hold that migration decreases with distance because of increased costs of transport and less availability of information about conditions in more distance destinations. The Soviet Union was and Russia has become the world's largest country. These factors combined with others, such as a rigid housing market, have always given the population of the FSU a reputation as a country with rather low rates of migrateability. Migration is broadly defined as any permanent change in residence, and migrateability is the tendency of a person or group of people to migrate. People in the Soviet Union, as opposed to say those in the United States, tended to migrate less often and tended to remain in the regions in which they were born. More than half the people of the FSU continue to live in the region where they were born, a measure of lifetime migration.[3] One of the key questions to be examined in this chapter is how many people across the successor states have migrated in the face of changing circumstances.

Economic and political characteristics of regions or countries have a strong impact on migration of people into or out of them. The Soviet state attempted to optimize the spatial distribution of the population for reasons of economic efficiency. It did this by restricting entry into cities, introducing wage and other incentives to induce people to move to areas designated for priority development, organized recruitment of recent graduates, limiting migration into or out of the country, and the above-mentioned *propiska* system. These measures affected the distribution of the population among and within the fifteen successor states to the Soviet Union. The focus of this chapter is on migration movements among the fifteen successor states and between them and the rest of the world. This is not to ignore some of the large migration movements that have taken place at other geographic scales, such as out of the Russian north or the concentration of population into many of the capital cities, but full treatment of these flows is beyond the scope of this chapter.[4]

The Soviet Union was a complex system of ethnic homelands, which has an effect on migration patterns in several ways. When the Soviet Union was disbanded, there were fifty-three different ethnic homelands, fifteen of which became independent sovereign states. Because of past migration movements, differential growth rates of different nationalities, and other factors, in 1989 the proportion that the titular group made up of its homeland ranged from 93 percent in Armenia to just 40 percent in Kazakhstan. Many thought that "return migration" to ethnic homelands of diaspora groups would dominate post-Soviet migration patterns. This included migration to homelands external to the Soviet Union, such as Israel for Jews and Germany for Germans. Politically, the Soviet successor states have embarked on quite divergent paths, ranging from the Baltic states, which joined the European Union in May 2004, to Belarus and Turkmenistan, which have become forms of dictatorship. The types of government adopted have had an impact on rates of economic growth and thus on migration rates. They have also adopted different policies toward levels of promotion of the titular nationality and inclusion or exclusion of minority groups. This was reflected in the language and citizenship laws that each country adopted as well as the migration polices of each new state. For a period immediately after the breakup of the Soviet Union, migration was highly unregulated (making it difficult to measure) but has become increasingly formalized and in many cases rather restrictive.

People who migrate are favorably self-selected compared with those who remain in their place of origin. Migrants tend to be more ambitious, aggressive, entrepreneurial, and in general more able.[5] In the Soviet Union, certain ethnic groups had higher levels of "migrateability" as a result of having many of the socioeconomic characteristics associated with migration. These included Russians, other Slavic groups, Tatars, Jews, and "mobilized Europeans"—Armenians, Georgians, Latvians, and Estonians.[6] Once migration processes are under way, they often persist because of the existence of ethnic enclaves in foreign countries, whose residents provide feedback to those in the home country and help ease transition into destination countries. In many cases, the existence of a core number of members of an ethnic group abroad as a result of past migrations makes it difficult for governments to later reduce or prevent the migration of such groups. An example is that of Mexican migration to the United States, which started as a temporary program in 1917; today, however, with nearly 10 million Mexicans in the United States, it would be difficult to stem this flow, even if that was the goal of either Mexico or the United States. Because of the past migrations across the Soviet Union, there are a number of large diaspora populations that could serve to fuel further migration of their ethnic kin in the post-Soviet period.

The Soviet Union attempted to equalize the standard of living among regions and between urban and rural areas.[7] Though this ideal was never fully realized, income levels among the Soviet republics and oblasts were narrower than what they might have been had the country operated under market conditions. This had the effect of limiting migration because of narrow differences in regional standards of living. Under the centrally planned economy of the Soviet Union, most prices were administratively set, and as a result the income distribution among sectors and occupations was rather narrow, and differences in the cost of living among regions were rather small. This was partially accomplished with a massive and elaborate system of subsidies, which caused certain sectors to be "overvalued" and others to be "undervalued." This included a set of regional wage coefficients designed to induce people to migrate to and work in priority sectors and regions. Due to the regional concentration of industry, this system benefited some regions more than others. When prices were liberalized in 1992 and most subsidies were removed, this caused a rapid rise in income distribution and greatly increased differentiation in the cost of living among the countries. From the discussion above on migration theory, this very quickly caused a change in the variables in peoples' migration cost/benefit equation.

One part of the social contract in the Soviet Union was the maintenance of full employment. Under market conditions, open unemployment has become a reality and also a factor in migration, where it was not previously. The structural changes in the economies of the successor states have also influenced migration patterns through differential influences on the supply and demand for labor, with some states becoming consumers of domestic and foreign capital and others becoming suppliers of labor, resulting in the development of several levels of dual labor markets across the post-Soviet space.

Soviet enterprises had limited involvement in foreign trade or international institutions, and there was little exchange of ideas, capital, goods, or people with the outside world. With the opening of these economies, there has been increased involvement, including foreign direct investment, which has further exacerbated differentiation among countries and regions. World systems theory holds that as capitalist economies penetrate into peripheral noncapitalist countries, a mobile population is created. This has happened both between the Soviet Union and countries in the "far abroad" and also among the successor states, with some countries becoming part of a more advanced core and others being relegated to a periphery that exports only raw materials and low-skilled labor.

Population Movements across the Post-Soviet Space

This analysis of migration and population changes among the Soviet successor states begins at a broad level before moving onto a more nuanced analysis and examination of the causes of migration. Table 1.1 shows the population change for each country from 1989, the date of the last Soviet population census, to the beginning of 2004, disaggregating that population into natural increase (or decrease) and net migration. Of the fifteen states of the FSU, only five had population increases over the period: Azerbaijan and the four Central Asian states of Kyrgyzstan, Tajikistan, Turkmenistan, and Uzbekistan. These countries all have rather young age structures and continue to have high fertility rates and high rates of natural increase. In most FSU countries, positive natural increase is combined with net out-migration, as is the pattern for most countries in the world. This includes the five mentioned above plus Moldova, Lithuania, Armenia, Georgia, and Kazakhstan, though in this latter group, the populations of all declined because net out-migration exceeded natural increase. Three countries had both natural population declines and net out-migration—Ukraine, Latvia, and Estonia. Russia and Belarus had more deaths than births combined with positive net migration. However, for Belarus, immigration barely exceeded emigration.

It is Russia that has become the migration magnet within the post-Soviet space, with a documented gain of 5.8 million persons through migration over the period. Though this amounts to only 3.9 percent of its 1989 population, the issue of migration has become a rather common topic of political debate in the country. In part, this is because the estimated extent of illegal migration into Russia is roughly of the same magnitude as that of legal migration.[8] The extent of net out-migration was rather significant from a number of the states, with Armenia, Georgia, Kazakhstan, and Tajikistan showing that 15 percent or more of their populations had migrated out of the country on a permanent basis. These large population losses from migration actually understate their true impact on the economies and societies of these countries because those leaving are disproportionally young and better educated than those who remain.

Table 1.1. Population Change in the States of the Former Soviet Union, 1989–2004 (beginning of year)

	Total Population (thousands)		Absolute Change (thousands)			Percent Change		
State	1989	2004	Total	Natual Increase	Migration	Total	Natural Increase	Migration
Russia	147,400	144,534	–2,866	–8,635	5,769	–1.9	–5.9	3.9
Ukraine	51,707	47,442	–4,265	–3,482	–782	–8.2	–6.7	–1.5
Belarus	10,152	9,849	–303	–332	29	–3.0	–3.3	0.3
Moldova	4,338	4,247	–91	147	–238	–2.1	3.4	–5.5
Latvia	2,667	2,319	–347	–149	–199	–13.0	–5.6	–7.4
Lithuania	3,675	3,446	–229	6	–235	–6.2	0.2	–6.4
Estonia	1,566	1,351	–215	–62	–153	–13.7	–4.0	–9.8
Armenia	3,449	3,212	–236	399	–635	–6.9	11.6	–18.4
Azerbaijan	7,021	8,266	1,245	1,476	–232	17.7	21.0	–3.3
Georgia	5,401	4,544	–857	242	–1,099	–15.9	4.5	–20.4
Kazakhstan	16,465	14,951	–1,513	1,892	–3,406	–9.2	11.5	–20.7
Kyrgyzstan	4,254	5,037	783	1,174	–390	18.4	27.6	–9.2
Tajikistan	5,109	6,640	1,531	2,302	–771	30.0	45.1	–15.1
Turkmenistan	3,518	5,158	1,640	1,269	371	46.6	36.1	10.6
Uzbekistan	19,882	25,707	5,825	7,125	–1,300	29.3	35.8	–6.5

Sources: Data on population, births, and deaths were taken from a variety of different sources produced by the respective national statistical offices of the states of the former Soviet Union. Net migration was computed via the "residual method." All population figures have been adjusted following the censuses conducted in 1999 to 2002.

As elsewhere in the world, a combination of demographic and economic factors will continue to determine migration patterns among the post-Soviet countries, with demographic factors being more of a longer-term factor and economic factors determining more immediate population movements. In 2001, the number of deaths exceeded the number of births in the three Slavic and three Baltic states and Moldova. Georgia and Armenia are expected to join this group in the near future. These trends of negative natural decrease are expected to continue well into the future in all these states because of their older age structures and low fertility rates. Meanwhile, in Central Asia and Azerbaijan, with higher fertility rates and younger age structures, the populations are expected to continue to grow considerably.

The net migration figures shown in table 1.1 are computed via the "residual method," where the difference between the number of births and deaths is subtracted from total population change and net migration is a "residual."[9] This method is commonly used either in the absence of migration data or where migration data are thought to be unreliable or unrepresentative. This method requires that both population estimates and data on births and deaths be reasonably accurate. In the case of the former Soviet states, there are well-known problems with data on births and deaths.[10] However, in spite of these problems, it was felt that the vital statistics registration system deteriorated far less than the systems for measuring migration. Nearly all the FSU states have now conducted their first population censuses as independent states, which have allowed them to calibrate and adjust their population totals. Those census population totals are reflected in the population change figures given in table 1.1. Analysis of migration from this method is just one means, and given the nature of migration movements across the post-Soviet space, several methods need to be employed and triangulated against each other to gain a true picture of the migration situation in the region. Before moving on to some of this analysis, it is helpful to briefly discuss the measurement of migration among the post-Soviet states and the veracity of FSU migration data.

Measuring Migration in the Former Soviet Union

Even developed countries with good statistical systems often have difficulty fully measuring all migration movements across their borders. This is especially the case in countries with open borders and a high volume of migration. The countries of the FSU have faced more challenges than most countries in measuring migration movements across their external borders and among regions within them. The major factor was that migration went from being mostly internal within a country and being under a system that exerted considerable control over the movements of its population to being international across fifteen newly independent states that had much less control over their external borders and in some cases no control over people's spatial movements. When the Soviet Union was dissolved in 1992, the republic statistical offices, which had been branch offices under the control of the USSR statistical committee, had to quickly become independent national statistical offices. Their ability to do so varied widely because of the differing financial, human, and other resources that they had at their disposal. In the harried environment of state building that they were faced with in the early 1990s, reforming statistical systems and the proper measurement of migration often fell far down on the new governments' list of priorities.

In the Soviet Union, the *propiska* or resident permit system required persons to register before being allowed to migrate to a new location.[11] Though this system did not completely capture all migration flows, it was a useful tool in tracking migration flows. Migration into and out of the Soviet Union was limited, and there were few refugees or internally displaced persons (at least in the sense that the rest of the international community would define them). Remnants of the *propiska* system still exist in some of the countries, although in most cases, it is a simple declaratory process. Some of the countries have been able to erect the necessary administrative procedures and institutions to be able to manage and count migration. Much of this migration-management capacity building was done with the assistance of the international community, most notably the International Organization for Migration, following the Commonwealth of Independent States (CIS) Conference in 1996.[12] For example, the three Baltic states needed to align their visa regimes, reinforce border controls, and improve migration data collection as one of the many preconditions for accession to the European Union. Conversely, in some countries that went through periods of war and social unrest, migration movements into and out of the country went unrecorded for periods of time.[13] The visa-free travel among the CIS states for most of the 1990s contributed to an environment of rather porous borders, which made the recording of migration flows rather difficult. The extent to which the successor states have instituted systems to properly measure total migration flows and to disaggregate these flows by age, gender, nationality, and other useful characteristics necessary for both analysis and policymaking varies considerably.

Thus, when analyzing migration across the FSU, it is necessary to be transparent about data sources and to triangulate migration flows from several different sources. Migration data from these countries should not and cannot be completely discarded but should be approached with more than the usual degree of caution. Migration data derived via the residual method only produce an estimate of the crude net migration rate. In practice, there are a number of reasons why migration data do not equal net migration derived via the residual method. For example, in Georgia, the residual method produced an estimate of emigration from 1989 to 2000 of 1,080,000, while migration statistics showed emigration of 240,000. Armenia was another country, like Georgia, where migration flows went unrecorded for extended periods as a result of armed conflict and economic collapse. According to official data, the population of Armenia grew from 3,449,000 at the time of the 1989 census to 3,802,000 in 2001.[14] There was a natural increase of the population of 374,000, implying net emigration of just 20,000, a figure that most knew to not represent the true picture of the migration reality in the country.[15] The census conducted in October 2001 produced a figure of 3,001,000 for the de facto population, implying net emigration of 830,000, which is a more plausible figure given the economic situation in the country and migration figures from Armenia, using mirror statistics from major migration partners such as Russia.

Turkmenistan might be the most egregious example, where migration statistics show net emigration of 63,000 while the residual method produces net immigration of 786,000, a difference of nearly one-quarter of the population and an indication of manipulation of the population or migration figures, or both. Even countries in the region with seemingly well-developed statistical systems often are not able to record migration completely. For instance, in Lithuania, there was a downward adjustment of the population of more than 200,000, or more than 5 percent of the population, following the census conducted in April 2001.[16] Roughly the same magnitude of adjustment took place in Estonia following its March 2000 census, when it adjusted the population total downward by 67,000, or about 5 percent.[17] Among the surprises in the Russian census conducted in October 2002 was that the total population was 1.2 million higher than the previous estimate, due mainly to an undercount of migration.[18] There was an effort in the census to enumerate foreigners living temporarily in Russia, but this produced a total of only 250,000, because many foreigners in Russia are living there illegally and do not wish to be captured by the statistical system. Migration destinations such as Moscow were found to have populations much higher than precensus estimates, while regions with large amounts of out-migration such as those in the Far East were found to have populations lower than the estimates. In both cases, this was due to the fact that in-migration is generally better recorded than out-migration figures because many social benefits are tied to place of residence, giving people more incentive to register when moving to a location.[19]

These differences between population estimates and census figures in the FSU countries should be compared with those of the United States, long a traditional migration destination. Before the 2000 census in the United States, the population was estimated at 275 million, but the census revealed a count of 281 million, a difference of 6 million, almost all attributable to an undercount of the huge migration into the United States during the 1990s. The United States has long grappled with an issue that the FSU states are only beginning to deal with in trying to estimate temporary or circular migration. Estimates are that between 7 and 9 million foreign-born persons in the United States are unauthorized in some way, and each year another 350,000 to 500,000 illegal aliens, undocumented workers, and other persons in violation of immigration law enter the country.[20] Until recently, most of the FSU states only recorded only long-term or permanent moves, and many of the movements over the past decade are of a temporary or circular nature.

Migration Turnover in the Former Soviet Union

It has often been said that population of the Soviet Union was rather immobile because of the legal restrictions on mobility, the lack of a flexible housing and mortgage market, the sheer size of the country, the lack of wide geographic disparities in income, and other factors. As mentioned above, there has been a dramatic change in factors at the macroeconomic level in the FSU that have an impact on migration. An interesting question to ask is how many people have migrated in response to the changes in these factors. From the data available on migration in the former Soviet states, it is not possible to get a conclusive answer to this question. However, it is possible to gain some insight into migration turnover at the individual level.

It is difficult to compare levels of population mobility over time and across space between different countries. This is because of differing systems for collecting migration data (survey vs. administrative), differing time periods for measuring moves, and differing distance or geographic boundaries as to what constitutes a move. The general definition of the mobility rate is the number of movers as a share of the population at risk. Rates of in-migration and out-migration are computed by comparing the numbers of these groups to the average population of an area.[21] The crude net migration rate is total out-migrants minus total out-migrants as a share of the average population. This is the statistic shown in table 1.1. These are migration flow statistics and are usually computed over a period of time, such as year. Other common migration statistics are measures of lifetime migration. In recent Soviet censuses and some of the censuses conducted in the successor states, there was a question asking whether you were living in the place where you were born.

From data available for the late Soviet period, it is possible to get some idea of migration turnover just before the breakup of the Soviet Union.[22] Based on data for arrivals, in 1987 there were 55 migrants per 1,000 persons, meaning that about 5.5 percent of the Soviet population had moved in that year. During the 1980s, migration turnover steadily declined, so that by 1989, only 4.1 percent of the population migrated. In that year, Kazakhstan and Kyrgyzstan had the highest turnover rates and Armenia and Georgia had the lowest. It might not be an entirely fair and accurate comparison because of methodological reasons, but in the United States in 2003, 40.1 million persons moved, or 14.2 percent of the population.[23] This proportion is down from about 17 percent in the early 1990s and 20 percent when measurement started in 1948. It is also not fair because the U.S. population has a long history of being one of the most mobile in the world.

The last two Soviet censuses included a question on place of birth that was used to measure lifetime migration. In 1979, 52.9 percent of the Soviet population still lived in the place where they were born.[24] In 1989, this share had risen to 55.1 percent, consistent with the trend of decreasing mobility in the last decade of the Soviet Union's existence.

Uzbekistan, Azerbaijan, and Tajikistan had the least mobile populations, with all having more than three-quarters of their populations still residing in their places of birth.[25] Latvia and Lithuania had the most mobile populations according to this measure, with 45 percent of their populations still residing in their place of birth. This obviously reflects the postwar migration of Russians and Russian speakers into these republics. Again, this is perhaps an unfair comparison, but the 2000 U.S. census includes a question about residence five years previously. The census found that 45.1 percent of the population had moved in just the previous half decade.[26] According to the 1979 USSR census, only 16 percent of the population had moved in the previous five years, and in 1989, only 13 percent had. In the 1989 census, it was also possible to deduce migration within the past year and compare it with migration turnover from administrative data. The census data show that 3.3 percent of the population had moved in the previous year. This is slightly lower than administrative data because it includes the rural population, which tends to have lower mobility rates.

Figure 1.1 shows migration turnover in Russia during the 1990s.[27] The data include all persons who moved—within a region, across regions, or internationally. The migration rates indicating that about 3 percent of the population of Russia moved in 1991 is roughly consistent with both the migration flow data presented above as well as the 1989 census data. The data clearly show a downward trend in mobility during the 1990s and after 2000. In fact, the number of people moving halved over the period, so that in 2005, only 1.5 percent of the population migrated.

Figure 1.1. Migration Turnover in Russia, 1991–2005

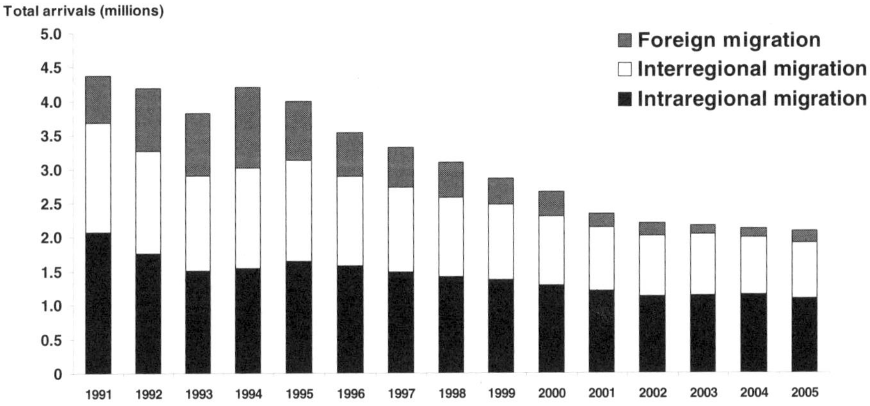

Source: Goskomstat Rossii, *Demograficheskiy yezhegodnik Rossii,* selected years.

Limited data for the other CIS states indicate roughly the same levels and trends as in Russia. Around 1990, migration rates combining both internal and international moves indicated that between 4 percent (in Belarus) and 1 percent (in Georgia) of persons moved.[28] According to these data, it appears that as time went on an increased share of the total migration turnover was confined to within countries as opposed to across international borders. For all twelve CIS countries, the share of arrivals from other parts of the country increased from 1991 to 2001. For nearly all the countries, the share of departures to other parts of the country, as opposed to other countries, also decreased. The only exceptions are Armenia, where the share of outmigrants going to other parts of Armenia decreased from 58 percent in 1991 to 31 percent in 2000. Likewise, for Tajikistan, the share of persons going to other parts of Tajikistan decreased from 50 to 40 percent from 1991 to 1995, and likely much further if more recent data were available. For both these countries, people increasingly looked abroad for work, as measured by both these official data and unofficial or anecdotal data.

During the course of the 1990s, international migration rates for different CIS countries showed a similar trend of an increase to a peak at the middle of the decade followed by declines to the present. In 1993 in Latvia and Estonia, both home to sizable Russian populations, emigration amounted to more than 1 percent of the population. From Armenia in 1993 and 1994, the worst years of its steep economic decline, more than 1 percent of the population was leaving, according to these data. In Russia, the recipient of the bulk of these migrants from the other CIS countries followed this same general trend in its immigration rate, although at its peak in 1994, the population increase from migration was only 0.5 percent of the Russian population. In all countries, the migration turnover declined roughly by half during the 1990s, as in Russia.

Though the picture of mobility in the post-Soviet space is somewhat clouded by the poor-quality data, it is possible to draw some tentative conclusions from the data that are available. These point to trends of decreasing levels of population mobility, at least on a permanent basis, which is what most of the above figures encompass. As will be discussed below, there is considerable evidence of increased rates of mobility on a temporary basis. The statistical systems of the successor states have been slow to begin to capture these new temporary, circular, and often illegal flows. In the early 1990s, more of the migration that did place was international, while after 2000, much of the recorded migration is within countries. This would seem to indicate that in the early 1990s, much was diaspora migration of people moving to ethnic homelands and that this tapered off as diaspora populations sought different accommodations. By 2000, an increasing portion of migration was economically motivated. The overall decreased mobility rates point to an inability of the population of the FSU states to adjust to regional economic change. This might be due to a lack of financial resources to be able to move, a lack of information about destination regions, or slowness in the development of housing and mortgage markets, which enable mobility. This inability to migrate away from regions with deteriorating economies has led to pockets of increased poverty but also temporary labor migration in search of work in other regions and other countries.

Changes in the Ethnic Composition of the Post-Soviet States

The Soviet Union was a multiethnic country that disbanded along its ethnic seams and may not be done breaking apart along those lines. It became this way through centuries of expansion of Tsarist Russia and later the Soviet Union that incorporated lands of non-Russian groups. This was accompanied by both spontaneous and state-sponsored out-migration of Russians and other groups into the non-Russian, non-Slavic periphery and the mixing of members of these groups within the closed migration space of the

Soviet Union. The result of these centuries of ethnic mixing are contained in table 1.2, which shows the distribution of the titular nationalities across the fifteen successor states that emerged from the breakup of the Soviet Union at the time of the 1989 USSR population census, conducted just before the dissolution.

Following the 1926 census, one's nationality became an important social marker that was stamped on a person's passport. The Soviets used the results of this census to draw the boundaries of the homelands of the groups that had come under their control, provided they were geographically concentrated and constituted a majority of the population in their homeland. There was both conscious and unconscious gerrymandering in the demarcation of these homelands. Because of this fact, as well as migration out of their homelands, in-migration of other groups, differential rates of natural increase, ethnic reidentification, and differing ways in which nationality data were collected and compiled in subsequent censuses, the shares that the titular groups made up of their homelands and their concentration within them varied considerably at the end of the Soviet period.

For the fifteen newly independent states, the share that the titular population made up of their homelands ranged from Armenians, who made up 93 percent of Armenia, to Kazakhs, who totaled just 40 percent of Kazakhstan, although this was up from a low of 30 percent at the time of 1959 census. The only other groups that made up more than four-fifths of their own homelands were Azeris, who were 83 percent of the population of Azerbaijan, and Russians, with 82 percent of the population of the Russian Soviet Federated Socialist Republic. Both Latvians and Kyrgyz constituted only 52 percent of their homelands. In most cases, Russians were the largest minority group, with a range from 1.6 percent of the population of Armenia to 38 percent of the population of Kazakhstan and 20 percent or more of the populations of Estonia, Kyrgyzstan, Latvia, and Ukraine.

The titular groups of the three Caucasus states were somewhat disbursed among them, with the population of Georgia being 8 percent Armenian and 6 percent Azeri, and Azerbaijan being 6 percent Armenian. The latter figure was probably higher before the 1989 census, which was conducted after the hostilities between Armenia and Azerbaijan over Nagorno-Karabakh had started. The titular groups of the three Baltic states were much less spread out among each other, and Russians were the main minority group, although there were small Ukrainian and Belarusan populations in each and a sizable Polish minority in Lithuania, part of which had been Poland. Central Asia, because of the more recent development of ethnic consciousness and bor-

Table 1.2. Ethnic Composition of the USSR by Union Republic, 1989 (thousands)

Union republic	Total	Armenians	Azeris	Belarusians	Estonians	Georgians	Kazakhs
USSR	285,743	4,623	6,770	10,036	1,027	3,981	8,136
Armenia	3,305	3,084	85	1	0	1	0
Azerbaijan	7,021	391	5,805	8	0	14	2
Belarus	10,152	5	5	7,905	1	3	2
Estonia	1,566	2	1	28	963	1	0
Georgia	5,401	437	308	9	2	3,787	3
Kazakhstan	16,464	19	90	183	3	9	6,535
Kyrgyzstan	4,258	4	16	9	0	1	37
Latvia	2,667	3	3	120	3	1	1
Lithuania	3,675	2	1	63	1	1	1
Moldova	4,335	3	3	20	0	1	1
Russia	147,022	532	336	1,206	46	131	636
Tajikistan	5,093	6	2	7	0	1	11
Turkmenistan	3,523	32	33	9	0	1	88
Ukraine	51,452	54	37	440	4	24	11
Uzbekistan	19,810	51	44	29	1	5	808

Source: Goskomstat SSSR, *Natsional'nyy sostav naseleniya SSSR* (Moscow: Finansy i statistika, 1991).

ders not drawn to match homelands, had more diverse populations, with Uzbeks making up 9 percent of the population of Turkmenistan, 13 percent of Kyrgyzstan, and 24 percent of Tajikistan. Uzbekistan itself had significant minority populations of Kazakhs and Kyrgyz. Always the outlier, Moldovans made up just two-thirds of the population of Moldova, with Russians and Ukrainians both constituting about 13 percent.

In terms of the concentration of ethnic groups within their own homelands, Armenians were the least concentrated, with one-third of Armenians in the Soviet Union living outside Armenia, in spite of making up the largest share of their own homeland. Of course, because of the changing borders of the Armenian homeland and other historical factors, there is a large Armenian diaspora population both elsewhere in the Soviet Union as well as outside. Tajiks had the second-lowest share residing within their homeland, with three-quarters in Tajikistan and another 22 percent in Uzbekistan. At the other extreme, more than 90 percent of Estonians, Latvians, Lithuanians, Georgians, and Turkmen resided in their homelands. For most groups, if there was significant spreading of their diaspora group, it was to Russia, where 12 percent of Armenians and Belarusans and 10 percent of Ukrainians lived. Russians were in the middle in terms of concentration within their homeland, with 82.6 percent of Russians living in the Russian Soviet Federated Socialist Republic, 8 percent in Ukraine, and 4 percent in Kazakhstan.

Kyrgyz	Latvians	Lithuanians	Moldovans	Russians	Tajiks	Turkmen	Ukrainians	Uzbeks	Other
2,529	1,459	3,067	3,352	145,155	4,215	2,729	44,186	16,698	27,778
0	0	0	1	52	0	0	8	0	72
0	0	1	2	392	1	0	32	1	372
1	3	8	5	1,342	1	1	291	4	577
0	3	3	1	475	0	0	48	1	40
0	1	1	3	341	1	0	52	1	454
14	3	11	33	6,228	26	4	896	332	2,078
2,230	0	0	2	917	34	1	108	550	348
0	1,388	35	3	906	0	0	92	1	110
0	4	2,924	1	344	1	0	45	1	285
0	0	1	2,795	562	1	0	600	1	347
42	47	70	173	119,866	38	40	4,363	127	19,369
64	0	1	1	388	3,172	20	41	1,198	179
1	1	0	2	334	3	2,536	36	317	129
2	7	11	325	11,356	4	3	37,419	20	1,735
175	1	2	6	1,653	934	122	153	14,142	1,684

Before moving on to an analysis of migration trends by nationality and changes in the nationality composition of the Soviet successor states in their first decade of independence, it is useful to place this information on the ethnic composition in 1989, on the eve of the breakup of the Soviet Union, in some historical perspective. Russians had been expanding into the non-Russian periphery of the Tsarist Empire for centuries, but this outward migration greatly accelerated during the early period of the Soviet Union. There were signs that this expansion was in reverse in the latter part of the Soviet period. Overall, the Russian Federation had net out-migration vis-à-vis the non-Russian republics for most of the Soviet period until 1975, when the net migration became positive in favor of Russia. From that year until the Soviet Union disbanded, Russia gained an average of 165,000 persons a year from the other republics through migration. The proportion of Russians in the population of the fourteen non-Russian republics peaked in 1959 at 19.6 percent and had declined to 18.2 percent by 1989.[29] However, this trend differed between the six European republics (the three Baltics, Ukraine, Belarus, and Moldova) and the eight southern republics (the three Transcaucasian and five Central Asian). In the six European republics collectively and each individually, the Russian shares of the total populations continued to rise throughout the Soviet period, from 9.0 percent of the population of these states in 1926 before peaking at 20.3 percent in 1989. This was because Russian migration continued into these states throughout the Soviet period and Russians had rates of natural increase much closer to the titular populations of these republics. For the southern republics, the Russian share was 10.5 percent in 1926, rising to a peak of 22.1 percent in 1959, before declining to 15.9 percent in 1989. The Russian share peaked in 1959 in all these republics, except for Armenia and Azerbaijan, where it peaked even earlier, in 1937. The reasons for this earlier peak in the Russian shares was partially a reversal of migration of Russians and partly because the southern nationalities had much higher rates of natural increase than the Russians.

More comprehensive measures of ethnic mixing confirm that much of the observed Russification in the non-Russian republics occurred early in the Soviet period, before 1959.[30] Various measures of concentration and dissimilarity all point to decreased mixing of nationalities. Looking at the territorial concentration of nationalities within their homelands during the Soviet period, evidence suggests that there was a trend of increasing concentration. Only Russians and Belarusans show significant declines in the portions residing in their homelands. The share of Russians residing in Russia declined from 93 percent in 1926 to 83 percent in 1989, while the share of Belarusans living in Belarus fell from 85 to 79 percent over the same period.

Although the evidence presented above points to increased concentrations of ethnic groups in their homelands and overall decreased levels of ethnic mixing, these levels should be placed in an international context. Each of the successor states to the Soviet Union emerged with significant minority populations, and nearly all the new states had significant diaspora populations in the other states. Overall, 43 million members of the titular groups of the fifteen successor states resided outside their homelands when the Soviet Union dissolved (see table 1.2). With independence, many of the new states sought to elevate members of the titular group above minorities through the institution of exclusionary citizenship and language laws.[31] In other ways, the minority groups in the newly independent states felt real or perceived discrimination. Possible job loss or the need to learn often linguistically distant languages were factors in individuals' migration cost/benefit equation that pushed them to make the decision to leave. Likewise, many members of these diaspora groups thought that migrating to their homelands would enhance their life chances. This has both economic and noneconomic causes. Most people have a desire to live with people like themselves, whether those with similar economic levels, similar ethnic and cultural groups, or similar political views. Witness the increased geographic concentration of Americans into "red" (Republican) and "blue" (Democratic) states, counties, and even neighborhoods. Cultural as well as economic factors drove the migration of groups with external homelands such as Germans and Jews. To what extent has this theorized concentration within ethnic homelands taken place?

Table 1.3 shows data on net migration of the FSU titular and other major nationalities with Russia since the time of the 1989 census. The pattern is rather clear because, for most of the larger ethnic groups, there was positive net migration to Russia. In the period 1989–93, just before and after the breakup of the Soviet Union, patterns of overall and ethnic migration were difficult to discern. Since 1994, however, there has been a clear pattern of immigration to Russia of all the non-Russian FSU titular groups except Belarusans. Armenians stand out as the only non-Russian titular group with positive migration to Russia in every year from 1989 to 2005. Armenians, along with Azeris, Georgians, and Tajiks, have considerably increased as a share of their 1989 totals in Russia as the result of migration. However, comparing the numbers who have migrated to the numbers in Russia in 1989 might not be entirely correct, because these were not the base populations at risk of migrating. Of the titular populations outside Russia in 1989, of the fifteen titular nationalities, 13 percent of the Russian population outside Russia has migrated to Russia, as has 9 percent of the Armenian population. Others, though positive, have seen smaller amounts of their total populations migrate to Russia, at least on a full-time permanent basis.

Figure 1.2 shows the net migration of Russians with each of the non-Russian FSU states since 1989. A rather clear pattern emerges as to the percentage of the Russian population that has left each state. From the three Transcaucasian states and Tajikistan, half or more of the Russian population have left. In all these states, there have been periods of ethnic violence coupled with steep economic downturns. From the Central Asian states, besides Tajikistan, about a quarter of Russians have left. From the Baltic states and Moldova, roughly one in eight Russians have left, and from the other two Slavic states, there has been minimal migration of the Russian populations. As mentioned above, there has been net migration of about 13.8 percent of the 25.3 million people in the Russian diaspora. This consists of an immigration to Russia of 5.5 million and an emigration of 2 million; thus, though the overall migration balance of the Russian diaspora has been positive, there is evidence of considerable churning.

Table 1.4 updates the ethnic composition of the union republics shown in table 1.2 by compiling the distribution of the titular nationalities of the

Table 1.3. Nationality Composition of Migration between Russia and the States of the Former Soviet Union, 1989–2005 (thousands)

		In Russia		Outside Russia	
	Net Migration, 1989–2005	Numbers of Each Nationality, 1989	Net Migration, 1989–2005, as percentage of 1989 Total	Numbers of Each Nationality, 1989	Net Migration, 1989–2005, as percentage of 1989 Total
Total	5,221	147,400	3.5		
Russians	3,341	119,866	2.8	25,289.5	13.2
Ukrainians	304	4,363	7.0	39,823.1	0.8
Belarusans	32	1,206	2.6	8,830.0	0.4
Moldovans	14	173	7.9	3,179.7	0.4
Latvians	1	47	1.7	1,412.2	0.1
Lithuanians	–1	70	–1.4	2,997.0	–0.0
Estonians	1	46	2.6	980.3	0.1
Armenians	373	532	70.1	4,090.8	9.1
Azeris	92	336	27.2	6,434.5	1.4
Georgians	50	131	38.5	3,850.4	1.3
Kazakhs	–10	636	–1.5	7,500.0	–0.1
Kyrgyz	–2	42	–4.4	2,487.2	–0.1
Tajiks	37	38	96.8	4,177.2	0.9
Turkmen	0	40	–0.5	2,689.2	–0.0
Uzbeks	21	127	16.5	16,570.9	0.1
Jews	8	537	1.4	841.2	0.9
Germans	84	842	10.0	1,196.7	7.0
Ossetians	49	402	12.1	195.7	24.9
Tatars	268	5,522	4.8	1,126.9	23.7
Bashkir	38	1,345	2.8	103.7	36.8
Other	380				

Sources: For 2005: Goskomstat Rossii, *Demograficheskiy yezhegodnik Rossii 2005* (Moscow: Goskomstat Rossii, 2006), 515–26. For 2004: Goskomstat Rossii, *Chislennost' i migratsiya naseleniya Rossiyskoy Federatsii v 2004 godu: Statisticheskiy byulleten'* (Moscow: Goskomstat Rossii, 2005), 86–91. For 2003: Goskomstat Rossii, *Chislennost' i migratsiya naseleniya Rossiyskoy Federatsii v 2003 godu: Statisticheskiy byulleten'* (Moscow: Goskomstat Rossii, 2004), 82–87. For 2002: Goskomstat Rossii, *Chislennost' i migratsiya naseleniya Rossiyskoy Federatsii v 2002 godu: Statisticheskiy byulleten'* (Moscow: Goskomstat Rossii, 2003), 80. For 2001: Goskomstat Rossii, *Demograficheskiy yezhegodnik Rossii* (Moscow: Goskomstat Rossii, 2002), 368–71. For 1994–2000: Goskomstat Rossii, *Demograficheskiy yezhegodnik Rossii* (Moscow: Goskomstat Rossii, 2000), 354–57. For 1989–93: Goskomstat Rossii, *Chislennost' i sotsial'no-demograficheskiye kharakteristiki Russkogo naseleniya v respublikakh byvshego SSSR* (Moscow: Goskomstat Rossii, 1994), 28–29.

newly independent states across the fifteen FSU successor states based on the 2000 round of population censuses. A number of qualifiers must be made before any conclusions can be drawn from these data on changes in the ethnic composition of the successor states. The first is that the population censuses were not conducted at the same time (the dates of the censuses are

Figure 1.2. Net Migration of Russians with Russia, 1989–2005

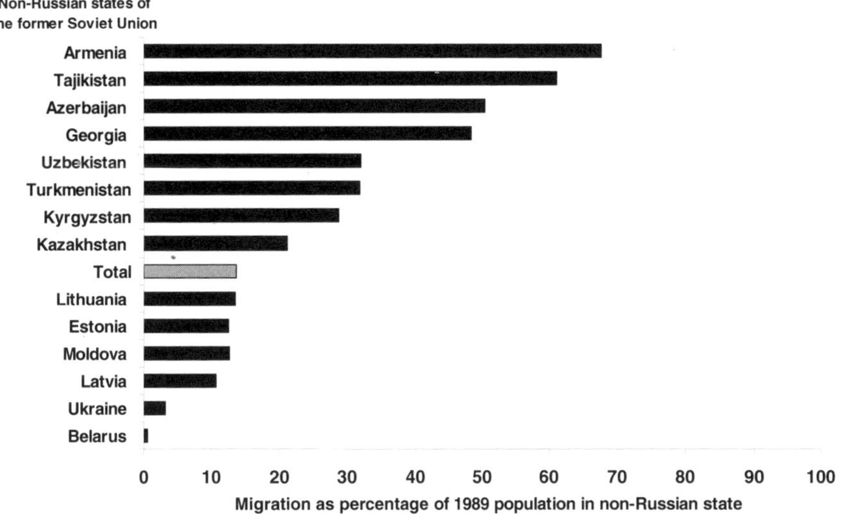

Source: Goskomstat Rossii, *Chislennost' i migratsiya naseleniya Rossiyskoy Federatsii,* various years.

noted in the table). Thirteen of the fifteen countries conducted their first censuses as independent states between January 1999 and October 2002, with Turkmenistan and Uzbekistan being the outliers. Turkmenistan conducted a census in 1995, and Uzbekistan has yet to conduct its first post-Soviet census. A few of the countries followed the schedule of the USSR, which had conducted recent censuses in years ending in "9." Others had intended to do so but encountered financial or technical difficulties. Two of the countries, Moldova and Uzbekistan, have yet to conduct their censuses and publish results based on them. For these two countries, estimates of the nationality composition were made based upon data on migration and natural increase by nationality.

With the USSR republic statistical offices becoming independent national statistical offices, there were obvious variances in census methodology. Though all the countries followed the pattern of previous USSR censuses and included a question on nationality, there were a number of deviations that could affect comparison of the results with the last Soviet census. These included changes in the exact wording of the question on nationality, changes in the order in which the question appeared on the census

Table 1.4. Ethnic Composition of the Soviet Successor States, 1999–2002 (thousands)

Country (Census Data)	Total	Armenians	Azeris	Belarusians	Estonians	Georgians	Kazakh
Former USSR	284,667	4,856	8,324	9,547	966	3,920	9,745
Armenia (October 2002)	3,213	3,145	0	0	0	0	0
Azerbaijan (January 1999)	7,953	121	7,206	1	0	15	0
Belarus (February 1999)	10,045	10	6	8,159	0	3	1
Estonia (March 2000)	1,370	0	0	17	930	0	1
Georgia (January 2002)	4,372	249	285	0	0	3,661	0
Kazakhstan (February 1999)	14,953	15	78	112	2	5	7,985
Kyrgyzstan (March 1999)	4,823	1	14	3	0	1	43
Latvia (March 2000)	2,377	3	2	97	3	1	0
Lithuania (April 2001)	3,484	1	1	43	0	0	0
Moldova (January 1999)	4,293	0	0	0	0	0	0
Russia (October 2002)	145,164	1,130	621	815	28	198	655
Tajikistan (January 2000)	6,127	1	1	0	0	0	1
Turkmenistan (January 1995)	4,418	34	37	4	0	1	87
Ukraine (December 2001)	47,843	100	45	276	3	34	6
Uzbekistan (January 1999)	24,231	47	29	20	0	0	966

Note: 0 indicates that the data rounded to less than 1,000.

Sources: Armenia: National Statistical Service of the Republic of Armenia, *The Results of the 2001 Census of the Republic of Armenia (Figures of the Republic of Armenia)* (Yerevan: National Statistical Service of the Republic of Armenia, 2003), 362–63. Azerbaijan: Goskomstat Azerbaijan, *The Population Census of the Azerbaijan Republic 1999* (Baku: Goskomstat Azerbaijan, 2001), 381. Belarus: MinStat Belarus, *Statistical Yearbook 2001* (Minsk: MinStat Belarus, 2001), 70. Estonia: Statistical Office of Estonia, *2000 Population and Housing Census: Citizenship, Nationality, Mother Language, and Command of Foreign Languages* (Tallin: Statistical Office of Estonia, 2001), vol. 2, 14. Georgia: State Department of Statistics of Georgia, http://www.statistics.ge. Kazakhstan: Agenstvo po statistike Kazakhstan, *Natsional'nyy sostav naseleniya Respubliki Kazakhstan* (Almaty: Agenstvo po statistike Kazakhstan, 2000), vol. 1, 6–7. Kyrgyzstan: Natskomstat Kyrgyzstan, *Osnovnyye itogi pervoy national'noy perepisi naseleniya Kyrgyzskoy Respubliki 1999 goda* (Bishkek: Natskomstat Kyrgyzstan, 2000), 26. Latvia: Central Statistical Bureau of Latvia, Results of the 2000

Kyrgyz	Latvians	Lithuanians	Moldovans	Russians	Tajiks	Turkmen	Ukrainians	Uzbeks	Other
3,490	1,414	3,009	3,457	133,978	6,299	3,602	42,161	21,378	28,519
0	0	0	0	15	0	0	2	0	51
0	0	0	0	142	0	0	29	0	440
0	2	6	4	1,142	1	1	237	2	471
0	2	2	0	351	0	0	29	0	37
0	0	0	0	68	0	0	7	0	102
11	2	7	19	4,480	26	2	547	371	1,292
3,128	0	0	1	603	43	0	50	665	271
0	1,371	33	2	703	0	0	64	0	99
0	3	2,907	1	220	0	0	22	0	285
0	0	0	2,997	484	0	0	552	0	260
32	29	45	172	115,868	120	33	2,943	123	22,352
66	0	0	0	68	4,898	20	4	937	131
2	0	0	2	299	3	3,402	23	407	118
1	5	7	259	8,334	4	4	37,542	12	1,212
250	0	0	0	1,202	1,204	140	110	18,861	1,401

Population and Housing Census in Latvia: Collection of Statistical Data (Riga: Central Statistical Bureau of Latvia, 2000), 142–43. Lithuania: Statistics Lithuania, http://www.std.lt/web/main.php. Moldova: Estimates for 1999 are from "The End of an Empire: Migration and the Changing Nationality Composition of the Soviet Successor States," by Timothy Heleniak, in *Diasporas and Ethnic Migrants: Germany, Israel and Post-Soviet Successor States in Comparative Perspective,* ed. Rainer Munz and Rainer Ohliger (London: Frank Case, 2003), 131–45. Russia: Goskomstat Rossii, Broshyura "Osnonvyee itogi Vserossiyskoy perepisi naseleniya 2002 goda," http://www.gks.ru, table 7. Tajikistan: Goskomstat Tajikistan, *Naseleniye Respubliki Tadjikistan 2000 po itogam perepisi 20–27 yanvarya 2000 g.* (Dushanbe: Goskomstat Tajikistan, 2002), 155. Turkmenistan: Goskomstat Turkmenistan, *Brief Results of the 1995 National Population Census of Turkmenistan* (Ashgabat: Goskomstat Turkmenistan, 1997), 12. Ukraine: Derzhgomstat Ukraine, *Vseukrainskiy perepis naseleniya 2001* (www.ukrstat.gov.ua). Uzbekistan: Estimates for 1999 are from Heleniak, "End of an Empire," 131–45.

form (being before or after the question on language being most crucial), changes in whether there was a list of nationalities to choose from, and changes in how the results were processed and presented (the most crucial being the combining or separation of ethnic groups). As in the case of other countries, there were also attempts by political and ethnic leaders to influence the results of the ethnic composition for or against certain groups.

There are three components of change in the ethnic composition of any region between censuses: natural increase, net migration, and ethnic reidentification. The last pertains to persons who identify themselves as one nationality in one census and a different nationality in a subsequent census. None of the successor states followed the U.S. example in the 2000 census and allowed people to identify as more than one race, even though many persons in the FSU are the product of mixed marriages and could have legitimately claimed more than one nationality. "Ethnicity" and "nationality" are rather fungible concepts, and people's perceptions of which group they identify with change over time. This was certainly the case in the immediate post-Soviet years, when there was rapid social change and the relative position of nationalities vis-à-vis each other was changing.

An example of this is Russians in Ukraine. It is impossible to determine the exact extent of ethnic reidentification, but some inferences can be made. In comparison with other pairs of nationalities found across the USSR, Russians and Ukrainians are linguistically, culturally, and in many other ways rather close. In 1989, there were 11.4 million Russians in Ukraine, constituting 22 percent of the population. There were 37.4 million Ukrainians in Ukraine, making up 72.4 percent of the population. For Russians in Ukraine, during the intercensus period from January 1989 to December 2001, there was an estimated excess of deaths over births of 515,000 and an estimated net emigration of 339,000.[32] If these figures are close to the actual situation, this indicates a Russian population at the time of the December 2001 census of 10.5 million. However, the census found only 8.3 million, or more than 2 million less than expected. During the same period, there was an estimated natural decrease of the Ukrainian population of Ukraine of 1,955,000 and net immigration of 500,000, which combined would indicate a Ukrainian population of 36.0 million. The census enumerated 37.5 million Ukrainians, about 1,577,000 more than expected. Though, admittedly, there could have been some error in either the natural increase or net migration figures, it is not likely that they would have been large enough to produce these large discrepancies in the numbers of Ukrainians and Russians enumerated in the census. The bulk of these differences must be attributable to persons in Ukraine who identified themselves as Russian during the last Soviet census in 1989 but who choose to designate themselves as Ukrainian in the first census conducted in independent Ukraine. In both cases, they identified themselves as belonging to the titular nationality, on the assumption that Russians were the titular nationality in the USSR. Though difficult to prove precisely, it is likely that this trend of ethnic reidentification toward the titular group occurred in the censuses of many of the other FSU states.

With these qualifiers in mind, the data do offer a reasonable enough picture of changes in the nationality composition of the FSU states during their first decade of independence to be able to draw conclusions and make some inferences about the migration patterns that influenced these changes. Before the 1989 USSR census, there was a fear that the results would reveal that Russians were no longer the majority in the Soviet Union. Though this did not prove to be the case, they were a thin majority, at 50.8 percent. According to the collective census results, the Russian share of the FSU states has fallen below a majority, to 47 percent. Though this might have less relevance now that they are not part of one country, as has become clear, the successor states seem to be constituting a common migration space, while other attempts at economic integration through the CIS and other mechanisms seem to have failed. These differential rates of population growth among countries and nationalities will play a role in driving future migration trends because, at the same time that the Russian share has declined, the share of the five Central Asian titular groups has increased from 12.0 to 15.6 percent of the combined population of the FSU states.

The titular share of each of the fifteen successor states, with the exception of Russia, increased between the 1989 and the later censuses, with especially large increases in Tajikistan, Kazakhstan, Georgia, and Kyrgyzstan. The share of Russians in Russia fell slightly, from 81.5 to 79.8 percent, in spite of the net migration of 3.4 million Russians from the other states. This is because of some out-migration of Russians to the states beyond the FSU, likely an element of reidentification away from the Russian nationality between censuses, and also a much higher rate of natural increase than the non-Russian groups. For the other Slavic states, the Baltics, and Moldova, these increases in the titular share represent a sharp reversal of lower titular shares over most of the Soviet period. For the Central Asian and Caucasus states, these increased titular shares are a sharp acceleration that has been under way since the 1950s. For all except Kazakhstan and Kyrgyzstan, the titular shares recorded are higher than recorded during any Soviet census.

With rising titular shares, the Russian shares declined in every successor state, including, as mentioned above, in Russia. The largest percentage declines were from those states where the Russian out-migration was the highest—the three Transcaucasian states and Tajikistan. The other two Slavic nationalities, Ukrainians and Belarusans, had also been quite spread throughout the Soviet Union outside their homelands. For both, their numbers declined in even larger percentages outside their homelands than Russians. This was presumably because they felt even less secure about their future prospects than did Russians as these states took steps to elevate their titular nationalities. Another contributing factor was the fact that the size of their ethnic enclaves in these states was smaller than that of Russians. The long-term trends in the shares of Russians in the non-Russian states mirrors that of the titular groups. Declining Russian shares in the six European successor states is a reversal of a long-term trend, but there remain significant Russian minorities in all of them, with only Lithuania having less than a 10 percent Russian population. The declining Russian shares in the eight southern states is a continuation of a long-term trend, and only in Kazakhstan and Kyrgyzstan do Russians still make up more than 10 percent of the population. Other noticeable shifts include the large increase within Russia of Tajiks, Armenians, Azeris, and Georgians. The Tajik population more than tripled from 38,000 to 120,000, and the already sizable Armenian population more than doubled from 532,000 to 1.1 million.

In terms of the theorized increased concentration of titular groups within their homelands, this seems to be confirmed as all but two groups increased their share residing in their homeland.[33] The two exceptions are Armenians, who went from having 66.7 percent of Armenians residing on a permanent basis in Armenia to 64.8 percent. Likewise, Georgians fell from having 95.1 percent of all Georgians residing in Georgia to 93.4 percent. For Armenians, the share of all FSU Armenians residing in Russia increased from 11.5 to 23.3 percent. Part of this was due to the fact that many Armenians who left Azerbaijan during the conflict over Nagorno-Karabakh went to Russia instead of Armenia. The share of all Armenians in the successor states residing in Azerbaijan declined from 8.4 to just 2.5 percent, or from 391,000 to 121,000. Not surprisingly, it was the most disbursed groups who had the largest increases in concentration in their homelands—all three Slavic groups, Moldovans, and Uzbeks who were spread among a number of other Central Asian states.

Another qualifier to the above discussion is that many of these data on changes in the nationality composition of the FSU successor states are based on counts of the permanent population. Many of the available data on the nationality composition of migration are based on long-term, permanent, legal migration. Illegal, irregular, and various forms of temporary or circular migration have not been well captured in the migration statistics of the FSU states (nor have they been in many other countries with well-developed statistical systems). Much of the previous analysis of concentrations within homelands is based on those who reside *permanently* in their homelands.

In the last few decades of the Soviet Union's existence, there was growing concern about the spatial mismatch between industrial resources and additions to the labor force. The bulk of the Soviet Union's industrial infrastructure was located in central Russia, the Urals, Ukraine, and Belarus. Meanwhile, most of the increments to the labor force were coming from the Central Asian states. For decades, additions to the labor force had been a major factors fueling Soviet economic growth. There was a rather rigorous debate as to whether more investment should be made in the republics of Central Asia, where the populations were growing the fastest, or to induce young Central Asians to migrate to and work in central Russia and other more industrialized regions of the Soviet Union. One element of this debate was whether Central Asians would even migrate out of Central Asia in large enough numbers to labor-deficit regions. Western observers were also engaged in this debate. On the one side were those who argued that Central Asians would not migrate out of the region in large numbers because of cultural factors.[34] These include a lack of Russian language skills, educational differences, religion, and other traditional beliefs such as family formation preferences.

Others have argued that because of more universal laws governing migration, economic considerations would outweigh cultural factors and induce Central Asians to migrate to other regions of the Soviet Union in search of employment because the expansion of their own economies would not be sufficient to accommodate all the surplus labor.[35] From the summary above on migration theory, it should be apparent that both economic and noneconomic factors both weigh in an individual's cost/benefit equation on whether to migrate or not. Though the Central Asian republics and Russia are no longer part of one country, it has become apparent that they continue to constitute one migration space with many of the same regional development and labor supply issues that they inherited from the Soviet period. Observers on neither side of this argument in the 1970s could have foreseen the events of the 1990s and the twenty-first century, but it appears that both sides have a claim to having been partially correct in their predictions.

The number of persons of the Central Asian titular nationalities living *permanently* in Russia increased moderately from 882,000 in 1989 to 963,000 in 2002, with about half this increment attributable to migration. However, there is considerable evidence that the number of Central Asians who are migrating to Russia on a *temporary* basis for labor purposes has increased considerably. In the early period following the breakup of the Soviet Union, ethnic considerations and a desire to be in one's homeland may have dominated migration decisions. But in the second half of the 1990s, economic considerations and the desire to feed one's family took over. In each year since 1994, there has been positive net migration into Russia of each of the Central Asian titular ethnic groups. This encompasses legal, recorded immigration. If illegal, temporary migration were added, the evidence would point to what could be termed a massive migration to Russia, with economic considerations being primary and cultural considerations a distant second. For many Central Asians, Russia has become a major migration destination to an extent that Soviet planners and Western Sovietologists could have never imagined. The exact causes of this and other migration streams under way in the post-Soviet space is examined more thoroughly in the next section.

Causes of Migration across the Post-Soviet Space

The discussion of migration theory above showed that potential migrants weigh the costs and benefits of their current location and move if the incomes of other locations outweigh those in their current location by more than the cost of the move. Factors other than wages are explicitly or implicitly factored into this cost/benefit equation. These rising income differentials among the FSU states and among the regions within them can explain much of the post-Soviet migration that is taking place. The absence of appropriate migration legislation in the early period of independence explains why much of the migration was undocumented, illegal, or quasi-legal. In recent years, there has been an increased effort on the part of the successor states to regulate migration movements across their borders. Ethnic or cultural factors and a desire to maintain ties to one's homeland can explain much of the temporary nature of the migration that is taking place.

An International Labor Organization study estimated that there are between 3.0 and 3.5 million illegal guest migrants in Russia.[36] Only about 300,000 guest workers possessed proper documentation.[37] A person can become illegal through illegal entry, residence, or activity; but in the early period of independence, these categories were murky at best. About a half million of the total were persons who entered Russia illegally with the goal of seeking asylum but who were denied. The bulk, between 2.0 and 2.5 million, were those who entered through visas or legally without needing a visa and who are working in violation of their visa status. An estimated 2 million of these undocumented labor migrants are from Central Asia.[38] This includes an estimated 600,000 Tajiks, which is 10 percent of the Tajik population, roughly comparable to the share of the Mexican population working in the United States. Like other non-Russian ethnic groups in the FSU, most Tajiks speak at least some Russian, and most view their stay in Russia as temporary and intend to return.[39] The permanent legal net migration of Tajiks to Russia during the 1990s was only 5 percent of this total. There are estimates of up to 500,000 Kyrgyz working in Russia as well, although the Kyrgyz Embassy claims only 30,000, with the true number lying somewhere between the two. Between 600,000 and 700,000 Uzbeks are working aboard as well. From Moldova, 600,000 individuals, or 14 percent of the population, are working aboard, with more than half in Russia but many others in Western European countries.[40] In Armenia, there is a well-developed seasonal pattern of migration, mostly to Russia, where people leave from January to August for seasonal work in agriculture and construction and return between the months of September and December.

On the demand side, these persons are filling a niche in the Russian labor market by accepting jobs that the growing Russian middle class does not want, with many working in construction, household services, and in the street markets in Moscow and other large cities in Russia. Labor migration and the remittances that these people send home have become a survival strategy and informal social safety net. The size of these remittances is quite significant, with estimates of 4 to 7 percent of gross domestic product in Georgia, Armenia, and Tajikistan according to official International Monetary Fund balance-of-payments statistics.[41] There is the usual caveat that official remittances grossly understate unofficial totals. Regardless, their size and importance are such that groups such as the International Organization for Migration are attempting to funnel remittances into development projects.[42]

Much of this legal, illegal, and temporary migration among the FSU states can be explained by the growing economic disparities among them. As stated above, there were attempts to equalize living standards among Soviet regions and republics; and though not entirely equal, the Soviet

Union had one of the lowest income distributions in the world.[43] This was true across regions as well, limiting the influence of regional disparities on migration. Table 1.5 shows some economic indicators for the FSU states that have an impact on migration. The ratio of the countries with the highest and lowest gross domestic product among FSU states widened from 4.9 in 1990 to 12.5 in 2002. More comprehensive measures, such as the coefficient of variation, show the same rise, from 0.50 in 1990 to 0.73 in 2002.[44] In most of the Central Asian and Caucasus states, which are losing people in large numbers, their transition depressions were much steeper and lasted much longer than in Russia. Unemployment rates and, more important in these relatively young populations, youth unemployment rates are very high. Real wages in most of these countries have fallen considerably and have yet to recover.

A number of factors influencing migration patterns among the FSU states both explain the immediate economic disparities in these states and also shed some light on possible future economic development.[45] Initial conditions in the transition states explained output declines in the early 1990s, but reform policies explain output variation thereafter. Seven of the eight central Asian and Caucasus states are classified as noncompetitive political or war-torn regimes. In the former, political power is concentrated in the executive branch (or ruling family, in some cases), which has stifled economic reform. In many of these countries, social spending on health and education has fallen to very low levels. Many of these countries are stuck in a no man's land between plan and market. Many of the landlocked central Asian and Caucasus states do not have good neighbors like some of the countries recently acceding to the EU, which benefit both economically and politically.

Four of the international financial institutions have come to realize the effects that the external shocks and poor reform policies have had on the poorest of the FSU states and have developed the CIS-Seven initiative, a combination of both strengthening reform efforts and debt relief in Armenia, Azerbaijan, Georgia, Kyrgyzstan, Moldova, Tajikistan, and Uzbekistan. A report on this initiative concluded that these countries all face difficult fiscal and external outlooks in the future.[46] Inequality has not declined in recent years despite economic growth, and many of the nonincome dimensions of poverty, such as access to social services, might be worsening. These dim economic prospects and worsening social indicators factor into the migration equations of people in these countries in favor of decisions to migrate elsewhere.

Table 1.5. Selected Economic Indicators for the States of the Former Soviet Union, 2002

State	GDP per Capita (current international dollars) 1990	GDP per Capita (current international dollars) 2002	Real GDP Growth (Index: 1989 = 100)	Cumulative Output Decline (percent)	Annual Registered Unemployment Rate (average percentage of labor force)	Registered Unemployed Age 15–24 Years (percentage of total annual unemployed)	Real Wages (Index: Base Year = 100)
Russia	8,340	8,230	74.9	40	1.8	20.7	63.9
Ukraine	6,930	4,870	49.5	59	3.8	N.A.	81.1
Belarus	4,310	5,520	97.1	35	3.0	36.7	N.A.
Moldova	3,040	1,470	40.7	63	1.9	31.6	62.9
Latvia	8,570	9,210	81.6	51	8.9	14.0	74.5
Lithuania	9,230	10,320	81.4	44	11.3	10.9	49.7
Estonia	8,050	12,260	97.0	35	5.9	17.9	79.9
Armenia	2,700	3,120	84.8	63	10.8	6.4	44.1
Azerbaijan	N.A.	3,210	70.3	60	1.4	19.4	81.1
Georgia	4,060	2,260	41.0	78	1.2	13.1	122.7
Kazakhstan	4,620	5,870	93.6	41	2.9	30.1	58.7
Kyrgyzstan	1,980	1,620	73.3	50	3.1	23.4	67.9
Tajikistan	1,880	980	61.3	50	2.5	39.3	31.6
Turkmenistan	4,640	4,250	99.4	48	N.A.	N.A.	66.5
Uzbekistan	1,490	1,670	107.0	18	0.4	56.3	22.5

Note: GDP = gross domestic product; PPP = purchasing power parity; N.A. = not available.
Sources: GDP: World Bank, *World Development Indicators 2004,* CD-ROM. Cumulative output decline: World Bank, *Transition: The First Ten Years—Analysis and Lessons for Eastern Europe and the Former Soviet Union* (Washington, D.C.: World Bank, 2002), 5. Real GDP growth, unemployment rates, and real wages: UNICEF, *Inncoenti Social Monitor 2004* (Florence: UNICEF, 2004), 91–95.

Another factor to be considered when examining causes of migration among the post-Soviet states is the role of the state. In the early 1990s, people could travel visa free across most of the post-Soviet space, and the successor states played a minimal role in directing migration movements.[47] Starting in the late 1990s and continuing after 2000, there was a growing trend of delimiting borders and restricting freedom of movement, especially attempts to control and regulate increasingly common irregular, undocumented, or illegal migration. This was accomplished through the passage and implementation of citizenship and related language laws and other aspects of migration policy. Because most of the FSU states were new, they had to adopt citizenship laws defining a body of citizens. For some, such as the Latvia and Estonia, this had an explicit migration focus.[48] Of course, a major actor in the region is the Russian government and its migration policy. Russia passed a rather restrictive citizenship policy in 2002.[49] Since then, however, the migration debate has continued in light of Russia's falling population size and was highlighted in Vladimir Putin's speech to the State Duma in May 2006, along with policies for increasing the birthrate.

The fifteen FSU successor states have followed divergent paths in migration trends, with some becoming countries of high immigration, some becoming major migrant-sending countries, and some becoming major routes of transit migration. Because of these differences, they have adopted varying migration policies appropriate to their situations. Migrant workers and the remittances they produce have become a key concern for many of the major migrant-sending countries.[50] A number of countries have signed bilateral agreements regulating and regularizing labor-related migration, many of these with Russia.[51] Most have also become signatories to major international migration agreements, such as those dealing with migrant workers, trafficking, and refugees. However, as with other countries, these migration policy instruments are often ineffectual or meet with limited success, especially in achieving desired levels of immigration or emigration, because economic factors often outweigh state intervention. An example is Latvia, where most of the Russians remain despite being denied citizenship because economic conditions are better than in Russia.[52]

The Future of Migration in the Former Soviet Union

As demonstrated above, economic factors such as differences in per capita income are driving migration patterns among the post-Soviet states in the short term. These will continue to be important, but demographic factors will play an important role as well. Figure 1.3 shows the population of the FSU states over the period 1950 to 2050—the past half century and next half century. The countries are grouped into the northern FSU states (the Slavic and Baltic states and Moldova) and the southern FSU states (Central Asia and the Caucasus). The northern states as a group are characterized by continued low fertility, aging populations, an excess of deaths over births, and declining populations. The population of the group and all countries individually peaked in 1990 and is expected to decline over the next half century by about one-third, to 149 million. By contrast, the southern FSU states have younger populations, above-replacement-level fertility, and continually growing populations. As a group, these countries nearly tripled in size, from 25 million in 1950 to 72 million in 2000. Though growth is declining,

Figure 1.3. Populations of the Northern and Southern States of the Former Soviet Union, 1950–2050

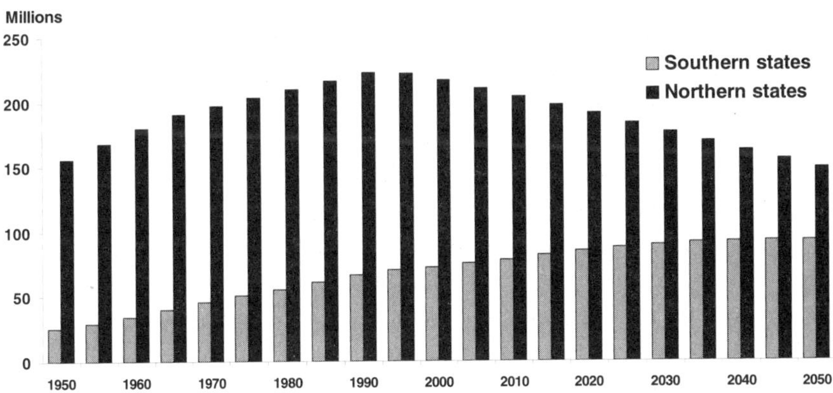

Note: The northern states consist of Russia, Ukraine, Belarus, Moldova, Latvia, Lithuania, and Estonia. The southern states consist of Armenia, Azerbaijan, Georgia, Kazakhstan, Kyrgyzstan, Tajikistan, Turkmenistan, and Uzbekistan.
Source: United Nations Population Division, *World Population Prospects: The 2002 Revision* (http://www.un.org/esa/population/unpop.html).

the momentum built into the age structure of these populations will cause their continued growth—to a projected 93 million in 2050.

Migration is the most volatile and difficult component of population change to project, and until recently the UN and other agencies that do projections simply built in the assumption that net migration would be zero in the very near future. More recent UN projections have relaxed this assumption, because zero net migration is simply not the experience of most countries in the world. The assumption embodied in these projections is that all the FSU states except Russia are expected to have moderate population losses from migration over the next half century, whereas Russia is expected to have a very moderate increase from migration.

Differential rates of population growth (or decline) do not necessarily imply that there will be migration from the high-growth to low-growth areas but does present that precondition. Though the northern FSU states will have declining working-age populations in even greater numbers than their overall population declines, most of the southern FSU states, with their "youth bulges," will have growing working-age populations with economies not growing fast enough to supply jobs. Given their geographic proximity and common historical legacy, it would be only natural that the youth of the southern FSU states would look north for jobs, and, as mentioned above, there is ample evidence that they are doing so. If so, they would be following the pattern of other empires, where members of the periphery followed the colonial powers home after independence. In contrast to the former British and French empires, the Soviet Union was not an overseas empire, which helps to facilitate migration, but an almost self-contained migration space—and that historical legacy causes people to favor destinations in the FSU region over others.

A recent United Nations study examined the issue of using "replacement migration" as a policy measure to address declining and aging populations.[53] (Replacement migration refers to using international migration to offset declines in total population, working-age population, or population aging.) Russia was included in the study, along with other countries that face similar trends of declining and aging populations, including Italy, Germany, France, the United Kingdom, Japan, South Korea, and the United States. Most of the other northern FSU countries face similar issues, with projected population declines by 2050 of between 17 percent (Moldova) and 52 percent (Estonia). Countries with aging and/or declining populations face a number of policy dilemmas, including appropriate retirement ages, pension system reform, and health care for the elderly; support levels and ratios between working and pension-age populations; labor force participation; and possible replacement migration and the integration of these immigrant populations. Governments have three levers at their disposal to offset population aging. One is to increase mortality—obviously not an option, socially or morally. The second is to increase fertility. Most of the northern FSU states, and the other countries in the UN study, have fertility rates in the range of 1.1 to 1.3 children per woman, far below the necessary replacement level of about 2.1. Most do not believe that these rates will get back up to the replacement level any time in the near future. Thus, the governments of these countries with aging populations have replacement migration as a possible policy option.

Russia, under the medium-variant scenario used in the study, is projected to have net migration of 5.4 million between 2000 and 2050.[54] To maintain its same 1995 population, there would have to be net migration of 24.9 million; and to maintain its same working-age population, there would need to be net migration of 35.8 million.[55] In contrast, there was net migration of about 3.3 million into Russia during the 1990s, a period of extraordinary change and unprecedented migration that is not likely to be repeated. With the exception of the United States, the number of migrants needed to maintain the total population is significantly higher than the numbers assumed in the medium-variant scenario. For Russia to maintain a constant working-age population between 2000 and 2050 would require it to have average annual net migration of 4.9 persons per 1,000 current inhabitants. This is about the same required level of migration as for Japan and Europe as a whole. Because of their older age structures, Germany and Italy would require average annual migration of 6.0 and 6.5 persons per 1,000 inhabitants, respectively, whereas the United States, with its younger age structure, would require only 1.3 migrants per 1,000 inhabitants. With the slowdown in migration to Russia in recent years, migration has been less than 1 migrant per 1,000 inhabitants.

For Russia, as well as the other nations with large aging and declining populations analyzed in the UN study, it is obvious that the needed levels of replacement migration are far below the experience of the recent past and far above levels that are politically and socially plausible. In recent years in Europe, the United States, Australia, and Russia, right-wing politicians advocating severe restrictions on migration, to the point of outright bans, have been able to cultivate significant followings among large segments of society. Even low levels of migration will require very careful political and social balancing acts in Russia, the other northern FSU countries, and other major migration destinations. Policies must be designed to accommodate these new migration realities in both destinations and origins—and, most important, between the two. Mexico and the United States, which is home to 10 percent of the Mexican population, have been carrying on a regular dialogue over this large migration stream for decades, which was temporarily interrupted after the terrorist attacks of September 11, 2001. There is evidence that Russia and some of the other FSU states are facing up to this new migration reality in the region and taking steps to regularize it. For instance, agreements on labor migration have been concluded between Russia and Tajikistan and Kyrgyzstan.

It appears that people across the post-Soviet space are responding to migration signals like people are elsewhere in the world and that there is not a separate "post-Soviet migration theory." There were some unique aspects to migration in the Soviet Union, such as the extreme level of state intervention and the fact that the country was an almost completely closed migration space. Yet in spite of recent efforts to influence migratory movements, the role of the FSU successor states in controlling migration is far less than that of the Soviet Union. Some features of the post-Soviet migration experience have also been unique to that region, such as the return of displaced peoples—for example, Crimean Tatars returning across what are now international borders, because their original forced migration was within one country.

Migration was central to the making of Tsarist Russia and the Soviet Union and the accompanying mixing of ethnic groups. It appears to also be playing a central role in the post-Soviet states. Even after barely a decade since the Soviet Union's breakup and the onset of the transition to capitalism, people in the successor states seem to be responding to the same economic and demographic signals that drive migration streams elsewhere in the world. Thus, established migration theory can guide analysts and policymakers in the FSU countries in forecasting the future scope, direction, and composition of these population movements across the post-Soviet space.

Notes

1. In fact, because of the breakup of the country, the results of the 1989 USSR population census were never completely published by the USSR statistical committee.

2. Douglas S. Massey et al., "Theories of International Migration: A Review and Appraisal," *Population and Development Review* 119, no. 3 (September 1993): 431–66.

3. CIS Statistical Committee and East View Publications, *1989 USSR Population Census, CD-ROM* (Minneapolis: Eastview Publications, 1996).

4. Timothy Heleniak, "Out-Migration and Depopulation of the Russian North during the 1990s," *Post-Soviet Geography and Economics,* April–May 1999, 155–205; and MONEE Project on CEE/CIS/Baltic States, "Migration Trends and Policy Implications," in *Innocenti Social Monitor 2004,* by Innocenti Research Center, UNICEF (Florence: UNICEF, 2004), 29–42.

5. Barry R. Chiswick, "Are Immigrants Favorably Self-Selected? An Economic Analysis," in *Migration Theory: Talking across Disciplines,* ed. Caroline B. Brettell and James F. Hollifield (New York: Routledge, 2000), 61–76.

6. Robert A. Lewis, Richard H. Rowland, and Ralph S. Clem, *Nationality and Population Change in Russia and the USSR: An Evaluation of Census Data, 1897–1970* (New York: Praeger Publishers, 1976), 45.

7. Michael J. Bradshaw and Karen Vartapetov, "A New Perspective on Regional Inequalities in Russia," *Eurasian Geography and Economics* 44, no. 6 (September 2003): 403–29.

8. Eugene Krassinets, *Illegal Migration and Employment in Russia,* International Migration Paper 26 (Geneva: International Labor Organization, 1998), 10–11.

9. Formally, this is computed by rearranging the population equation from $P_0 + B - D + I - O = P_1$ (where P = population, B = births, D = deaths, I = in-migrants, O = out-migrants) or $P_0 + B - D + NM = P_1$ by combining in-migrants and out-migrants (where NM = net migration) to $P_1 - P_0 - (B - D) = NM$.

10. E.g., Tajikistan recently revised its time series upward on the number of births

for the period 1994–99. For 1999, this upward revision was by 60 percent. This was done because of a known undercount in the number of births, apparently because women were beginning to be charged for the registration of births. For a more complete discussion of some aspects of birth registration, see "Special Feature: Counting Infant Mortality and Accounting for It," chap. 6 in *Innocenti Social Monitor 2003,* by UNICEF (Florence: UNICEF, 2003), 33–51.

11. International Organization for Migration, *Migration Trends in Eastern Europe and Central Asia: 2001–2002 Review* (Geneva: International Organization for Migration, 2002), 169.

12. The full name of the conference was "The Regional Conference to Address the Problems of Refugees, Displaced Persons, Other Forms of Involuntary Displacement and Returnees in the Countries of the Commonwealth of Independent States and Relevant Neighboring States." It was held in Geneva, May 30–31, 1996.

13. UN Population Division, *International Migration from Countries with Economies in Transition: 1980–1999* (New York: United Nations, 2002), 9.

14. These numbers are based on the de facto measure of the population. The figure of 3,449,000 itself was an upward adjustment by the Armenian statistical office from that tabulated at the time of the USSR census. This was because of an undercount of the population in the area around Spitak, the site of a large earthquake in December 1998 just before the census conducted in January 1989 as well migration movements between Armenia and Azerbaijan over the region of Nagorno-Karabakh that had started before the 1989 census.

15. The National Statistical Service of Armenia was quite aware of this situation regarding its population estimates and was quite transparent regarding them, citing as evidence a survey of arrivals and departures from the airport showing that there had been 618,400 more departures than arrivals, a good indicator of migration in a landlocked country such as Armenia.

16. The previous series can be found in Lithuania Department of Statistics, *Statistical Yearbook of Lithuania 2001* (Vilnius: Statistics Lithuania, 2001), 31. The adjusted series can be found at the Lithuania Department of Statistics Web site, http://www.std.lt.

17. Population totals for the years 1990 to 2000 were adjusted slightly based on the results of 2000 population census (Statistical Office of Estonia Web site, http://www.stat.ee). Previous figures are from various Estonian statistical yearbooks.

18. Timothy Heleniak, "The 2002 Census in Russia: Preliminary Results," *Post-Soviet Geography and Economics,* September 2003, 430–42.

19. International Organization for Migration, *Migration Trends in Eastern Europe and Central Asia,* 169.

20. Philip Martin and Elizabeth Midgley, "Immigration: Shaping and Reshaping America," *Population Bulletin* (Population Reference Bureau) 58, no. 2 (June 2003): 9, 20.

21. It must be noted that technically the gross rate of in-migration as defined as the total in-migrants into an area as a percentage of the average population is not a true measure of those at risk of moving. See John R. Weeks, *Population: An Introduction to Concepts and Issues,* 8th ed. (Belmont, Calif.: Wadsworth-Thomson Learning, 2002), 251.

22. Goskomstat SSSR, *Demograficheskiy yezhegodnik SSSR 1990* (Moscow: Finansy i statistika, 1990), 508–23. The data are only for moves involving an urban area and exclude rural-to-rural migration. However, these flows are rather minimal, and thus the data available capture the vast majority of migration.

23. U.S. Census Bureau, *Geographic Mobility: 2002 to 2003,* Current Population Report (Washington, D.C.: U.S. Government Printing Office, 2004). The data are collected from the Current Population Survey.

24. CIS Statistical Committee and Eastview Publications, *1989 USSR Population Census CD-ROM* (Minneapolis: Eastview, 1996). Data for Armenia, Turkmenistan, and Estonia were missing from the original source.

25. Data for Armenia, Turkmenistan, and Estonia were missing from the original source.

26. U.S. Census Bureau, *Migration and Geographic Mobility in Metropolitan and Nonmetropolitan America: 1995 to 2000,* Census 2000 Special Reports (Washington, D.C.: U.S. Government Printing Office, 2003).

27. Though Russia abolished the *propiska* system in 1993, persons are still required to register with the Ministry of Internal Affairs when migrating to a new location because various social benefits are tied to residence. Because of the incentives to register at the destination location data on in-migrants tend to higher than for out-migrants. For this reason, at the regional level in Russia, regions with high rates of out-migration tended to have lower population figures in the 2002 Russian census than the estimated populations while those with high rates of in-migration tended to have higher census population totals than expected. Also, the under count of the immigration to Russia from the non-Russian FSU states are not properly reflected in these data. Apparently, following complete compilation of the census results, adjustments will be made to both population and migration figures for the intercensus period. See Heleniak, "2002 Census in Russia."

28. Interstate Statistical Committee of the CIS, *Commonwealth of Independent States in 2001: Statistical Yearbook* (Moscow: Interstate Statistical Committee of the CIS, 2002), 116–17. In some cases the sum of internal and international migrants do not sum to the total because people did not indicate their place of previous residence. Interstate Statistical Committee of the CIS, *Naseleniye i usloviya zhizni v Stranakh SNG: Statisticshekskiy sbornik* (Moscow: Interstate Statistical Committee of the CIS, 1998), 26. International migration data are only with other CIS countries.

29. Chancy D. Harris, "The New Russian Minorities: A Statistical Overview," *Post-Soviet Geography* 34, no. 1 (January 1993): 1–27.

30. W. Ward Kingkade, "The Demographic Development of Soviet Nationalities: Post Mortem," in *Migration, Population Structure, and Redistribution Policies,* ed. Calvin Goldscheider (Boulder, Colo.: Westview Press, 1992), 249–79.

31. W. Rogers Brubaker, "Citizenship Struggles in Soviet Successor States," *International Migration Review* 26, no. 2 (1992): 269–91.

32. Timothy Heleniak, "The End of an Empire: Migration and the Changing Nationality Composition of the Soviet Successor States," in *Diasporas and Ethnic Migrant: German, Israel, and Post-Soviet Successor States in Comparative Perspective,* ed. Rainer Ohliger and Rainer Munz (London: Frank Case, 2003), 131–54.

33. Of course this excludes any migration of groups to outside the former Soviet Union where they would not be captured in these censuses. However, for most of these groups, this appears to have been minimal, because most of the migration seems to have been confined to within the post-Soviet space.

34. Murray Feshbach, *Prospects for Massive Out-Migration from Central Asia during the Next Decade,* ed. Foreign Demographic Analysis Division, U.S. Census Bureau (Washington, D.C.: U.S. Government Printing Office, 1977).

35. Lewis, Rowland, and Clem, *Nationality and Population Change in Russia and the USSR.*

36. Krassinets, *Illegal Migration and Employment in Russia.*

37. "Russia, Tajikistan Spar over Illegal Labor Migration," Eurasianet.org, May 10, 2004.

38. UN Office for the Coordination of Humanitarian Affairs, "Central Asia: Special Report on Labour Migration in Russia," March 17, 2004.

39. Monica Whitlock, "Russia Signs Tajik Migrant Deal," BBC News, October 18, 2004.

40. Nora Dudwick and Akshay Sethi, "Migration: Coping with Economic Hardships," background paper prepared for World Bank Moldova poverty assessment.

41. UNICEF, *Innocenti Social Monitor 2004,* 37.

42. United Nations, "Tajikistan: IOM Announces New Programme of Labour Remittances," November 2, 2004.

43. World Bank, *Transition: The First Ten Years—Analysis and Lessons for Eastern Europe and the Former Soviet Union* (Washington, D.C.: World Bank, 2002), xiv.

44. The coefficient of variation is the standard deviation divided by the mean. A higher number indicates more disparity.

45. World Bank, *Transition.*

46. International Monetary Fund and World Bank, "Recent Policies and Performance of the Low-Income CIS Countries: An Update of the CIS-7 Initiative," April 23, 2004, available at http://www.cis7.org.

47. International Organization for Migration, *Migration Trends in Eastern Europe and Central Asia,* 19.

48. Brubaker, "Citizenship Struggles."

49. Timothy Heleniak, "Migration Dilemmas Haunt Post-Soviet Russia," *Migration Information Source,* October 2002, http://www.migrationinformation.org/Profiles/display.cfm?ID=62.

50. International Organization for Migration, *World Migration 2005: Costs and Benefits of International Migration* (Geneva: International Organization for Migration, 2005), 154.

51. International Organization for Migration, *Migration Trends in Eastern Europe and Central Asia,* 178.

52. Timothy Heleniak, "Latvia Looks West, but Legacy of Soviets Remains," *Migration Information Source,* February 2006, http://www.migrationinformation.org/Profiles/display.cfm?ID=375.

53. United Nations Population Division, *Replacement Migration: Is It a Solution to Declining and Ageing Populations?* (New York: United Nations, 2001).

54. The UN Population Division revises its population projections every two years. For the study on replacement migration, the 1998 revision was used; United Nations Population Division, *World Population Prospects: The 1998 Revision* (New York: United Nations, 1999). Population projections vary considerably from one revision to the next because of the incorporation of data on recent demographic trends. The medium variant of the 1998 revision projected that the Russian population would be 121.3 million in 2050 while the medium variant in the 2004 revision, used in figure 1.3, projects a much lower population of 101.5 million in 2050.

55. The study uses the same working ages for all countries of fifteen to sixty-four years, regardless of national definitions.

2

Post-Soviet Migration: New Trends at the Beginning of the Twenty-First Century

Andrei V. Korobkov

The dissolution of the USSR and creation of the Commonwealth of Independent States (CIS) in December 1991 represented a significant political achievement:[1] A huge, nondemocratic, multiethnic[2] state fell apart without a major external or civil war. Nevertheless, the transition period brought about the collapse of the previous political and economic systems and created a new socioeconomic situation. Considering the complexity of the post-Soviet transition, experts both in the former Soviet Union and in the West envisioned the development of large-scale migrations in the period following the USSR's dissolution. Figures approaching 25 million migrants were frequently cited.[3]

In the period 1992–2006, Russia alone received more than 11 million migrants from the post-Soviet states (with net immigration of 4.8 million—compared with 1.5 million in 1981–90).[4] During the initial postdissolution period, the scale and direction of migration flows were defined primarily by ethnic and political factors. The nationalizing governmental policies in many newly independent states (NIS) harshly interfered with the lives of millions of people who frequently found themselves as aliens in the countries they used to perceive as their own. Thus, immigration flow to Russia was completely dominated by the migrants from the post-Soviet states; during the period 1989–2002, only 50,500 came to the Russian Federation (RF) from outside the former Soviet Union.[5]

Forced migration flows were especially painful. Already, by the fall of 1991, there were 710,000 forced migrants in the USSR territory, mostly coming from Azerbaijan, Armenia, and some ethnic regions of Russia.[6] With the dissolution of the Soviet Union, the problem of refugees started to concern those countries that became the sites of large-scale military conflicts. In 2003, in Tajikistan, Azerbaijan, and Armenia, for instance, 1 out of 10 residents was a refugee or a forced migrant;[7] and in Georgia, about 6 percent. The largest number of refugees was recorded in Russia—1,191,900 at the beginning of 1998—but in relation to the whole population they accounted for only about 0.7 percent.[8] After that, the number of refugees started to decline due both to the political stabilization in most NIS and the toughening of the immigration legislation in Russia and other migrant-receiving countries. By the beginning of 2004, the overall number of refugees and forced migrants in the RF was 360,800, or 3.3 times lower than in 1998.[9]

The dramatic increase in migration after 1991 was to a large extent the result of the combined heritage of authoritarianism, ethnic inequality, and Soviet policies, which created a complicated multilevel ethnic federal structure.[10] By the end of the Communist period, the USSR included fifteen union republics as well as twenty lower-positioned autonomous republics, seven autonomous oblasts, and ten autonomous okrugs (districts). Each ethnic unit had its titular nationality (or nationalities) and a specified set of symbols of statehood or national autonomy. Many of these lower-positioned ethnic units were located within the RF (sixteen autonomous republics, five autonomous oblasts, and all ten autonomous okrugs).[11]

The application of the ethnic federalism model in the framework of the Communist state and ideology was originally designed to form local ethnic professional and cultural elites interested in strengthening the central power and the existing sociopolitical system as protectors of their own privileges. The hierarchical Soviet federal system played a primary role in the legal differentiation of ethnic groups; thereafter, the opportunities for the development of an ethnic culture depended on the group's position in the complex structure of Soviet federalism. This became especially visible during the post-Stalinist, politically more relaxed period, from 1953 to 1985. The partial decentralization and liberalization of the regime expanded the powers of local ethnic elites, allowing them to grant preferential treatment to "their" groups by restricting educational and career opportunities for nontitular minorities. These quota-based policies became a mechanism of differentiation and discrimination against local, nontitular minority groups and simultaneously assisted in the creation of power bases for titular ethnic elites.

Essentially, local governments sponsored the intensive replacement of Russian-speaking professionals with those from the titular ethnic groups. In 1989 in Buryatia, an autonomous ethnic republic of the RF, for instance, the share of the titular nationality among upper-level management reached 36.7 percent, compared with its share in the population of 24.0 percent. In Tatarstan, another of Russia's ethnic autonomous republics, the respective shares were 64.1 and 48.6 percent.[12] In Kyrgyzia in 1989, there were 197 Kyrgyz and 105 Russian research workers and university professors per 10,000 employees of each of these nationalities. For those working in the fields of literature and the arts, these figures were 129 and 67; for physicians, 205 and 98; and for lawyers, 38 and 16.[13] Though the Russians' share in the urban population was around 40 percent, they accounted for 29 percent of those engaged in literature and journalism. At the same time, Russians, constituting 21.5 percent of the population of Kyrgyzia in 1989, accounted for 60 percent of industrial engineers and 57 percent of managers,[14] being increasingly pushed into the industrial sphere.

This "cultural division of labor" in the post-Stalinist period led to dissatisfaction among both titular and Russian elites, and it was particularly troublesome for nontitular nationalities. Within the national republics, educational opportunities for titular ethnic groups increased interethnic competition for high-level jobs. As Roeder contends, the inability of members of the educated titular group to secure employment and compensation commensurate with their education increased ethnic hostility, stimulating intrarepublican policies of "ethnic succession."[15] The situation was further aggravated by economic decline and the stagnant personnel policies of the 1980s, making the educated elites the driving force of discontent in the ethnic republics and creating ethnically based tensions.

These trends stimulated the emigration of Russian speakers from the ethnic republics, primarily to the Russian-speaking regions of the RF, Ukraine, and Belarus, and increased the percentage of the titular nationalities in the general population and especially among the political and professional elites of many ethnic regions. One of the visible results of this process was the change in the direction of a number of migration flows. Beginning in the 1970s, Russians and Russian speakers started to leave the most nationalistic and culturally distinct republics of the USSR and a number of ethnic regions of the RF. From 1959 to 1974, Russia's population loss to other Soviet republics amounted to 2.1 million, but after 1975, the internal Soviet migration balance of the RF became positive; between 1976 and 1990, net immigration amounted to 2,534,000.[16] In the period 1979–88, Armenia alone lost about 33 percent of its Russian population; Azerbaijan, about 25 percent; and Georgia, 15 percent.[17]

With the achievement of independence in 1991, "ethnic succession" became the major element of state- and nation-building policies in many NIS. Considering the fact that 54.3 million (or 19 percent) of the USSR's citizens lived outside their titular states (see tables 2.1 and 2.2), these policies became the major factor triggering the first postdissolution migration wave.[18]

The result was the increasing population homogenization of the absolute majority of the post-Soviet states and the growing shares of the titular majorities. During the period 1989–2000, the number of Russians in the post-Soviet states outside Russia declined by 4,675,000, or by 18.5 percent (see table 2.3). By 2005, this number further declined to 18 million, including

Table 2.1. Shares of Titular Nationalities, Russians, and Other Ethnic Groups in the Population of the Former Soviet Republics (1989 census data)

	Percentage of the Total Population			Percentage of the Capital's Population		
Republic	I	II	III	I	II	III
Russia	81.5	N.A.	18.5	89.7	N.A.	10.3
Ukraine	22.1	72.7	5.2	20.9	72.5	6.6
Belarus	13.2	77.9	8.9	20.2	71.8	8.0
Uzbekistan	8.3	71.4	20.3	34.0	44.2	21.8
Kazakhstan	37.8	39.7	22.5	59.1	22.5	18.4
Azerbaijan	5.6	82.7	11.7	16.5	66.0	17.5
Moldova	13.0	64.5	22.5	25.3	51.3	23.4
Kyrgyzstan	21.5	52.4	26.1	55.7	22.9	21.4
Tajikistan	7.6	62.3	30.1	32.4	39.1	28.5
Armenia	1.6	93.3	5.1	1.9	96.4	1.7
Turkmenistan	9.5	72.0	18.5	32.3	50.9	16.8
Georgia	6.3	70.1	23.6	10.0	66.1	23.9
Lithuania	9.4	79.6	11.0	20.2	50.5	29.3
Latvia	34.0	52.0	14.0	47.3	36.5	16.2
Estonia	30.3	61.5	8.2	41.6	46.8	11.6

Note: Column I: Russians; column II: titular nationality; column III: other ethnic groups. N.A. = not available.

Source: Goskomstat SSSR, *Natsional'nyi sostav naseleniia SSSR* (Moscow: Finansy i statistika, 1991), 5–8, 34–140.

Table 2.2. Concentration of the Major Post-Soviet Ethnic Groups in Their Titular Republics, 1989

Ethnic Group	Lived in the Native Republic (percent)	Lived outside the Republic (percent)	Lived outside the Republic (thousands)
Russians	82.6	17.4	25,289
Ukrainians	84.7	15.3	6,767
Belarusans	78.8	21.2	2,131
Uzbeks	84.7	15.3	2,556
Kazakhs	80.3	19.7	1,601
Azerbaijanis	85.7	14.3	965
Moldovans	83.4	16.6	557
Kyrgyz	88.2	11.8	299
Tajiks	75.3	24.7	1,043
Armenians	66.7	33.3	1,539
Turkmen	93.0	7.0	192
Georgians	95.1	4.9	194
Lithuanians	95.3	4.7	143
Latvians	95.1	4.9	71
Estonians	93.8	6.2	64

Source: Data from 1989 census; Goskomstat SSSR, in *Natsional'nyi sostav naseleniia SSSR* (Moscow: Finansy i statistika, 1991), 5–19.

8.2 million in Ukraine, 4.1 million in Kazakhstan, 1.2 million in Belarus, and 1 million in Uzbekistan. Their shares in the population in all the post-Soviet states also declined.[19] It should be mentioned, however, that this decline in the number of ethnic Russians in the post-Soviet states results not only from their emigration but also from formal changes of nationality by people of dual ancestry (usually, to that of the titular nation of a particular state). This process was highly visible in those countries where the shares of ethnically mixed marriages were very high (see table 2.4).

The share of ethnic Russians in the immigration inflow to the RF has steadily declined over the past two decades—from 81 percent in 1989–92 to 64 percent in 1993–2000, 59 percent in 2001–4, and 53 percent in 2005.[20] Most experts expect that not more than 4 million Russians will migrate to the RF in the foreseeable future, mostly from Kazakhstan and Uzbekistan.[21] About 12 percent of the migration inflow is made up of the members of Russia's other titular groups, first of all, Tatars. During the period 1989–2002, another 17.3 percent of legal migrants to Russia represented members of the CIS titular nations.[22] Thus the immigration inflow to the RF became increasingly heterogeneous in ethnic, racial, and religious respects. The pace of migration within post-Soviet space slowed in the later 1990s, with the

Table 2.3. Regional Distribution of the Ethnic Russian Population in the USSR and Russia, 1897–2005

Group	1897	1917	1926	1939	1959	1989	1996	2000	2005
Ethnic Russians (thousands)	55,457	76,507	78,357	100,609	114,114	145,155	N.A.	N.A.	N.A.
Lived outside Russian Republic (thousands)	4,501	7,652	5,764	10,681	16,250	25,289	23,130	20,614	18,000
Lived outside Russian Republic (percent)	8.1	11.1	7.9	11.9	16.6	17.4	N.A.	N.A.	N.A.

Note: N.A. = not available.

Sources: Vladimir M. Kabuzan, *Russkie v mire: Dinamika chislennosti i rasseleniia (1719–1989)—Formirovanie etnicheskikh i politicheskikh granits ruskogo naroda* (Saint Petersburg: Izdatel'stvo Russko-Baltiiskii informatsionnyi tsentr "BLITS," 1996), 279; Vladimir Mukomel', "Migratsionnyi potentsial i perspektivy immigratsii sootechestvennikov iz gosudarstv SNG i Baltii," *Etnopanorama,* no. 3 (2001): 47; Vladimir Mukomel' and E. A. Pain, eds., *Nuzhny li immigranty Rossiiskomu obshchestvu?* (Moscow: Fond Liberal'naia missiia, 2006), 21; Goskomstat SSSR, *Natsional'yi sostav naseleniia SSSR* (Moscow: Finansy i statistika, 1991), 5–19; S. S. Savoskul, ed., *Russkie v novom zarubezh'e: migratsionnaia situatsia, pereselenie i adaptatsiia v Rossii* (Moscow: Institut etnologii i antropologii RAN, 1997), 23; Mikhail Tul'skii, "Istinnoe litso demograficheskoi katastrofy," *Nezavisimaia gazeta,* July 19, 2001.

Table 2.4. Ethnically Mixed Families in the Former Soviet Republics, 1989

Republic	Families, Thousands	Ethnically Mixed Families: Thousands	Ethnically Mixed Families: Percent
Russia	40,246	5,916	14.7
Ukraine	14,057	3,556	25.3
Belarus	2,796	688	24.6
Uzbekistan	3,415	434	12.7
Kazakhstan	3,824	914	23.9
Azerbaijan	1,381	109	7.9
Moldova	1,144	281	24.6
Kyrgyzstan	856	141	16.5
Tajikistan	799	118	14.8
Armenia	559	21	3.8
Turkmenistan	598	80	13.3
Georgia	1,244	152	12.2
Lithuania	1,000	128	12.8
Latvia	732	201	27.5
Estonia	427	74	17.3
USSR, total	73,078	12,887	17.5

Source: Data from 1989 census, cited by L. Semenchuk, "Poistine odna sem'ia," *Pravda,* February 24, 1991.

Table 2.5. The Dynamics of Russia's Migration Exchange with the Post-Soviet States, 1992–2004 (percent)

Period	Immigration	Emigration	Net Migration
1992–95	55.9	61.2	53.3
1996–2000	35.4	30.1	38.1
2001–4	8.7	8.7	8.6
1992–2004	100.0	100.0	100.0

Source: Vladimir Mukomel, *Migratsionnaia politika Rossii: Postsovetskie konteksty* (Moscow: Institut sotsiologii RAN, 2005), 51.

number of registered migrants decreasing more than four times between 1989 and 2000.[23] While, initially, net migration inflow to Russia was expected to be on the level of 200,000 to 300,000 annually until approximately 2015,[24] it declined from 213,610 in 2000 to 35,126 in 2003.[25] Emigration from the RF has also declined more than twentyfold (see table 2.5).[26]

This contraction of migration activity also concerned external emigration outside the post-Soviet region; the number of emigrants from Russia peaked at 100,000 in 1995, declining to just 42,000 in 2004 and 33,000 in 2005. Simultaneously, external emigration started to lose its ethnic character; in 2004, for example, the share of ethnic Russians in this group of migrants was 45.7 percent (compared with 24.0 percent in 1993), whereas the share of the Jews declined from 15.8 percent in 1993 to 1.7 percent in 2004 (see table 2.6). Of the major minority groups, only Germans retained their high share among emigrants (29 percent in 2004). To understand the reasons for this drastic decline, it is necessary to consider the relationship of the major factors defining the character of post-Soviet migration.

The Dynamics of Post-Soviet Migration

Post-Soviet migrations evolved in five major stages, clearly distinguishable in both the scale and the character of migration flows. In the years surrounding the dissolution of the USSR (1991–92), the scale of the population movement remained at approximately the same level as at the end of the 1980s. At the time, migrant motivations were predominantly political and ethnic. The dissolution of the USSR led to mass repatriation resulting from the fear of ethnic discrimination by the NIS governments on the part of the newly formed ethnic minorities and their desire to return to their titular ethnic states.[27] During this period, the first large-scale refugee flows

Table 2.6. Emigrants from Russia outside the Newly Independent States by Nationality, 1993–2004

	1993		1995		1998		2000		2001		2002		2003		2004		1993–2004	
Nationality	Thousands	Percent	Thousands	Percent	Thousands	Percent	Thousands	Percent	Thousands	Percent	Thousands	Percent	Thousands	Percent	Thousands	Percent	Thousands	Percent
Russians	21.3	24.0	28.8	28.8	29.3	36.4	25.8	41.4	24.0	41.0	21.7	40.4	19.8	42.1	19.2	45.6	307.5	35.0
Germans	47.5	53.5	51.3	51.3	28.3	35.2	22.6	36.3	21.7	37.0	18.3	34.1	14.9	31.6	12.2	29.3	360.5	40.9
Jews	14.0	15.8	12.8	12.8	7.3	9.1	4.5	7.2	2.8	4.8	1.5	2.8	1.0	2.1	0.7	1.7	89.2	10.1
Others	6.0	6.7	7.1	7.1	15.5	19.3	9.4	15.1	10.1	17.2	12.2	22.7	11.4	24.2	9.9	23.4	123.3	14.0
Total	88.8	100.0	100.0	100.0	80.4	100.0	62.3	100.0	58.6	100.0	53.7	100.0	47.1	100.0	42.0	100.0	880.5	100.0

Note: This table includes officially registered emigrants, that is, those who received exit permits and abandoned their residence registration.

Sources: A. G. Vishnevskii, ed., *Naseleniie Rossii 2000: Vos'moi ezhegodnyi demograficheskii doklad* (Moscow: Tsentr demografii i ekologii cheloveka, Institut narodnokhoziaistvennogo prognozirovaniia RAN, 2001), 140; A. G. Vishnevskii, ed., *Naseleniie Rossii 2001: Deviatyi ezhegodnyi demograficheskii doklad* (Moscow: Tsentr demografii i ekologii cheloveka, Institut narodnokhoziaistvennogo prognozirovaniia RAN, 2002), 115–16; A. G. Vishnevskii, ed., *Naselenie Rossii 2002: Desiatyi ezhegodnyi demograficheskii doklad* (Moscow: Tsentr demografii i ekologii cheloveka, Institut narodnokhoziaistvennogo prognozirovaniia RAN, 2004), 150; A. G. Vishnevskii, ed., *Naseleniie Rossii 2003–2004: Odinnadtsatyi-dvenadtsatyi ezhegodnyi demograficheskii doklad* (Moscow: Nauka, 2006), 328.

were formed and the mass movement of military servicemen started (following the dissolution of the Soviet armed forces into fifteen separate militaries). This was the only period when Russia was losing the titular nationalities of the former Soviet Union republics (except for Armenians).

The second period (1993–95) was marked by the formation of unidirectional flows within the post-Soviet space. Emigration from Russia declined drastically while the migration inflow to that country steadily increased; essentially, the contraction of emigration, not the inflow of immigrants, was the real cause of the RF's net migration gains. Another new feature was the fact that this trend concerned both Russians and other Russian speakers[28] (who often feared discrimination in the newly formed states) as well as the residents of all other CIS titular nations, now motivated by political as well as economic considerations (a relatively more stable economy and higher living standards in the RF).

The third period started in 1996 and continued until 2000. It was marked by a relative stabilization of the migration situation in the post-Soviet space. Its major features were the general contraction of intraregional migration activity, the relative increase in the importance of external emigration, and the growing role of socioeconomic factors in defining the character and intensity of the new migration flows.

The forced migration that dominated the post-Soviet migration flows in the initial postdissolution years declined dramatically and lost its defining character. Overall, in Russia during the period 1992–2003, 1,637,600 people were registered as either refugees or forced migrants, of whom 1,392,400 came from the post-Soviet states and 243,100 moved among the RF regions. In the 2000s, the number of refugees and forced migrants was continuously declining due to both administrative restrictions in the RF and the stabilization of political situations in a number of post-Soviet states.[29]

Overall, after 1996, various types of temporary, labor, and undocumented migration grew in importance. These changes were based on political stabilization in many post-Soviet states, moderation of governmental policies toward minorities, exhaustion of the reserves of mobile population,[30] including ethnic Russians and Russian-speakers, and the inhospitable social and political atmosphere for migrants in many migrant-receiving countries (including Russia and—following the September, 11, 2001, terrorist attacks—the West). This latter factor led to the rapid growth of undocumented migration—it represents both a diagnostic feature of the socioeconomic and legal environment in the NIS and one of the major problems currently encountered by those states. Stimulating the new forms of migration is also the realization by the majority of the NIS populations of the inability and the unwillingness of their states to provide them with the social and economic support.

The fourth period (2000–5) was characterized by the attempts of the new Vladimir Putin administration to develop the institutional foundations for migration policy in Russia. Unfortunately, these attempts were oriented primarily toward the strengthening of the law enforcement aspects of migration policy, including the transfer of the Federal Migration Service to the jurisdiction of the Interior Ministry in February 2002. Although the adoption of numerous legislative acts provided better legal and structural foundations for migration policy,[31] many of these acts complicated the position of migrants, further forcing many of them out of the legal space. In general, migration policy concentrated on two major problems: the position of refugees and forced migrants, and illegal immigration; in both cases, state policy was aimed at limiting the numbers of migrants belonging to these groups.

During this period, permanent and ethnically motivated migration flows continued to shrink,[32] while temporary and labor migration continued to expand.[33] Simultaneously, the disproportionate influence exercised by Russia on the formation of migration flows in the region became even more visible.[34] Having remained the major recipient of migrants, Russia increasingly plays a role as supplier of labor migrants to the West and acts as a "bridge" for those attempting to reach Western Europe.

In March 2005, the new, fifth period started. Its distinguishing features included the general liberalization of migration policy, aimed at increasing permanent immigration, improvements in migration statistics, the expansion of the legal space for temporary labor migration, a limited legalization of undocumented migrants, and the creation of stimuli for the immigration of highly qualified labor resources.[35]

This turnaround of migration policy seems to be based on the realization by the Putin administration of the severity of the demographic crisis that Russia faces. Ironically, the execution of the new migration policy remains in the hands of the same people (first of all, the deputy head of the presidential administration, Viktor Ivanov) who in the previous years were pursuing an openly anti-immigrant course. Respectively, despite the proclamation of a new migration policy and the introduction of some stimuli for the repatriation of compatriots from the CIS, as well as simplifying the processes of entrance and naturalization for such categories of migrants as students and foreigners serving in the Russian armed forces, it is not yet clear how effective the newly revised migration policy will be. Overall, the recent migration situation in the post-Soviet region is characterized by shifts from registered to unregistered migration flows, from political to socioeconomic motivations, and from permanent to increasingly temporary migration within and outside the region.

Labor Migration in the Post-Soviet Space

The rapid expansion of labor migration in the post-Soviet space is frequently viewed as a temporary and crisis-caused phenomenon, yet labor migration is essential for open societies and market economies. There exist huge socioeconomic disparities not only between the post-Soviet states and the outside world but also within the NIS group itself as well as within some of the post-Soviet states, especially Russia. These involve such indicators as the levels of unemployment, gross domestic product (GDP) per capita, hourly wages, and the availability of welfare services. The differentiation goes even further, involving the division of the NIS into countries with weak economies and quickly growing populations and those that face quick population declines and labor force shortages.[36] Russia is the primary example of the latter group (see table 2.7). Since 1992, immigration has been the only source of population growth in the RF, compensating in 1992–94 for up to 80 percent of the losses resulting from the natural decline of the population; in 1996–98, for about 40 percent of these losses; and in 1999–2000, for about 20 percent of these losses.[37]

Nevertheless, even this small-scale permanent immigration flow is important for Russia; the economically active population makes up about two-thirds of the inflow.[38] This is especially important considering the fact that in 2007, Russia started to lose its economically active population. In addition, external immigrants on average are much better educated than the Russian population as a whole; 19.0 percent have university diplomas and 32.8 percent have an associate degree, compared with the Russian averages of 16.2 and 27.5 percent, respectively.[39]

Given present economic conditions in the CIS, it is difficult to imagine that permanent migration will become more important than temporary labor migration in the near to middle terms. Indeed, due to the complexity of movement to Russia, the major migrant-receiving country in the region, permanent immigration is out of necessity increasingly complemented and to a large extent substituted for with a number of temporary forms.[40] Thus not only the dynamics and the relationship of the major factors causing mi-

Table 2.7. Russia's Population Dynamics

Population Group	Millions
1989 census data	147.0
2002 census data	145.2
Population decline, 1989–2002	–1.8
Natural decline	–7.4
Net migration inflow	+5.6
Immigration	+11.0
Emigration	–5.4

Source: V. I. Mukomel and E. A. Pain, eds., *Nuzhny li immigranty Rossiiskomu obshchestvu?* (Moscow: Fond "Liberal'naia missiia," 2006), 8.

gration are changing but also its forms. Temporary, labor, and undocumented migration cohorts have seen a rapid growth during the 1990s and 2000s. There are 3 to 4 million labor migrants in the Russian territory. Of them, at least 1 million come from Ukraine and 1.5 million from Transcaucasia. Labor migration from Central Asia is quickly growing and is expected to exceed that from Transcaucasia in the foreseeable future.[41]

Labor migration had become the most massive migration flow in Russia by the second half of the 1990s. The reasons for that included the exhaustion of the reserves of ethnic repatriates, the moderation of the NIS minority policies, the official recognition of the freedom to exit and (to a lesser extent) to enter, and the beginning of market reforms. Simultaneously, falling living standards, the erosion of the welfare state, and growing unemployment forced many NIS residents to seek sources of income independent from their states. Thus the leading causes of immigration to Russia at present are economic, resulting from the economic crisis in many NIS and huge disparities among them in levels of income and the intensity of economic activity.[42] Among the NIS labor migrants, only 30 percent had permanent jobs at home, while 16 percent had temporary jobs. About 20 percent were students. Thus labor migration became a separate and significant sphere of employment. Following the USSR's dissolution, differences in the character and the pace of reforms, the existing economic structures, and the levels of natural resource endowment resulted in a quick differentiation among the CIS states. The energy-importing countries have experienced a shock resulting from the shift toward more market-based prices of energy products. Another major negative effect stemmed from the termination of fiscal transfers from Moscow, which for some smaller CIS countries amounted to a significant share of their GDP. The industrial structure of the CIS economies was closely integrated, and many of the traditional production and trade links were disrupted by the radical institutional changes in all the post-Soviet states. The result was the drastic decline of economic co-operation in the region; the share of the CIS countries in Russia's foreign trade declined from 66 percent in 1991 between 17 and 18 percent at the beginning of the current century (in 2003, they accounted for 15 percent of Russia's exports and 23 percent of its imports).[43] Finally, in several CIS countries, civil wars and regional conflicts also led to economic disruptions.

All the CIS and the Baltic countries experienced a large decline in GDP, on average by about 54 percent by the middle of the 1990s.[44] By 2002, only Belarus, Kazakhstan, and Uzbekistan were able to reach the GDP per capita levels of 1990 (see table 2.8). The temporary stabilization of 1996–97 was interrupted by the devastating Russian financial crisis of 1998. Most of the CIS countries were severely affected by the collapse of their trade with Russia and were forced to adjust their exchange rates in response to the devaluation of the Russian ruble. During this period, the smaller CIS countries, including Armenia, Georgia, Kyrgyzstan, Moldova, and Tajikistan, were affected more than the other CIS members. More than 50 percent of their population was driven below the poverty threshold. The breakup of the USSR and the subsequent economic developments have led to noticeable disparities in the living standards of the CIS countries. The gap in average wages (see table 2.9) has been mentioned above, and if one uses market exchange rates, the disparity is even more visible; GDP per capita in Tajikistan is 15 times smaller than in Russia, and Russia has a GDP per capita 5.5 times larger than the average for the five aforementioned smaller CIS states.[45]

When they achieved independence, many post-Soviet states found themselves in a precarious situation. On the one hand, the RF took responsibility for all the former USSR debts. Thus a "zero option" was created for the other post-Soviet states; they started their independent existence without any external debts. On the other hand, they immediately encountered a deep economic crisis, caused by both the breakup of the previous economic system and the destruction of their traditional economic ties. Respectively, those states started to quickly accumulate huge external debts. In these circumstances, many CIS members, and first of all Armenia, Georgia, Kyrgyzstan, Moldova, and Tajikistan—essentially went bankrupt.[46]

Under the conditions of the resulting economic collapse and the erosion of social welfare mechanisms, the quickly developing labor migration not only became a means of personal survival but also provided an important economic and financial support pillar for many CIS countries, creating a new economic infrastructure at the grassroots level. Labor migration stim-

Table 2.8. Gross Domestic Product (GDP) per Capita Dynamics in the Countries Belonging to the Commonwealth of Independent States

	1990		2002		
Country	Dollars	Percentage of Russia's GDP per capita	Dollars	Percentage of Russia's GDP per capita	Percent, 2002/1990
Russia	9,490	100.0	7,100	100.0	74.8
Georgia	8,065	85.5	2,560	36.1	31.7
Belarus	6,830	72.0	7,620	107.3	111.5
Ukraine	6,618	69.7	4,356	61.4	65.8
Turkmenistan	6,538	69.0	4,320	60.8	66.1
Kazakhstan	6,286	66.2	6,500	91.5	103.4
Moldova	4,910	51.7	2,150	30.3	43.8
Azerbaijan	4,146	43.7	3,090	43.5	74.5
Kyrgyzstan	3,488	36.8	2,750	38.7	78.8
Armenia	3,266	34.4	N.A.	N.A.	N.A.
Uzbekistan	2,389	25.2	2,460	34.6	102.9
Tajikistan	2,308	24.3	1,170	16.4	50.7

Note: N.A. = not available.
Source: G. A. Vlaskin and E. B. Lenchuk, *Promyshlennaya politika v usloviyakh perekhoda k innovatsionnoi ekonomike: Opyt stran Tsentral'noi i Vostochnoi Evropy i SNG* (Moscow: Nauka, 2006), 13.

ulated the formation of various segments of the market, including the labor market, and generated new large-scale financial flows, supporting the weak economies of the migrants' home states.

Meanwhile, in recent years, migration has become increasingly difficult due to growing limitations on entering particular countries both within and outside the CIS as well as the mounting hostility toward immigrants, even ethnic co-nationals. The impoverishment of potential migrants also complicates their movement. Educational migration, previously a major component of population flows in the region, has declined markedly.[47]

Migration always is at least to some extent labor related; travel in search of a new job usually is one of the major reasons for relocation. To some extent, this was also true for the population movement in the USSR. State-directed migrations of that period were at least partially motivated by economics. The territorial redistribution of the workforce was, in Stephen Kotkin's words, "viewed as an integral part of central planning" and in this sense, represented one of the major mechanisms promoting growth in the planned economy.[48] This territorial movement of the population was frequently implemented with no regard for the social or cultural needs of mi-

Table 2.9. Monthly Wages in Selected Newly Independent States

	Average Monthly Wage (dollars)	
State	2000	January 2004
Russia	79	202
Ukraine	42	92
Azerbaijan	50	N.A.
Moldova	33	N.A.
Kyrgyzstan	26	42
Tajikistan	9	17
Armenia	42	60
Georgia	37	60

Note: N.A. = not available.
Sources: Interstate Statistical Committee of the Commonwealth of Independent States, *Labour Market in the CIS Countries* (Moscow: Interstate Statistical Committee of the Commonwealth of Independent States, 2004), 95; Elena Tiuriukanova, *Forced Labour in the Russian Federation Today: Irregular Migration and Trafficking in Human Beings* (Moscow: International Labor Organization, 2004).

grants. Blair Ruble, in particular, emphasizes that economic migrations in the USSR were "driven more by bureaucratic and administrative policies and directives than by market forces or individual preference."[49] In the modern situation, labor migration is mostly voluntary and frequently does not imply a permanent change of residence, at least initially. Labor migrants move to another country for a limited period and travel there periodically, without intent to permanently resettle. This group includes both those engaged in hired labor activities and merchant migrants (the so-called *chelnoki,* or shuttles, widespread in the 1990s).[50]

Labor migration exists in both legal and illegal forms. To retain legal status, a migrant (if he or she is a foreigner) needs to have permits to enter the country, stay in it for a particular period, and engage in labor activity. If one of those requirements is not fulfilled, the migrant is considered illegal.[51] However, this model requires at least two qualifications.

First of all, contrary to a popular stereotype, about a quarter of migrants in Russia have labor permits, while the overwhelming majority enters the country legally.[52] At the same time, a large share of labor trips is either never registered (this is typical for migrations within the CIS) or is conducted under the disguise of tourism or study (primarily involving migrants from outside the CIS). The major reason is the rigidity of the legislative systems in the post-Soviet states (e.g., the RF still to a large extent operates on the basis of the 1970 Soviet Labor Code), especially in the areas of labor and migration regulation, opening the door for the widespread corruption of state officials and abuse by employers. The latter get used to hiring nonlocals and to engaging in activities outside the legal field. This approach gives them additional flexibility, a cheap labor force, and low social expenditures, and allows them to avoid paying taxes. According to the estimates of Galina Vitkovskaia, the average migrant's workweek is fifty-three hours, while Elena Tiuriukanova estimates it at sixty-six hours. V. Moshniaga and G. Rusnak claim that 79 percent of Moldovan construction workers in Russia work twelve or more hours a day.[53] Thus a particular regime is being created and reproduced, providing for the targeted hiring of migrants. The combination of these factors results in the frequent violations of the legislative norms of the receiving states both by the illegal migrants and the local employers and state officials.

Second, the use of the very term "illegal" is questionable, because migrants tend to enter legally but are then improperly registered after their arrival. Most frequently, violations of legal status concern a mismatch between visa type and actual activities, such as entering with a tourist or student visa but primarily engaging in economic activity. Another frequent violation is the visa overstay. Only about 10 percent of illegal migrants do not work. Thus, of the three components of illegal migration (illegal entry, illegal stay, and illegal employment), the most frequent in Russia is illegal employment,[54] and in most cases, it would be more correct to talk about the undocumented or irregular rather than illegal migration.[55] The problems related to the status of the majority of migrants belonging to this category originate primarily in the ineffectiveness and the discriminatory character of the receiving CIS members' legislation, not in the migrants' intention to engage in illegal activities.

Increasingly, the RF labor market is structured in accordance with the patterns typical for the majority of the migrant-receiving countries, including the formation of a division of labor based on ethnic, racial, and gender segregation. Most frequently, labor migrants are employed in the least regulated job markets, including retail, which employs 30 percent of all working migrants; services, 25 percent; and construction, 20 percent. About 60 percent of labor migrants work as a hired force. Of them, about a half have more or less permanent jobs. Forty percent of migrants are ready to take any jobs. Overall, the migrant niche primarily involves labor of either average (52 percent) or low qualifications (27 percent).[56]

Labor migration has played the important role of social stabilizer, allowing many post-Soviet societies to avoid mass hunger and poverty under the conditions of economic collapse and growing unemployment. Migration, almost exclusively based on people's grassroots initiative, has assisted in rebuilding and expanding the consumer market in the post-Soviet space and has created new employment spheres. Of special importance is the issue of migrants' remittances. More than 30 percent of migrants send some part of their earnings home. According to Russian sources, during the period of stay in Russia, an average migrant sends home approximately $1,700, or about $80 monthly. A recent International Monetary Fund study has shown that in 2003, gross remittances sent to Moldova amounted to about 25 to 30 percent of its GDP, one of the highest levels in the world.[57] The size of the remittances was comparable to that of exports of goods and services, and dwarfed foreign direct investment in and official development assistance to that low-income country, considered the poorest in Europe. A similar 2002 survey carried out in Georgia by the International Organization for Migration evaluated the size of remittances at about $480 million, or approximately 20 percent of that country's GDP.[58] Overall, in the poorer CIS countries, such as Armenia, Georgia, Kyrgyzstan, Moldova, and Tajikistan, the amount of incoming remittances is comparable to the value of exports.[59]

Initially, few CIS countries actively pursued policies regarding remittance flows, although the encouragement of international actors such as the World Bank and IMF has prompted countries such as Moldova and Tajikistan to begin exploring policies to harness the development potential of remittance flows. For the most part, migrants continue to avoid official channels when sending money home. Thus numerous legal problems arise, including tax evasion, the proliferation of organized crime, and opening up potential channels of financial support for other illegal activities, including international terrorism. This is often viewed as a security threat to Russia. In addition, it is frequently claimed that migrants' remittances take large amounts of money out of the Russian economy.[60] Meanwhile, it is obvious that monetary transfers also play an important role in the relative socioeconomic and political stabilization of the CIS. They provide economic support for a large share of the CIS population, thus contributing to Russia's economic and political stability. This issue thus calls for immediate attention from the national authorities and requires regional cooperation between the migrants' source and destination countries as well as broader international cooperation.

In Russia, about 10 percent of households include labor migrants—a total of more than 5 million people, of whom between 1.5 and 2 million travel outside the Russian territory while the remainder moves within Russia. The volume of internal Russian labor migration is comparable to that of labor immigration from the CIS countries. Russian labor migrants represent a significant segment of the Russian labor market: 15 percent of the state-sector employees, 8 percent of those employed in the economy, and more than one-third of those engaged in the informal economic sectors. If external labor immigrants are added to this group, the share of labor migrants among those employed in the Russian economy is at least 12 percent.[61]

Labor migration represents an effective means of dealing with poverty and serves as an important generator of the middle class in the country (due to its influence, in the RF this population group has expanded by at least 4 million) and a business and market relationships "school" (every fifth migrant household in Russia has started its own business). Between a fifth and a quarter of labor migrants have solved their housing problems. Thus labor migration represents one of the major social mechanisms for the transition to a market economy. Immigrants bring with them important skills and are frequently eager to take the jobs that are not considered prestigious and thus are rejected by the local population. They provide financial support for their families at home; their financial transfers also help their home countries' economies. No less important are the professional skills and business experience that they acquire in the receiving countries. The analogous experiences of other countries also show the political importance for migrants' home states of the ethnic diasporas formed in the migrant-receiving countries.

An important component of the labor migration flow is intellectual migration. The desire of academics and students to go abroad and stay there for a relatively long time is based on a number of push and pull factors originating in the social environment in both the post-Soviet states and the migrant-receiving countries. The push factors include low salaries and social standing, the absence of demand for scholars' abilities, poor access to modern equipment and academic sources, and unclear prospects at home.[62] Characteristic, in this sense, is the fact that the external emigration of scholars is paralleled by a large-scale "internal emigration" into activities that do not correspond to their education and professional qualifications.[63] In the West, the major pull factors include higher living standards, respect for professionals, and the opportunity to continue professional activity in one's field of study.

Labor migration represents the most frequent strategy for scientists' permanent emigration, allowing them to retain their opportunities to continue their professional activity. The labor migration of scholars also benefits their home countries, offering a reliable way of establishing effective international contacts, the academics' inclusion in the global intellectual labor market, and the universalization of science and knowledge. In the long run, the free movement of scholars can be seen as the most important precondition for the development of science.

According to the Russian expert S. Egerev, the overall number of Russian scientists working abroad at the end of 1998 was about 30,000, of whom 14,000 to 18,000 were engaged in the fundamental sciences.[64] Other estimates show between 20,000 and 200,000 Russian academics working abroad.[65] Still, it is hard to distinguish between those who became real emigrants (i.e., acquired a permanent living permit) and those who are legally considered temporary migrants, but essentially live abroad permanently.[66]

The issue of "brain drain" has been traditionally highly politicized, causing a sharply negative reaction in Russia and many other NIS. Yet, in 2002, using official channels, 2,922 Russian researchers from 324 organizations (or just 0.7 percent of the overall number of researchers and 0.8 percent of the listed organizations in their fields of study) traveled abroad for a term between three months and three years.[67] It is hard to describe such contacts as intensive. These figures create some doubts about the seriousness of the frequently cited brain drain from Russia.

Of those who left, every third is a physicist; every fourth, a biologist; and every tenth, a mathematician. Specialists in these fields have much more intensive foreign contacts than anyone else. Overall, basic sciences accounted for 77 percent of those who left. Working abroad, for example, are about a half (out of 300) of the leading Moscow mathematicians. It is much harder to find a job abroad for those working in other branches of science, especially for specialists in agriculture, the social sciences, and the humanities.[68]

The major destination points for Russian scholars include Western Europe (42.4 percent, with Germany accounting for 19 percent); and North America (30.4 percent, with the United States accounting for 28.7 percent). Also visible in the flow are the countries of Asia and Scandinavia. Meanwhile, Russia's academic interaction with its former satellites—the countries of Eastern Europe and the post-Soviet states—has practically stopped. The flow to Eastern Europe is equal to that to Africa, while the flow to the post-Soviet states is just a little bit smaller than that to Latin America. Overall, though seventy-three states received Russian scholars, ten countries—the United States, Germany, France, the United Kingdom, Japan, Sweden, India, Italy, the Netherlands, and China—account for three-quarters of the academic flow from the RF.

Nevertheless, the development of intellectual migration is significantly slowed down by NIS governmental policies. Academic interaction remains limited to a small number of institutions and the major regional centers. In the RF, Moscow and Saint Petersburg with the surrounding oblasts and Novosibirsk account for three-quarters of overall Russian intellectual labor migration,[69] whereas the majority of academic institutions have practically no access to colleagues abroad. Thus, overall, regardless of the highly segmented brain drain from a limited number of schools, the scale of Russia's intellectual exchange with the outside world remains inadequate, hurting the RF's ability to become an effective part of the international academic market. The same could be said about Russian students abroad; in the middle of the 1990s, 13,000 of them were studying in the universities of thirty-three countries, although more than 80 percent lived in four states—the United States, Germany, France, and the United Kingdom. Still, in Germany, the Russians' share among foreign students was just 2.1 percent; in the United States and France, 1.2 percent; and in the United Kingdom, 0.25 percent.[70]

The real problem seems to be the issue of the "internal migration" of Russian academics into jobs not related to their professional skills and the low level of investment in the academic sphere; at the beginning of the current century, the share of research and development (R&D) expenditures in the Russian GDP was 1 percent, compared with 2.69 percent in the United States and 2.98 percent in Japan. Russia's share of the world's information equipment exports was 0.04 percent, compared with the United States' 13 percent. Russia ranked seventieth in the world in the competitiveness of its industrial products.[71] Since 1999, Western support for Russian science has also been declining.[72]

Conclusion

During the last fifteen years, migration patterns in the post-Soviet space have changed drastically. Particularly visible are signs of political stabilization and the improvement in the position of minorities (simultaneously with their declining shares in the population of most NIS), including the decreasing numbers of refugees and the low intensity of emigration outside the post-Soviet region. Thus, the political factors for migration have to a large extent lost their importance. At the same time, the continuous economic crisis in many NIS and the disparity in living standards have led to the formation of new, economically based migration flows. The generally low levels of migration activity also seem to testify to the spread of poverty throughout the region.

Meanwhile, the inflow of migrants has allowed many Russian enterprises and small businesses to survive and has protected a significant portion of the population from poverty under crisis conditions. More than that, most migrants have not received any support from their states but have frequently become pioneers in the development of various private activities. During the 1990s, for example, only 350,000 out of 11 million migrants to Russia, or about 3 percent, received some housing support from the state.[73] The immigrant labor force was especially effective in supporting the development of private retail, services, and construction activities.

Nevertheless, neither Russia nor other NIS were ready or willing to deal with the new migration problems. The post-1991 position of the Russian government, for instance, generally was that the migration issue was of secondary importance for the Russian state. Respectively, the RF's policies were mostly reactive and usually marked by a negative approach to immigration and immigrants. The results of this approach included the continuous bureaucratic reorganizations, low planned budgetary expenditures, and a chronic underfulfillment of even those inadequate budgetary goals.[74] Especially harmful was the absence of understanding that labor migrants represent an important segment of the labor market and the market system in general. Thus the solution of labor migration problem requires much wider and more radical reforms of the economic system in general, including the requirement of transparency in economic activity. The policy changes of 2005–8 give some hope for the improvement of this situation, although the consistent strengthening of executive power, and specifically law enforcement bodies, complicates the achievement of officially proclaimed goals.

The situation at the CIS level remains very similar to that inside particular NIS. There exists a visible discrepancy between the CIS's declarations and practical policies. Although the CIS's official declarations proclaim the necessity of forming a single labor market and providing for freedom of movement inside it, its practical policies are marked by the constant introduction of various limitations on such movement under the pretext of containing illegal migration and organized crime. The situation is further aggravated by the general underestimation of the significance of labor migration and its impact on the labor markets and economies of the migrant-receiving countries as well as by the willingness of many Russian politicians to use anti-immigrant rhetoric in their political goals (the recent anti-Georgian campaign serves as an effective illustration of this trend).

This is a very dangerous trend, because labor migration provides a source of income for a large number of families in the CIS. An additional complicating factor is the fact that many Russian media outlets and politicians consistently emphasize the negative, sensational aspects of the migration problem, including the proliferation of undocumented immigration (practically always characterized as illegal) and its potential links to such phenomena as corruption, organized crime, and terrorism, while ignoring such issues as the existence of a common cultural and historical heritage and the economic role of migrants.[75] Also ignored are such issues as the stabilizing effect of labor migration and migrants' remittances on the home economies of migrants and the well-being of particular migrant families in both the home and host countries.

Governmental bodies frequently support such claims. These actions result in increasing public hysteria and create a negative stereotype of ethnic migrants. If, in 1990, 52 percent of the Russian population condemned any expressions of ethnic phobias, by 2004, 68 percent were negatively viewing any ethnic immigrants.[76] In 2005, 50 percent supported limiting the number of migrants from the Caucasus living in Russian territory; and 58 percent expressed their support for the slogan "Russia for Russians," compared with 20 to 25 percent in the middle of the 1990s.[77] In October 2006, 38 percent of the surveyed were ready to support the deportation from Russia of all Georgians, including those who were the RF citizens.[78] In addition, the Russian government does not effectively suppress the xenophobic anti-immigrant movements developing in the country.[79] The number of ethnically motivated hate crimes is growing. According to the SOVA Center for Monitoring and Analysis, in 2004, there were 46 racially motivated murders and 208 beatings in Russia; in 2005, respectively, 32 and 386; and in 2006, 57 and 377.[80]

No less important is the weakness of the legislative base of migration policy—a chronic problem for Russian politics. The creation of such a legal base is a complicated task, because a large share of the labor market remains in the "shadow zone"—and this is to a large extent not the fault of migrants. Labor migration, more than any other type of population movement, requires the development of effective, simple legal procedures and transparency in the work of both private businesses and governmental institutions—and this is the only practical way to guarantee the effective control of this sphere. The adoption of a number of important legislative acts at the beginning of this century and the policy changes of the last three years give some hope for the improvement of the situation. Nevertheless, migration policy is still plagued by another Russian political "illness": the discrepancy between the written law and its understanding and implementation by state officials and the general disrespect for the law by all groups in society.[81]

In addition, attempts to prevent illegal immigration by dealing solely with the migration issue and ignoring the restructuring of the labor market or avoiding the reform of housing registration and work permit procedures will inevitably fail. These goals cannot be achieved in the absence of a free market (including the labor market) and the elements of civil society in the post-Soviet space. It is impossible to imagine migrants effectively defending their rights and expressing their views on the issues of importance to them without the free development of public organizations and media outlets that are independent from the state and the expansion of the powers and independence of the courts. Unfortunately, recent political trends in Russia hardly support the development of such institutions.

Notes

1. At present, the CIS includes twelve of fifteen former Soviet republics. Three Baltic republics—Estonia, Latvia, and Lithuania—did not join this organization.

2. The last, 1989 Soviet population census officially recognized 128 nationalities living in the USSR. The Russians' share in the population was at that time 50.8 percent. Goskomstat SSSR, *Natsional'nyi sostav naseleniia SSSR* (Moscow: Finansy i statistika, 1991), 5. The 2002 Russian Federation Census recognizes already 182 separate ethnic groups living in Russia alone. Meanwhile, the share of ethnic Russians in the Federation is much higher than it was in the Soviet Union as a whole: 79.83 percent in 2002, although it has declined compared with 81.53 percent in 1989. A. G. Vishnevskii, ed., *Naseleniie Rossii 2003–2004: Odinnadtsatyi-dvenadtsatyi ezhegodnyi demograficheskii doklad* (Moscow: Nauka, 2006), 67, 72.

3. See, e.g., Congress, *Forced Migration,* Congress, House, Subcommittee on International Operations and Human Rights, *Forced Migration in the Newly Independent States of the Former Soviet Union,* 104th Cong., 2nd sess., May 22, 1996, 4, 9; "Kontseptsiia gosudarsvennoj migratsionnoj politiki Rossijskoj Federatsii: Proekt," *Migratsiia v Rossii* 1 (October-November 1999): 11; Sergei Khetagurov, "Regulirovat' protsessy migratsii v interesakh grazhdan i Rossii," *Migratsiia v Rossii* 2 (April–May 2000): 4; and Galina Vitkovskaia and Sergei Panarin, eds., *Migratsiia i bezopasnost' v Rossii* (Moscow: Interdialekt+, 2000), 169.

4. Considering the negative migration balance with the Old Abroad, the overall net immigration amounted to 3.9 million. *The Demographic Yearbook of Russia: Statistical Handbook* (Moscow: Federal Statistical Service, 2006), 425; *Chislennost' i migratsiia naseleniia Rossiiskoi Federatsii v 2006 godu: Statisticheskii biulleten'* (Moscow: Federal'naia sluzhba gosudarstvennoi statistiki, 2007), 28; A. G. Vishnevskii, ed., *Naseleniie Rossii 2000: Vos'moi ezhegodnyi demograficheskii doklad* (Moscow: Tsentr demografii i ekologii cheloveka, Institut narodnokhoziaistvennogo prognozirovaniia

RAN, 2001), 125; A. G. Vishnevskii, ed., *Naseleniie Rossii 2001: Deviatyi ezhegodnyi demograficheskii doklad* (Moscow: Tsentr demografii i ekologii cheloveka, Institut narodnokhoziaistvennogo prognozirovaniia RAN, 2002), 138, 147; and A. G. Vishnevskii, ed., *Naseleniie Rossii 2002: Desiatyi ezhegodnyi demograficheskii doklad* (Moscow: Tsentr demografii i ekologii cheloveka, Institut narodnokhoziaistvennogo prognozirovaniia RAN, 2004), 132–33, 148.

5. Vishnevskii, *Naselenie Rossii 2003–2004,* 308.

6. Vladimir Mukomel, *Migratsionnaia politika Rossii: Postsovetskie konteksty* (Moscow: Institut sotsiologii RAN, 2005), 14.

7. According to the 1967 United Nations definition, considered as a *refugee* can be "any person . . . [located] outside the country of his nationality . . . because he has or had well-founded fear of persecution by reason of his race, religion, nationality, membership of a particular social group or political opinion and is unable or, because of such fear, is unwilling to avail himself of the protection of the government of the country of his nationality [here, citizenship]"; Guy S. Goodwin-Gill, *The Refugee in International Law* (Oxford: Clarendon Press, 1983), 5–6. The postdissolution Russian legislation distinguishes between *refugees,* who were forced to cross the international border and lacking citizenship of the receiving country; *forced migrants,* who were compelled to cross the international border and having citizenship of the receiving country; and *displaced persons,* who were forced to move inside the borders of their country. Vladimir Mukomel', "Vynuzhdennaia migratsiia v SNG," *Migratsiia* 2 (January–March 1997): 7. The existence of the latter category is based on Russia's ethnofederal structure and the legal limitations on the movement and stay of the Russian citizens within the RF borders. During the transition period, many Russian citizens and legal residents were forced by circumstances to move among the federal units of the RF.

8. Andrei V. Korobkov and Zhanna A. Zaionchkovskaia, "The Changes in the Migration Patterns in the Post-Soviet States: The First Decade," *Communist and Post-Communist Studies* 37 (2004): 484.

9. Vishnevskii, *Naseleniie Rossii 2003–2004,* 340.

10. For the discussion of the Soviet ethnic and migration policies, see Andrei Korobkov, *State and Nation Building Policies and the New Trends in Migration in the Former Soviet Union,* Carl Beck Papers in Russian and East European Studies (Pittsburgh: University of Pittsburgh Press), 2003.

11. The post-Soviet RF also retained the complex ethnofederal structure: according to the 1993 RF Constitution, along with fifty-seven Russian-speaking units, it included thirty-two ethnic units: twenty-one republics, ten autonomous okrugs, and one autonomous oblast. In 1989, in these ethnic units lived 22 percent of the RF population. Goskomstat SSSR, *Natsional'nyi sostav naseleniia SSSR,* 9, 34–48. Currently, President Putin's administration is cutting the number of the RF ethnic federal units by merging them with the economically stronger and politically easier controllable Russian-speaking oblasts and krays.

12. *Sotsial'noe razvitie SSSR, 1989: Statisticheskii sbornik* (Moscow: Finansy i statistika, 1991), 63.

13. Sergei S. Savoskul, ed., *Russkie v novom zarubezh'e: Sredniaia Aziia: Etnosotsiologicheskii ocherk* (Moscow: Institut etnologii i antropologii RAN, 1994), 32–35.

14. A. G. Vishnevskii, ed., *Naselenie Rossii 1996: Chetvyertyi ezhegodnyi demograficheskii doklad* (Moscow: Tsentr demografii i ekologii cheloveka, Institut narodnokhoziaistvennogo prognozirovaniia RAN, 1997), 139.

15. Philip G. Roeder, "Soviet Federalism and Ethnic Mobilization," *World Politics* 43 (January 1991): 213–14.

16. Vishnevskii, *Naselenie Rossii 1996,* 6, 13.

17. A. G. Vishnevskii, ed., *Naseleniie Rossii 1999: Sed'moi ezhegodnyi demograficheskii doklad* (Moscow: Tsentr demografii i ekologii cheloveka, Institut narodnokhoziaistvennogo prognozirovaniia RAN, 2000), 134.

18. Including 25.3 million Russians, or 17.4 percent of the Russian nation, and more than 4 million of the representatives of other ethnic groups having their state formations in the Russian territory. Goskomstat SSSR, *Natsional'nyi sostav naseleniia SSSR,* 5–19.

19. V. I. Mukomel and E. A. Pain, eds., *Nuzhny li immigranty Rossiiskomu obshchestvu?* (Moscow: Fond "Liberal'naia missiia," 2006), 21.

20. Vishnevskii, *Naselenie Rossii 2003–2004,* 322; A. G. Vishnevskii, ed. *Naselenie Rossii 2005: Trinadtsatyi ezhegodnyi demograficheskii doklad.* (Moscow: Izdatel'skii dom GU VShE, 2007), 200.

21. Mukomel and Pain, *Nuzhny li immigranty Rossiiskomu obshchestvu?* 21.

22. Vishnevskii, *Naseleniie Rossii 2003–2004,* 322.

23. The movement of military servicemen and prisoners was not reported by the Soviet statistical authorities. Their number was at least 1.6 million. If one takes this group into account, the decline was fivefold. Korobkov and Zaionchkovskaia, "Changes in the Migration Patterns in the Post-Soviet States," 485.

24. Aleksandr Blokhin, "Nasha kontseptsiia odnoznachna—povernut'sia litsom k nuzhdam pereselentsev," *Migratsiia v Rossii* 2 (December 2000): 2; Aleksandr Blokhin, "Obsuzhdaem 'Kontsetsiiu gosudarstvenoj migratsionnoj politiki RF,'" *Migratsiia v Rossii* 2 (January 2000): 20.

25. In 2002, net migration inflow was twelve times lower than in 1990. Vishnevskii, *Naseleniie Rossii 2002,* 141. During 1992–2000 alone, migration to Russia from Estonia declined twenty-nine times; from Latvia, twenty times, and even from Kyrgyzstan, nine times; Vladimir Mukomel', "Migratsionnyi potentsial i perspektivy immigratsii sootechestvennikov iz gosudarstv SNG i Baltii," *Etnopanorama* no. 3 (2001): 47, 51. Net immigration increased somewhat after 2005, reaching 132,319 in 2006. Still, at present, migration inflow continues primarily from Kazakhstan and Central Asia; see http://gks.ru/free_doc/2007/b07_11/05-09.htm.

26. Vishnevskii, *Naseleniie Rossii 2003–2004,* 309.

27. With a partial exception of Russia (*Rossiia*), all Soviet republics bore the names of their official nationalities, even though on average, ethnic minorities accounted for 31.7 percent of their populations. The shares of nontitular groups were especially high in Kazakhstan, 60.3 percent; Latvia, 48 percent; and Kyrgyzstan, 47.6 percent. Goskomstat SSSR, *Natsional'nyi sostav naseleniia SSSR,* 5–19. Minority shares were particularly high among the professionals and industrial workers and, respectively, in the population of capitals and major industrial centers (see table 2.1).

28. Living in the non-Russian ethnic areas people of nontitular ethnic groups, communicating primarily in the Russian language.

29. Vishnevskii, *Naseleniie Rossii 2003–2004,* 340. In 2006, only 6,876 people were newly registered as forced migrants in Russia; see http://www.gks.ru/free_doc/2007/b07_11/05-10.htm.

30. This latter factor is based on the fact that the representatives of the most mobile population groups have already moved during the initial period of migration, leaving be-

hind those belonging to demographic, educational, and professional groups that are less competitive on the labor market.

31. These included, among others, the Concept of the RF Demographic Development until 2015 (September 2001), the Concept of the RF Demographic Development until 2025 (October 2007), the Concept of Migration Processes Regulation in the RF (March 2003), the Law on Citizenship of the RF (May 2002; significantly revised and liberalized in November 2003), the Law on the Legal Status of Foreign Citizens (July 2002; revised in November 2003), and the revised version of the Law on Entrance and Exit (January 2003). Also significant were the introduction in 2002 of migration cards for all foreign citizens arriving in Russia and of a diversified visa system in 2003. In 2004, the CIS Concept of Cooperation in Preventing the Illegal Migration was adopted.

32. In 2004, only 4.4 percent of migrants to Russia in the age of fourteen or older claimed the worsening interethnic relations as the major reason for their decision to migrate, compared with close to two-thirds in 1991. Mukomel, *Migratsionnaia politika Rossii,* 52.

33. Compared with the peak, 1994, migration inflow to Russia from the post-Soviet states has declined more than tenfold; net migration in 2004 was 74,000 compared with 914,000 in 1994. Mukomel, *Migratsionnaia politika Rossii,* 50.

34. Russia's share of the immigrants received by the CIS countries increased from 42 percent in 1989 to 73 percent in 2000. Vishnevskii, *Naseleniie Rossii 2001,* 168.

35. In the framework of this new policy, on June 22, 2006 Vladimir Putin signed the decree on "Measures Supporting the Voluntary Resettlement to the Russian Federation of Compatriots Living Abroad." On June 21, 2007, it was followed by another decree, "On the Creation of the 'Russian World' Foundation." Among the foundation's stated goals—spreading the Russian culture, establishment of ties with the Russian-speaking diaspora abroad, and the encouragement of the return of Russians and Russian speakers to the RF.

36. E.g., the population of Russia is declining since 1992, when it reached 148.2 million. By November 1, 2007, the population declined to 142.0 million, or by 6.2 million (a 4.2 percent decline as compared with 1992); see http://www.gks.ru/bgd/free/b07_00/Isswww.exe/Stg/d110/08-0.htm, and Mukomel and Pain, *Nuzhny li immigranty Rossiiskomu obshchestvu?* 7, 9. According to the UN estimates, during the period 2000–50, the population of Russia, Georgia, and Latvia might decline by about 30 percent; Ukraine, by approximately 40 percent; and Estonia, by close to 50 percent. In Russia, the share of people in the age groups of sixty years or older might increase from 18.5 percent in 2000 to 37.2 percent in 2050. United Nations, *World Population Prospects: The 2000 Revision* (New York: United Nations, 2001), vol. 1, *Comprehensive Tables.* This issue is important for the majority of the post-Soviet states; except for Azerbaijan and four states of Central Asia, they are currently losing population. As a result of these unfavorable demographic trends and out-migration, during the period 1991–2001, the CIS as a whole has lost 1.6 million, or 0.6 percent of its population. Anatolii Topilin, "Demograficheskaia situatsiia v stranakh SNG," *Demoscope* 2 (2002): 63–64; available at http://www.demoscope.ru. The situation in the Baltic states is even more extreme; the annual population loss in Latvia is 0.6 percent, and in Estonia, 1.1 percent—one of the highest figures in the world. "Estonia—samaia bystro vymiraiushchaia strana mira," *Demoscope* 2 (2002): 91–92.

37. Ol'ga D. Vorob'yeva, "Trud i migratsia: Transformatiia zaniatosti naseleniia i migrationnykh protsesov v Rossii v 90-kh godakh," *Migratsiia v Rossii* 2 (2000): 44–50. Overall, during the period 1989–2002, immigration compensated about 75 percent of the natural population decline; respectively, 5.4 million and 7.4 million. Mukomel and Pain,

Nuzhny li immigranty Rossiiskomu obshchestvu? 8. The compensation ratio declined to 7.7 percent in 2001 and less than 5 percent 2003–2004, bouncing back to 48.9 percent in January–October 2007. Overall during 1992–2006, immigration compensated for 46.3 percent of the natural population decline. Vishnevskii, *Naselenie Rossii 2005,* 7. "Na postsovetskom prostranstve sformirovalis' poliusa 'pritiazheniia' i 'vytalkivaniia,'" *Demoscope* 2 (2002): 51–52; "Migratsiia sokrashchaetsia povsemestno," *Demoscope* 3 (2003): 95–96; "Chislennost' naseleniia Rossii—144,5 milliona chelovek," *Demoscope* 3 (2003): 123–24; http://www.gks.ru/bgd/free/b07_00/IssWWW.exe/Stg/d110/08-0.htm.

38. Mukomel and Pain, *Nuzhny li immigranty Rossiiskomu obshchestvu?* 10.

39. *Chislennost' i migratsiia naseleniia Rossiiskoi Federatsii v 2006 godu: Statisticheskii biulleten'* (Moscow: Federal'naia sluzhba gosudarstvennoi statistiki, 2007), 63, 117; Vishnevskii, *Naseleniie Rossii 2003–2004,* 311–13.

40. According to Elena Tiuriukanova, the average duration of stay of temporary labor migrants in Russia is 8.7 months. Elena Tiuriukanova, *Prinuditel'nyi trud v sovremennoi Rossii: Nereguliruemaia migratsiia i torgovlia liud'mi* (Moscow: Mezhdunarodnaia organizatsiia truda, 2004), 45.

41. E.g., every third household in Armenia and Azerbaijan has a labor migrant working in Russia. Vishnevskii, *Naseleniie Rossii 2003–2004,* 344–35.

42. The gap between the NIS with the highest (Russia) and the lowest (Tajikistan) monthly wages increased from 9.3 in 2000 to 11.9 in January 2004 (see table 2.9).

43. G. A. Vlaskin and E. B. Lenchuk. *Promyshlennaya politika v usloviyakh perekhoda k innovatsionnoi ekonomike: Opyt stran Tsentral'noi i Vostochnoi Evropy i SNG* (Moscow: Nauka, 2006), 179.

44. Stanley Fischer and Ratna Sahay, 2000. "The Transitional Economies after Ten Years," *IMF Working Paper WP/00/30.*

45. These figures are quite comparable with the gap between the United States and Mexico: in 2002, the US GDP per capita was about four times that of Mexico, generating a huge labor migration flow (primarily, undocumented) from that country to the United States (Samuel P. Huntington. "The Hispanic Challenge." *Foreign Affairs* [March-April], 36).

46. Thomas Helbling, Ashoka Mody, and Ratna Sahay, *Debt Accumulation in the CIS-7 Countries: Bad Luck, Bad Policies, or Bad Advice?* IMF Working Paper WP/04/93 (Washington, D.C.: International Monetary Fund, 2004).

47. In Russia, for instance, the share of the young people in the most mobile age groups (fourteen to twenty-nine years old) in the internal migration flows has fallen from above 70 percent in the 1980s to 47 percent in 2000. Among those arriving in Russia from the other NIS, this share declined to 28 percent even though the RF borders with most of those countries remained practically open. Zhanna Zaionchkovskaia, "Migratsionnye trendy v SNG: Itogi desiatiletiia," in *Migratsiia v SNG i Baltii: Cherez razlichiia problem k obshchemu informatsionnomu prostranstvu,* ed. Zhanna Zaionchkovskaia and Galina Vitkovskaia (Moscow: Adamant, 2001), 178.

48. Stephen Kotkin, *Magnetic Mountain: Stalinism as a Civilization* (Berkeley: University of California Press, 1995), 103.

49. Ruble specifically emphasizes the impact on the territorial movement of Soviet labor resources of such policies as "a system of residency permits [*propiska*]; . . . [limitations on the movement of rural residents based on] internal passport system; . . . [forced migrations of the purged people; and creation of settlements in] otherwise unsustainable locations." In his opinion, many of these measures were aimed at meeting

"the needs of central planners." U.S. Congress, House Subcommittee on International Operations and Human Rights, *Forced Migration in the Newly Independent States of the Former Soviet Union,* 104th Cong., 2nd sess., May 22, 1996, 35–36. The introduction of the internal Soviet passports in 1932 served as one of the most effective measures, enhancing bureaucratic control over population movement.

50. According to the estimates by Tatiana Ivanova, in 1995–96, up to 30 million people were involved in such *shuttle* merchant activity in Russia, while the annual volume of trade within this sphere amounted to $30 billion. Mukomel, *Migratsionnaia politika Rossii,* 31.

51. Russian governmental sources claim between 1.5 million and 15 million illegal immigrants from approximately sixty states in the Russian territory. Meanwhile, some estimates give figures of even in excess of 19 million people living in Russia without a proper legal status. See, e.g., V. Ivanov, "19 millionov inostrannykh rabochikh—zapal sotsial'noj miny, vzryv kotoroj mozhet progremet' do kontsa desiatiletiia," 2002, http://www.voskres.ru; "Terrorist ne budet prosit' grazhdanstvo," *Rossiiskaia gazeta,* September 18, 2004; Elena Tiuriukanova, *Forced Labour in the Russian Federation Today: Irregular Migration and Trafficking in Human Beings* (Moscow: International Labour Organization Office, 2004); and Vladimir Volokh, "Nezakonnaia immigratsiia: prichiny i sledstviia," *Migratsiia v Rossii,* January 2000. As in the case of illegal immigration to the United States (where the numbers of illegal migrants provided by different sources vary from 5 to 20 million), the estimates of the number of illegal immigrants (especially when they are provided by politicians or governmental officials) are frequently biased in accordance with the political preferences of their authors. According to Mukomel, the real average number is somewhere between 3.2 and 3.9 million and varies significantly, depending on the season, from 2.0 to 4.6 million. Mukomel, *Migratsionnaia politika Rossii,* 194, 197.

52. Vishnevskii, *Naseleniie Rossii 2003–2004,* 345.

53. Mukomel and Pain, *Nuzhny li immigranty Rossiiskomu obshchestvu?* 107; V. Moshniaga and G. Rusnak, *My stroim Evropu: I ne tol'ko* (Chisineu: CEP USM, 2005), 27. Discrimination and violations of the law also have an impact on the working conditions of migrants. A total of 23 percent of labor migrants in Russia live on the worksite, 39 percent experienced underpayment or delays in payment, and 24 percent lacked payment altogether. A total of 38 percent performed involuntary work and services, and 20 percent experienced restricted freedom of movement, Tiuriukanova, *Forced Labour in the Russian Federation Today,* 9; Zaionchkovskaia, "Migratsionnye trendy v SNG."

54. The legalized labor migration on the basis of contracts and licenses constitutes a relatively insignificant portion of the overall migration flow: In 2000, 213,300 foreign workers came to Russia on the basis of official labor contracts (0.9 percent more than in 1999). In 2001, this figure increased to 283,700, or by approximately one-third. By 2003, the number of legal labor migrants was about 380,000. Labor immigration flows from the CIS countries (99,100 in 1999, 108,800 in 2000, 148,600 in 2001, and 180,000 in 2003) and from other countries (respectively, 104,500, 135,100, 112,200, and 200,000) were roughly equal in size. Vishnevskii, *Naseleniie Rossii 2003–2004,* 345.

55. In this sense, Russia's problems are to some extent similar to those facing the United States with regard to labor migrants from Latin America.

56. Andrei V. Korobkov and Zhanna A. Zaionchkovskaia, "The Post-Soviet Labor Migrations: The Socio-Economic, Legal, and Financial Aspects," paper presented at the International Studies Association Forty-Fifth Annual Meeting, Montreal, March 2004.

57. International Monetary Fund, *Republic of Moldova: 2004 Article IV Consulta-*

tion—Staff Report; Public Information Notice on the Executive Board Discussion; and Statement by the Executive Director for the Republic of Moldova, IMF Country Report 05/48 (Washington, D.C.: International Monetary Fund, 2005); International Monetary Fund, *Republic of Moldova: Selected Issues,* IMF Country Report 05/54 (Washington, D.C.: International Monetary Fund, 2005).

58. International Organization for Migration and Association for Economic Education, *Labour Migration from Georgia* (Tbilisi: International Organization for Migration and Association for Economic Education, 2003).

59. Andrei Korobkov and Lev Palei, "The Socio-Economic Impact of Migrant Remittances in the CIS," *International Migration Trends* 15 (MAX Press, Moscow), 140.

60. According to Zhanna Zaionchkovskaia, annual transfers from Russia amount to about $5 billion, or approximately 60 percent of all migrants' transfers received by the CIS countries. Vishnevskii, *Naseleniie Rossii 2003–2004,* 347–48. In his turn, Mukomel estimates annual transfers at $3.7 billion. Mukomel, *Migratsionnaia politika Rossii,* 201.

61. Vishnevskii, *Naseleniie Rossii 2003–2004,* 345–46.

62. Russia's share in the world high-technology production is currently below 1 percent, compared with 36 percent for the United States and 30 percent for Japan. During the post-Soviet period, R&D expenditures declined more than fivefold and have reached the level of the beginning of the 1960s. In 2002, the per capita R&D expenditures in Russia were about ten times lower than in the United States ($98.6 and $964 respectively), G. A. Vlaskin and E. B. Lenchuk, *Promyshlennaya politika v usloviyakh perekhoda k innovatsionnoi ekonomike: Opyt stran Tsentral'noi i Vostochnoi Evropy i SNG* (Moscow: Nauka, 2006), 200; Galina Vitkovskaia and Sergei Panarin, eds., *Migratsiia i bezopasnost' v Rossii.* (Moscow: Moscovskii tsentr Karnegi, 2000), 109–51. The level of research equipment endowment is 80 times lower than in the West, while in terms of Western research literature accessibility, the gap reaches 100 times. O. Zharenova, N. Kerchil, and E. Pakhomov, *Intellektual'naia mi gratsiia Rossiian: Blizhnee i dal'nee zarubezh'e* (Moscow: Tsentr politicheskoi informatsii, 2002), 8–9.

63. During the period 1991–2003 alone, the number of employees in the research sphere declined from 1,496,000 to 870,800, while the number of researchers declined from 878,000 to 409,800. Vlaskin and Lenchuk, *Promyshlennaya politika v usloviyakh perekhoda k innovatsionnoi ekonomike,* 126. At the same time, just one out of ten academics leaving the research sphere is migrating abroad. I. G. Ushkalov and I. A. Malakha, *Utechka umov: Masshtaby, prichiny, posledstviia* (Moscow: Editorial URSS, 1999).

64. S. Egerev, "Mozgi utekaiushchie: Interv'iu S. Egereva N. Davydovoi," *Moskovskie novosti,* no. 46 (1998).

65. Vlaskin and Lenchuk, *Promyshlennaya politika v usloviyakh perekhoda k innovatsionnoi ekonomike,* 203.

66. According to some estimates, the number of academics working abroad on the basis of a temporary contract is four times larger than of those who officially emigrated to the West. Irina Dezhina, "Rossiiskaia nauka kak factor mirovoi politiki," *Kosmopolis* 2, no. 4 (Summer 2003): 66. In addition, permanent emigration does not by itself guarantee getting a job corresponding to one's qualification. E.g., among those highly qualified specialists who came to Israel, only 27.8 percent worked in their field and at a level corresponding to their qualification after three years of living in that country. Z. Eckstein and Y. Weiss, *The Absorption of Highly Skilled Immigrants: Israel 1990–1995* (Tel Aviv and Boston: Tel Aviv University and Boston University, 1997), 6–7.

67. If one relates the number of those traveling abroad to the overall number of re-

searchers employed by the organizations sending people on such trips, the share will visibly increase—to 5 percent. This is a rather large number, especially considering the length of their absence from the worksite. This is based on a 2002–3 study by the Russian State Committee on Statistics, *O chislennosti sotrudnikov, rabotavshikh za rubezhom v 2002 godu,* Indeks 3808, kod raboty 1512003, 10 vols. (Moscow: Goskomstat Rossii, 2003).

68. Egerev, "Mozgi utekaiushchie."

69. Andrei Korobkov and Zhanna Zaionchkovskaia, "The Intellectual Migration from Russia," paper presented at the Fifth International CISS Millennium Conference, Salzburg, July 2004.

70. Of those, the desire to return to Russia was expressed by 18 to 25 percent. L. I. Ledeneva and E. V. Tiuriukanova, *Rossiiskie studenty za rubezhom: Perspektivy vozvrashcheniia v Rossiiu* (Moscow: Strakhovoe reviu, 2002), 22, 27, 101.

71. Vlaskin and Lenchuk, *Promyshlennaya politika v usloviyakh perekhoda k innovatsionnoi ekonomike,* 13.

72. In 1999, the share of Western sources in the overall financial support for the Russian science peaked at 16.9 percent and has been declining ever since. Dezhina, "Rossiiskaia nauka kak factor mirovoi politiki," 71.

73. Mukomel and Pain, *Nuzhny li immigranty Rossiiskomu obshchestvu?* 20.

74. E.g., in 1994–98, the Federal Migration Service received only 47.9 percent of the originally designated budgetary funds. V. Brovkin, "FMS Rossii: Itogi 1999," *Migratsiia v Rossii* 2 (2000): 6–7.

75. Meanwhile, statistical data indicate that foreign citizens accounted for just 1.5 percent of crimes committed in the RF in 2005. Of special interest in recent years is also the consistent exaggeration of the scale of the Chinese immigration; though the number of Chinese labor migrants is estimated at 250,000 to 500,000, both Russian media and politicians talk about millions of Chinese illegally living in Russia. Mukomel and Pain, *Nuzhny li immigranty Rossiiskomu obshchestvu?* 25–26, 104; Vishnevskii, *Naseleniie Rossii 2003–2004,* 346.

76. Mukomel, *Migratsionnaia politika Rossii,* 67.

77. Mukomel and Pain, *Nuzhny li immigranty Rossiiskomu obshchestvu?* 38, 54, 59, 63.

78. *Obshchestvennoe mnenie—2006* (Moscow: Levada-Tsentr, 2006), 182, 192.

79. Characteristically, in October 2006, State Duma member Nikolai Kur'ianovich met in the Russian parliament with David Duke, a former KKK leader, to discuss such issues as "the illegal immigration, the demographic crisis of the white population, etc."; http://kuriyanovich.ru/news/?id=460&n_action=read.

80. SOVA Center for Monitoring and Analysis, http://sova-center.ru. The Moscow Human Rights Bureau lists 51 murders and 310 beatings in 2006; see http://www.antirasizm.ru. The Russian Interior Ministry estimates are similar: 130 extremist (mostly ethnically or religiously based) crimes in 2004, and 356, in 2007. "V Rossii rezko vozroslo chislo prestuplenii ekstremistskogo kharaktera"; see http://lenta.ru.

81. Characteristic in this sense is the fact that 65 percent of Russians do not have any faith in the Russian police. Lev Gudkov and Boris Dubin. "Privatizatsiia politsii." *Vestnik obshchestvennogo mneniia.* 1(81) 2006. According to the July 2005 Levada Center survey data, Russian population considers police officers to be representatives of the most criminalized profession, followed (with a large gap) by civil servants and legislators and (only afterward!) professional criminals; http://www.levada.ru/press/2005080901.html.

3

The Russian State and Migration: A Theoretical and Practical Look at the Russian Federation's Migration Regime

Andrew Robarts

Over the course of the last fifteen years, the territory once controlled by the Soviet Union has been transformed into one of the world's principal migration systems.[1] Structural legacies, including a shared colonial experience, a common language, and established communication and transportation links, combined with the porosity of newly constructed internal postimperial land borders have generated and allowed for large-scale population movements among the republics of the former Soviet Union.[2] Of these republics, the Russian Federation—as the core Eurasian political entity, the heir to the decolonized Soviet Union, possessor of the strongest regional economy, and home to the global city of Moscow—has assumed the role of a migration magnet within the Eurasian migration system.[3] In the face of increasing migratory pressures, including well-endowed social capital among ethnically based migration networks, the Russian state has faced exceptional difficulty in developing a comprehensive and effective migration regime. From the reasonably stable Baltic countries to the less stable Muslim-Turkic belt from Azerbaijan to Kazakhstan, the Russian Federation shares a border with more countries (fourteen) than any other country in the world. Despite 450 official border-crossing points, Russia's 20,000-kilometer-long land borders are not easily monitored and are generally characterized as "porous."[4]

After giving an overview of the development of Russia's legislative initiatives and administrative practices concerning refugees, asylum seekers, and migrants in the post-Soviet period, this chapter focuses on the state-society nexus in the formulation of migration policies in the Russian Federation. Because Muslim migrants from the former Soviet republics in the Caucasus and Central Asia constitute a readily available source of migrants to offset population decline in the Russian Federation, this chapter concerns itself primarily with this sizable element of Russia's migrant population. Societal attitudes toward Muslim migrants and the influence of these attitudes on state migration policy in the Russian Federation are addressed. The chapter concludes with a discussion on the choices before the Russian government concerning immigration, the options available to the Russian government in arresting population decline through migration, and the potential consequences of the decisions the Russian government will be forced to make regarding migration in the coming decade.

Russian Legislative Initiatives and Administrative Practice Concerning Refugees and Migrants in the Post-Soviet Period

There are two fundamental aspects of the development of Russian legislation: first, policies, and second, administration concerning refugees and migrants in the post-Soviet period. First, the Russian Constitution and subsequent legislation on refugee and migrants, until very recently, tended toward decentralized control in dealing with migration issues. This decentralization has allowed ample space for autonomous action, often in contravention of federal and international law, by regional (territorial) and municipal actors. Second, after a brief period characterized by a liberal and humanitarian attitude toward refugees and migrants, the Russian Federation's legislative initiatives and administrative actions concerning refugees and migrants have grown more restrictive. Restrictive refugee and migration legislation, coupled with the disconnect between federal, regional (territorial), and local application of Russian legislation pertaining to refugees and migrants, will, if continued, have negative consequences for the Russian Federation's ability to attract migrants.

The Constitution of the Russian Federation

The Constitution of the Russian Federation entered into force on December 25, 1993.[5] The preamble highlights the principle of human rights and human liberties, and the text of the Constitution refers repeatedly to the multinational character of the Russian Federation. Articles 4, 72, 73, and 76 pertain to the relationship between federal and regional (territorial) authorities—a relationship that the Russian constitutional scholar Gennady Danilenko terms "unclear."[6] Article 73(b) states that these jurisdictions overlap in the areas of "protection of the rights and freedoms of man and citizen; protection of the rights of ethnic minorities; ensuring legality, law and order, and public safety; and border zone regime." Article 76 maintains that where federal or joint-jurisdictional law is silent, the subject (i.e., a territorial governing entity) can "effect their own legal regulation, including the adoption of laws and other regulatory legal acts." Article 27 confers the right of the freedom of movement to those who are lawfully in the territory of the Russian Federation.

The Amended Law of the Russian Federation on Forced Migrants

According to Arthur Helton, the December 28, 1995, Amended Law of the Russian Federation on Forced Migrants,[7] by creating a specific legal category for "forced migrant," had no analogue in international law. This law was created to give status initially to ethnic Russian nationals of the former Soviet Union and subsequently to nonethnic nationals of the former Soviet Union. Reflective of the duality of authority over migration and asylum issues, the law confers authority in these matters on federal executive bodies as well as on executive bodies of the subjects of the Russian Federation. "Local bodies" also have authority in applying the regulations of the law on forced migrants, although the nature of this authority is not defined in the body of the law.

The Amended Law of the Russian Federation on Refugees

The Amended Law of the Russian Federation on Refugees,[8] of July 3, 1997, in comparing the categories of forced migrants to refugees, is more restrictive in its definition of a refugee and in the procedure for obtaining refugee status. Limitations on the refugee definition include those "whose rights and obligations arising from the citizenship of the State of his/her former residence have been recognized by the competent authorities of the said state." Though the ambiguous nature of this proviso lends itself to a variety of interpretations, one possible meaning is that if the Russian state still considers the asylum seeker to be a citizen of his or her country of origin, then Russia has the right to refuse that individual refugee status. Students from Africa—who came to study in Russia under the communist government, remained after the collapse of the Soviet Union to complete their studies, and are afraid to return to their home country due to a well-founded fear of persecution—could be excludable under this interpretation. Moreover, the determination on the part of the decisionmaker as to what constitutes the competent authority of the state from which the refugee has fled opens up the possibility for an arbitrary dismissal of the asylum claim.

The last few articles in the law on refugees attempt to delineate the federal, territorial, and local areas of authority in implementing the law. These levels and lines of authority, however, are ill defined and rely upon a variety of interactions between federal, territorial, and local actors, including "border control organs." Finally, the government of the Russian Federation reserves the right to distribute refugees and those accorded temporary asylum to various parts of the country on a quota basis.

The Resolution on the Granting of Temporary Asylum in the Territory of the Russian Federation

Adopted on April 9, 2001, Resolution 274, On the Granting of Temporary Asylum in the Territory of the Russian Federation,[9] further develops article 12 of the refugee law, titled "Provision of Temporary Asylum to a Foreign National or Stateless Person." Temporary asylum is reserved for those who have no grounds to be recognized as a refugee but cannot be deported due to "humanitarian reasons." The decision on the grant of temporary asylum resides with the "territorial authority of the Ministry for the Federation, National, and Migrations Policy." As will be addressed below, this ministry was dissolved and folded into the Ministry of the Interior in February 2002. Temporary asylum can be granted for one year and may be extended for "each following year" by the territorial migration authority on the receipt of a written application by the asylee. The law does not address whether or not those under temporary asylum have the opportunity to make a refugee claim either during or at the cessation of temporary asylum. The mechanism and the authority for deciding on cessation are unclear in the law.

The Law on Citizenship of the Russian Federation

Another federal law, On Citizenship of the Russian Federation,[10] came into force on May 15, 2002. Foreign nationals and stateless persons "possessing legal capacity" are eligible to apply for citizenship as long as they have resided in the Russian Federation for five years, "have a lawful source of existence," and "know the Russian language." Reflective of the government's priorities in migration and citizenship matters, the residence requirement can also be shortened for those who possess "high achievements in science, technology or culture . . . of interest to the Russian Federation." Initially hailed as a positive development in Russian migration legislation, the 2002 citizenship law and its November 2003 amendments have, according to the Office of the United Nations High Commissioner for Refugees (UNHCR), "negatively affected" certain categories of migrants in the Russian Federation. The law stipulates that to be eligible for citizenship, former citizens of the USSR must have been legally resident in Russia as of July 1, 2002. Because many migrants in the Russian Federation lack proper police registration in their place of residence, they cannot verify their resident status and therefore are denied access to the naturalization procedure.[11]

The Securitization of Migration

The move to a more restrictive policy toward refugees in Russian legislation coincided with the first Chechen War (1994–96). In 1994, the Federal Migration Service declared that "uncontrollable migration is acquiring a threatening character, aggravating the epidemiological, criminal and social situation in major cities and causing harm to the security of the country."[12] In the mid-1990s, the Federal Migration Service began to reorient its priorities from providing aid and assistance to migrants to controlling immigration flows into the Russian Federation. Linking the external threat of terrorism to migration, Russia's migration regime began to be securitized as migrants, in Russia's political and social discourse, were increasingly viewed as threats to Russia's national security.

The 1990s also saw a shift in the discourse among Russian politicians, journalists, and scholars concerning migration and its role in Russia. During the initial wave of ethnic Russian migration in the early part of the decade, migration was perceived as a positive contributing factor to Russia's socioeconomic development. As this source of migration was exhausted, however, the Russian nationalist media and segments of the scholarly community, viewing an influx of nonethnic Russians as destabilizing and as an unhealthy addition to the demographic composition of the nascent Russian nation-state, began to grow more alarmist in tone and called upon the Russian state to take efforts to control migration. The Russian Federation's trend toward a more restrictive immigration regime is in step with the increasingly anti-immigrant posture adopted by the United States and Europe in the last few years.

The Ministry of the Interior

In the post-Soviet period, federal authority over migration and asylum matters in Russia has shifted repeatedly. From 1997 to 2000, the chronically underfunded Federal Migration Service was in charge of the asylum and refugee regime in Russia at the federal level. In 2000, authority passed to the Ministry of Federal Affairs, National, and Migration Policy. In his February 23, 2002, decree "On Streamlining State Management in the Sphere of Migration Policy,"[13] President Vladimir Putin dissolved this ministry, and federal authority over asylum and refugee issues was incorporated into the Ministry of the Interior (MOI). The decree "On Streamlining State Management in the Sphere of Migration Policy" constituted a clear attempt by President Putin to consolidate and even federalize control over migration, including asylum and refugee matters, within one executive ministry. The decree explicitly stated that the MOI would act as the federal executive migration service agency and that the "territorial bodies of the disbanded Ministry for Federal Affairs, National, and Migration Policy of the Russian Federation shall be transformed into migration units under the ministries of interior and the directorates or chief directorates of interior of the Russian Federation's constituent members."

The MOI is charged with developing state migration policies and proposing legislative improvements. In clear language, the MOI is directed to implement Russian Federation legislation on refugees and forced migrants and to participate in procedures for granting political asylum. The MOI is also charged with immigration "control," which includes the "prevention" and reduction of illegal migration. In assuming leadership over migration matters, the MOI, as Eric Lohr demonstrates in chapter 5 of this volume, has reclaimed a position it held in late Imperial Russia. The migration policies of the contemporary incarnation of the MOI are as restrictive as those maintained by its Imperial ancestor.

Asylum Seekers and Refugee Recognition

By all accounts, Russia's procedures to determine refugee status, which have been in place since 1997, remain slow and often result in high rates of rejection. It can take anywhere between eighteen and twenty-four months before an asylum application is even considered,[14] and over the course of the last five years, only 500 individuals from non Commonwealth of Independent States countries have received refugee status.[15] Denial rates run, on average, at 95 percent.[16] According to Amnesty International, 50 percent of all denials are based on two grounds taken from article 5 of the refugee law. The first ground is the "safe third country" principle, whereby applicants are denied if they arrive from a country where they had the "opportunity" to be recognized as a refugee. Second, from among asylum seekers who arrived illegally and subsequently applied for refugee status, many are rejected for not applying within twenty-four hours of arrival. Amnesty International notes the arbitrary nature of this provision, because asylum seekers generally do not know about this requirement and nongovernmental organization assistance agencies are not always available to help asylum seekers to adhere to this requirement.[17] Additionally, of the 450 official border-crossing points in the Russian Federation, only 114 have a "Point of Immigration Control" where requests for asylum can officially be lodged.[18]

Society, State, and Migration: Making a "Home" for Migrants in the Russian Federation?

Despite a well-articulated federal legislative framework and the imposition, albeit in an ad hoc and uneven manner, of restrictions on migration at the regional and municipal levels, the Russian government is still in the process of constructing a comprehensive and effective migration regime. Two factors, one specific to the Russian context and one affecting states in general, have impeded progress toward this goal. First, as Hilary Pilkington has noted, the Russian Federation did not inherit an existing migration regime from the Soviet Union.[19] Timothy Heleniak similarly asserts that, "when the Soviet Union broke up, . . . Russia needed to fundamentally reform its migration policy . . . as it had no legislative base or institutional experience in dealing with refugees."[20]

Second, over the last few decades, a whole field of international migration theory has been developed that convincingly deemphasizes the role of the state in international migration and denies the state's ability to stem, in any significant or comprehensive way, international migration flows.[21] As a state that came into existence in the late twentieth century without a recognizable migration regime, the Russian Federation offers a clear example of the ineffectiveness of states in the face of powerful structural forces. Moreover, according to international migration theory, the ability of the state to control migration is further weakened when potential migrants exist in relative geographic proximity to the receiving country, communication and transportation links are well established between sending and receiving countries, and the psychological costs of learning a new language or new culture in the target migration country are reduced. As Heleniak demonstrates in chapter 1 of this volume, all three of these factors obtain in the post-Soviet space and, by lessening "transaction costs" for potential migrants, serve to promote migration to the Russian Federation.

However, according to Douglas Massey, "even though governments may not be able to control fully the powerful forces surrounding international migration fully, state policies clearly have an influence in determining the size and composition of immigration."[22] With this influence, government's can promote one of three types of migration regimes: a receptive regime, an indifferent regime, or a hostile regime.[23] As detailed above, over the last ten years federal laws pertaining to migrants in the Russian Federation has become increasingly restrictive. According to migration theory, in attitudes and policies toward migration, "the state is merely a reflection of societal interests."[24] What, then, is the attitude of Russian society toward migrants and migration, what are the nature and level of debate in Russian society concerning immigration, and what influence do societal attitudes have on the formulation of migration policies in the Russian Federation?

To address these questions, this chapter now turns to the case of Muslim migration in the Russian Federation. The reasons for this case study are twofold: Muslim migrants constitute the largest potential migrant population in the Russia; and the issue of Muslim migration highlights the interconnection between religion, national identity, and the formulation of migration policy in the Russian Federation. Additionally, an analysis of the Islamic factor in the Russian Federation's discourse on migration will direct us toward an answer to the question of what type of migration regime the Russian Federation is in the process of constructing.

The Islamic Factor in the Russian Federation's Discourse on Migration

There are two divergent views on the relationship between Orthodox Russians and Muslims in Eurasia. One view holds that, historically, relations between Orthodox Russians and Muslims have been characterized by benign coexistence and periods of cooperation. Centered on the key symbiotic relationship between the Russian metropole (Moscow) and the Muslim capital of Eurasia (Kazan), dating from the Muscovite state's absorption of the Khanate of Kazan in 1552, it is argued that the Russians have consistently pursued a pragmatic and flexible policy toward Muslims. In turn, Muslims in Russia have historically accommodated themselves to Russian national hegemony and, in a moderated manner, adhered to a distinct version of Islamic modernism (*Jadidism*) that sought linguistic, religious, and cultural autonomy within the political framework of the Russian state.

The contrary view to this assessment of Russian-Muslim relations, and the one that has gained the upper hand in contemporary political and social discourse in the Russian Federation, contends that the relationship between Orthodox Russians and Muslims in Eurasia has been and will continue to be essentially hostile. From the thirteenth-century Mongol yoke down to the current war in Chechnya, Orthodox Russians have constructed a vision of Muslims as a hostile "other." Increasingly robust links between Muslims in Russia and their coreligionists in the Middle East—through educational exchange, religious training, and access to Arabic and Iranian media—are viewed as conduits for the dissemination of Islamic extremism and the export of terrorism to Russia. Through this lens, Muslims in Russia are undifferentiated, from the settled populations in the Middle Volga, to migrants from the former Soviet republics in the Caucasus, to refugees from Somalia, Afghanistan, and Iraq. Muslims in Russia, it is argued, pose a potential threat to Russia's territorial integrity and national identity.[25]

For the purposes of this discussion, this reification of religion and national identity in Russia has an impact on the issue of Muslim migration, the largest potential source for population replacement in Russia, in two ways. First, at the international level, Russian nationalists have historically viewed the Russian state as an outpost of Christianity in an otherwise hostile region and as the defender of Christianity against Muslim "hordes" from the south and east. In a particularly poignant iteration of this historical vision that stretches back to the time of Kievan Rus', Vitalii Tretyakov, the founder of *Nezavisimaya gazeta,* declared, in the immediate wake of the Beslan tragedy, that "Russian soldiers in the Caucasus are defending the values of Christian civilization and the Euro-Atlantic world, including the freedom and security of Europe."[26] Second, at the domestic level, it is estimated that there are between 15 to 20 million Muslims in the Russian Federation, constituting 12 to 14 percent of the Russian Federation's current population. Because the overall population of the Russian Federation is expected to drop to about 120 million by 2020 and the Muslim population, due to natural increase and migration, is expected to increase to at least 30 million by 2030, during the next two to three decades, the Muslim portion of the total population of the Russian Federation is projected to double to roughly 20 to 25 percent.[27] In this sense, besides constituting a threat to the Russian Federation's cultural and territorial security, increasing Muslim migration and the subsequent imbalance in ethnic Russian-Muslim population growth rates threaten to dilute the ethnic Russian component of the Russian Federation and pose a demographic threat, in the view of Russian nationalists, to the perceived core Russian national identity of the Russian Federation.

Although neo-Malthusian migration theory would dictate that xenophobia and racism would be most prevalent in cities with high concentrations of migrants,[28] it is apparent that negative societal attitudes toward Muslim migrants are not confined to Moscow and Krasnodar Kray, the two regions most heavily affected by migration in the Russian Federation. Discrimination, restrictive policies and, occasionally, violent attacks against Muslims and foreigners have recently been reported in—among other cities, towns, and regions—Saint Petersburg, Voronezh, Yakutia, Rostov, Yaroslavl, Ulyanovsk, Irkutsk, Kazan, Chelyabinsk, Tobolsk, Yekaterinburg, Nizhniy Novgorod, Omsk, Orel, Kursk, Vladimir, Komi (Syktyvkar), and Lipetsk. According to Oleg Orlov, the head of the Memorial Soviet Human Rights Center and a member of President Putin's Council for the Development of Civil Society Institutions and Human Rights, in Russia "today, xenophobia is a widespread phenomenon, and not mainly at the state level."[29] This situation is perhaps not surprising given the fact that only three regions in the Russian Federation (Kamchatka, Magadan, and Sakhalin) have not experienced an increase in population as a result of migration in the post-Soviet era.[30] In short, "shifting demographics are focusing the ethnic Russian majority to confront a restive Muslim minority in a surprisingly broad swath of provinces."[31]

The Russian Media and the Russian Orthodox Church

The exigencies of globalization combined with postimperial structural forces have frustrated efforts to construct and territorialize a national identity for the Russian Federation. In this context, Russian Orthodoxy and its institutional manifestation, the Russian Orthodox Church, have become influential political and social actors in post-Soviet Russia. Orthodoxy has historically been equated with the notion of "Russianness." For Russian nationalists, the "first act of Russian national consciousness was a religious act—the adoption of Orthodoxy."[32] According to Hunter, in the Russian context, a "symbiotic" relationship has historically existed between Orthodoxy and Russian nationhood and, in time, Orthodox Christianity became "inextricably linked to Russia's cultural heritage and its national identity."[33]

The Russian media and the Russian Orthodox Church echo societal attitudes toward Muslim migrants, refugees, and foreigners in the Russian Federation. The UNHCR has noted that press articles "concerning 'far abroad' refugees and asylum-seekers do not promote tolerance and a negative attitude towards refugees often predominates."[34] A number of scholars have noted the negative stereotyping of Caucasian peoples by Russian journalists and the generally anti-Islamic tone of the Russian media.[35] The Russian migration analyst F. M. Mukhametshin writes that the Russian media represents Islam as an ideology of fanaticism.[36]

Although the Russian Orthodox Church officially emphasizes Russia's historical tolerance of Islamic populations, indirectly, through cultural and religious pronouncements, certain elements within the Russian Orthodox Church both contribute to and reflect Islamophobia in Russian society.[37] For example, in the 1990s, during a debate over the construction of an Islamic cultural center in Moscow, Father Georgy of the Church of the Archangel Saint Michael, declared, "Moscow has always been and will continue to be a holy city for the Orthodox Christians. . . . But they want to make us into nobodies with no heritage. We pray to God that everything turns out alright. But all the same, Moscow is the Third Rome not the Second Mecca."[38] And in the context of increased Muslim migration in Moscow, Deacon Andrei Kurayev, a professor of theology at Saint Tikhon's Theological Institute, has asserted, "We must oppose the growing influence of alien religion and culture."[39] Although the Russian Constitution provides for the separation of church and state, it is apparent that distinctions between official Orthodoxy and the state apparatus in Russia have become increasingly blurred.[40] According to Alexei Malashenko, the Russian Orthodox

Church plays a significant role in state ideology and exercises considerable influence in Russian policymaking.[41] The U.S. Department of State reported in 2003 that the Russian Orthodox Church, to ensure the "spiritual security" of the Russian Federation, has entered into a number of formal and informal agreements to cooperate on law enforcement and customs with representatives of the Russian police and the Federal Security Service.[42] Additionally, in the Duma, the Rodina Bloc and deputies from the People's Party are considered to be lobbyists for the Russian Orthodox Church.[43]

There is evidence that Islamophobic views are becoming increasingly mainstream in Russia society. The results of recent surveys conducted to gauge societal attitudes toward Muslims, migrants, and foreigners support this assertion. In a survey conducted in early 2004 by the Ekspertisa Institute, out of 2,500 respondents, 60 percent held negative opinions toward people from the Caucasus and 47 percent expressed negative opinions toward people from Central Asia.[44] In the results of a survey conducted in October 2004, out of 1,600 respondents polled in thirty-nine different regions of the Russian Federation, 34 percent felt that ethnic Russians should have more rights than other people in Russia and 11 percent believed that Russia should only be inhabited by ethnic Russians.[45] In light of the rise of more robust Russian nationalist sentiment in the Russian Federation, the consequences of a migration regime that is receptive to Muslim migration would be profound and potentially destabilizing because the resulting change in Russia's overall ethnic and religious composition would be perceived as a threat to the core Orthodox and Slavic components of Russian national identity.

Migration in the Russian Federation: Policy Considerations

This section begins with an analysis of a detailed plan developed by two Russian migration scholars, V. A. Modenov and A. G. Nosov, for the construction of Russian migration regime. The purpose of this discussion is twofold: to show how, even in a balanced and dispassionate scholarly treatise, historical and societal factors concerning Islam and migration are reflected in specific policy proposals; and to highlight the complexity and magnitude involved in constructing an effective migration regime in a postimperial context. Throughout their proposal, Modenov and Nosov maintain a relatively balanced view on migration that, in its moderation and tone, is sensitive to the real concerns that a good portion of Russian society hold regarding migration and migrants. These scholars consistently reiterate the point that migrants should be viewed as a positive resource whose contributions to the Russian economy and society will help offset Russia's demographic decline. Noting that the initial wave of ethnic Russian migration in the 1990s, which masked a precipitous decline in Russia's natural population replacement rate, has been exhausted, they acknowledge that future migrants to Russia will speak a different language and adhere to different religious and cultural traditions than the ethnic Russian population in the Russian Federation. Therefore, the Russian migration regime should not discriminate against migrants based upon religion or ethnicity. Russian Federation citizenship, however, in their view, should be restricted to those migrants who are able to speak Russian.[46]

In terms of specific policy proposals, Modenov and Nosov's analysis is informed by a relatively pragmatic approach to migration in Russia that acknowledges both the demonstrated need for migration as a population replacement and the consequences of a receptive migration regime for the Russian Federation's ethnic composition and national identity. After asserting that for the first time in Russian history the Russian state has been unable to effectively control migration and arguing that it is "premature" to say that the Russian state has implemented a well-developed and comprehensive migration regime, these scholars maintain that the acuity of Russia's migration problem is just now beginning to be realized and addressed at the highest levels of the Russian government.[47] They unveil a series of specific policy proposals designed to promote migration as an important socioeconomic engine for Russia's continued growth and as a fundamental remedy to Russia's impending demographic crisis.

A variety of specific proposals put forth by Modenov and Nosov assume a certain level of state migration control, organizational capacity, and financial resources. For example, these scholars argue for the strengthening and extension of border crossing posts, especially along the Russian-Kazakh border; the establishment of a central database of registered migrants (to allow for the identification and deportation of illegal migrants); an integrated network of information exchange between central and regional-level migration agencies to vet migrants for possible connections to international terrorist networks; a mechanism to distribute migrants where they are needed most; the establishment of regional migration quotas, especially to repopulate low population density areas, such as Siberia;

and the issuance of a migrant identification card containing a variety of personal information, including knowledge of Russian. Modenov and Nosov acknowledge the financial costs involved in implementing their proposed migration regime but argue that in the long run migrants will make positive contributions, overall, to Russia's economy and socioeconomic development. They also advocate farming out some migration functions to the private sector.[48]

Noting that the Russian Federation's population is declining by an estimated 700,000 to 900,000 a year and is projected to fall from 140 to 120 million by 2020 and to between 80 and 90 million by 2050,[49] Modenov and Nosov argue that the Russian government should set an annual goal of attracting and permitting 1 million legal migrants to settle and establish residency in Russia.[50] The number of Muslims should be kept relatively low, according to the scholars, to minimize the risk of importing terrorist networks, fundamentalist religious movements, or political extremism to Russia.

In their hesitancy toward Muslim migrants, Modenov and Nosov reflect a relatively mainstream opinion of Russian society regarding these migrant groups. They caution that looking beyond ethnic Russians from the Commonwealth of Independent States for population replacement could violate Russia's ethnic, religious, and cultural balance; lead to irreversibly negative demographic consequences; and cause serious social conflict.[51] However, this is a risk worth taking, because, according to these scholars, the establishment of an effective and comprehensive migration regime is essential for Russia's reclamation of Great Power status.[52] Therefore, they argue, it is the responsibility of the Russian state to plan for and implement effective mechanisms for migration regulation to maintain its national security, defend its territorial integrity, ensure its social stability, and promote its ethnic and demographic balance.[53]

Economy and Demography

Debates about national identity and "ideational," cultural, and ethnic factors often trump strictly "instrumental" economic or demographic factors in the formulation of state immigration policies.[54] In Europe and the United States, policymakers and civil society actors constantly engage in vigorous and ongoing debates regarding the nexus between immigration, economic policy, and the question of national identity.[55] In Russia, this debate is nascent and is dominated by "ideational" factors and nationalist discourse.

Fueled by the heavily labor-intensive and robust energy sector, the Russian economy grew by 7.4 percent in the second quarter of 2004,[56] and it averaged 7 percent growth in 2005 and 2006.[57] The Russian economy is expected to grow at a rate of 6 percent in 2007.[58] The Russian Federation ranks ahead of Spain, the Czech Republic, Canada, and Brazil in forecasts of nations that will receive the most foreign direct investment in the coming decade.[59] By 2040, it is forecast that size of the Russian economy, in terms of gross domestic product (GDP), will exceed that of Germany, Britain, and France.[60] Russia will need foreign labor and migrants to maintain these economic growth rates;[61] its impending demographic crisis has been well documented. The projected decline in its population—especially because it will severely affect the most productive, energetic, and entrepreneurial segment of the population (males between the ages of twenty and fifty years)—will, pending any sudden reversal in the decline its population, have serious implications for its economic competitiveness.

Russian government officials readily acknowledge the bleak demographic situation in the country and are clearly cognizant of the consequences attendant with demographic decline. In his first state of the union speech in 2000, President Putin noted the country's alarming demographic situation, listed population first among sixteen problems that he would address during his presidency, and cited negative population trends as a threat to the nation's national security. Again, in March 2005, he declared, "Today's most important goal is the stimulation of the immigration process. The demographic situation in the country had dictated the necessity of calculated measures to attract foreign labor to the Russian economy."[62] In 2002, Yevgeny Primakov, the former Russian prime minister, declared that "the issue of demographics will be one of Russia's biggest problems for years to come."[63] And in March of 2005, Regional Development Minister Vladimir Yakovlev, after reciting a litany of negative indicators concerning the decline of the Russia's able-bodied male population, declared, "In the very near future, we will simply have no labor force at all, as the losses among the male population are comparable to those the USSR suffered during World War II."[64]

The Putin Administration

With regard to immigration policy, the political rhetoric of Russian officialdom has not been matched by political action. For example, it is difficult to envision how Putin can achieve, much less sustain, the level of GDP growth envisioned for the labor-intensive Russian economy (one of his stated goals is to double Russian GDP by 2010) with a labor force that is declining in number. Additionally, the Russian Army faces severe shortages in the quantity and quality of recruits.[65] The weakness of Russia's armed forces contrasts with Russia's ongoing military commitment in the Caucasus and contradicts President Putin's statements regarding the reclamation of Russia's Great Power status.

To date, in Russia, nationalism has trumped economic pragmatism, and anti-immigration forces have captured, or are in the process of capturing, the Russian state. According to a poll conducted in late September 2004 by the Levada Analytical Center, 89 percent of the 1,600 respondents polled in 128 cities in the Russian Federation supported the implementation of tighter measures for document checks and searches and 60 percent favored the temporary restriction of some civil rights, including freedom of movement.[66] President Putin consistently emphasizes the traditional centrality of Orthodoxy to Russia's national and historical development. The imperative of state cohesion, in his estimate, overrides the introduction of policies aimed at forging an inclusive national identity for the Russian Federation.[67] These types of pronouncements provide cover if not encouragement for the intensification of parochial and nationalist attitudes in Russian society. Three-quarters of Putin's top advisers (*siloviki*) have a law enforcement, intelligence, or military background and support Putin's view that migrants and refugees in Russia, together with Islamic elements along the nation's southern tier, pose a serious threat to its territorial integrity.[68] In the Russian Duma, reflective of the general populace's attitude toward migration in the country, the anti-immigration lobby is ascendant and negative opinions and attitudes toward Muslims and Muslim migrants receive official sanction.[69]

It is apparent that the Ministry of the Interior is not positively disposed toward migration in the Russian Federation and considers refugees and asylum seekers to be undifferentiated from the larger category of "illegal migrants." The language of an MOI press release preceding a conference on illegal migration organized by the International Organization for Migration in September 2003 typifies the MOI's attitude toward migration in Russia. According to the MOI, illegal migration is a threat to Russia's security and stability and illegal migrants are a source of crime in Russia. According to the MOI, there are six types of illegal migrants in Russia: persons arriving with student and tourist visas who outstay the terms of their visas; transit migrants; economic migrants in search of work; those who have outstayed work visas (Vietnamese and Koreans); former students from Afghanistan, Iraq, and Ethiopia who do not want to return to their home country; and any individual seeking refugee status.[70]

Conclusion

Going forward, the Russian government is faced with a stark choice in the formulation of a migration regime. It can impose a hostile migration regime, suffer the consequences of demographic decline, and attempt to cope with the economic and military challenges that will ensue. Or it can turn to the population that has demonstrated a willingness to migrate to Russia—Muslim migrants from the former Soviet Union—as the means to offset Russian demographic decline. In the short and medium terms, it can plausibly be argued that political initiatives and financial resources will be directed toward monitoring the activity of Muslim migrants in Russia as an increasingly authoritarian Russian government that utilizes the threat of terrorism to countenance extralegal measures attempts to protect its borders, restrict the immigration of Muslims to Russia, and impede the free movement of migrants and refugees within Russia.[71] Whether or not the Russian government will succeed in its project to build a less porous and more secure migration regime is an open question, and, as this chapter has argued, due to a weak institutional base, a lack of experience, powerful structural forces, and postimperial circumstances, likely to be only marginally successful. At the state-society nexus, growing official and popular Islamophobia and vitriolic state-sanctioned societal attitudes toward Muslims and Muslim migrants will further threaten "to undermine the lengthy traditions of positive cohabitation between Russians and Muslims" and put into jeopardy "Russia's future development as an ethnically and confessionally pluralistic state."[72]

The tragedy in Beslan in September 2004, following a history of increasingly brazen terrorist acts on Russian soil, resulted in calls from government officials and security service personnel for greater monitoring of, and greater control over, the movement and activities of Muslim migrants in the Russian Federation. To demonstrate control over migration, symbolic political and administrative measures are likely to increase. These measures will include prolonged detentions and well-publicized deportations undertaken by state security and migration authorities targeting less integrated and more vulnerable migrant populations in Russia—refugees, asylum seekers, and Muslim migrants from Caucasus and Central Asia. In a post-Beslan era of political and social discourse that equates Islam with terrorism in a region with a large and mobile Muslim population, the interplay between an increasingly authoritarian government, a weak migration regime, and a more xenophobic society raises serious questions about the future for Muslim migrants in the Russian Federation.

Tough decisions regarding migration, its impact on the Russian economy and military, and the construction of a migration regime (receptive, indifferent or hostile) that matches Russia's long-term economic and political goals have yet to be made. If and when these decisions are made, their impact will be felt not only in Russia but in Eurasia and internationally. Since the fall of the Soviet Union, it has been argued that Russia's ability to absorb surplus labor from the Caucasus and Central Asia has had a "stabilizing effect in the Eurasian region as a whole." A move toward a more restrictive migration regime in Russia would reduce this important "outlet for hundreds of thousands of people who would be unemployed in Central Asia and the Caucasus" and result in increased instability in Eurasia.[73]

Although muted in the Russian discourse on migration, advocates for the adoption of a more receptive migration regime, or at least the formulation of more pro-immigrant policies, do exist in the Russian government. Officials within the Russian Ministry of Labor were among the first to publicly address the nation's demographic crisis and have been among the most outspoken advocates for migration as means to replenish its dwindling labor force. In 2003, the head of the Demographic Policy Unit of the Ministry of Labor argued that the Russian Federation needed to actively recruit migrants to shore up its dwindling labor resources. Ideally, it was argued, these migrants would possess, "contemporary education, professional training, and a mentality which suits Russian conditions."[74] In late 2005, Vyacheslav Postavnin, a labor migration official within the Federal Migration Service, announced a plan to provide amnesty to illegal migrants in the Russian Federation. Asserting that Russia is a tolerant country, Postavnin indicated that this amnesty would be extended to roughly 1 million illegal migrants.[75]

Recently, the Russian military initiated a program, on a pilot basis, that seeks to recruit up to five hundred young male migrants annually from the former Soviet republics into the Russian Army. In line with the contractual nature of this program, upon completion of their tour of duty, these migrant recruits will obtain Russian citizenship. As of 2005, 250 Azerbaijanis had applied for this program. The Russian military approved 45 of these applications.[76]

At the nonfederal level, Russian analysts of the situation in the Russian Far East have raised concerns about the depopulation of Siberia and the demographic vacuum that exists in this part of the Russian Federation. Arguing that the federal government does not pay enough attention to the demographic situation in the Far East, these analysts advocate for a more proactive immigration policy to encourage migration to Siberia and warn that, in the absence of attention from Moscow and given the failure to reverse downward population pressures, the secession of the Russian Far East from the Russian Federation remains a possibility in the long term.[77] Already, as Seema Iyer points out in chapter 4 of this volume, regionalization is occurring in the Russian Far East. Though population trends elsewhere in Siberia are decidedly negative, the Irkutsk Oblast, she notes, is gaining population.

It might be stretch to claim that the combination of officials within the Labor Ministry, a smattering of local officials in Russia's regions, parts of the military establishment, and some migration scholars constitute a "pro-immigrant lobby" in Russia. However, it is apparent that there are policy-makers and political analysts in Russia who are willing to discuss, in the interests of the Russian economy, military, and territorial sovereignty, policies that entail a certain amount of receptiveness toward migrant populations. The existence of these voices and the potential coalescing of public opinion around the idea of a more receptive migration regime raise the possibility of developing a more balanced debate on migration in the Russian Federation.

Notes

1. Although Douglas Massey et al. fail to address the former Soviet Union, the migration systems they describe, in their development and structure, resemble the migration dynamics in the post-Soviet space. See Douglas S. Massey, Joaqufn Arango, Graeme Hugo, Ali Kouaouci, Adela Pellegrino, and J. Edward Taylor, *Worlds in Motion: Understanding International Migration at the End of the Millennium* (Oxford: Clarendon Press, 1998). I refer specifically to the definition of migration system outlined on pp. 60 and 61.

2. International migration theory indicates the strong correlation between migration and the structural links between former colonies and the Imperial metropole. See, e.g., Massey et al., *Worlds in Motion,* 41. Though the Soviet Union as empire question is one of considerable scholarly debate, I agree with Shireen Hunter's assessment that in its multinational, multireligious, and multiethnic composition, the Soviet Union, as the territorial successor to the Tsarist Russian Empire, "culturally and politically resembled a colonial empire." See Shireen Hunter, *Islam in Russia: The Politics of Identity and Security* (Armonk, N.Y.: M. E. Sharpe, 2004), 128; and also see 281–82, Hunter's discussion on the imperial characteristics of the Soviet Union and the Russian Federation.

3. Timothy Heleniak, "Migration Dilemmas Haunt Post-Soviet Russia," *Migration Information Source,* October 2002, http://www.migrationinformation.org/Profiles/display.cfm?ID=62, 6. Moscow's Muslim population (roughly 1.5 million) is larger than that of any city in Europe; see Algis Prazauskas, "Russia and Islam," Vytautas Magnus University, Kaunas, Lithuania.

4. Heleniak, "Migration Dilemmas," 1; and Julie DaVanzo, Olga Oliker, and Clifford Grammich, "Too Few Good Men: The Security Implications of Russian Demographics," *Georgetown Journal of International Affairs,* Summer–Fall 2003, 23.

5. The text of the Constitution of the Russian Federation can be found at the UNHCR Web site, http://www.unhcr.ch/research/legal/htm.

6. Gennady Danilenko, "The New Russian Constitution and International Law," *American Journal of International Law,* no 88 (1994): 457.

7. The text of this law can be found in *Forced Displacement and Human Security in the Former Soviet Union: Law and Policy,* by Arthur Helton and Natalia Voronina (Ardsley, N.Y.: Transnational Publishers, Inc., 2000), 215–27.

8. The text of this law can be found in ibid., 229–57.

9. The text of this resolution can be found at the UNHCR Web site, http://www.unhcr.ch/research/legal/htm.

10. The text of this law can be found at the UNHCR Web site, http://www.unhcr.ch/research/legal/htm.

11. UNHCR, "Russian Federation," in *UNHCR Global Report 2003* (Geneva: Office of the United Nations High Commissioner for Refugees, 2003), 398.

12. Hilary Pilkington, *Migration, Displacement, and Identity in Post-Soviet Russia* (New York: Routledge, 1998), 71.

13. The text of this decree can be found at the UNHCR Web site, http://www.unhcr.ch/research/legal/htm.

14. UNHCR, "Russian Federation," in *UNHCR Global Report 2002* (Geneva: Office of the United Nations High Commissioner for Refugees, 2002), 407.

15. "Dokumenty: Discrimination on the Grounds of Race in the Russian Federation" *Amnesty International,* 2002, page 58.

16. UNHCR, "Russian Federation," in *UNHCR Global Report 2002,* 408.

17. Amnesty International, "*Dokumenty: Discrimination on the Grounds of Race in the Russian Federation* (London: Amnesty International, 2002), 60.

18. Merrill Smith, ed., *World Refugee Survey 2003* (Washington, D.C.: U.S. Committee for Refugees and Immigrants, 2003), 217. The U.S. Department of State asserts that Point of Immigration Control officials have never accepted or recognized asylum seekers. U.S. Department of State, *U.S. State Department Human Rights Report, 2003* (Washington, D.C.: U.S. Government Printing Office, 2003).

19. Pilkington, *Migration,* 89.

20. Heleniak, "Migration Dilemmas," 3.

21. See, e.g., Charles Keely, "Demography and International Migration," in *Migration Theory: Talking across Disciplines,* ed. Caroline B. Brettell and James F. Hollifield (New York: Routledge, 2000), 53; and Barbara Schmitter Heisler, "The Sociology of Immigration," in *Migration Theory,* ed. Brettell and Hollifield, 87. See also Massey et al., *Worlds in Motion,* 45–46.

22. Ibid., 281.

23. Heisler, Sociology of Immigration," 83.

24. James F. Hollifield, "The Politics of International Migration," in *Migration Theory,* ed. Brettell and Hollifield, 145.

25. Hunter, *Islam in Russia,* xxii.

26. *RFE/RL Newsline,* September 8, 2004.

27. Hunter, *Islam in Russia,* 44. One Russian analyst, Paul Goble, has gone so far to say to that in "several decades," the majority of the population in the Russian Federa-

tion will be Muslim. Goble is quoted by Merdith Buel, "Analyst Predicts Muslim Majority in Russia within 30 years," Voice of America, February 28, 2006.

28. According to Hollifield, "An alternative to the Smithian or Durkheimian arguments draws heavily on social geography and has a distinctive Malthusian ring to it. This is the idea that the spatial concentration of immigrants triggers a xenophobic reaction in the native population which fears being overwhelmed by the other." Hollifield, "Politics of International Migration," 171.

29. Catherine Fitzpatrick, "New Rights Council Sparks Debate about Cooptation," *RFE/RL Newsline,* November 10, 2004. See also data collected by the Feniks Center for New Sociology and the Novyi region news agency indicating that "nationalist youth groups are springing up not only in large cities but also in the provinces." *RFE/RL Newsline,* November, 9, 2004.

30. Pilkington, *Migration,* 90.

31. Graeme Smith, "Tensions Rise in Lenin's Hometown: Ethnic Friction Up as Muslims Buck Population Slide," *Globe and Mail,* April 25, 2006.

32. Viktor Aksiuchits, leader of the Christian Democrat Party in Russia, as quoted by Hunter, *Islam in Russia,* 178.

33. Ibid., 142, 148.

34. UNHCR, *UNHCR Country Operations Plan 2005: Russian Federation* (Geneva: Office of the United Nations High Commissioner for Refugees, 2005), 3.

35. See, e.g., Hilary Pilkington and Galina Yemelianova, eds., *Islam in Post-Soviet Russia: Public and Private Faces* (New York: RoutledgeCurzon, 2003), 228, 239; and "Survey of Russia," *The Economist,* May 22, 2004, 13.

36. F. M. Mukhametshin, "Islam v Sovremennom Rosiiskom Obshchestve," in *Musulmane Izmeniaiushcheisia Rossii* (Moscow: Rosspen, 2002), 31.

37. Hunter, *Islam in Russia,* 158.

38. As quoted in ibid., 118–19.

39. As quoted by Smith, "Tensions Rise."

40. An example is the creation of a Russian Orthodox political association, the Corporation for Orthodox Action, composed of high-level and influential political lobbyists and well-known clerics of the Russian Orthodox Church. *RFE/RL Newsline,* August 12, 2004.

41. Alexei Malashenko, "Islam i Politika v Sovremennoi Rossii," in *Musulmane Izmeniaiushcheisia,* 18.

42. U.S. Department of State, *United States Department of State Annual Report on International Religious Freedom* (Washington, D.C.: U.S. Government Printing Office, 2004), Russia Section II, 2–3.

43. Ibid., 2.

44. *RFE/RL Newsline,* April 5, 2004.

45. All-Russia Center for the Study of Public Opinion survey, as reported in *RFE/RL Newsline,* November 17, 2004.

46. V. A. Modenov and A. G. Nosov, *Rossiia i Migratsia* (Moscow: Prometei, 2002), 228.

47. Ibid., 6–7.

48. Ibid., 283–85.

49. Ibid., 253. According to scholars at the RAND Corporation, it is projected that by 2040 the population of the Russian Federation will drop below that of Bangladesh, Nigeria, the Democratic Republic of Congo, Mexico, and the Philippines. Julie DaVanzo,

Olga Oliker, and Clifford Grammich, "Too Few Good Men: The Security Implications of Russian Demographics," *Georgetown Journal of International Affairs,* Summer–Fall 2003, 17.

50. A similar argument is made by Zhanna Zayonchkovskaya of the Institute for Economic Forecasting, *RFE/RL Newsline,* October 10, 2004, and by experts at the Center for Human Demographics and Ecology in *ECRE Country Report: Russian Federation, 2003,* ed. European Council on Refugees and Exiles (Brussels: European Council on Refugees and Exiles, 2003), 144.

51. Charles Keely makes a similar point. According to Keely, "large, sustained immigration flows . . . are not politically sustainable because they would probably change other compositional aspects of a country's population, such as ethnicity, religion, or race, thus altering their identity." Keely, "Demography and International Migration," 55. See also Massey et al., *Worlds in Motion,* 55.

52. Modenov and Nosov, *Rossiia,* 215.

53. Ibid., 252–55.

54. Hollifield, "Politics of International Migration," 161–63. Or, in the words of Howard Chang, "xenophobia and intolerance . . . have always exerted a powerful influence on the formulation of immigration policies." Howard Chang, "The Economic Analysis of Immigration Law," in *Migration Theory,* ed. Brettell and Hollifield, 225.

55. Examples in Europe: with regard to the discussions regarding whether or not to place Turkey on the list of candidates for membership in the European Union; the adoption, upon the decision to open negotiations on Turkey's EU candidacy, of a clause to limit migration for a specified period of time should Turkey ever be offered EU membership; the decision to deny central Europeans the right to travel visa free within the Schengen Zone until 2007 at the earliest; and immigration as one of the key political issues in the British elections of May 2005. Examples in the United States: ongoing debates about what is an acceptable level of illegal immigration in the United States; proposals to grant amnesty and eventual citizenship to illegal immigrants who have been in the United States for more than three years; calls by congressional representatives and business leaders to raise the quotas for H1B visas; and the occasional relaxation of immigration enforcement to allow for increases in seasonal migrant laborers on an as-needed basis.

56. *The Economist,* September 18, 2004.

57. *The Economist,* April 15, 2006, and September 16, 2006.

58. *The Economist,* April 22, 2006.

59. *The Economist,* January 22, 2005.

60. "The New Titans: A Survey of the World Economy," *The Economist,* September 16, 2006.

61. The United Nations estimates that to sustain the Russian economy, the Russian Federation will require 2 million additional workers a year. Russian officials acknowledge the need for an additional 700,000 workers a year. Victor Yasmann, "Russia: Immigration Likely to Increase, Mitigating Population Deficit," *RFE/RL Newsline,* November 10, 2005.

62. Ibid.

63. Quoted by Nicholas Eberstadt, "The Demographic Factor as a Constraint on Russian Development: Prospects at the Dawn of the Twenty-First Century," in *The Sources and Limits of Russian Power,* ed. Eugene B. Rumer and Celeste A. Wallander (Washington, D.C.: National Defense University Press, forthcoming).

64. Quoted in *RFE/RL Newsline,* March 31, 2005.

65. DaVanzo, Oliker, and Grammich, "Too Few Good Men," 23.

66. As reported in *RFE/RL Newsline,* October 6, 2004.

67. Hunter, *Islam in Russia,* 423.

68. "Survey of Russia," *The Economist,* May 22, 2004, 6, 16.

69. Heleniak, "Migration Dilemmas," 9. In the December 2003 elections, neither S. A. Kovaliov nor V. V. Igrunov of the Memorial Human Rights Center was reelected to the State Duma. According to the European Council on Refugees and Exiles, this development "considerably reduced any possibility of defending the interests of migrants in parliament"; *ECRE Country Report: Russian Federation, 2003,* 144. See also Hunter, *Islam in Russia,* 157–58.

70. Ministry of the Interior, Russian Federation, press release issued at the International Organization on Migration Conference on Illegal Migration in Russia: Conditions, Problems, and Outlook, September 2003.

71. In the weeks after the Beslan tragedy, it was reported that upon the start of the Duma's fall session later in September, the government intended to introduce legislation to increase funding for defense and security. The Duma, closely studying antiterrorism measures introduced in other countries, such as the codification of staged terrorist threat levels, would discuss ways to increase security at airports, in subway systems, and in other public places, and would debate the formal introduction of domestic travel restrictions. The Duma would also accept legislation intended to strengthen the southern state border, including the creation of two new border posts in the Caucasus. In Moscow, the City Duma began preparing legislation to "sharply curtail entry into the city by nonresidents," including allowing access only to members of those ethnic groups who make up at least 10 percent of the city's population (*RFE/RL Newsline,* September 8, 9, and 12, 2004). Additionally, following the Beslan tragedy, the Russian government invited members of the U.S. 9/11 Commission to consult with state security and migration authorities on the implementation of antiterrorist measures (*RFE/RL Newsline,* November 3, 2004), and the minister of the interior asked Israeli security forces officials to provide antiterrorist training to ministry personnel (*Washington Post,* September 28, 2004).

72. Pilkington and Yemelianova, *Islam in Post-Soviet Russia,* 57.

73. See the remarks made by Fiona Hill in a lecture titled "Eurasia on the Move: The Regional Implications of Mass Labor Migration from Central Asia to Russia," delivered at the Kennan Institute of the Woodrow Wilson International Center for Scholars, Washington, September 27, 2004.

74. Quoted by Murray Feshbach, *Russia's Health and Demographic Crisis: Policy Implications and Consequences* (Washington, D.C.: Chemical and Biological Arms Institute, 2003), 74.

75. Yasmann, "Russia: Immigration Likely to Increase."

76. *RFE/RL Newsline,* March 15, 2005.

77. Paul Goble, "Is Moscow Letting Russian Far East Slip Away?" *RFE/RL Newsline,* May 2, 2005.

4

The Permanence of the "Frostbelt" in Post-Soviet Russia: Migrant Attraction to Cities in the Irkutsk Oblast, 1997–2003

Seema Iyer

One of the most dramatic outcomes of the forced migration (and exile) of people during the Soviet period was the high levels of urbanization and settlement in Siberia and the Russian Far East. Since the dissolution of the Soviet Union in 1991, many scholars have argued that this inherited state of development represents a severe "misallocation" of labor, capital, and infrastructure;[1] this premise suggests that the inordinate resources needed to sustain overpopulated settlements in the coldest, most isolated parts of what is today the Russian Federation has stunted Russia's ongoing transformation into an efficient market economy. As expected, several studies on migration patterns in the 1990s show extremely high out-migration from the remotest areas in the North;[2] however, instead of moving to the European/western parts of Russia (i.e., Russia's "sunbelt"), migrants have chosen to relocate to larger urban areas in the southern parts of Siberia and the Far East (see appendix A for specific subjects). "Most Russian migrants in the 1990s did not make it as far as the sunbelt. Instead, they moved from the Permafrost Belt to the Frostbelt."[3] As the designation suggests, Russia's

"Frostbelt" is still a very cold place; the mean January temperature for cities along the Trans-Siberian Railroad, which serves as the major artery through southern Siberia and the Far East, ranges from –14° C in Vladivostok to –21° C in Irkutsk.[4] In contrast to the severe depopulation of the North, many Siberian and Far Eastern regions have experienced both high out-migration *and* higher-than-expected in-migration (see appendix A for details). Therefore, Russia's Frostbelt exhibits many of dynamic demographic processes posited by classical migration theory, including depressed areas along with growth poles as well as a large stock of both "stayers" and highly mobile migrants.[5]

Although net migration to the region has been negative overall, migration rates into the region's cities, particularly the larger ones (population 500,000+), have been positive and rising since 2000.[6] Several explanations exist as to why these large settlements continue to persist:

- the attractiveness to potential migrants of urban services and amenities built during the Soviet period that continue to function;
- the adoption by the federal government of the Siberian Development Strategy in 2002, which decreases transportation and energy tariffs and invests in education and high-technology industries;
- a lack of assistance for migrants in other/potential receiving destinations;
- residents' reluctance to abandon well-established personal safety nets and means of subsistence;
- migration restrictions in Moscow specifically, which is the largest (and really only) area experiencing economic growth; and
- the "permanence" of places, particularly large cities, which simply tend not to lose population.

The permanence of cities in Russia's Frostbelt is also a function of the region's history and natural endowments. First, the development and settlement of Siberia span several centuries, due to population and economic objectives of not only the Soviet regime but also the preceding Tsarist regime. To extract the otherwise unreachable resources endowed to the region, both regimes significantly expanded the infrastructure necessary to move raw materials, epitomized by the two major rail lines laid in the region: the Trans-Siberian Railroad, completed in 1917; and the Baikal-Amur Mainline, completed in 1984. Of course, the natural resources of the area (oil, gas, timber, nonferrous and ferrous metals) continue to provide wealth, legally and illegally, not only to the country's gross domestic product but more immediately to people living there. For example, as the rate of manufacturing growth in neighboring China increases, the southern parts of Siberia and the Far East are becoming large exporters of raw materials, particularly timber.[7] The costs of entering the raw timber market are relatively low because extraction and transportation are easy, whereas the enforcement of illegal logging is difficult.[8]

In addition to physical and natural capital, Russia's Frostbelt is rich in other spheres of capital as well. Given the long history of movement into the area, a significant proportion of people living in Siberia today have multigenerational tenure of residence; the ancestral connection to place means that moving out of the region would bankrupt accumulated social capital.[9] The development of the region, particularly during the Soviet period, also emphasized human and intellectual capital. For example, Akademgorodok, the Siberian City of Science,[10] was planned and located in Siberia as an oasis of academic and research freedom; moreover, nearly all the capital cities in Siberia became regional centers of higher education during the Soviet period and remain magnets for university-age students.[11] Finally, the devolution of power that began during the mid-1980s under Mikhail Gorbachev regionalized and, to a lesser extent, localized political capital; therefore, permanence of place is also a function of urban politics and the innovative leaders who actively work to maintain a city's position within an urban network.[12] For example, during the 1990s, local and regional politicians and planners in the Irkutsk Oblast (see figure 4.1) successfully obtained funds from the Federal Road Agency to build a bridge across the Angara River in the city of Irkutsk that would facilitate Trans-Siberian road traffic and thereby *increase* network capacity in the region.[13]

Therefore, the conundrum posed in this chapter concerns the ability of cities in this purportedly "economically inefficient" region to attract migrants since the end of communism. The purpose of this chapter is to explore the capacity of certain types of cities in Russia's Frostbelt (specifically within the Irkutsk Oblast[14]) to "pull" migrants from other parts of the country. Although the urban areas in Irkutsk have decreased in population since 1991, most cities continue to attract migrants both within the region and from other parts of the Russian Federation; and, as the analysis in this chapter attempts to show, aggregated migration patterns exhibit self-selectivity by migrants to different types of cities; that is, certain types of cities are attracting certain types of migrants. The migrants' choice of destination is altering the demographic composition of the receiving locations so that des-

Figure 4.1. Map of Irkutsk Oblast (with All 14 Cities, Lake Baikal, and Ust-Ordinski Buryatski Autonomous Okrug)

tinations need to understand what type of migrant (i.e., economic, social, ethnic, aging) they are attracting today to accommodate their new constituencies. The analysis in this chapter indicates a waning influence of "transitional" forces on migration that occurred in the 1990s (i.e., movement from remote locations subsidized during the Soviet period, selling or bequeathing of housing in newly high-valued areas, or reclaiming ancestral land/deeds) and emerging market and social forces influencing migration decisions since 2000. This shows that even though the region is deemed "inefficient," any national policy on migration needs to acknowledge the fact that a significant number of migrants are choosing cities in Russia's Frostbelt based on a priori push/pull factors, such as expected wages, urban amenities, and social ties. The findings, which are based on city types, also contribute to the conceptualization of Russia as an "archipelago" of metropolitan areas or city types serving as nodes of viable development (economic production and consumption, diversity, and "favorable" migration) separated by an off-network, nonintegrated hinterland.[15]

"Phases" of Migration Decisionmaking

During the Soviet period (1917–91), population redistribution in Russia via the migration system resulted in the intensive urbanization of cities in Siberia and the Far East that were created, located, and planned to meet national economic objectives (e.g., heavy industrialization, resource extraction) and represent socialist ideals (e.g., equal distribution of urban life and urban land).[16] Since the dissolution of the Soviet Union, demographic processes throughout Russia's Frostbelt have altered as migrants have responded to political decentralization, economic marketization, and the end of administratively managed migration.

Mitchneck and Plane suggest that analyzing the post-Soviet migration system in "phases" shows how migrants have altered their responses to economic and political uncertainty in accordance with the maturity of the Russian transition.[17] Studies of internal migration in post-Soviet Russia during the *early phase* of the Russian transition (1991–94) have shown some reversals of *pretransition* trends: movement away from remote regions in Siberia and the Far East and out of areas no longer heavily subsided,[18] deceleration of urbanization or deurbanization altogether as many urban residents chose to move to rural areas,[19] and a decrease in the population size of many large cities, including Moscow and Saint Petersburg.[20]

Studies of migration streams during the *later phase* of the Russian transition (1994–99) have focused on regional variations in employment, wages, and climate as a catalyst for migration;[21] interrepublic migration and the return of ethnic Russians from former Soviet republics;[22] and the suburbanization of large cities with the rise in single-family dwellings and private automobile ownership.[23] In the *posttransition* phase (since 2000), favorable migration seems to be occurring toward certain "nodes" around the country that are in the network in terms of emerging technologies, foreign investment, and economic development; many of the large settlements in Siberia and the Far East are becoming a node in Russia's emerging urban network and, therefore, attracting young, well-educated migrants to the Frostbelt.

Therefore, since the dissolution of the Soviet Union in 1991, the migration system in Irkutsk Oblast has passed through three phases: "chaotic" migration in the early 1990s, due to economic and political uncertainties; "reverse" migration in the late 1990s, as Soviet-era forces affecting population movement unraveled; and new market and social determinants of migration since 2000.

Types of Russian Cities

At the time of the dissolution of the Soviet Union in 1991, its cities exhibited a remarkably high degree of uniformity with respect to size, administrative status, and age primarily due to the central planning of the urbanization process during the Soviet period.[24] For the purposes of this study, the cities in the Irkutsk Oblast are categorized by administrative status and era of creation, which is a common delineation in the literature of Soviet-era urban development:[25] administrative capitals, Soviet-era company towns, and prerevolutionary (1917) towns. With respect to an urban hierarchy, these three categories represent urban areas in decreasing size, political status, and economic power. The first city type consists of capitals of the subjects of the Russian Federation (krays, republics, oblasts) that experienced growth during the Soviet period, despite official rhetoric against large-city growth, due to the embeddedness of industrial decisionmaking within the political infrastructure.[26] Greater political power captured greater economic opportunity and therefore attracted or demanded more labor. Since the dissolution in 1991, the administrative capitals, particularly in Russia's Sunbelt and Frostbelt, have become a "second tier" of metropolitan areas next to the prime cities, Moscow and Saint Petersburg; they literally rank "second" with respect to natural gas consumption, monetary expenditures on retail trade, access to education, existence of a middle class, and Internet connectivity.[27] Most administrative capitals in the Russian Federation experienced a population decrease immediately after the dissolution in 1991; but in the posttransition phase, these cities have begun to grow again.

The second city type includes Soviet-era new towns, which were planned to meet national economic objectives and promote socialist ideology. These new towns were occasionally conceived as ideal types (e.g., Akademgorodok), but for the majority of those built, particularly in Siberia and the Far East, the primary objective was resource extraction and mineral processing. Most of the new towns founded during the Soviet period were dubbed "company towns," because one industrial establishment typically served as the hub of the town around which workers' housing and all other urban activities revolved. The state ensured the growth of these towns by not only heavily subsidizing the industrial production but also providing incentives to potential migrants such as higher wages or larger living accommodations.[28] Although these towns experienced rapid and intense population growth during the Soviet period, many of them had general urban development plans (*genplans*) that forecasted even more growth than was realizable after 1991;[29] therefore, these towns had an excess supply of housing at the time of the USSR's dissolution.

The third city type includes cities that existed before the 1917 Bolshevik Revolution but are not administrative capitals.[30] The growth of these cities during the Soviet era occurred with little integration into the existing functionality or usage of the town, making the juxtaposition of old and new extremely acute. For example, the original city of Usole-Sibirskoye in the Irkutsk Oblast began along the banks of the Angara River; however, a Soviet-style center square (*ploshchad*) was built farther inland closer to the Trans-Siberian Railroad soon after 1917. Since 1991, the land in the older part of town has been the source of attraction for in-migrants with claims (real or perceived) to ancestral or family-owned land; however, given the ambiguity of deeds, ownership of the parcels is heavily disputed. In Siberia and the Far East, many of these towns have, on average, experienced population decline and are graying as pensioners come for the low cost of housing.

On the basis of a previous analysis of *propiska* (residency registration form) data from the Irkutsk Oblast between 1997 and 1999, all three city types were distinguishable with respect to self-selection among migrants; distinct flows of migrants could be identified to each type of city.[31] As the administrative capital of the oblast, which became the place of concentrated business expertise, culture, and opportunity, the city of Irkutsk attracted migrants who were younger and ethnically non Russian, and who moved to the city for educational and/or employment opportunities. The Soviet company towns in the Irkutsk Oblast not only retained underemployed workers who stayed with the town's enterprise to continue receiving social benefits.[32] They also, because of an abundant and rapidly privatizing housing stock, attracted older migrants who could capitalize on more profitable housing in areas experiencing development pressure and move to these towns with an abundant housing stock.[33] The prerevolutionary towns experienced population decline as highly specialized personnel assigned to these remote locations after graduation returned to their previous place of residence; however, these cities did attract migrants, who tended to be ethnically Russian and claimed an ancestral connection to the town, either socially (family) or physically (land).

As will be shown in this chapter, longitudinal comparative analysis indicates that city types continue to be distinguishable with respect to the type of migrant they attract. However, the capital is much more separable from both Soviet company towns and prerevolutionary towns than these latter two are from each other, further suggesting that (1) Soviet-era urban distinctions are becoming less important and (2) the administrative capitals are distinct "nodes" within a broader national urban network.

Registration Data

To determine what types of migrants were attracted to specific destinations in Russia's Frostbelt, *propiska* (again, registration) data from the Irkutsk Oblast (see appendix B) were analyzed across two time periods: 1997–99 and 2002–3. Because *propiska* forms serve as the source of data, the decision to move by an individual migrant has already been made; therefore, the outcome of interest is the choice of destination among different migrant types. The sample taken from this data set consists of all in-migrants to the oblast during the month of April,[34] from 1997 to 1999 and from 2002 to 2003. As the reasons for and enforcement of registration have relaxed since the dissolution in 1991, migrants who register have tended to be permanent residents, as opposed to temporary migrants, who are obligated to register in order to work, occupy an apartment, or attend school in the new place of residence.[35] Therefore, the sample is highly biased toward not only permanent migrants but also migrants who are required or compelled by other reasons to officially register. These tend to be *non-elite* migrants who cannot build homes or work without official permission.[36]

Within this sample, the absolute number of registration forms during the month of April in the first time period (1997–99) decreased more than 5 percent each year (see table 4.1), which is more likely a function of fewer people registering rather than such a precipitate drop in annual migration.[37] However, since 2000, the number of *propiska* records in the month of April sharply increased for those in-migrating from outside the oblast; the number of records nearly doubled from 710 in April 1999 to 1,373 in April 2000. Although overall migration rates in the Russian Federation have steadily been declining (as shown in chapter 1 of this volume), migration into all urban areas has sharply risen since 2000.[38] And for cities that have retained Soviet-era migration restrictions, there appears to be greater enforcement of registration procedures under Vladimir Putin's presidency and also due to security concerns and rising xenophobia that surged after the 2000 terrorist bombings in Moscow (see chapter 3 of this volume).

Unfortunately, due to repository space limitations, not all the information reported on the *propiska* is archived by the Oblast State Statistical Committee (Oblastnoi komitet gosudarstvennoi statistiki, Oblkomstat). From 1997 to 1999, only 7 questions from the *propiska* forms were recorded (sex, year of birth, previous and current place of residence, reason for leaving, ethnicity, and number of children); starting in 2002, level of education was also recorded.[39] Although limited, these data do account for the personal characteristics of each migrant (age, gender, number of children, and education) and the characteristics of the move itself (distance,[40] a move either within the Irkutsk Oblast or from other parts of the Russia Federation, and reason for moving). The migrant's stated reason for moving serves as a proxy for otherwise unavailable information about the migrant and the destination itself.[41] For example, a migrant who states "school" as his or her reason for moving suggests that he or she is a student and the destination is attractive for its educational opportunities. Similarly, the other reasons for moving—work, personal/family, and return to previous place of residence—suggest the destination's attractiveness due to employment opportunities, social ties, and ancestral connection to place, respectively.

Table 4.1. Number of Propiska Records in the Month of April for Migrants 16 Years and Older by Type of Migration to All Cities (Goskomstat Level 401 and Above) in the Irkutsk Oblast, 1997–2003

Year	From within Oblast	From Other Parts of Russian Federation	From other CIS Countries	International Immigration
1997	1,375	766		
1998	1,319	692		
1999	1,177	710		
2000	1,426	1,373	192	28
2001	1,129	1,292	81	20
2002	1,032	1,232	123	18
2003	970	1,276	5	15

Note: CIS = Commonwealth of Independent States.
Source: Irkutsk Oblast, *Irkutsk Oblastnoi komitet gosudarstvennoi statistiki (Oblkomstat), 1997–2003* (Irkutsk: Irkutsk Oblast, 2003).

Description of Destination Cities

The destination cities are all located within the Irkutsk Oblast, a Siberian province heavily urbanized during the Soviet period. Nearly half the cities in this region were incorporated after 1945 to meet national planning objectives and epitomize socialist ideals.[42] For example, Angarsk grew on the basis of a large, state-owned aluminum smelter; Shelekhov was planned as a satellite city to limit growth in the capital; and Sayansk was conceived as a pristine bedroom community for communist "enthusiasts" seeking an environmentally and aesthetically pleasing location. All of these post–World War II towns experienced rapid rates of population growth until the perestroika and glasnost programs of the mid-1980s.

The capital city, Irkutsk, has a unique position in the province aside from its administrative functions. Since 1991, the city maintained a high level of industrial production even during a time of transitional recession.[43] This reflects not only the varying fortunes of key enterprises throughout the region but also the concentration of oblast and foreign investment in the city, including foreign credit.[44] The city has also managed to increase knowledge-sector infrastructure (though not employment) at a rate higher than the national average.[45] Its strategic location at the junction of the Trans-Siberian and Trans-Mongolian rail lines has enabled commercial trade with China, such as in timber and food; and, its role as the "gateway" to Lake Baikal has generated a thriving tourist industry within the city.

Categorization by city type secondarily orders the cities by population size (see table 4.2); as in other subjects of the Russian Federation, the capital city of Irkutsk is much larger than the other cities in the oblast, and the Soviet company towns are on average larger than the prerevolutionary towns. Demographic processes since the dissolution of the Soviet Union have altered the urban transition of each city type. Between 1989 and 1999, the city of Irkutsk and the prerevolutionary towns suffered significant population loss (–4.7 and –5.7 percent, respectively). However, the Soviet company towns actually *increased* their average population by 3.8 percent. Positive growth occurred in (1) Sayansk, which had the highest rate of housing privatization in the oblast (65 percent by 1999); and (2) Shelekhov, whose proximity to the capital, coupled with the rise in private automobile ownership, made it a more attractive place of residence for commuters to the capital.[46]

According to the 1999 vital statistics given in table 4.2, all city types suffered negative natural increase;[47] however, in 1999, the city of Irkutsk was able to offset its rate of natural decrease (–4.1) with a positive rate of net

Table 4.2. Population Figures for City Types in the Irkutsk Oblast, 1989, 1999, and 2002

Demographic Characteristic	Mean for All Cities	City Type: Capital	Soviet Company Town	Prerevolutionary Town
Population, 1989[a]	127,566	626,135	117,178	56,591
Population, 1999	124,821	596,400	118,000	54,183
Percent change in population between 1989 and 1999	–0.9	–4.7	3.8	–5.7
Population, 2002[a]	122,590	593,604	115,234	52,671
Percent change in population between 1999 and 2002	–1.8	–0.5	–1.7	–2.0
Birthrate, 1999	9.4	9.9	8.9	9.8
Death rate, 1999	14.8	14.0	12.3	17.8
Natural increase rate, 1999	–5.4	–4.1	–3.4	–7.9
Net migration rate, 1999	–2.5	3.9	–2.9	–3.3

[a]Population figures in 1989 and 2002 are from census data.

Source: Irkutsk Oblast, *Dinamicheski ryadi, chislennost i pocelkam gorodckogo tipa irkutskoi oblasti 1999* (Irkutsk: Irkutsk Oblast, 1999).

migration (3.9). Therefore, cumulatively, between 1999 and 2002, the capital lost only 0.5 percent of its total population. The Soviet company towns reversed their previous trend of population growth between 1989 and 1999, with an overall –1.7 percent population *decrease* between 1999 and 2002; and the prerevolutionary towns continued to lose population, albeit a smaller proportion (–2 percent).

One of the greatest enablers of migration throughout the Russian Federation has been the growth in the housing market, most immediately via housing privatization. An examination of housing stocks and residential markets in the cities of the Irkutsk Oblast offers some explanation for the ability of migrants to find affordable or abundant housing (figure 4.2). During the Soviet period, an acute housing shortage especially in Siberia and waiting-list procedures for acquiring housing served as deterrents to mobility.[48] Since 1991, housing privatization and new construction have been the primary generators of a housing market in Russia, which has enabled and increased residential mobility.[49] In the capital city of Irkutsk, per capita living space increased from 16.1 square meters in 1999 to 18.5 square meters in 2002, reflecting a surge in new construction of both apartments and single-family homes (see table 4.3).[50] In the Soviet company towns, per capita living space did not significantly change between 1999 and 2002; however, these towns decidedly have the highest rate of privatization (an average of 56.1 percent since 1991), which is attributable to their excess supply of housing. For prerevolutionary towns, the rise in per capita living space between 1999 and 2002 was the result of a decline in population over the period.

Common Migration Characteristics across All City Types

The subsequent discussion in this chapter is based upon an analysis of *propiska* data over two time periods (1997–99 and 2002–3), which correspond to two distinct periods in Russian migration patterns. This section describes common features of migration and migrants across all cities in the Irkutsk Oblast, and the next section shows differences by city type.

For the oblast as a whole, the profile of migrants is unique for those moving within the oblast (regional migrants) and for those moving from other parts of the Russian Federation (national migrants), and each of these profiles has changed over time (see table 4.4). In the first period (1997–99), migration within the oblast accounted for 64 percent of all migration, with the remaining 36 percent coming from other parts of the Russian Federation;

Figure 4.2. The City of Irkutsk Has Experienced a Housing Construction Surge since 2000

all three city types attracted more migrants from within the oblast than from outside. In the second period (2002–3), this proportion was nearly reversed, with only 47 percent of migrants coming from within the oblast and 53 percent from outside. As discussed above, this reversal is a function of both a rise in urban migration since 2000 and greater enforcement of registration

Table 4.3. Average Housing Statistics in the Irkutsk Oblast by City Type

		City Type		
Characteristic	Mean for All Cities	Capital	Soviet Company Town	Prerevolutionary Town
Per capita living space, 1999 (square meters)	18.5	16.1	18.4	19.1
Per capita living space, 2002 (square meters)	19.3	18.5	18.6	20.1
Percent increase in living space, 2001 to 2002 (square meters)	0.28	1.12	0.25	0.17
Percentage of all apartments privatized by 2002	51.4	46.0	56.1	46.8

Source: Irkutsk Oblast, *Zhilishchno-kommunal'noye khozyaistvo Irkutskoi oblasti, 2002* (Irkutsk: Irkutsk Oblast, 2002).

Table 4.4. Descriptive Statistics of All Migrants according to Those Who Moved Either within the Irkutsk Oblast or from Other Parts of the Russian Federation, 1997–99 and 2002–3

	Within Irkutsk				Other Parts of Russian Federation			
	1997–99		2002–3		1997–99		2002–3	
Descriptive Statistic	Number	Percent	Number	Percent	Number	Percent	Number	Percent
City Type								
Capital	1,527	38.7	613	30.6	778	35.5	840	33.5
Soviet company towns	1,602	40.6	912	45.6	1,049	47.9	1,277	50.9
Prerevolutionary towns	816	20.7	477	23.8	364	16.6	391	15.6
Gender								
Male	1,926	48.8	936	46.8	1,058	48.3	1,262	50.3
Female	2,019	51.2	1,066	53.2	1,133	51.7	1,246	49.7
Ethnicity[a]								
Russian	3,588	91.4	1,809	93.5	1,936	88.4	2,007	88.5
Non-Russian	339	8.6	126	6.5	253	11.6	261	11.5
Education								
At least some college	N.A.		466	23.3	N.A.		627	25.0
No college	N.A.		1,536	76.7	N.A.		1,881	75.0
Origin region								
Northwest	N.A.		N.A.		225	10.3	428	17.1
Southwest	N.A.		N.A.		211	9.6	411	16.4
Siberia and Far East	N.A.		N.A.		1,755	80.1	1,669	66.5
Reason for moving								
School	664	16.8	257	12.8	234	10.7	215	8.6
Work	1,587	40.2	568	28.4	857	39.1	438	17.5
Previous place of residence	428	10.8	353	17.6	326	14.9	486	19.4
Family/personal	967	24.5	776	38.8	528	24.1	1,242	49.5
Other	299	7.6	48	2.4	246	11.2	127	5.1
Total	3,945		2,002		2,191		2,508	

Note: N.A. = not available.

[a]A significant number of records from 2002 to 2003 (67 within the Irkutsk Oblast and 240 from other parts of the Russian Federation) do not contain information on migrants' *natsionalnost'*. Between 1997 and 1999, only a handful of records have missing information.

Source: Propiska data, Irkutsk Oblkomstat.

procedures, particularly for national migrants. Only the prerevolutionary towns did not receive more national migrants than regional migrants (391 migrants from outside the oblast and 477 migrants from within), reflecting these cities' lack of attractiveness beyond the oblast. The characteristics and reasons for moving of regional migrants tend to differ from those of national migrants; the overall shift in the *origin* of moves has an impact on the aggregated characteristics for all destinations.

The capital city of Irkutsk attracted approximately one-third of all migrants from inside and outside the oblast in both time periods; however, a greater proportion of *propiska* records were from national rather than regional migrants in the second period (33.5 and 30.6 percent, respectively). The Soviet company towns altogether attracted the largest *share* of migrants (at least 40 percent) both within and from outside the oblast; and the share of migrants to Soviet company towns actually increased in the second period (2002–3), from 41 to 46 percent regionally and from 48 to 51 percent nationally. Most of this increased share is attributable to the rise in *propiska* records for the city of Bratsk,[51] which is the oblast's second-largest city and the location of Russia's largest aluminum smelter, Bratsk Aluminum Works.[52] This appears consistent with Bratsk's demographic trends; between 1999 and 2002, the city experienced an overall population *increase* of 2.7 percent.

In the first period (1997–99), the proportion of migrants by gender was similar for moves within and from outside the oblast (48 percent male, 51 percent female). In the second period (2002–3), a greater proportion of migrants within the oblast were female (53 percent), whereas from outside the oblast, the proportion of male migrants increased so that the proportion of male and female migrants was roughly 50/50. Therefore, though women seem to have the capacity to make short-distance moves, men seem to have the capacity to move across the country to Siberia, perhaps as a place to accumulate wealth.

With respect to the ethnic background of migrants, the *propiska* records reflect a bias toward the respondent not identifying his or her *natsionalnost'* (ethnicity). In addition to the dramatic rise in the number of *propiska* records beginning in 2000, a significant number of migrants did not self-identify their ethnicity (*natsionalnost'*). For records in the first period (1997–99), fewer than 1 percent of the records did not have a migrant's stated *natsionalnost'*. In the second period (2002–3), more than 7 percent of the records have no information on *natsionalnost'*. This presents an interesting juxtaposition; with the rise of xenophobia since 2000 and greater enforcement of registration procedures, many non-Russians may have chosen to register without self-identification for fear of ethnic "labeling."[53] On the basis of reported data, ethnic Russians make up the vast majority of all registered migrants to the Irkutsk Oblast; and, the proportion of Russian migrants within the oblast increased over time (from 91 percent in the first period to 94 percent in the second). This reflects the overall "Russianization" of the oblast itself since the USSR's dissolution in 1991. Between the

1989 and 2002 censuses, the proportion of the country's population claiming Russian ethnicity actually *decreased* from 81.5 to 79.8 percent (see table 4.5); the Irkutsk Oblast, however, *increased* in the proportion of ethnic Russians from 88.5 percent in 1989 to 91.8 percent in 2002, well above the national average. The Irkutsk Oblast appears to be one of the regions in the country where ethnic Russians are "gathering in" (see chapter 1 of this volume). Of the non-Russian migrants coming to Irkutsk, most include titular nationalities from the neighboring republics of Buryatia and Sakha.

The reason for moving as stated on the *propiska* form dramatically shifted from "work" in the first period (approximately 40 percent of both regional and national migrants reported moving for work between 1997 and 1999) to "family/personal" in the second period (39 percent of regional migrants and nearly 50 percent of national migrants reported moving for personal reasons between 2002 and 2003). As will be shown in the next section of this chapter, this shift toward "social" migration occurs for migration to all city types. Among the other possible reasons for moving, the proportion of school-related moves has declined over the two periods (from 17 to 13 percent for regional migrants, and from 11 to 9 percent for national migrants), while the proportion of migrants returning to a "previous place of residence" has increased (from 11 to 18 percent for regional migrants and from 15 to 19 percent for national migrants).

Across both periods, the average age of national migrants remained roughly at thirty-six years; whereas, the average age of regional migrants increased from thirty-three to thirty-five years. The lower average age of migrants from within the oblast is primarily due to a greater proportion of

Table 4.5. Population by Ethnicity for the Russian Federation and the Irkutsk Oblast, 1989 and 2002

Ethnicity and Jurisdiction	1989	2002
Percent Russian		
Russian Federation	81.5	79.8
Irkutsk Oblast	88.5	91.8
Percent Buryat		
Russian Federation	0.3	0.3
Irkutsk Oblast	2.7	1.1

Note: Although the country as a whole has become less ethnically Russian since the dissolution of the Soviet Union in 1991, the Irkutsk Oblast appears to be one region where ethnic Russians are "gathering in" (see chapter 1 by Heleniak in this volume).

Sources: Russian censuses, 1989 and 2002.

school-related moves within the oblast. The distance of moves within the oblast has significantly shortened over time, from an average of 313 kilometers in the first period to 216 kilometers in the second period; this indicates that *the more remote, northern parts of the oblast are no longer disproportionately sending migrants to the southern parts.* Surprisingly, moves from outside the oblast were significantly *longer*-distanced (3,238 to 3,725 kilometers across the two periods), indicating an increased *attractiveness of the oblast for migrants from the European part of Russia.*

Two final characteristics shape the nature of change in overall migration to Irkutsk. First, across all city types, migrants moved with significantly fewer children in the second period (2002–3), which is of course consistent with the general decline in birthrates throughout Russia. Of course, as is typical of most migrations, the vast majority of migrants did not migrate with any children[54] (85 percent of migrants in the first period and 88 percent of migrants in the second reported moving with no children). Longitudinal comparisons of educational attainment are not available; however, the aggregated data show that in the second period (2002–3), roughly a quarter of both regional and national migrants had at least some college education. But the proportions are significantly different across city type; the proportions of college-educated migrants to the capital, Soviet company towns, and prerevolutionary towns were one-third, one-fifth, and one-sixth, respectively.

Therefore, the overall changes in migration across all city types include the following: more migrants moving into the oblast from other parts of the Russian Federation, an increasing attractiveness of the region to migrants from European Russia, a "gathering in" of Russians into the oblast, and a shift in the reported reason for moving from economic-related to social-related factors.

Migration by City Type

In a previous analysis of the *propiska* data from 1997 to 1999,[55] each of the three different types of cities in the Irkutsk Oblast were distinguishable with respect to the types of migrants they tended to attract. Migrants to the capital tended to be younger and more ethnically non-Russian; migrants to Soviet company towns tended to be older migrants being "pushed" out of cities more attractive to younger migrants, such as the city of Irkutsk;[56] and migrants to prerevolutionary towns tended to be ethnic Russians returning to their previous place of residence where they have familial ties or an ancestral claim to property. In this subsequent analysis, which compares Irkutsk *propiska* data over two periods, statistical differences in proportions/means tests show that distinctions have collapsed into two categories: capital city and noncapital cities. The capital city is attracting migrants with what are generally considered "favorable" characteristics (male, educated, labor-related). The unique self-selection of migrants to the other two city types is less discernable in the second period (2002–3); Soviet company towns are no longer attracting the oldest migrants, and the reasons stated for moving to both the Soviet company towns and prerevolutionary towns have become very similar.[57]

Migration to the Capital—the City of Irkutsk

Migrants to the capital of the Irkutsk Oblast in the posttransition phase (2002–3) continued to be younger than migrants to the other city types, with a greater proportion of them being non-Russian (see table 4.6). The average age of migrants in the second period was slightly older (from an average of 29.1 to 31.7 years for regional migrants and from 33.1 to 34.2 years for national migrants), primarily as a result of fewer school-related moves, but still lower than that for the other two city types. With respect to the ethnic profile of migrants to the capital, there were significant differences according to the origin of the move. Of the moves *within* the oblast in the second time period (2002–3), 91 percent of migrants to the capital were ethnic Russians, which is slightly lower than the overall proportion stated previously (93.5 percent of all migrants within the oblast were ethnically Russian). Of the moves from *other parts* of the Russian Federation, the capital received a *significantly* lower proportion of ethnic Russians (83.9 percent), in comparison with not only the overall average in this period (88.5 percent) but also the proportion of ethnic Russians in the first period (87.4 percent). Therefore, the capital has become an *even greater magnet* since 2000 for ethnically non-Russian migrants from other parts of the Russian Federation.

In other respects, migration to the capital has distinctly altered across the two periods. For migration within the oblast, the move itself became shorter-distanced (from 384 to 234 kilometers), indicating that movement from remote northern parts of the oblast has declined. In the first period (1997–99), 48 percent of both regional and national migrants were male; however, in the second period (2002–3), the gender structure of migration differs by origin of move. A significantly greater proportion of males moved to the capital from outside the oblast (53 percent) and a lower proportion of

Table 4.6. Summary of Propiska Data for Migrants to the Capital, the City of Irkutsk, 1997–99 and 2002–3

Statistic	Place of Origin	1997–99	2002–03	ToD[a]
Mean age of migrant	Within Irkutsk	29.1	31.7	***
	Other Russian Federation	33.1	34.2	
Mean number of children	Within Irkutsk	0.17	0.13	*
	Other Russian Federation	0.19	0.12	***
Mean distance (kilometers)	Within Irkutsk	384.1	233.6	***
	Other Russian Federation	2,762.0	3,602.5	***
Male (percent)	Within Irkutsk	48.3	43.9	
	Other Russian Federation	47.6	52.9	
χ^2			***	
Russian (percent)	Within Irkutsk	89.3	91.0	
	Other Russian Federation	87.4	83.9	*
χ^2			***	
At least some college (percent)	Within Irkutsk	N.A.	30.2	
	Other Russian Federation	N.A.	36.1	
χ^2			**	
Old region (percent)				
Northwest	Other Russian Federation	7.5	17.3	
Southwest	Other Russian Federation	6.7	14.0	
Siberia and Far East	Other Russian Federation	85.9	68.7	***
Reason for moving (percent)				
School	Within Irkutsk	33.4	27.7	
	Other Russian Federation	24.0	12.6	**
Work	Within Irkutsk	41.1	34.6	*
	Other Russian Federation	40.1	21.9	***
Previous place of residence	Within Irkutsk	2.2	7.2	
	Other Russian Federation	4.5	16.5	
Family/personal	Within Irkutsk	15.5	28.5	***
	Other Russian Federation	20.3	43.3	***
Other	Within Irkutsk	7.8	2.0	
	Other Russian Federation	11.1	5.6	

Note: $^*p < .1$, $^{**}p < .05$, $^{***}p < .01$; χ^2 represents chi-square test of association for a given variable in a given year. N.A. = not available.

[a]ToD: Test of difference between 1997–99 and 2002–3 (means for age, number of children, and distance; proportions for male, Russian, at least some college, old region, and reason for moving).

Source: Propiska data, Irkutsk Oblkomstat.

males moved from within (44 percent). As Pilkington suggests, without institutional help in the process of long-distance moves, many households send a "forward search party" (typically the male spouse) to secure housing prior to the family's joining them.[58] The data do provide some evidence to support this profile of male labor migrants moving nationally; in comparison with male migrants from within the oblast, males from outside the oblast tended to be older (33.5 vs. 30.8 years), and a slightly smaller proportion migrated with children (2 vs. 3 percent).[59]

As stated above, data regarding the educational attainment of migrants only became available starting in 2002, which means that changes in migrants' education levels cannot be determined here. However, the data do show differences in migrant profiles across type of city and type of move. In comparison with other city types, the capital attracted the highest proportion of educated migrants; 30 percent of migrants from within the oblast and a significantly greater proportion (36 percent) of migrants from outside the oblast had at least some college education. Table 4.7 shows that education levels vary by gender. Of the female migrants to the capital, roughly a third had at least some college education, regardless of the move's origin. Male migrants, conversely, differed according to place of origin. For male migrants within the oblast, only 24 percent already had some college education; given these migrants' primary reasons for moving (work for those with at least some college, and school for those with no college[60]), the *capital city appears to be a magnet for Irkutsk men seeking to increase their*

Table 4.7. Profile of Migrants to the Capital, the City of Irkutsk, Based on Educational Attainment, 2003–4

Characteristic	Place of Origin	Percent with at Least Some College	Percent with High School Education or Less
Male***	Within Irkutsk	24.2	75.8
	Other Russian Federation	38.3	61.7
	Total	33.0	67.0
Female	Within Irkutsk	34.9	65.1
	Other Russian Federation	33.6	66.4
	Total	34.2	65.8
Males with children	Within Irkutsk	3.1	2.5
	Other Russian Federation	2.9	1.5
Females with children	Within Irkutsk	25.0	11.6
	Other Russian Federation	17.3	17.5
		Mean Age (years)	
Males	Within Irkutsk	33	30
	Other Russian Federation	35	33
Females	Within Irkutsk	32	33
	Other Russian Federation	33	36

Note: *$p < .1$, **$p < .05$, ***$p < .01$; significance of χ^2 test of association for a given variable. A significantly greater proportion of males and migrants moving for work from outside the oblast reported having at least some college than from within the oblast.
Source: Propiska data, Irkutsk Oblkomstat.

own human capital. For male migrants from other parts of the country, 38 percent had at least some college education, which means that the capital city is not only the recipient of "favorable" migrants from outside the oblast who are not likely to burden the city's resources but also is capable of signaling "rational" expectations of economic benefit to potential migrants.[61] In a study of labor migrants in Russia, including those to and from Irkutsk, these migrants were in fact typically male heads of households with higher education.[62] For women, however, across both types of migration and irrespective of educational level, the primary reason stated for moving to the capital was "family/personal"; whether females are moving to join their spouse is unknown based on the available *propiska* data.[63]

Migration to Soviet-Era Company Towns and Prerevolutionary Towns

During the first period for which *propiska* data were collected (1997–99), migration flows to the other cities in the Irkutsk Oblast were distinct according to whether the cities were created during the Soviet period or existed before 1917. The Soviet company towns attracted the oldest migrants within the oblast, and the prerevolutionary towns attracted the highest proportion of Russian migrants both regionally and nationally (see table 4.8). In the posttransition phase (2002–3), these distinctions were no longer discernible. The average age of regional migrants to the prerevolutionary towns increased, making the average age for both city types roughly thirty-six years; and the proportion of ethnic Russian migrants to the Soviet company towns increased (significantly for national migrants, from 87.9 percent in the first period to 90.5 percent in the second), lessening the gap between the two city types. Previously, the two city types were additionally distinguishable according to the reasons stated for moving, with a greater proportion of migrants to the prerevolutionary towns returning to a previous place of residence (most likely to join family members or lay claim to ancestral property). However, in the posttransition phase, the reasons for moving to these towns also became increasingly similar; the most frequently stated reason for both towns was "family/personal" (43 percent for regional migrants and more than 50 percent for national migrants), with similar proportions across all other categories.

The proportions of male versus female migrants to these two city types marginally differentiate these types. For the Soviet company towns, between 48 and 49 percent of all migrants (over time and regardless of origin)

Table 4.8. Summary of Propiska Data for Migrants to Soviet-Era Company Towns and Prerevolutionary (1917) Towns

Characteristic	Place of Origin	Soviet Company Towns			Prerevolutionary Towns		
		1997–99	2002–3	ToD[a]	1997–99	2002–3	ToD[a]
Mean age of migrant	Within Irkutsk	35.9	35.8		33.5	35.9	**
	Other Russian Federation	37.7	37.8		40.0	39.9	
Mean number of children	Within Irkutsk	.23	.13	***	.23	.20	
	Other Russian Federation	.21	.15	***	.22	.15	*
Mean distance (kilometers)	Within Irkutsk	289.1	228.2	***	225.8	170.0	***
	Other Russian Federation	3,544.7	3,850.5	***	3,375.0	3,580.9	
Male (percent)	Within Irkutsk	48.9	48.7		49.2	46.8	
	Other Russian Federation	48.4	48.3		49.9	51.4	
χ^2							
Russian (percent)	Within Irkutsk	92.4	94.0		93.2	95.7	*
	Other Russian Federation	87.9	90.5	*	92.3	92.0	
χ^2		***	***			**	
At least some college (percent)	Within Irkutsk	N.A.	22.9		N.A.	15.1	
	Other Russian Federation	N.A.	20.1		N.A.	17.1	
χ^2							
Old region (percent)							
Northwest	Other Russian Federation	13.0	18.2		8.3	12.8	

Southwest	Other Russian Federation	12.1	17.5		8.5	17.6	
Siberia and Far East	Other Russian Federation	74.9	64.2	***	83.2	69.6	***
Reason for moving (percent)							
School	Within Irkutsk	6.8	8.0		5.9	2.9	
	Other Russian Federation	3.9	7.6		1.7	3.1	
Work	Within Irkutsk	41.5	24.7	***	36.9	27.5	*
	Other Russian Federation	40.2	14.7	***	35.3	16.9	***
Previous place of residence	Within Irkutsk	14.1	21.2	*	20.8	24.3	
	Other Russian Federation	19.2	21.7		25.3	17.9	
Family/personal	Within Irkutsk	31.9	43.3	***	27.4	43.2	***
	Other Russian Federation	26.3	51.5	***	26.2	56.3	***
Other	Within Irkutsk	5.6	2.9		9.0	2.1	
	Other Russian Federation	10.4	4.5		11.6	5.9	

Note: $*p < .1$, $**p < .05$, $***p < .01$; χ^2 represents chi-square test of association for a given variable in a given year. N.A. = not available.

[a]ToD: Test of difference between 1997–99 and 2002–3 (means for age, number of children, and distance; proportions for male, Russian, at least some college, old region, and reason for moving).

Source: Propiska data, Irkutsk Oblkomstat.

were male. These same percentages held true for the prerevolutionary towns in the first period (1997–99); but in the second period (2002–3), a slightly smaller proportion (47 percent) of males migrated within the oblast and a larger proportion migrated from outside (51 percent). Although this phenomenon also occurs in migration to the capital, the difference here is not statistically significant. Only migrants' level of education is a genuinely distinguishable characteristic of migration to the two city types during the second period (2002–3); the proportion of migrants with at least some college education was one-fifth to the Soviet company towns but only one-sixth to the prerevolutionary towns.

Of course, the profile of migrants to both the Soviet company towns and prerevolutionary towns in the Irkutsk Oblast do remain significantly distinguishable from the profile of migrants to the capital. The former two city types received migrants who were on average older, with a greater proportion being ethnically Russian, less educated, and moving for social reasons (family/personal or previous place of residence) rather than economic reasons (school or work).

Conclusions

Since the dissolution of the Soviet Union in 1991, the southern parts of Siberia and the Far East have (quietly) experienced both high out-migration and high in-migration rates, which has resulted in a slower-than-expected depopulation of some of the coldest parts of the Russian Federation. And though the region overall is declining in population, some of its *urban areas* have actually experienced positive net migration since 2000. The demographic "story" of this region, therefore, is much more complex than one of simple depopulation. With respect to the urban areas in Russia's Frostbelt that continue to maintain a large migrant stock, several historical, social, and economic factors contribute to their "permanence." The confluence of these factors in part determines the ability of cities to attract *in*-migrants both regionally and nationally; the purpose of this chapter has been to identify unique migrant self-selection factors for different types of cities in order to explain why and to whom they serve as magnets. As the analysis in this chapter shows, migrants' choices among destinations in the Irkutsk Oblast have altered not only over time but also by city type.

On the basis of *propiska* records in the Irkutsk Oblast, this chapter has analyzed the self-selectivity of migrants by city type across two periods:

first, during the later transition phase (1997–99); and second, during the posttransition phase (2002–3). The oblast as a whole has become more ethnically Russian and appears to be a place where Russians are "gathering in" and non-Russians are staying away. In the first period, the three city types (capital, Soviet company town, and prerevolutionary town) within the Irkutsk Oblast were distinct with respect to the types of migrants they tended to attract. From 1997 to 1999, the capital attracted younger and/or ethnically non-Russian migrants; also, the overall migration pattern within the oblast flowed from northern, more remote areas toward the capital in the south. Migrants to Soviet company towns tended to be older, as retirees sold or bequeathed their homes in areas highly valued in the new real estate market and moved to cities with abundant and cheaper housing. In contrast, prerevolutionary towns attracted primarily ethnically Russian migrants returning to their previous place of residence to be closer to family or to claim ancestral property.

Migration patterns and migrant profiles to cities in the Irkutsk Oblast changed in the second period (2002–3). First, the proportion of regional versus national migrants nearly reversed; the majority of migrants came from *outside* the Irkutsk Oblast in the second period. This reflects an increased attractiveness to the cities of the region, not only for migrants from the "Permafrost Belt" but also from European Russia. A final difference in overall migration patterns concerns the disparity in gender composition between regional and national migrants. Previously, the ratio of male to female migrants was approximately the same regardless of origin; in the second period, a higher proportion of women moved regionally, whereas a (slightly) higher proportion of men moved nationally.

In the second period (2002–3), the previous trichotomy of city types with distinguishable migrant self-selection essentially collapsed into a dichotomy of capital and noncapital cities, further establishing the conceptualization of Russia as an "archipelago" of development whereby the administrative capitals are connected into a broader web of "networked" place. The capital continued to attract the youngest migrants and a substantially above-average proportion of non-Russian migrants, particularly from outside the oblast. However, the previous southward flow of migrants from the oblast's remote northern regions declined; this, of course, reflects the lesser importance of migration that "reverses" Soviet-era legacies as well as the greater proportion of migration to Soviet company towns, Bratsk in particular. The data also show that the capital attracted a greater proportion of migrants with at least some college education. Educational level, however, varies by gender and by origin of move. For females, the same proportion of college-educated migrants moved regionally and nationally; and the most frequently stated reason for moving was "family/personal," regardless of educational level. For men within the region, the capital city also appears to be the place to gain human capital and then possibly move on to Moscow or abroad. This two-stage /multistage migration phenomenon also occurs in remote regions in the United States. In a study by Markusen and her colleagues, students receiving an education from Midwestern (i.e., the U.S. Frostbelt) colleges and universities migrated to more populated regions on either the West or East coast upon graduating.[64] For male migrants moving from outside the oblast, the capital appears to be the destination of labor migrants, indicating that the city of Irkutsk has the ability to pull migrants from across the country seeking economic opportunities. In addition to the perceived and/or actual expectations of finding work, movement to the capital has been facilitated by an increased housing stock, mostly by private developers building apartments and/or elite residents building single-family homes.

Whereas migrant self-selectivity to the capital could be described as economically favorable, migration to the noncapital cities is clearly based on social ties and cheaper, more abundant housing. The in-migration of older, less educated, and predominantly Russian migrants suggests that these cities are becoming enclaves of a graying, ethnically homogeneous population. One of the significant findings in this chapter is that the distinctions in migration between the cities in the oblast created during the Soviet period and those that existed before the 1917 Revolution have subsided, which is a sign of the lessening effects of the Soviet era.

The overall results of the analysis in this chapter show that migrant self-selection differs between the city of Irkutsk and other cities in the oblast. Whereas in-migration to noncapital cities does not offset population decline, in-migration to the capital has staved off reduction in the capital's size. Hill and Gaddy assert that the permanence of urban areas in Russia's Frostbelt represents a profound market inefficiency, and they question whether continued subsidization and plans to restructure the region are economically "worth it."[65] The chapter attempts to show that the migrants who are choosing the region as a destination are making "rational" decisions that go beyond simple subsidization:

- Housing at varying levels of affordability exists throughout the region; in the capital, the housing market is a generator of economic wealth for private developers and the city itself. In the noncapital towns, both Soviet-era housing and ancestral land are attractive to those with limited incomes and/or strong family resources.

- Educational and economic opportunities exist, particularly in the capital city; transportation infrastructure via rail and potentially road plus the existence of raw materials demanded by neighboring China have provided incomes for workers and entrepreneurs. Higher education institutions and technological connectivity mean that the city is "on the network"; geography and climate are irrelevant.

A national migration policy that attempts to dismantle or disregard the existence of these realities may actually be more inefficient than a policy that tailors resources to migrants choosing Russia's Frostbelt as a destination. For example, the national migrants coming to the capital tend to be well educated; programs that incubate entrepreneurialism may help ensure sustainable economic ventures that do not result in overly long family dislocations or illegal resource extraction. In the noncapital towns, planning for decline, graying, and/or homogenization may help bridge any informational, economic, and diversity gaps that seem to be widening within the Russian archipelago. Russia's coldest regions will most likely continue to depopulate, both for natural and migration reasons; but it is unlikely that a new generation of migrants, accustomed to making free and independent decisions, will comply with a policy that "unnaturally" speeds up this process.

Appendix A: Subjects of the Russian Federation in the "Frostbelt"

In this chapter, the Russian "Frostbelt" consists of the southern regions of Siberia and the Far East. The Russian North has been officially and differentially defined by both the World Bank and the Russian government.[66]

Table 4.A.1 shows that in both the Frostbelt and Permafrost Belt, the population of the administrative centers (capital cities) is becoming a much larger share of the region as a whole because of the urban and "network" amenities located there. Between 1989 and 2003, capital cities in the Frostbelt increased by an average of 2 percent and those in the Permafrost Belt increased by an average of 5.7 percent; for the rest of Russia, the centers only averaged an increase of 0.6 percent.

Perhaps more surprising, however, is the high rates of both in- and out-migration that the Frostbelt has experienced since 1993. Internal in-

Table 4.A.1. Migration Statistics for Regions in Russia's Frostbelts and Permafrost Belts

Economic Region/Subject	Designation	Administrative Center as Share of Total Oblast Population		Percentage-Point Increase	Internal In-Migration, 1993–2003 (percentage of 1993 population)	Internal Out-Migration, 1993–2003 (percentage of 1993 population)
		1989	2003			
West Siberia						
Tyumen	Oblast	15.4	15.6	0.3	14.8	16.0
Omsk[a]	Oblast	53.6	54.5	0.9	5.8	5.9
Novosibirsk[a]	Oblast	51.7	53.0	1.3	7.8	6.7
Altai kray[a]	Kray	22.8	23.1	0.4	6.6	6.9
Altai republic	Republic	24.1	25.7	1.6	12.5	11.9
East Siberia						
Khakassia[a]	Republic	27.0	30.3	3.3	15.4	13.3
Tuva[b]	Republic	27.3	34.1	6.8	4.9	7.9
Krasnoyarsk	Kray	30.0	30.7	0.7	8.1	10.2
Irkutsk	Oblast	2.0	23.0	1.0	6.5	7.8
Ust-Ordinski Buryatski	Autonomous Okrug	N.A.	N.A.	N.A.	4.6	4.6
Buryatia	Republic	33.9	36.6	2.7	7.5	10.6
Chita	Oblast	26.4	27.5	1.1	6.6	10.9
Far East						
Amur	Oblast	19.4	24.2	4.8	9.6	13.2
Khabarovsk	Kray	37.4	40.6	3.2	9.8	12.9
Birobidzhan	Autonomous Okrug	38.8	40.0	1.2	15.7	16.1
Primorski	Kray	28.0	28.6	0.6	7.1	10.0
"Frostbelt" average		30.5	32.5	2.0	9.0	10.3
"Permafrostbelt" average		29.5	35.2	5.7	8.1	19.3
All others average		32.9	33.4	0.6	7.3	6.6

Note: All others are defined as "regions equivalent" to the Russian North by the Russian government. N.A. = not available.

[a]Not defined as Russian North by either the World Bank or the Russian government.

[b]Defined as Russian North by the World Bank.

Sources: Goskomstat Rossii, *Demograficheskiy yezhegodnik Rossiyskoy Federatsii 1993–2003;* raw data provided by Timothy Heleniak.

migration to the Frostbelt between 1993 and 2003 was highest among all regions (an average of 9 percent of the 1993 population). Of course, out-migration was also high (10.3 percent of the 1993 population) and in the middle were the percentages of the Permafrost Belt (19.3 percent) and other regions (6.6 percent).

Although the Frostbelt's in-migration and out-migration rates have been steadily declining since 1994, they have consistently been higher than those

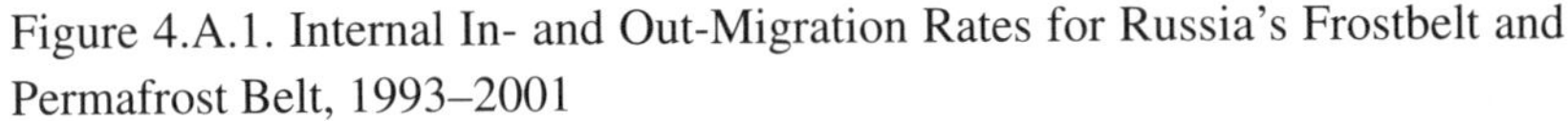

Figure 4.A.1. Internal In- and Out-Migration Rates for Russia's Frostbelt and Permafrost Belt, 1993–2001

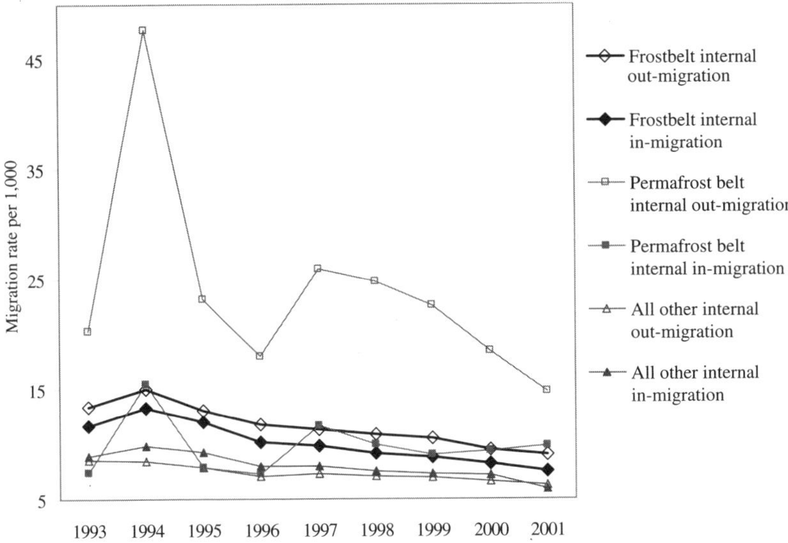

for nonremote regions (see figure 4.A.1). Migration rates for the Permafrost Belt have been much more volatile during the transition, although in-migration rates have been higher than the Frostbelt's rates since 1997.

Appendix B: Registration Form (*Propiska*) for the Irkutsk Oblast, 2000

Migration data for the Irkutsk Oblast come from vital registration records at the time of the move. Heads of households of in-migrants and out-migrants are required to fill out a registration form (*propiska* and *vypiska,* respectively), which in Irkutsk contains twenty-two items of demographic and geographic information. The data include age, sex, place of birth, previous (or future) place of residence, length of stay, reason for leaving, occupation, education, marital status, and number of children (see table 4.B.1). Although registration by in-migrants and out-migrants occurs at the local passport/visa office, all statistical information within the oblast is subsequently sent to the Oblast State Statistical Committee (Oblastnoi komitet gosudarstvennoi statistiki, Oblkomstat) on a monthly basis.

Table 4.B.1. Contents of the In-Migration Registration Form (Propiska) for the Irkutsk Oblast (only italicized data are archived for reporting purposes at the Oblast Statistical Committee, or Oblkomstat)

1. Last name	
2. First name	
3. Middle name	
4. Date of birth (day, month, year)	
5. Place of birth:	State (country); republic, kray, oblast, okrug; *raion,* city *raion* (okrug); city, urban settlement; rural settlement
6. Sex: Male—1, Female—2	
7. Citizenship (indicate country), if dual citizenship, indicate citizenship	
8. Nationality (ethnicity)	
9. New place of residence:	*Republic, kray, oblast, okrug; raion, city raion (okrug); city, urban settlement; rural settlement*
10. Previous place of residence:	*State (country); republic, kray, oblast, okrug; raion, city raion (okrug); city, urban settlement; rural settlement*
11. Length of stay at previous place of residence since ______ year	
12. Main circumstance provoking the necessary migration:	*In connection with studies—1, in connection with work—2, return to previous place of residence—3, due to aggravation of interethnic relations—4, due to aggravation of criminal conditions—5, ecological hazards (non-well-being)—6, disparity in natural-climate conditions—7, personal reasons of a family matter—8, other reason—9*
13. Occupation in previous place of residence:	Until the migration I worked in the branch of the economy: industry—100, agriculture—200, transportation and communication—500, construction—600, trade and services—700, information-computing service—820, public heath—915, education—920, culture and arts—930, science and scientific service—950, finance, credit and insurance—960, government—970, other branch—999, studying—001, at this time in college—002, did not work—003
14. Type of work	Work for hire in the capacity of: director—1, specialist—2, other employee (technical performer)—3, worker—4; independent provided with self-employment—5
15. Type of special provision in the previous place of residence	Received pension as a senior citizen—1, disability—2, toward promotion years—4, allowance for unemployment—12, other pensions and allowances—7
16. Education	*1 University, 2 Some university, 3 Specialty/technical education, 4 Completed high school, 5 Did not complete high school, 6 four grades of elementary school or below, 7 PhD, 8 Candidate of science*
17. Marital status	Married—1, never been married—2, divorced—3, widowed—4
18. If you lived with your family until migrating, then are you arriving: with the whole family—1, with part of the members of the family—2, alone—3, was living without the family—4	
19. Do some family members already live in the new place of residence? yes—1, no—2	
20. How many children under the age of 14 have arrived together with you? ______ Number of children and their names on record as shown in the passport of one of the parents (guardian, trustee).	

Appendix C: Summary of Moves to Rural Areas in Irkutsk and the Ust-Ordinski Autonomous Okrug

The focus of the analysis in this chapter has only been on urban areas. However, information from *propiska* data is able to show migration patterns in rural areas of the Irkutsk Oblast as well as the Ust-Ordinski Autonomous Okrug (AO) that is within its borders.

Moves to Rural Areas

Moves to the rural (*raiony*) areas of the Irkutsk Oblast accounted for 46 percent of all regional migration and 32 percent of all national migration. Across both types of moves, rural areas received the smallest proportion of college-educated migrants (only 12 percent of migrants within the oblast and 13 percent of migrants from outside the oblast had at least some college education). Rural areas attracted a relatively low proportion of ethnic Russians, particularly from other parts of the Russian Federation (only 78.4 percent of national migrants were ethnic Russians). This may be due to the attractiveness of collective farms in Siberia, which are being vacated by Russian youths, to older, minority migrants.[67] Also see table 4.C.1.

The Ust-Ordinski Buryatski Autonomous Okrug

In April 2002 and 2003, the Ust-Ordinski Buryatski AO received a total of 221 migrants from within the Irkutsk Oblast and 144 migrants from other parts of the country, mostly from the neighboring Republic of Buryatia. The AO received the smallest proportion of migrants who were ethnically Russian (63 percent from within the oblast and 28.5 percent from outside). Of the non-Russians migrants, 86 percent were ethnically Buryat. The proportion of college-educated national migrants to the AO was similar to that of all migrants to the oblast (27 percent). However, within the oblast, the proportion of college-educated migrants was much lower (11.3 percent). Other characteristics of regional migrants to the AO include the youngest average age (29.9 years), and a significant plurality (40.7 percent) reported moving to return to "previous place of residence." Also see table 4.C.2.

Table 4.C.1. Summary of Propiska Data for Migrants to Rural (Raiony) Areas

Characteristic	Place of Origin	2002–3
Total number of migrants	Within Irkutsk	1,688
	Other Russian Federation	1,184
Mean age of migrant (years)	Within Irkutsk	35.4
	Other Russian Federation	38.5
Mean number of children	Within Irkutsk	.17
	Other Russian Federation	.17
Mean distance (kilometers)	Within Irkutsk	174.9
	Other Russian Federation	3,155.5
Male (percent)	Within Irkutsk	51.8
	Other Russian Federation	50.5
χ^2		
Russian (percent)	Within Irkutsk	89.6
	Other Russian Federation	78.4
χ^2		***
At least some college (percent)	Within Irkutsk	12.0
	Other Russian Federation	13.3
χ^2		
Old region (percent)		
Northwest	Other Russian Federation	9.8
Southwest	Other Russian Federation	15.7
Siberia and Far East	Other Russian Federation	74.5
Reason for moving (percent)		
School	Within Irkutsk	4.6
	Other Russian Federation	6.2
Work	Within Irkutsk	22.2
	Other Russian Federation	19.0
Previous place of residence	Within Irkutsk	25.8
	Other Russian Federation	22.9
Family/personal	Within Irkutsk	42.5
	Other Russian Federation	47.6
Other	Within Irkutsk	4.9
	Other Russian Federation	4.4

Note: $*p < .1$, $**p < .05$, $***p < .01$; χ^2 represents chi-square test of association for a given variable.
Source: Propiska data, Irkutsk Oblkomstat.

Table 4.C.2. Summary of Propiska Data for Migrants to the Ust-Ordinski Autonomous Okrug

Characteristic	Place of Origin	2002–3
Total number of migrants	Within Irkutsk	221
	Other Russian Federation	144
Mean age of migrant (years)	Within Irkutsk	29.9
	Other Russian Federation	34.1
Mean number of children	Within Irkutsk	.21
	Other Russian Federation	.17
Mean distance (kilometers)	Within Irkutsk	103.8
	Other Russian Federation	1,240.3
Male (percent)	Within Irkutsk	54.8
	Other Russian Federation	47.9
χ^2		
Russian (percent)	Within Irkutsk	63.3
	Other Russian Federation	28.5
χ^2		***
At least some college (percent)	Within Irkutsk	11.3
	Other Russian Federation	27.1
χ^2		***
Old region (percent)		
Northwest	Other Russian Federation	.7
Southwest	Other Russian Federation	4.2
Siberia and Far East	Other Russian Federation	95.1
Reason for moving (percent)		
School	Within Irkutsk	6.8
	Other Russian Federation	11.1
Work	Within Irkutsk	23.1
	Other Russian Federation	25.7
Previous place of residence	Within Irkutsk	40.7
	Other Russian Federation	29.2
Family/personal	Within Irkutsk	28.1
	Other Russian Federation	31.9
Other	Within Irkutsk	1.4
	Other Russian Federation	2.1

Note: $*p < .1$, $**p < .05$, $***p < .01$; χ^2 represents chi-square test of association for a given variable.
Source: Propiska data, Irkutsk Oblkomstat.

Notes

1. Fiona Hill and Clifford Gaddy, *The Siberian Curse: How Communist Planners Left Russia Out in the Cold* (Washington, D.C.: Brookings Institution Press, 2003); John S. Strong and J. R. Meyer, *Moving to Market: Restructuring Transport in the Former Soviet Union* (Cambridge, Mass.: Harvard University Press, 1996).

2. Timothy Heleniak, *Migration from the Russian North during the Transition Period,* Social Protection Paper 9925 (Washington, D.C.: World Bank, 1999); D. Sutherland and P. Hanson, "Demographic Responses to Regional Economic Change: Inter-Regional Migration," in *Regional Economic Change in Russia,* ed. Philip Hanson and Michael Bradshaw (Cheltenham, U.K.: Edward Elgar, 2000).

3. Hill and Gaddy, *Siberian Curse,* 130.

4. Ibid., 228.

5. David Plane and Peter Rogerson, *The Geographical Analysis of Population: With Applications to Planning and Business* (New York: John Wiley & Sons, 1994).

6. Ira N. Gang and Robert C. Stuart, *Russian Cities in Transition: The Impact of Market Forces in the 1990s,* IZA Discussion Paper 1151 (Bonn: IZA, 2004), http://ftp.iza.org/dp1151.pdf.

7. A total of 28 percent of the timber exported to China comes from the Irkutsk oblast alone (source: Russian Federation Custom electronic database of customs declarations in 2002, provided by Josh Newell).

8. Josh Newell, ed., *The Russian Far East: A Reference Guide to Conservation and Development* (McKinleyville, Calif.: Daniel & Daniel, 2004).

9. These personal safety nets have become even more important after the dissolution with the dismantling of state social welfare, according to Nancy Reis, as paraphrased in Hill and Gaddy, *Siberian Curse.*

10. P. Josephson, *New Atlantis Revisited: Akademgorodok, the Siberian City of Science* (Princeton, N.J.: Princeton University Press, 1997).

11. According to a rating by *Ekonomika Rossii: XXI Veka,* thirteen of the top fifty Russian universities in 2003 were located in Eastern Russia. Of the rest, fifteen were in either Moscow or Saint Petersburg. Irkutsk State University ranked thirty-three on the list.

12. Michael Pagano and Ann Bowman, *Cityscapes and Capital: The Politics of Urban Development* (Baltimore: Johns Hopkins University Press, 1995); John Logan and Harvey Molotch, *Urban Fortunes: The Political Economy of Place* (Berkeley: University of California Press, 1987).

13. "Feel Like Going for a Drive?" *RFE/RL Newsline—Russia,* September 19, 2002. S. Iyer, "'Coping with Uncertainty in Planning' Applied to Post-Soviet Russia: Evidence from Building the Angara Bridge in the City of Irkutsk," paper presented at the AAASS meeting, 2004.

14. Hill and Gaddy, *Siberian Curse,* list the city of Irkutsk as one of the major *negative* contributors to "temperature per capita," an index developed in their book. The lower the temperature, the higher the costs are to maintain a population's existence.

15. Leslie Dienes, "Reflections on a Geographic Dichotomy: Archipelago Russia," *Eurasian Geography and Economics* 43, no. 6 (2002): 443–58; Y. Perfiliev, "Development of the Internet in Russia: Preliminary Observations on Its Spatial and Institutional Characteristics," *Eurasian Geography and Economics* 43, no. 5 (2002): 411–21.

16. Several authors have shown that administratively managed migration lacked ef-

fectiveness for achieving the expressed intentions of population redistribution. See C. Buckley, "The Myth of Managed Migration: Migration Control and Market in the Soviet Period," *Slavic Review* 4, no. 4 (1995): 896–916; R. A. Lewis and R. H. Roland, *Population Redistribution in the USSR: Its Impact on Society, 1897–1977* (New York: Praeger, 1979). However, the confluence of policies adapted to disperse the population within a centralized, hierarchical administrative structure did result in a social geography unique in the Former Soviet Union; George J. Demko and Roland J. Fuchs, eds., *Geographical Studies on the Soviet Union: Essays in Honor of Chauncy D. Harris,* Research Paper 211 (Chicago: Department of Geography, University of Chicago, 1984).

17. B. Mitchneck and D. Plane, "Migration Patterns during a Period of Political and Economic Shocks in the Former Soviet Union: A Case Study of Yaroslavl' Oblast," *Professional Geographer* 47, no. 1 (1995): 17–30.

18. T. Heleniak, "Internal Migration in Russia during the Economic Transition," *Post-Soviet Geography and Economics* 38, no. 2 (1997): 81–104; D. Sutherland and P. Hanson, "Demographic Responses to Regional Economic Change: Inter-Regional Migration," in *Regional Economic Change in Russia,* ed. Hanson and Bradshaw, 76–96.

19. Yuri Medvedkhov and Olga Medvedkhov, "Turning Points and Trends in Russia's Urbanization," in *Population under Duress: The Geodemography of Post-Soviet Russia,* ed. George Demko, Grigory Ioffe, and Zhanna Zayonchkovskaya (Boulder, Colo.: Westview Press, 1999); Mitchneck and Plane "Migration Patterns."

20. Gang and Stuart, *Russian Cities;* Goskomstat Rossiya, *Chislennost' naseleniya Rossiyskoy Federatsii po gorodam, robochim poselkam i rayonam na 1 Janvarya 1994 g.* (Enumeration of the Population in the Russian Federation by Cities, Workers' Settlements, and Rayons on January 1, 1994) (Moscow: Goskomstat Rossiya, 1994).

21. Sutherland and Hanson, "Demographic Responses."

22. H. Pilkington, *Migration, Displacement and Identity in Post-Soviet Russia* (London: Routledge, 1998).

23. R. Rowland, "Metropolitan Population Change in Russia and the Former Soviet Union," *Post-Soviet Geography and Economics* 39 (1998): 271–96.

24. R. A. French, *Plans, Pragmatism, and People: The Legacy of Soviet Planning for Today's Cities* (Pittsburgh: University of Pittsburgh Press, 1995).

25. William Taubman, *Governing Soviet Cities: Bureaucratic Politics and Urban Development in the USSR* (New York: Praeger, 1973).

26. G. Huzinec, "The Impact of Industrial Decision-Making upon the Soviet Urban Hierarchy," *Urban Studies* 15 (1978): 139–48.

27. Dienes, "Reflections on a Geographic Dichotomy."

28. B. Mitchneck and D. Plane, "Migration and the Quasi-Labor Market in Russia," *International Regional Science Review* 18, no. 3 (1995): 267–88.

29. Seema D. Iyer, "The Urban Context for Adjustments to the Planning Process in Post-Soviet Russia: Responses from Local Planners in Siberia," *International Planning Studies* 8, no. 3 (August 2003): 201–22.

30. All cities within a province are classified by their subordination status, either to the province or to the districts within the province (*raions*). The cities considered in this chapter are province-level prerevolutionary towns.

31. Seema D. Iyer, "Urban Transition in Post-Soviet Russia: Adjustments to the Planning Process in Different Urban Contexts," PhD dissertation, University of Michigan, 2003.

32. M. Field, "The Health and Demographic Crisis in Post-Soviet Russia: A Two-

Phase Development," in *Russia's Torn Safety Nets: Health and Social Welfare during the Transition,* ed. M. Field and J. Twigg (New York: St. Martin's Press, 2000).

33. S. G. Lehmann and B. Ruble, "From 'Soviet' to 'European' Yaroslavl: Changing Neighborhood Structure in Post-Soviet Russian Cities," *Urban Studies* 34, no. 7 (1997): 1085–1107.

34. April was chosen as a month of "moderate" migration over the course of a year. Moves in September overly bias school-age migrants; moves in June overly bias seasonal workers.

35. M. Matthews, *The Passport Society: Controlling Movement in Russia and the USSR* (Boulder, Colo.: Westview Press, 1993).

36. "In Elite Homes, People Live without Residential Permits or Rights to Property," May 31, 2003; http://virk.ru/news/article.aspx?nodeid=46676f23-bb71-4d3c-905e-71a651245353.

37. To correct for the autocorrelation across years with respect to the decline in the number of migrants reporting a move, the registration data are presented as a *sum* of all months rather than the *mean.*

38. Gang and Stuart, *Russian Cities.*

39. *Propiska* data from 2002–3 also include migration to both *raions* (rural areas) and Ust-Ordinsk Buryatski Autonomous Okrug. Summaries of migration to these destinations are provided in table 4.C.2.

40. The distance of each move was calculated using the difference in latitude and longitude between the origin and destination of each move. The degree distance between two sets of coordinates was calculated using the Pythagorean theorem ($D = \sqrt{(Lat_{origin} - Lat_{destination})^2 - (Long_{origin} - Long_{destination})^2}$). At 50° N, the length of a degree of latitude is approximate to 111.20 kilometers; so the multiple $D * 111.20$ kilometers yields the distance of the move in kilometers; Glenn Trewartha, Arthur Robinson, and Edwin Hammond, *Elements of Geography, Fifth Edition* (New York, McGraw-Hill, 1967). All the destinations in the data set are cities to which point coordinates were assigned (source: Names and geographic coordinates repository of the National Imagery and Mapping Agency, http://www.nima.mil/gns/html). This treatment introduces a slight bias to the distance of moves in different parts of the country. In Western Russia, the geographic and population centroids often coincide, so that the coordinate represents the average distance of a move from the province; however, in Eastern Russia, the geographic centroid can be quite disparate from populated areas, so that the coordinate introduces a bias for long-distanced moves from areas in Siberia and the Far East. Source: Environmental Systems Research Institute, "Digital Map of the World," 1993, a product originally developed for the U.S. Defense Mapping Agency using its data.

41. There is a second bias in the sample toward a disproportionate number of *propiska* registrants moving for school or work. Migrants who officially register their move typically do so to provide official documentation required by many places of school or work. This appears to be especially true in *propiska* records between 1997 and 1999. Beginning in 2000, the number of migrants reporting personal or other reasons for moving has dramatically increased.

42. Angarsk, Bratsk, Sayansk, Ust-Ilimsk, Ust-Kut, and Shelekhov were all incorporated after 1945. Taishet, incorporated in 1938, is also included with Soviet company towns because of its location at the junction of two major raillines (TransSiberian and Baikal Amur Mainline).

43. Michael Bradshaw, Alexandr Chernikov, and Peter Kirkow, "Irkutsk and Sakhalin," in *Regional Economic Change in Russia,* ed. Hanson and Bradshaw.

44. Alexander Chernikov, "Resource-Rich Regions: Irkutsk Oblast' on the Road to the Market," *Communist Economies & Economic Transformation* 10, no. 3 (1998): 375–89.

45. Perfiliev, "Development of the Internet in Russia."

46. According to propiska data in this first time period (1997–99), Shelekov was the only city to receive more migrants from than sent to the capital.

47. As has been well-documented, the death rate exceeds the birthrate in post-Soviet Russia leading to negative natural increase in population. See Field, "Health and Demographic Crisis in Post-Soviet Russia."

48. French, *Plans, Pragmatism, and People;* Lisa Lee and Raymond Struyk, "Residential Mobility in Moscow during the Transition," *International Journal of Urban and Regional Research* 20, no. 4 (1996): 656–70.

49. R. Struyk and C. Romanik, "Residential Mobility in Selected Russian Cities: An Assessment of Survey Results," *Post-Soviet Geography* 36 (1995): 58–66.

50. Interviews with Evgenii Tretyakov, chief architect, city of Irkutsk, and Alexsy Ivonine, deputy director, Irkutskmoststroy, April 2004.

51. Across the two time periods (1997–99 and 2002–3), the share of migrants to Bratsk increased from 11 to 13 percent regionally and from 14 to 18 percent nationally. The city of Bratsk attracted a higher proportion of men (both with respect to women and over time) from within the oblast yet a higher proportion of women from outside the oblast.

52. Chernikov, "Resource-Rich Regions."

53. However, no protocol could be established as to the ethnic profile of nonrespondents; therefore, these records were treated as missing data when reporting summaries of *natsionalnost'*.

54. The exact question on the *propiska* form reads: "How many children under the age of 14 have arrived together with you?" (see Appendix B).

55. Iyer, "Urban Transition in Post-Soviet Russia."

56. Lehmann and Ruble suggest that the older, more desirable housing in historic districts were home to both the political elite and pensioners who maintained their residence. Many of these pensioners have privatized their apartments, bequeathed them to younger generations, and moved to areas with cheaper housing. Lehmann and Ruble, "From 'Soviet' to 'European' Yaroslavl."

57. The previous analysis of *propiska* data simultaneously tested for the likelihood of migrants choosing a particular destination via multinomial logistic regression; Iyer, "Urban Transition in Post-Soviet Russia." The models using the 1997–99 data produced modest measures of goodness-of-fit and predictability. Similar models using data from 2002–3 failed to statistically distinguish between Soviet company towns and prerevolutionary towns.

58. Pilkington, *Migration, Displacement and Identity.*

59. A gender disparity (men migrating with fewer children than females) is true across all city types, both because of the high number of female-headed households throughout the country and the tendency for women and children to join the male head of household who migrated first.

60. Of the college-educated males moving to the capital, 60 percent stated work as the reason for moving. Of the males without college education, 34 percent reported moving to the capital for educational purposes and 40 percent reported moving for work.

61. Barry R. Chiswick, “Are Immigrants Favorably Self-Selected? An Economic Analysis,” in *Migration Theory: Talking across Disciplines,* ed. Caroline Brettell and James Hollifield (New York: Routledge, 2000), 61–76.

62. Irina M. Baldyshtova, “Characteristics of Labor Migrants’ Households in Russia,” *Sociological Research* 43, no. 1 (January–February 2004): 46–61.

63. Question 18 on the *propiska* form asks if the registrant is moving to join family members, but the responses are not archived at Oblkomstat.

64. Ann Markusen, Peter Hall, Scott Campbell, and Sabina Deitrick, *The Rise of the Gunbelt: The Military Remapping of Industrial America* (New York: Oxford University Press, 1991).

65. Hill and Gaddy, *Siberian Curse,* 164; “Federal Government Approves Subsidies for Regions,” *RFE/RL Newsline—Russia,* December 3, 2004.

66. Timothy Heleniak, “Out-Migration and Depopulation of the Russian North during the 1990s,” *Post-Soviet Geography* 40, no. 3 (1999): 157.

67. James Brooke, “New Face of Farming in Russia’s Far East,” *New York Times,* July 8, 2004.

Part II

Historical Legacies

People have chosen, or been compelled, to move from place to place since the beginning of human history, and historic patterns of migration can help to explain the aspects of current migration flows that economic analyses cannot. Today's migrants are influenced—consciously or unconsciously—by networks and migration patterns that have developed over generations. Policymakers charged with regulating migration must contend with the legacies of historical population policies and long-held popular perceptions.

No analysis of migration in Eurasia would be complete without an examination of the important role that the state has played in regulating and directing migration in the region during the past century. More than most other states, the Soviet Union, and the Russian Empire before it, implemented very specific, and sometimes coercive, policies designed to encourage some types of migration and limit others. In addition, Russian and Soviet policies that were not specifically intended to deal with migration have nonetheless continued to influence migration flows in the post-Soviet era. Soviet policies for dealing with ethnic diversity, which tied personal identity to specific "national homelands," provided incentives for ethnically motivated migration when the Soviet Union collapsed. The tightly integrated economy that developed under Soviet central planning has also encouraged post-Soviet migration.

The chapters by Eric Lohr, Bruce Adams, and J. Otto Pohl that make up part II demonstrate three often-conflicting motivations for migration policies in the Russian Imperial and Soviet states: concerns about ethnic composition and cultural identity, economic interests in maintaining access to labor, and security concerns related to population settlement of often-remote border regions. As Lohr demonstrates in chapter 5, population policies in the Russian Empire often arose from conflicts among these three motivational forces. The treatment of some ethnic groups, such as the Jews, highlights how labor concerns can be overshadowed by ethnic policies. For economic reasons, the goal of most officials was to increase the empire's population, and citizenship laws therefore made emigration effectively illegal. Nevertheless, Jewish citizens—widely seen as undesirable—were occasionally allowed to emigrate.

Soviet policies also targeted specific ethnic groups. The most brutal example of this was the mass deportation of entire ethnic groups from central Russia and the Caucasus to Central Asia during and after World War II. In chapter 7, Pohl examines the history of three deported groups—Volga Germans, Meskhetian Turks, and Crimean Tatars—that were not allowed to return to their homelands after Stalin's death. The potential for members of these groups to return in large numbers to their historic homeland following the collapse of the Soviet Union has fueled some of the most bitter post-Soviet debates over citizenship and migration policies in Russia, Ukraine, Georgia, and Germany.

A second way in which the state can influence migration is economic policies. In chapter 2 of this volume, Andrei Korobkov demonstrated that contemporary Russian policymakers are torn between promoting migration to increase the size of the labor force and facilitate economic growth, and restricting migration in the name of ethnic and cultural homogeneity. Lohr shows us that these debates are far from new—officials in the Russian Empire faced a similar conflict between the desire to populate their vast lands and the desire to promote Russian cultural hegemony. Today, as in the past, immediate economic concerns often take precedence.

Finally, the state can influence migration, intentionally and unintentionally, through foreign policy. The Soviet state, by attempting to collectivize Central Asian agriculture, settle nomadic tribes, and harden its border with

China, disrupted lifestyles and migration patterns that had existed in Central Asia for centuries. According to Adams in chapter 6, during the 1930s, as many as 300,000 people left the Soviet Union for China's Xinjiang Province, where they became trapped in the complex ebbs and flows of Sino-Soviet relations. Though increasing tensions between Moscow and Beijing made life harder for Soviet expatriates in Xinjiang and gave them additional incentives to return to the Soviet Union, the tensions also made it more difficult to acquire the necessary permissions for repatriation.

States do not have complete control over the migration flows across their borders. In Adams's example, many of the emigrants from the Soviet Union to China, and some of those who returned to the Soviet Union, crossed the border unofficially or illegally. Nevertheless, state policies have had a considerable impact on the nature and direction of migration flows in Eurasia. In some cases, policymakers have intentionally tried to direct migration to populate remote regions or remove ethnic groups perceived as threatening from border areas. In other cases, economic policy and policies to manage ethnic diversity have had unintended results for migration. Even in the case of policies that specifically address migration, the policies have often had long-term consequences that were never anticipated by the officials who developed them. The Russian and Soviet states have left behind deep-seated and complex legacies of migration, mostly without intending to do so.

5

Population Policy and Emigration Policy in Imperial Russia

Eric Lohr

In a long-term perspective, the late Imperial period of Russian history saw a major shift in the general orientation of population policy, away from a strong traditional bias in favor of population increase and toward a more selective policy that imposed sharp restrictions on the immigration and rights of certain less-desired groups. In the most general sense, these emerging population policies aimed to influence the nationality balance of the country, particularly in borderland regions.[1] In the late Imperial period, Orthodox Slav emigration was nearly nonexistent, while Jews, Germans, Poles, and a few other minorities accounted for nearly all emigrants from the empire. In this context, official encouragement of emigration or even expulsion of unwanted minorities from the Russian Empire might appear to be conceivable and even consistent with broader policy trends.

Of all the minorities in the Russian Empire, the Jews would be the most likely target of such initiatives. The government had a long history of restricting Jewish residence, and even expelling Jews from one part of the empire to another. A series of nineteenth-century decrees had already expelled

Jews from the Russian countryside and banned their settlement in rural areas (both within the Pale and throughout the empire).[2] Strict quotas were maintained on Jewish migration to the cities of the empire outside the Pale. In 1892, the governors of Moscow and Saint Petersburg ordered the mass expulsion of thousands of Jews from their cities, and individual Jews always faced the threat of arbitrary expulsion. Though the government did not approve of the pogroms against Jews in 1881–82 and 1902–7 (at the highest level at least),[3] it certainly could have been more vigorous in its prosecution of the perpetrators. It was not just domestic Russian policies that made the forcible expulsion of Jews, or simply the encouragement of Jewish emigration, conceivable. International factors were important as well. One of the major events in the history of international migrations and their regulation in the late nineteenth century was the forcible expulsion of 20,000 (mostly Jewish and Polish) Russian subjects from Prussia in 1885. It is understandable that many contemporaries and later scholars believed that the rulers of Imperial Russia wanted to get rid of their Jews by emigration or expulsion.[4] However, as Hans Rogger has shown, there is no evidence from all the commissions on the Jewish question that expulsion was ever a seriously considered option. In fact, Imperial Russia never actually legalized emigration of Jews or any other group.[5] This chapter examines the origins of this outcome.

Russia's Population Policy Traditions

One of the distinguishing features of Russia's *longue durée* is the constant preoccupation with holding and increasing its population. In contrast to much of Europe, population, not land, was the scarce and most-valued commodity. Long after Europe moved away from serfdom, Russia introduced and deepened it in the fifteenth to the eighteenth centuries, largely to keep its peasants in place so that their surplus could be directed toward the building of armies and the few other things undertaken by the early modern Russian state.[6] If anything, the rapid expansion of the polity to the south and east during this period to incorporate the vast Eurasian steppe with its rich soils added to the overwhelming official desire to expand and hold the Russian Empire's population. For centuries, population drained from the poor gray forest soils to the rich black earth of the steppe, and, starting in the eighteenth century, the government launched an aggressive program of attracting farmers from Europe to settle the steppe as well. For Catherine the

Great and her physiocratic court economic philosophers, population was the source of wealth, and any person—even if Muslim, Lutheran, Mennonite, or Jewish—was worth keeping to expand the prosperity of the empire. Bodies were good, too, for security reasons. In the eighteenth century, the empire was desperate to populate and till the vast, largely uninhabited southern steppe to claim it for good from the Ottoman Empire and the nomadic societies that conducted pastoral migrations, long-distance trade, and the occasional raid or war against farming communities and their Russian sponsors. Russia's rulers also believed that the steppe had to be won to stop the evasion of Russia's attempts to hold its core population in place. Large and growing Cossack communities on the steppe not only preyed on Russian trade and settled communities but also provided a home for runaway serfs. Later, in the nineteenth century, concerns about the strength of the Russian hold over the Far East prompted a persistent drive to settle more people there.[7]

These general factors help explain the basic contours of Russian state policies toward international migration. First, beginning in the 1750s, the state embarked on a policy of attracting immigrants to the empire, offering strong incentives in the form of free land, exemptions from taxes, military service, and other privileges. In numerical terms, the vast majority of the immigration that resulted was composed of farmers, who gladly took the land offered by the tsar and played an important role in tilling and settling the steppe. A numerically smaller, but economically and culturally more significant, immigration began earlier, under Peter the Great, and it brought large numbers of merchants, entrepreneurs, skilled laborers, professionals, and the like to Russia's cities. The demand for these types of immigrant grew as Russia began to modernize.

The Russian Empire's emigration policies complemented its immigration policies. Given its strong bias toward population increase, it is quite logical that the regime opposed emigration as a matter of principle. Until the great reforms of the 1860s, the question of the legality of emigration was somewhat moot. Peasants were bound to their masters and could not leave without permission. Merchants, nobles, and servitors were all bound to the tsar. Departure from the empire without his permission was strictly prohibited, and rarely granted. Even temporary travel abroad was made difficult by the regime until the mid–nineteenth century. As in the famous case of Patrick Gordon, in the era of Peter the Great, even foreigners who came to Russia to serve the tsar could be refused permission to leave.[8] Of course, official policies did not entirely stop emigration. There was a constant flow of runaway serfs to the Cossack communities of the steppe, and mass emigrations of Kalmyk, Tatar, Nogai, and several other groups from the Caucasus to the Ottoman Empire occurred after Russian annexation. However, as a general rule, emigration was practically nonexistent as a regular yearly phenomenon before the 1860s.[9]

This encouragement of immigration and sanctioning of emigration combined to form a coherent and fairly stable Russian population policy. However, for several reasons, the middle to late nineteenth century proved to be a watershed in Russia's international migration policies. First, Russian and Ukrainian migration to the steppe combined with rapid population growth among all groups to reduce the need for immigrants. Second, the great reforms of the 1860s brought ideas of equalized rights and obligations for all groups. Though the regime had few problems preserving inequalities of rights, it no longer tolerated the exemptions from military service and other obligations that had been granted to draw immigrants in the previous century. The removal of exemptions from military service obligations in 1874 spurred a mass emigration of Germans and other groups. Third, from the 1860s to 1914, population growth led to an increasingly dire land shortage. Local reactions against immigrants correlated closely with land availability.[10] Finally, anti-immigrant initiatives were closely linked to the rising challenges of nationalism in the western borderlands, and the move of officials in the region toward attempts to transform demographic balances. In the wake of the 1863 Polish rebellion, the government not only expropriated a large number of Polish estates but also began a comprehensive campaign to increase the amount of land owned by Russians at the expense of the Poles. Likewise, in the 1880s, in the wake of the Temporary Laws of 1882, the government aggressively enforced and imposed further restrictions on the limited number of Jews in rural areas. An important part of the demographic and land struggles was a series of initiatives to limit immigration from abroad and to limit the rights of foreign-subject immigrants, Poles, and Germans to acquire or inherit land in the western borderlands.[11]

Although the domestic factors of land shortage, the challenges of the Polish movement, and general policies toward the Jews all were crucial, the emergence of a new kind of nationalistic population politics—especially in the sphere of immigration and emigration—was closely linked to international factors as well. One of the most important influences came from the emergence of fiercely nationalistic population policy in Germany in the 1880s, which led to a Prussian initiative in 1885 to expel all Russian subjects (roughly 20,000) from the country. Officially, the measure was directed against all Russian subjects, but the German authorities made clear that they were specifically targeting Poles and Jews as part of their own population policy in Germany, their own attempt to Germanize the land, not by assimilating foreign minorities but by transferring their lands and simply removing them. As the Russian Ministry of Foreign Affairs noted, this was also a landmark in the long history of Russian-German relations. For decades, Russia, Prussia, and Austria had all cooperated closely in matters of extradition, suppression of the Polish threat, and antirevolutionary police activities. This incident marked the beginning of much more hostile relations among these neighboring countries on these kinds of questions, and the first of several conflicts over attempts to expel unwanted groups.

The expulsion project was eventually negotiated to a solution, but roughly 8,000 Russian subjects were expelled and a much tighter system of controls was set up, making permanent emigration to Prussia much more difficult.[12] This incident directly caused the Ministry of Internal Affairs (Ministerstvo vnutrennikh del, MVD) to work out retaliatory measures against German immigration and land acquisition in the western borderlands.

The Ottoman Empire likewise had an influence. In the 1890s, an influx of 20,000 Turkish-subject Armenian refugees running from pogroms in Anatolia caused the Russian authorities in the Caucasus to try to seal the border to prevent further immigration. The Armenians were held in limbo for nearly a decade while diplomatic negotiations dragged out. Here too, neither side wanted to accept the Armenians based on considerations of land and demographics. In Anatolia, the sultan argued that he could not allow their return because Kurds had taken their lands and would not give them up without a fight, while in the Caucasus, the chief authority for civilian affairs argued that land was scarce and should be reserved for projects to settle Cossacks and other Russians rather than be given to the Armenians.[13]

These examples illustrate how the control of migration increasingly became entwined in the population policies of Russia and its neighbors. Though the numbers affected in these and other cases were in the thousands, it is important to remember that the actual demographic effects of emigration and immigration policies are much larger and are measurable only as counterfactuals, because we will never know how migrations would have differed in the absence of the policies.

Policy Responses in the Era of Mass Emigration

It was in the context of these important broad changes and trends in official population policy that emigration suddenly rose from insignificance to become a phenomenon of major scale. More than 4 million Russian subjects emigrated in the half century after 1861, and roughly 1.5 million of these emigrants were Jews. The causes of this large-scale emigrations varied. Identifying and ranking the causal variables explaining the emigration of various groups from the Russian Empire is a task in its own right that scholars have yet to systematically undertake. In the case of the more than 200,000 Nogai and Tatars who emigrated from Crimea to Turkey from 1859 to 1861, rumors and fears of government repression following the Crimean War and a movement among Muslim clerics in favor of departure for Turkey led to the exodus. For German colonists, Mennonites, and Dukhobors, the introduction of universal military service in 1874 was the key event. For the Jews, the pogroms of 1881 and the sharp repressive turn of government policy played a major role. Shortages of land, economic difficulties, and a lack of opportunities in education drove members of all groups to migrate. But we can also not forget the simple fact that cheap rail and steamship travel made the journey affordable and feasible. There may be no better explanation for the rise of emigration to the Americas from 4,900 during the decade 1816–70 to 68,000 from 1871 to 1880.[14]

One of the most remarkable aspects of emigration from the Russian Empire was the fact that only 1 to 3 percent of all emigrants from 1861 to 1914 were Russian—depending on how one defines "Russian." The United States had the largest number of ethnic Russian immigrants from the Russian Empire, at an estimated 40,000 (out of 1,732,000 natives of the Russian Empire in the United States in 1910), most of whom were members of the Molokane, Dukhobor, or Old Believer sects.[15] Thus, emigration was almost entirely a phenomenon of non-Russian minorities leaving the empire. This fact alone may help to explain much about emigration policy as a whole.

First, it helps to explain why the government took such a remarkable disinterest in the fate of emigrants from the empire. This disinterest was noted by the Ministry of Foreign Affairs (Ministerstvo Inostrannikh Del, MID) in its yearly report for 1887, which included a summary of its first major review of emigration policy within the ministry.[16] The report laid out the results in stark fashion. Consulates and embassies abroad seemed not even to consider tending to the needs and interests of Russian subject emigrants abroad to be within the scope of their concerns. When the minister of foreign affairs asked each to provide lists of Russian subjects within their jurisdictions and reports on the activities of the consulates, in many cases they could not even provide estimates of their numbers, much less their needs. MID called for changes in consular practice to address the problem.

But, tellingly, it was only with the first major emigration of ethnic Russians and Ukrainians—to Brazil and Argentina, in 1890–93—that MID and the MVD began to show a serious concern for the fate of emigrants after they emigrated. As both MID and MVD correspondence consistently pointed out, this emigration was different from previous ones in that it included many Russians and others "from the core peasant population." Several thousand ethnic Ukrainian, Lithuanian, Polish, and Russian peasants departed for South America, enticed by the promise of free land and government-subsidized travel. But the majority failed at subtropical farming, lacked money for needed investments, and succumbed to disease and other problems. Their position became desperate, leading MID to press the MVD to provide funding for impoverished emigrants to return to the empire. The MVD responded that emigration was illegal, and thus no funds could be provided to "criminal" emigrants. But given the scale of the tragedy and the fact that in this case Russians were also affected, the MVD relented—but allowed no assistance to be given to Jews.[17]

The decision to deny assistance to returning Jews was just one small example of what appears to have been a fairly consistent general emigration policy of encouraging the return of Russians and Slavic peasants but discouraging or even banning the return of other emigrants. In the cases of the mass emigrations of Nogai and Tatars from Crimea and of mountain peoples from the Caucasus, all were allowed to leave the country and Russian subjecthood, but only on the condition that they would not have the right to ever return to Russia.[18] German colonists were also required to leave Russian subjecthood upon departure from the country and in principle were not allowed to return, although in a number of cases, they did receive special permission to return.[19] Like all emigrants, Jews were subject to the law that anyone leaving the country illegally was to be removed from Russian subjecthood and face arrest upon return.

Because, by official MID estimates, as many as 90 percent of all emigrants left illegally,[20] nearly all faced much more serious consequences if they ever chose to return than was the case for emigrants from any other European country. Illegal emigrants were forced to pay the huge passport fees they had avoided upon return. Most seriously, if they missed their military call-up, they faced a whopping 300-ruble fine plus immediate induction.[21] The severity of these penalties and legal insistence on the irreversibility of emigration made little sense to international lawyers, the Ministry of Trade and Industry (which complained of the economic harm), and MID. They were glaringly out of tune with trends in urban Russia and the world of trade and industry. In these areas, Russia launched a major effort beginning in 1860 and 1864 to liberalize laws on immigration. On the whole, this drive to encourage the immigration of entrepreneurs, technicians, and skilled and unskilled foreign laborers was a resounding success.[22] The restrictive policies and the insistence on the irreversibility of emigration seem to make little sense in this context.

However, in the context of the emerging population policies promoted by the MVD, the context begins to make more sense. The regime certainly did little to explicitly thwart emigration. It allowed the Jewish Colonization Society to legally operate in the Russian Empire. This was a highly successful organization with more than four hundred offices by 1910; it spread news about emigration and gave assistance in purchasing tickets, arranged cheap lodging en route, and helped Jews plan for life in the new country. Tolerance of this organization's activities could be read as an indirect endorsement of Jewish emigration (despite the fact that all emigration was still technically illegal).[23] In 1881, the MVD proposed allowing emigration of Jews only as full families, in part to avoid having young wage-earning males go abroad while the old and infirm stayed behind, but also perhaps to ensure that the workers going abroad were permanently emigrating rather than just seeking temporary work. The evidence for a policy of encouraging emigration is compelling: a strong motive, a strong pattern of prior behavior, and plenty of circumstantial evidence.

But in practice, even the most anti-Semitic officials in the MVD did not fully endorse the emigration of Jews or other minorities.[24] Why? First, MVD officials believed that one of the main causes of emigration was the attempt to avoid military service. This was certainly accurate in the cases of German colonists, Mennonites, Dukhobors, and some of the other minorities that had either been exempt from military service before 1874 or opposed military service as a matter of principle.[25] Many Jewish emigrants also left to avoid conscription (though not nearly so universally, as MVD reports suggest). In any event, the authorities could have applied the common practice in other countries of simply requiring men of certain ages to fulfill their military requirements before acquiring legal permission to emigrate.

There were also economic arguments. The MVD pointed out that there was a sort of Darwinian process whereby the best workers left and succeeded abroad, while the least successful, the impoverished, orphans, widows, the infirm, the diseased, and the ruined all came back to Russia. Officials often complained that emigrants were mostly young men in their prime working years, while families stayed behind. When emigration was just becoming a mass phenomenon, the Department of Police wrote a memorandum in 1881 on the issue summarizing the MVD approach. It outlined the concerns above, focusing on the Jews, and argued that despite "all the improvements in the rights of Jews" over the past twenty years, they continued in all ways possible to "avoid carrying the burdens of state life," and that all the efforts to facilitate the assimilation (*sliianie*) of Jews with the rest of the population had failed. The memo concluded that "there was no reason to stop emigration, but that it wanted to be sure that state interests did not suffer as a result."[26] It turns out that in the era of rapid industrialization, mass conscript armies, and an alliance with France, the state's interests were well served by preserving a place for skilled workers and professionals, by keeping men in the army reserves, and by avoiding conflict with Russia's allies.

The conflicts between MID and the MVD over emigration continued right up to 1914. MID consistently argued that it was pointless to try to stop emigration through administrative measures, that it was driven primarily by economic factors, and that the state simply lacked the capacity to guard its borders and stop emigration.[27] MID, the Ministry of Finance, and the Ministry of Trade and Industry all argued strongly for legalizing emigration to reap the rewards of repatriated earnings from abroad and to bring some regulation and control over the process.[28] Because emigration remained illegal, illicit emigrant smuggling operations proliferated, leading to extensive bribery of Russian border officials and regional police authorities. It also led to widespread abuses of the emigrants by agents, who took advantage of the fact that emigrants feared reporting to the authorities because they themselves were breaking the law. The proponents of legalization argued that it would be the most effective way to end such abuses, much more effective than the periodic crackdowns on agents conducted by the MVD. The strongest proposal for legalization came in the early twentieth century from the Ministry of Trade and Industry's Division of the Merchant Marine, which presented all these arguments plus the consideration that all the profits from overseas emigration were going to foreign shipping and railroad companies. Legalization would enable Russian shipping companies to get these profits and would also simultaneously end the exploitation of emigrants by agents and by the German authorities in Prussia.[29]

Step by step, starting in the 1890s, temporary migration for work was gradually legalized (but not for Jews). Departures from Russia's ports (particularly from Libava) began to take on a significant scale after they were authorized to enter the emigrant transport business in 1905. But permanent emigration was never legalized; nor was the question of departure from Russian subjecthood ever legally solved. A major attempt to legalize emigration was initiated by MID in 1906. But, as the minister of foreign affairs bitterly wrote in 1907, the proposal, which had been developed through an interministerial committee, was stymied by the MVD, which did not clearly explain the reasons for its opposition.[30]

The failure to legalize emigration came at great cost. Studies by the Ministry of Trade and Industry showed that Russia was losing millions of rubles each year in potential repatriated earnings from abroad—even from as far abroad as the United States. Return migration was not an option, both because of the remarkable expenses involved for the majority of emigrants—who paid, on average, a hundred rubles to illegal emigration agents (a third of the average emigrant's annual salary)—and because of the legal uncertainties. One could argue that Russia not only lost potential repatriated earnings and returning skilled laborers but also lost an important opportunity to ease the pressures of overpopulation.[31]

The MVD was the main proponent of nationalistic population policies in many fields, from its leading role in enforcing and maintaining the limits on Jewish residence and landholding within the empire to new limits on Polish and foreign-subject landholding, and its attempts to limit immigration in the western regions, the Caucasus, and the Far East.[32] Thus, it is something of a mystery why it would so persistently oppose legalizing emigration right up to 1917. It not only blocked the proposals to draw up new emigration and naturalization laws in 1906–7 but also continued its administrative efforts to round up and arrest illegal emigration agents right up to 1914.[33]

There are a few possible explanations for this policy. The first relates to the dispute with the United States about Russian passport policies. This dispute centered on the refusal of the Russian government to allow Jews to leave Russian subjecthood. Legalizing emigration for Jews would mean legalizing departures from the country, and by necessity, legalizing exits from Russian subjecthood. Legally clarifying the situation of departing Jews could thus force the government to recognize the naturalization of its emigrants, which would give Jews a means to evade the myriad restrictions facing every Russian-subject Jew. Second, the MVD seems to have been more intent on preventing the evasion of obligations to the state (primarily military service) than in pursuing its population policy initiatives.

Conversely, one of the reasons for the MVD's policy may have been the often-stated fear that ethnic Russian emigration might suddenly rise (aided and encouraged, of course, by unscrupulous Jewish agents in illegal emigrant-running networks). The Department of Police pointed with alarm to figures indicating that, in fact, emigration from the core peasant population was increasing rapidly in the first decade of the twentieth century. Thus, the MVD's opposition to legalizing emigration in general may have been primarily aimed at preventing the exodus of its favored core populations.

The ambivalence of the Russian authorities played itself out in dramatic fashion in the spring and summer of 1915, when the high command turned to a policy of mass expulsion of the Jewish population from the front zones to the Russian interior ahead of retreating Russian troops, to prevent Jews from coming under the occupation regimes of enemy powers. Then, in an about-face in June and July, Army Headquarters sporadically drove Jews across the front lines to the enemy in selected areas, claiming that Jews were so exploitative and undesirable that it would be better to saddle the enemy with their presence than to keep them in the empire. This policy did not last long due to vehement opposition from all the ministers in the Russian government and the angry protests of Russia's allies. They argued against the policies not only on humanitarian but also even more on economic grounds. By August, the army settled on systematic policies of forced expulsions of Jews to the Russian interior.[34]

The divisions within the regime on emigration policy played out in another dramatic case during World War I, this time involving Chinese and other Asian laborers and small traders, who were referred to by officials as "workers and traders of yellow race" (*rabochie i torgovtsy zhel'togo rasa*).[35] In the decades before the war, the intense growth in the demand for labor in the Far East drew in a massive immigration of Chinese and Korean laborers. In the gold-mining industry alone, the number of Chinese workers grew quickly, from 5,933 in 1906 to 30,249 in 1909, making up 80 percent of the industry's workforce. Koreans, who were even more numerous, worked almost exclusively in agriculture, either as laborers or lease holders. Asian labor was particularly important in railroad construction, and the Ministry of Transport used Chinese labor throughout the empire. In addition, Chinese small traders flourished in the rapidly growing Siberian-Chinese border trade and made their way to cities throughout the empire to conduct small trade in the years before the war.[36]

The Ministry of the Interior and some Far Eastern officials were concerned about this "influx of the yellow element" ("*naplyv zheltogo elementa*") before the war, and they began an officially titled "war" against it."[37] However, the balance of power between police security concerns on the one hand and economic imperatives on the other was lopsidedly in favor of the latter, and the influx of Chinese and Koreans continued through the summer of 1914. This changed dramatically only days after the outbreak of war.

On July 25, 1914, the commander of the Southwest Front reported that Chinese traders were engaged in widespread spying for the Japanese and Germans, and he ordered their deportation from the entire military theater.[38] Army Headquarters sent a series of circular telegrams to the heads of military regions, informing them that Chinese traders were to be considered spies and deported. Small traders were quickly rounded up from the entire area under military rule and imprisoned in collection camps for deportation from the country.[39]

The Ministry of the Interior instructed governors throughout the country to establish close oversight over the Chinese in their regions, claiming that the Japanese were using them for spying, and ordered the deportation of any Chinese raising even the smallest suspicions.[40] Governors throughout the country responded in August 1914 with clean sweeps of Chinese traders from their jurisdictions.[41] However, China was officially neutral in the war, and its envoy protested vehemently against the internment of Chinese throughout the country. This led MID to insist that governors restrict their deportations only to those "suspected of spying." Nonetheless, broad interpretation of this clause led to the deportation of thousands of Chinese subjects from areas throughout the empire. In October 1914, the government categorically banned the entry of Chinese into the Russian Empire. Although China entered the war on Russia's side later in the same month, this ban was not lifted until 1916.[42]

Although the conviction that Chinese were prone to spying did not weaken in the army and police leadership, by 1916 economic forces regained the upper hand. Military call-ups and the pressures of defense production created a severe labor shortage, which led to a massive program to distribute prisoners of war and civilian deportees to firms, to state construction teams, and to farmers and local government institutions for work as agricultural laborers. By early 1916, 700,000 prisoners and deportees had been assigned to work, and those remaining were classified as incapable of work.[43] Shortages of workers became a major bottleneck in the armament industry, railroad construction, and agriculture. Petitions flowed into the Ministry of the Interior requesting permission to import Asian workers. Already in August 1915, a few contingents of Chinese and Koreans were allowed to enter the empire in exceptional cases for the construction of crucial railroads in European Russia.

The Council of Ministers officially allowed the importing of Asian workers in March 1916. Once the decision was made to allow Chinese and Korean subjects to enter the empire, they were imported in huge numbers. The Ministry of Transport requested more than 100,000 Chinese workers for its railroad construction projects, including 22,000 for the vital Murmansk Railroad.[44] The Ministry of Land Properties (Zemledelie) proposed a massive program of importing 200,000 Korean and Chinese to work as agricultural laborers in central Russia.[45] The main limiting factor to the inflow of Asian workers quickly became the transportation capacity of the Siberian Railroad (approximately 15,000 per month).[46]

Police and army officials remained suspicious of Chinese spying, and they argued throughout 1916 against importing Asian laborers to Petrograd and areas near the front.[47] Their arguments were mostly overruled in 1916, but by the summer and fall of 1917, economic conditions had begun to change drastically. Labor shortages eased considerably. In some areas, Asian laborers became unemployed, as in Petrograd, which reported 6,000 unemployed Chinese in the city.[48] In June 1917, the minister of labor argued that, given the condition of the labor market, it would be desirable to ban further entry of Asian laborers.[49] In September 1917, the proposal was officially accepted, and the importing of Asian workers was once again banned.[50] Workers were again imported during the 1920s, but once again in the 1930s, security and the police view prevailed, and Asians were deported en masse to Siberia.

Conclusions

This remarkable swing from massive immigration to mass deportation and back again illustrates how powerful the demand for labor could be as a motive in the formulation of official policies for international migration. It also illustrates how deep the divisions between the security, economic, and international branches of the Russian Empire's government ran on these issues.

Despite all the trends toward a population policy that might quite logically include dramatic measures like encouraging or forcing the emigration of the most unwanted minorities, the Russian Imperial regime never legalized emigration. One can perhaps read too much into its refusal to legalize emigration. After all, Jews and other minorities emigrated in the hundreds of thousands, evading official sanctions in myriad ways. The regime, as we have seen, even facilitated this emigration to a degree by allowing information centers to spread the word about the procedures involved. It seems that the value of labor and population, the desirability of continued state control over the process, the fear that many would emigrate to avoid state obligations, and other factors all played an important part in the decision. Perhaps more than anything, legalizing emigration in general would have opened the door to the emigration of Slavs. In this sense, the refusal to legalize emigration may have been as much a tool of the Imperial regime's emerging population policies as it was a limit upon their exercise.

Notes

1. For the concept of population policy, see Peter Holquist, "To Count, to Extract, to Exterminate: Population Statistics and Population Politics in Late Imperial and Soviet Russia," in *A State of Nations: Empire and Nation-Making in the Age of Lenin and Stalin,* ed. Ronald Grigor Suny and Terry Martin (Oxford: Oxford University Press, 2001), 111–44; and Eric Lohr, *Nationalizing the Russian Empire: The Campaign against Enemy Aliens during World War I* (Cambridge, Mass.: Harvard University Press, 2003), 163–65.

2. By some estimates, as many as 200,000 Jews were transferred from rural areas to towns by the 1840s. Hans Rogger, "Government, Jews, Peasants, and Land in Post-Emancipation Russia," *Cahiers du Monde Russe et Sovietique* 17, no. 1 (1976): 1–11.

3. This is the recently emerging consensus among scholars of the pogroms in Russia, who distinguish between officials at the ministerial level (who opposed pogroms as disruptive of public order) and governors and other lower-level officials (some of whom were complicit or passive in the pogroms). John D. Klier and Shlomo Lambroza, *Pogroms: Anti-Jewish Violence in Modern Russian History* (Cambridge: Cambridge University Press, 1992).

4. Hans Rogger, "Tsarist Policy on Jewish Emigration," *Soviet Jewish Affairs* 1 (1971): 26.

5. See ibid., 26–36; S. Ia. Ianovskii, "Russkoe zakonodatel'stvo i emigratsiia," *Zhurnal ministerstva iustitsii,* April 1905; "Pravo v'ezda v chuzhuiu stranu," *Zhurnal ministerstva iustitsii* 10 (December 1909): 107–34; "Emigratsiia s tochki zreniia prava (Po povodu zakonoproekta ob emigratsiia, razrabatyvaemogo osobym soveshchaniem pri Ministerstve Torgovli i Promyshlennosti)," *Zhurnal ministerstva iustitsii* 3 (March 1908): 31–66; and V. M. Gessen, *Administrativnoe pravo* (Saint Petersburg: G. Pozharova, 1903), 85–87.

6. Richard Hellie, *Enserfment and Military Change in Muscovy* (Chicago: University of Chicago Press, 1971).

7. Willard Sunderland, *Taming the Wild Field: Colonization and Empire on the Russian Steppe* (Ithaca, N.Y.: Cornell University Press, 2004); Roger P. Bartlett, *Human Capital: The Settlement of Foreigners in Russia, 1762–1804* (Cambridge: Cambridge University Press, 1979).

8. Patrick Gordon, *Passages from the Diary of General Patrick Gordon of Auchleuchries in the Years 1635–1699,* 1st ed., new impression (London: Frank Cass, 1968).

9. Before the Great Reforms, official yearly emigration figures for all groups were remarkably small, often numbering only in the hundreds per year. V. M. Kabuzan, *Emigratsiia i Reemigratsiia v Rossii v XVIII - nachale XX veka* (Moscow: Nauka, 1998), 47–48.

10. Dietmar Neutatz, *Die "deutsche Frage" im Schwarzmeergebiet und in Wolhynien: Politik, Wirtschaft, Mentalitäten und Alltag im Spannungsfeld von Nationalismus und Modernisierung (1856–1914)* (Stuttgart: Franz Steiner Verlag, 1993); Detlef Brandes, *Von den Zaren Adoptiert: Die Deutschen Kolonisten und die Balkansiedler in Neurussland und Bessarabien 1751–1914* (Munich: R. Oldenbourg Verlag, 1993); Victor Dönninghaus, *Revolution, Reform und Krieg: Die Deutschen an der Wolga im ausgehenden Zarenreich,* Veröffentlichungen zur Kultur und Geschichte der Deutschen im östlichen Europa, vol. 23 (Essen: Klartext, 2002).

11. Lohr, *Nationalizing the Russian Empire,* 84–120.

12. Arkhiv Vneshnei Politiki Rossiiskoi Imperii (hereafter, AVPRI), f. 137, op. 475, d. 100, l. 93ob.

13. Gosudarstvennyi Arkhiv Rossiiskoi Federatsii (hereafter, GARF), f. 102, II d-vo (1893), op. 50, d. 229 ch. 1.

14. Kabuzan, *Emigratsiia i Reemigratsiia.*

15. V. A. Iontsev, *Emigratsiia i repatriatsiia v Rossii* (Moscow: Popechitel'stvo o nuzhdakh rossiiskik repatriantov, 2001), 29. Canada saw a more substantial Slavic immigration, mostly of Ukrainians. Approximately 92,000 Slavs from the Russian Empire migrated to Canada between 1900 and 1913. Vadim Kukushkin, "Protectors and Watchdogs: Tsarist Consular Supervision of Russian-Subject Immigrants in Canada, 1900–1922," *Canadian Slavonic Papers* 44, no. 3/4 (September–December 2002).

16. AVPRI, f. 137, op. 475, d. 100, ll. 137–52.

17. AVPRI, f. 137, op. 475, d. 108, ll. 191–92ob; GARF, f. 102, op. 76a, d. 29, ll. 39–46ob.

18. AVPRI, f. 159, op. 502a, d. 932, l. 2ob; GARF, f. 102, op. 269, l. 52. The ban on returning was stamped on their foreign passports.

19. GARF, f. 102, II d-vo (1899), op. 56, d. 22 ch. 8, ll. 7–13.

20. AVPRI, f. 137, op. 475, d. 100, l. 148.

21. Kukushkin, "Protectors and Watchdogs," 210.

22. John McKay, *Pioneers for Profit: Foreign Entrepreneurship and Russian Industrialization 1885–1913* (Chicago: University of Chicago Press, 1970).

23. V. V. Engel', *"Evreiskii vopros" v Russko-Amerikanskikh otnosheniiakh: Na primere 'pasportnogo' voprosa 1864–1913* (Moscow: Nauka, 1998), 42–43; A. Ginzburg, "Emigratsiia evreev iz Rossii," in *Evreiskaia entsiklopediia* (Moscow: Terra, 1991), 264–67.

24. Rogger, "Tsarist Policy," 26.

25. Robert F. Baumann, "The Debates over Universal Military Service in Russia, 1870–1874," PhD dissertation, Yale University, 1982.

26. GARF, f. 102, op. 76a, d. 29, l. 35.

27. AVPRI, f. 137, op. 475, d. 139, ll. 20–29.

28. On the broader conflicts between the MVD and the Ministry of Finance in the nineteenth century, see Daniel Orlovsky, *The Limits of Reform: The Ministry of Internal Affairs in Imperial Russia, 1802–1881* (Cambridge, Mass.: Harvard University Press, 1981).

29. Rossiiskii Gosudarstvennyi Istoricheskii Arkhiv, P.Z. 2531, "Ocherk istorii i sovremennogo sostoianiia otkhoda na zarabotki za granitsu v zapadnoi evrope i v Rossii."

30. AVPRI, f. 137, op. 475, d. 139, ll. 20–29.

31. The idea that Russia is overpopulated has often been missed because of its vast size. But the livable areas and areas with reasonably good soils comprise only a small portion of the country, and by 1900, those areas were overpopulated by almost any measure. The resultant downward pressures on plot sizes and wages combined to comprise key sources of socioeconomic tension in the revolutionary era. The institutional constraints of the peasant commune (for Slavs) and the restriction of Jewish residence to the towns and cities of the Pale both exacerbated the problem. For an excellent recent contribution to the literature on overpopulation, see Fiona Hill and Clifford Gaddy, *Siberian Curse: How Communist Planners Left Russia out in the Cold* (Washington, D. C.: Brookings Institution Press, 2003). On the internal migration that resulted, see Barbara A. Anderson, *Internal Migration during Modernization in Late Nineteenth Century Russia* (Princeton, N.J.: Princeton University Press, 1980).

32. *MVD: Zhurnaly vysochaishe uchrezhdennoi komissii o merakh k preduprezhdeniiu naplyva inostrantsev v zapadnye okrainy—Otdel III vopros o priniatii i ostavlenii russkogo poddanstva* (Moscow: N.p., 1891).

33. GARF, f. 102, II d-vo (1890), d. 104 ch. 1, ll. 5, 16, 50–62.

34. Dokumenty o presledovanii evreev," *Arkhiv russkoi revoliutsii* 19 (1928): 249–50; Volodimir Sergiichuk, Pogromi v Ukraini, 1914–1920: Vid stuchnikh stereotipiv do girkoi pravdi, prikhovuvanoi v radians'kikh arkhivakh (Kiev, 1998), 104–5; Eric Lohr, "The Russian Army and the Jews: Mass Deportation, Hostages, and Violence during World War I," *Russian Review* 60 (July 2001): 409–13.

35. For background on the Chinese, see Lewis Siegelbaum, "Another 'Yellow Peril': Chinese Migrants in the Russian Far East and the Russian Reaction before 1917," *Modern Asian Studies* 12, no. 2 (1978): 307–30.

36. GARF, f. 102, II deloproizvodstvo, op. 75, d. 29, l. 122. Asians, as a proportion of the population in the Primorskii region made up 29 percent of the population in 1897. The Asian population grew by 11,000 by 1915 but fell to 19 percent of the population due to the faster in-migration of Slavic peasants. Foreign-subject Asians outnumbered Russian-subject Asians by a factor of two to one. Ministerstvo Zemledeliia, *Primorskii pereselencheskii Raion statisticheskii otdel: Naselennie i zhiliia mesta Primorskogo Raiona, Krestiiane, Inorodtsy, Zheltye Perepis' Naseleniia 1–20 June 1915 g.* (Vladivostok: N.p., 1915), 14.

37. Memo to the Main Administration of Army Headquarters on uprisings of Chinese troops and the situation on the Chinese border, 1911–1914, Rossiiskii gosudarstvennyi voenno-istoricheskii arkhiv (hereafter, RGVIA), f. 2000s, op. 2, d. 1028, ll. 1–10.

38. Kiev, Podolia and Volynia Governor General to the Chief of Staff of the regional military administration, secret, July 25, 1914, RGVIA, f. 1759, op. 3 dop., 1405s, l. 3. Army counterintelligence assumed that Germany used influence in Manchuria and their representatives there to recruit Chinese spies.

39. GARF, f. 102, II deloproizvodstvo, op. 71 (1914), d. 105, ll. 1–7. The Petrograd deportations of Chinese were completed by August 4, 1914. A circular of the General Staff on September 7, 1914, ordered the deportation of all Chinese subjects from all areas under military rule. Copy of secret circular correspondence of the Main Administration of the General Staff Headquarters, September 7, 1914, GARF, f. 102, II deloproizvodstvo, op. 75 (1916), d. 29, l. 9.

40. MVD Department of Police Secret Circular to governors and city heads, July 28, 1914, GARF, f. 102, II deloproizvodstvo, op. 71 (1914), d. 105, l. 98.

41. Full statistics on the number of Chinese deported from the country are not available. Several thousand were deported from areas under military rule, and 963 from Moscow. Numbers from provinces outside the area under military rule were usually in the tens or low hundreds. GARF, f. 102, II deloproizvodstvo, op. 71 (1914), d. 105.

42. Dzhunkovskii circular to governors and city heads, August 17, 1914, GARF, f. 102, II deloproizvodstvo, op. 71 (1914), d. 105, l. 9. Dzhunkovskii instructed governors not to use undue force against Chinese, to release those not suspected of spying, and to deport them from the country as quickly as possible.

43. P. D. Eropkin to director of the Department of State Landed Properties, March 31, 1916, GARF, f. 102, II deloproizvodstvo, op. 75, d. 29, l. 75. Slavic prisoners and deportees were used for labor in much larger proportion than Germans. Officers, according to international agreements, were not required to work. The prisoner-of-war workers were let out in teams with police or military guards.

44. Unmarked memo, GARF, f. 102, II deloproizvodstvo, op. 75 (1916), d. 29, l. 75.

45. GARF, f. 102, II deloproizvodstvo, op. 75 (1916), d. 10 ch. 7, l. 6. An interdepartmental commission was set up under the minister of landed properties to "render harmless" the allowance of Chinese and Koreans within the borders of Russia.

46. GARF, f. 102, II deloproizvodstvo, op. 75, d. 29, l. 76.

47. Deputy Minister of Internal Affairs A. Stepanov to Ministry of Transport, August 2, 1916, GARF, f. 102, II deloproizvodstvo, op. 75, d. 29, ll. 136–37ob.

48. Unmarked memo, GARF, f. 1791, op. 2, d. 4, l. 6.

49. Minister of Labor to Interdepartmental Committee for the resolution of questions on the acceptance and transfer of workers of yellow race, June 1917, GARF, f. 1791, op. 2, d. 4, l. 3.

50. Provisional Government Chancery to Minister of Finance, September 21, 1917, GARF, f. 1791, op. 2, d. 398, l. 2.

6

Reemigration from Western China to the USSR, 1954–1962

Bruce F. Adams

On several occasions, beginning in the late 1890s and ending in the early 1930s, more than half a million residents of the Russian Empire, and later of the Soviet Union's de facto empire, left their homeland and for a time lived in China. Many of these migrants eventually returned to the Soviet Union. Their choices to cross the border were strongly influenced by state policies. The political and economic climate in Russia, the USSR, and China went through many drastic changes in the second half of the nineteenth century and first half of the twentieth century. Before World War II, China's remote northern and western provinces were a promising destination for those who wished to escape the harsh measures of the Russian and Soviet states. After the war, return to the Soviet Union became an increasingly appealing choice as the policies of China's Communist government became more repressive. But returning was not a simple task. This chapter explores the complex process of negotiation that occurred between the Soviet and Chinese governments and the potential migrants, eventually allowing most to return by 1962.

Waves of Migration to China

Migration from Russia and the USSR to China occurred in several waves. The first influx of migrants came to build and run the Chinese Eastern Railroad (CER). The construction and operation of the CER brought more than 15,000 Russians to Harbin and several thousand more to the CER right of way before the Russo-Japanese War in 1904–5. About 80,000 soldiers, support personnel, and businessmen flocked to Harbin during the war, but most of them left when it ended in Russia's defeat. The area experienced considerable disorder and a brief recession after the evacuation, but between 1907 and 1914 the railroad, the region, and especially the city of Harbin prospered. On the eve of World War I, Harbin's population exceeded 67,000, of whom approximately 43,500 were Russian.[1]

The largest influx to northeastern China occurred toward the end of the Russian Civil War, mostly in 1920–21, when more than 200,000 refugees, possibly as many as 300,000, fled to the relative safety of Harbin and Manchuria. Although they were not all ethnically Russians, almost all of them were citizens of Tsarist Russia, which would cause them considerable inconvenience when Tsarist Russia ceased to exist and a few years later the Soviet Union claimed ownership of the CER.[2] As they could, tens of thousands left the overcrowding, unemployment, and other hardships of the region. Between the 1920s and 1949, most reemigrated to the United States, Australia, Canada, the Philippines, Brazil, and a few other countries. After the Japanese occupation of Manchuria in 1931, many resettled in other parts of China, with the greatest number relocating to Shanghai. In three waves in 1935, 1947, and 1954–55, tens of thousands also returned or emigrated to the USSR. By 1955 only a few thousand Russians remained in urban, eastern China.

Northwestern China, in contrast, was home to large numbers of emigrants from the Central Asian region of the Russian Empire / Soviet Union until the 1960s. Kazakh, Kyrgyz, Tadzhik, and Uigur nomads and farmers had lived on both sides of what became the Russian/Chinese border long before the border was firmly established. For centuries, people had moved east or west through the mountain passes to find greater security. The borders were porous and government control in the area was weak on both sides of the border into the nineteenth century. In the later nineteenth century and first half of the twentieth century, Russian governance grew firmer, but northwestern China was still far from centers of Chinese governance and weakly controlled. In that period most of the migrations moved from west to east into what in 1884 became Xinjiang (Sintszian) Province.

Small numbers of herders moved into China when Russian peasants began to settle and farm in Central Asia after the emancipation of the serfs in 1861. Larger numbers migrated in the years just before World War I, when the Stolypin land reforms claimed almost 19 million hectares (more than 73,000 square miles) of pasturage for new agricultural settlers. Another larger wave of migrants fled into Xinjiang in 1916, when the Tsarist government began to draft Muslim subjects into labor detachments for the world war. When the draft led to a revolt in the Fergana Valley and nearby areas in the steppe, the Russian governor-general punished the rebels by seizing their land and turning it over to Russian settlers. This prompted the flight of about 300,000 Muslim subjects into Xinjiang. The Chinese government feared the large number of new settlers for a variety of reasons, among them the concern that the expatriates would bolster Russian claims on parts of the province, and it was soon able to arrange amnesty for those who chose to return to Russia. By 1918, most of them had returned.[3]

A decade later, when the Soviet government began its collectivization campaigns, grain requisitioning, livestock confiscation, land redistribution, and collectivization efforts were initiated in the Central Asian steppe and valley regions. In 1930, when it was recognized how difficult and harmful collectivization efforts had been, the Soviet government compromised at forcing nomadic people into permanent settlements, which proved equally unpopular. The nomads and peasants in these areas reacted much as the peasants of European Russia had. They burnt their grain stores, and they sold or slaughtered huge numbers of their animals. In addition, many thousands fled. The size of herds plummeted, and famine became widespread.[4]

Just how many people migrated in these years and to where remains unclear. The population of the Central Asian republics dropped sharply between 1928 and 1932. It is unknown how much of this decline should be attributed to excess deaths by starvation, a much-increased infant and child mortality rate, a birthrate that was much lower than usual, a renewed Basmachi revolt, or out-migration. Martha Olcott wrote in 1987 that approximately 300,000 Kazakhs moved to Uzbekistan, more than 40,000 to Turkmenistan, and "thousands of Kazakhs set out for China, but less than a quarter of them survived the journey."[5] She now believes that the numbers of migrants was larger.[6] Linda Benson and Ingvar Svanberg think the greater movement from the steppe during these years was into Afghanistan and Xinjiang but do not hazard a number.[7] Soviet consular officials in Xinjiang would later claim that approximately 300,000 emigrants came from Soviet territory into Xinjiang, usually citing 1931 as the year of their arrival. There may have been reasons for the diplomats to exaggerate these numbers, which we will consider below, but it is also quite possible that the number is a good estimate. The Kazakhs who moved initially to Uzbekistan or Turkmenistan could not have found refuge there for long. It is quite possible that many of them made up the number arriving in Xinjiang in 1931.

There was very little movement back into the Soviet Union from Xinjiang until after 1950. Life for the newcomers could not have been easy in China, at least at first, but it was apparently preferable to that in the USSR. Most of the emigrants were able to live in Xinjiang much as they had in the Soviet Union. They often moved there as entire villages (*auls*) and usually settled in areas already populated by distant relatives. Nomads and farmers found themselves in similar, sparsely settled lands in the east and made themselves at home. Governance in the region was weak, and there was no significant resistance to the migrations from either side of the border.

Conversely, Xinjiang was itself an unstable region, and such large in-migrations must have added to ethnic tensions and contributed to the instability. Tensions between the Muslim nationalities and the Chinese rulers and population broke into open rebellion several times in the 1930s and 1940s. The earliest of these, in 1932–33, principally involved the Uigurs, who made up 75 percent of Xinjiang's population at that time, but other Muslim nationalities also joined in. The most noteworthy fact about the rebellion for our purposes is that the Soviet government intervened in 1933–34, probably to keep a pan-Turkic or pan-Muslim movement from spreading into its own territory and to create an ally against the possible expansion of the Japanese into the region. Soviet aid brought General Sheng Shicai to power as the next warlord/governor of Xinjiang, and Sheng maintained close relations with the USSR until 1942.[8] Some observers go so far as to say that Xinjiang was essentially a Soviet satellite during those eight years, much like Outer Mongolia.[9] Economic relations between Xinjiang and the USSR were strong and valuable to both during that period. Access to minerals was important to the Soviet government, but animals and the animal products produced by the nomads were the largest part of the trade. Good relations came to an end in 1942, when Sheng could not get much support from the war-torn USSR and thought it prudent to improve relations with the Kuomintang. The break was a serious blow to the herders' economy and of considerable concern to the Soviet government.

It is interesting that in the 1934–41 period, when Soviet influence was strong in Xinjiang, and when Soviet Army units and secret police were active in the region, that the Soviet government did not try to force the collectivization-era "exiters" to return. As far as I know, they did not even encourage repatriation. I have seen no government documents that explain this, but I think there were at least four good reasons for the Soviets to behave as they did. First, collectivization had been a disaster. The Soviet citizens in China had fled in opposition to the program and would likely flee farther into China and/or resist rather than be led docilely back. Second, a huge percentage of Xinjiang's exports were flowing to the USSR, including animals and animal products, which were being produced more abundantly in Xinjiang than they were in the areas the exiters had fled. Acquiescence was the cheaper way to acquire those goods. Third, Sheng apparently did not ask that the émigrés be removed, as his predecessors had done in 1916. Their presence contributed to Xinjiang's productivity and was apparently welcome. I think it is also possible that Sheng and the Soviet government saw one another as mutually important in discouraging a Japanese incursion into the region. Fourth and last, no one knew what the outcome of the struggle between the Japanese and Chinese would be. The presence of 300,000 émigrés in Xinjiang, or the claim that they were that numerous, may have strengthened some future Soviet claim to Xinjiang, which they coveted in much they same way they did Manchuria and Mongolia at various times.

The largest and most serious of the rebellions against Chinese government in Xinjiang coalesced during the particularly unstable time near the end of World War II. Known as the Ili Rebellion, it united much of the Turkic Muslim population against Han rule and created the East Turkestan Republic in Xinjiang from 1944 to 1949. On this occasion, the Soviet Union intervened militarily on the side of the Muslims in the Ili River Basin around Kul'dzha and helped create and govern the new republic, but as significant anti-Soviet rebellions broke out among Turkic Muslims in other parts of Xinjiang and the Chinese Communists were making headway in their Civil War against the Kuomintang, the Soviet government negotiated a peace agreement that allowed them to pull back from other parts of Xinjiang while continuing to dominate the Ili River region until the Communists came to power in 1949.[10]

Waves of Returning Emigrants

At the end of World War II, the Soviet government was deeply concerned about its disastrous loss of population during the war. It appealed to émigrés around the world to come home and help rebuild the motherland. The appeal was eagerly welcomed in parts of China. The Soviets were suspicious of the émigré population in Manchuria, which had been required to cooperate with Japanese occupation forces from 1931 to 1945, but they organized a large repatriation from Shanghai in 1947. Those who chose to reemigrate were motivated by the terrible conditions of unemployment and poverty they had experienced during and after the war, by the worsening tensions created by the Chinese Civil War, and by the growth of Soviet patriotism among them during the Great Patriotic War (i.e., World War II).[11] None of those factors was felt as strongly by the farmers and nomads in western China, only a few of whom had begun to inquire about returning to their homelands to the west by 1947.

Between 1947 and 1949, when the Chinese Civil War was at its peak, many Russians left China for countries other than the USSR, but a sizable community remained in Harbin and a smaller group stayed in Shanghai. Several hundred repatriated in 1951–52.[12] Many more applied to the Soviet consulates, but their petitions were denied, perhaps fortuitously, until 1954, a year after Joseph Stalin died. In that year, the Soviet government conducted another campaign, urging Russians living abroad to return. In the case of the Russians in China, a major reason for this campaign was to find people to work on the Virgin Lands project that was just beginning. In a very orderly exodus in 1954–55, 26,966 émigrés, most of the Russians remaining in eastern China who wished to enter the USSR, were brought to the Soviet Union and given residence in towns and villages in the Virgin Lands.[13]

In the years immediately after World War II, the Soviet authorities in Xinjiang were instructed to ask participants in the collectivization-era exodus if they would like to reclaim Soviet citizenship and to consider reemigration. Soviet officials, who staffed consulates in Urumchi, Kul'dzha, Kashgar, Chuguchak, and Shara-Sume, numbered the former-Soviet émigré population in Xinjiang at approximately 300,000. But response to the offer was slow, quite possibly in part because it did not reach everyone. Between 1947 and 1949, 86,524 people applied for Soviet citizenship. Because of a variety of problems, including the high rate of illiteracy in this population, the inability of Soviet consular officials to communicate in languages other than Russian, and a lack of transport, only 10,190 *sovzagranvidy* (special foreign residence permits) were granted in those years, and there was no legal reemigration.[14] According to a report from the consulate in Kul'dzha, dated October 16, 1950, 70 percent of the applicants in these years were from among the poorest of the former Soviet residents:

herders, peasants who had little land, unskilled laborers, and some craftsmen. Most of the remaining 30 percent were part of the "progressive intelligentsia," who may have seen what lay in the near future.[15] As the Chinese Communists took control of the region, they worked to instill feelings of Chinese nationalism and made life increasingly difficult and uncomfortable for non-Chinese citizens and ethnicities.

In 1949–50, former Soviet residents made up more than 12 percent of the population of Xinjiang and held a roughly proportional number of administrative positions throughout the province, including some of considerable power. Chinese Communist officials were uncomfortable with this and began to pressure non-Chinese administrators to take Chinese citizenship. At the same time they changed school curricula, removing instruction of Russian language, geography, and political studies, and requiring that all instruction be in Chinese. They also increased efforts to tax non-Chinese residents. As a consequence, requests increased at Xinjiang consulates for Soviet citizenship and reemigration. In his letter of October 16, 1950, the consul in Kul'dzha wrote that the appellants wished to "become active participants in socialist construction and contribute to the struggle to liquidate the consequences of the war." He added that such reemigration would not damage Sino-Soviet relations, while it would benefit the USSR. The brief response from the Consular Administration of the Ministry of Foreign Affairs (Ministerstvo Inostrannikh Del, MID) said simply, without explanation, that repatriation "at the current time is politically inadvisable."[16] The only organized repatriation that occurred in 1950 was of some 100 orphans of Soviet citizens who had been killed during the Chinese Civil War.[17] A similar effort was made for another 164 orphans in 1951.[18]

By 1953, although relations between Moscow and Beijing remained good, relations between the Chinese authorities and Soviet citizens in China had worsened considerably, as had the conditions in which those citizens lived. As MID prepared for the last major evacuation from the cities of eastern China, it also paid increasing attention to the large number of potential reémigrés living in Xinjiang. A report in MID's files for 1953 counted 146,969 Soviet citizens throughout China, including 84,769 in Xinjiang.[19] MID prepared a summary report, including information on their location in China, their occupation (or unemployment), and nationality. The Soviet deputy minister of foreign affairs, Valerian Zorin, forwarded this to Georgii Malenkov and Nikita Khrushchev for the Central Committee of the Communist Party in February 1954. His cover note mentioned that due to changing political conditions in China, Chou En Lai would like to have Soviet citizens moved from their present locations. Chou had apparently suggested that those who did not want to accept Chinese citizenship might be interned or repatriated.[20]

In March, the Central Committee instructed the Soviet ambassador in Beijing to visit Chou and inform him that Soviet authorities had looked into the matter and concluded:

> Considering that this question involves a large number of people (over 140,000) who have lived in China for a long while and that we have not yet sufficiently studied the matter, the Soviet government considers it sensible as a first step . . . to carry out the repatriation in 1954 from China to the USSR of 3,000 to 4,000 Soviet citizens and up to 1,000 orphans.[21]

Either these numbers grew considerably during 1954 or the number of citizens above referred to heads of households, not counting their dependents. A chart summarizing those repatriated from all parts of China in 1954 shows a total of 5,453 families and 587 individuals, totaling 26,966 people. The great majority of them came from cities of eastern China. Only 2,471 people returned from Xinjiang, all from Kul'dzha. The chart categorized the repatriates as engineers, technicians, doctors, clerks, or members of the free professions. Apparently this repatriation brought few if any farmers or herders back to the USSR, because almost all the adult males from Kul'dzha fit into the technical, medical, and office worker categories.[22]

Correspondence between the Soviet consulates in China and MID in late 1954 and 1955 indicates that many citizens of the USSR still in China were increasingly eager to reemigrate to the USSR and that Soviet authorities were increasingly inclined to want them, particularly if they could be useful in the Virgin Lands. In Harbin, for example, there were still 17,566 Soviet citizens. Of them, 4,000 had applied for permission to emigrate to the Virgin Lands but, the general consul explained, another 7,000 "reactionarily minded doctors, engineers, clergy, shopkeepers," and other "reactionary scum" were attempting to move their capital abroad illegally and hoped to emigrate to capitalist countries. Rumors "supported by American and English agents" held out hopes for migration to Brazil or Paraguay. Five thousand or so citizens who had not made up their minds were being deterred from reemigration by letters from friends who had already returned to the USSR that told of shortages of food and potable water in the Virgin Lands and of the arrest of some earlier repatriates. Other "slanderous information" circulating in Harbin said that there was forced labor in the Virgin Lands, that children were being separated from their parents, and that separate male and female concentration camps were being prepared. Moreover, everyone believed that there would be another opportunity to reemigrate in 1955, so they could afford to wait.[23]

In this they were correct. The 1955 repatriation was bigger. It brought back just about all the émigrés in Manchuria and eastern China who wished to go to the USSR. And it began the much larger removal from Xinjiang as well. By this time, the People's Republic of China (PRC) had completed pacification of Xinjiang. Local and provincial government provided some autonomy and representation for non-Chinese peoples, but it was clear that the People's Liberation Army and Han officials were in charge and that the already limited autonomy of non-Chinese nationalities was likely to deteriorate. In 1955, 115,000 people returned from the PRC, including 68,000 from Xinjiang.[24] The earlier removals had been logistically difficult and revealed many shortcomings both in transit and in situ, especially in the Virgin Lands. The Soviet government consequently planned more extensively for this much larger exodus. Twenty-nine officials from a dozen ministries, the State Bank, the Border Guards, and several other agencies met in Moscow on March 7, 1955, to coordinate the planning already going on in their many institutions. Among other complications, they were concerned about having enough truck and rail transport, sufficient food and water, and adequate health care and room (i.e., separate railcars) to isolate those who had contracted contagious diseases en route. The difficulty of transport in Xinjiang, where the roads were bad, the population was thin, and the mountains were tall, received particular attention. To overcome the problems that officials had anticipated, they decided they would have to know as precisely as possible the number of people traveling from each area, their routes of travel and points of entry into the Soviet Union, and their final destinations.[25] Orders were sent to all Russian consulates in China to begin to prepare.

During the year, additional problems were encountered in Xinjiang. One was that many families, anticipating the repatriation, were returning across the borders on their own. Border guards caught a Soviet citizen of Kazakh nationality—who was trying to arrange the illegal crossing of 500 Kazakhs—crossing the border from where he lived in the Chuguchak District. These Kazakhs had heard rumors that they would be sent to Kyrgyzstan but preferred to resettle in Kazakhstan. According to the report on the incident to MID from the Ministry of Internal Affairs (MVD, from its name in Russian), similar attempts were being made "in every settlement [*aul*]." The returnees' dual purpose in illegal repatriation was to keep their livestock, which they assumed would be confiscated either by the Chinese or the Soviets and made common property in a state farm, and to settle with clansmen where they had come from.[26] Another large set of problems, already noted in 1947–49, involved the languages, low level of literacy, and poverty of the would-be repatriates and the inadequate staffing and equipping of the Xinjiang consulates. A report from Kashgar admitted that in 1954 the consulate did not know how many Soviet citizens lived in its territory.[27] The records on hand were invented ("did not correspond to reality"), mistaken, or filed "chaotically." By the end of the year, the consulate staff had ascertained that there were approximately 500 Soviet families in the territory, numbering around 2,000 people. Almost half of them were Uzbeks; 20 percent, Uigur; 20 percent, Kyrgyz; and 10 percent, Kazakh; with a few Tatars, Ukrainians, and Russians. Many were so poor that they "had no shoes, practically no clothes, [and] no pot to cook in." Approximately 20 percent were unemployed or barely employed, and a majority were illiterate or barely literate. Many children had never attended school. The majority of the families wanted to return, but they had to complete applications for citizenship and have them approved before they could return, and the paperwork was a serious bottleneck:

> The archive of the general consulate is in chaotic disorder. Suffice it to say that a whole cabinet of about 3,000 documents is stuffed with applications, autobiographical sketches, and photos of people who had applied for Soviet citizenship between 1949 and 1953. Most of these were written in Uigur or in unbelievably mangled Russian on notebook paper, . . . and even on scraps of newspaper. . . . It gives the impression that these applications were accepted only to calm the applicants by giving them the false hope that they would be granted Soviet citizenship and then were quite calmly chucked in the cabinet.[28]

The report from Chuguchak helped explain what made some of the émigrés so anxious to return. As had happened in Harbin, Shanghai, and throughout eastern China, rumors circulated in Xinjiang about the terrible and dangerous conditions in the USSR; but conditions in China threatened to become even worse. As the report stated, "What occurred in the Soviet Union in the 1930s from which [these people] fled to China is now seen to be happening in the PRC." At first only the poorest émigrés had signed up, but life was getting harder for them in China every year. Moreover, the consulate had been conducted effective propaganda, using films, books, newspapers, and letters from relatives in the USSR, and the émigrés had come to believe that "socialism is already built in the USSR." The mistakes and difficulties, such as collectivization, had been experienced in the Soviet Union and were in the past, whereas in China the "socialist transformation" was only beginning and many of the same difficulties would recur. During the last several years, almost all Soviet citizens had requested repatriation.

The consul echoed another concern expressed in Kashgar. Almost 60 percent of the repatriates were Kazakhs (6,826 of 11,627). They insisted on being sent to Kazakhstan and vowed, if they were sent to Kyrgyzstan, to make their way back "to the place of their clan, that is, where their relatives live and from where they came to China." Applicants of all nationalities also threatened to return illegally if they were not permitted to go in the 1955 removal.[29]

The situation in Kul'dzha was similar.[30] The consul claimed that rumors of problems in the Soviet Union kept the number of applications low early in the year, but the consulate's effective "educational" work brought those numbers up in the spring. By April, almost all Soviet citizens had applied for repatriation. This report also says a little more about the reaction of Chinese officialdom to the removal. For the most part, the Chinese were content to see other nationalities leave. The remaining Chinese citizens reaped numerous benefits from the departure. In some instances, Chinese officials seized livestock, which were given to Chinese collective farms. In others, Chinese residents could purchase homes, livestock, and other possessions at desperately low prices. Chinese officials were concerned, however, that if too many people left at once, Xinjiang Province could not fulfill its economic plans. They were particularly concerned and asked that non-Chinese residents in management positions not be taken in 1955. The Soviet authorities cooperated with that request.

The resettlement of the returnees did not go smoothly. Already in 1955, repatriates were complaining to the consulate in Kul'dzha, to relatives who had stayed behind, and to the Chinese authorities about poor conditions and ill treatment in the Soviet Union. To investigate these allegations, the consul accompanied the last group to leave Xinjiang for the Kazakh Soviet Socialist Republic (SSR) in August 1955 and there visited several *sovkhozy* (state-operated agricultural estates). He reported upon his return that he had seen "the most heartless treatment of the people who came from the PRC." Not one in twenty families was well provided for, most lived in substandard structures, and some had no shelter at all. There were no beds or even cots prepared for them, and most slept on unpacked bags and boxes. He continued:

> No housing is being prepared for winter. There is no fuel. No salaries have been paid for two months. Necessary produce and other goods are unavailable and, if they do appear, are taken by the *sovkhoz* leadership and their cronies. The new arrivals have only what they brought with them from China to eat. They are not given loans to build houses or to obtain livestock. Medical help is not given. No political-educational work is being carried out.

Despite the presence of local officials, the new returnees "begged with tears in their eyes for help or for permission to return to the PRC."[31] There is no indication that anyone actually did return.

Despite reports of this sort, the desire to repatriate to the USSR remained strong. The repatriation of 1955 left approximately 30,000 Soviet citizens in Xinjiang and more than another 200,000, mostly Kazakh, farmers and herders. Most were exiters from the collectivization-era flights who possessed no citizenship, but they included other groups like the Kirei clan (*rod*) of Kazakhs who had migrated eastward into Chinese territory a century earlier. This whole clan of 22,000 prosperous herders wanted to resettle in Kazakhstan. Many of the other 200,000 were also by then requesting Soviet citizenship and repatriation. Nonetheless, according to a report written by the Soviet vice consul in Kul'dzha, dated January 19, 1957, repatriation in 1956 was guided by the Chinese officials' desire that the process be slowed. This was reflected in a Soviet government decision made in January 1956 and circulated by MID to the consulates in March. Altogether, only 14,456 people from this area were allowed back into the USSR in 1956.[32]

The Kul'dzha consular officials reported in August 1956 that they were doing their best to hold back the tide of would-be émigrés, dissuading them from selling their property and goods and from reemigrating illegally, but they warned that they could only be temporarily successful if conditions continued to worsen. They decided to at first repatriate only members of split families (those whose spouses or other close relatives had already left), the unemployed and underemployed, and all ethnic Russians. The Chinese authorities had particularly asked them to take as few Kazakhs and Uigurs as possible.[33] They also agreed to wait until after the spring sowing to begin their work and to accept applications only from people who had already received permission from the Chinese authorities to leave. Their work actually began only in May after the Chinese had conducted a campaign of "socialist reeducation," in which Soviet citizens "participated actively," and they stopped accepting applications on August 1. Most families who did leave thus had only one to three months to settle their affairs before they were trucked out to the border fifteen to thirty families at a time.

Of the 14,456 repatriates, 7,462 (51.3 percent) held Soviet passports, 6,977 (48.6 percent) were dependent family members, and 17 (0.1 percent) had Chinese passports. By nationality, 8,816 (61 percent) of them were Kazakh, 2,404 (16.6 percent) were Uigur, 1,707 (11.8 percent) were Russian, 529 (3.7 percent) were Kyrgyz, 490 (3.4 percent) were Uzbek, 307 (2.1 percent) were Tatar, 186 (1.3 percent) were Dungan, and 17 (0.1 percent) were Chinese. Most of them, 11,737 (81.2 percent), were resettled in Kazakhstan, 1,171 (8.1 percent) in Kyrgyzstan, 795 (5.5 percent) in Uzbekistan, 477 (3.3 percent) in the Russian Soviet Federated Socialist Republic, and the remaining 275 (1.9 percent) in other republics of the USSR. More than three-quarters (76.7 percent) had been engaged in herding and/or farming. The rest were laborers, tradesmen, clerical workers, small businessmen, unemployed workers, and their families. The vice consul claimed that the 1956 repatriation had been carried out with the complete cooperation of "our Chinese friends" and had benefited the local economy by reducing unemployment in the towns and the number of superfluous workers in the villages.

The Soviet government followed the same careful policy during the next two years, allowing rather small repatriations. According to a report issued by the Far Eastern Department of MID on April 11, 1957, "the Chinese side, as is apparent from conversations of Chinese officials with Consul General Kazanskii, . . . do not want to have people without citizenship or citizens of the PRC removed from that region." Nor do they want "Kazakhs or Uighurs, who are exiters from the USSR, [repatriated] as they have lived there a long while, have productive farms and close ties with the local population, and their departure might have a negative effect on the economy of Xinjiang."[34] Therefore, the Russian ambassador was instructed to inform the Chinese Ministry of Internal Affairs "that the Soviet government does not plan to carry out any more massive repatriations from Xinjiang." The consulates were told to inform any would-be repatriates who did not yet have Soviet citizenship that their cases would be considered only on a "strictly individual basis and with the permission of Chinese officials" and to tell Kazakh and Uigur applicants who were born in China that they should consider renouncing Soviet citizenship and accepting Chinese citizenship.[35] I did not find any documents enumerating repatriates in 1957, and from that and other evidence, I conclude that their number was very small. In 1958, only 790 families, fewer than 3,500 people, made the journey from Xinjiang to the Virgin Lands.[36]

Later Repatriation from Xinjiang Province

In 1959 and 1960, the number of repatriates was much greater. The Great Leap Forward, which began in 1958, brought an intensification of all the changes the non-Chinese peoples in Xinjiang feared. It brought a steady stream of young Han settlers, ended the autonomy of "minority" areas and groups, and pressed the collectivization of farmers and nomads. Collectivization led to extreme food shortages throughout Xinjiang.[37] As the proportion of the Han population and Chinese nationalism grew, the Chinese government's willingness to allow emigration evolved into an active desire to expel non-Chinese nationals from western areas. Planning for a larger repatriation in 1959 began in 1958. The Soviet consulates in western China were instructed to recruit repatriates by spreading the word of the benefits of resettlement in the Virgin Lands. The last point in these instructions was a reminder that "work on repatriation of Soviet citizens must be regarded as a serious political measure leading to the further strengthening of Soviet-Chinese friendship. This work must be conducted by the embassy and consulates in close contact with local Chinese authorities."[38]

The 1958–59 repatriations included approximately 1,500 people from Harbin and another 150 from Beijing, Shanghai, and Dalnii, but the great bulk were from Xinjiang, most of whom were evacuated through Kul'dzha.[39] In response to an order from MID, dispatched to Kul'dzha on September 25, 1958, that they evacuate about 10,000 families, numbering 60,000 to 65,000 people in 1959, the Kul'dzha Consulate drew up a detailed plan of their needs. Because the great majority of the would-be repatriates were non-Russian, the consulate asked for ten Kazakh-Russian interpreters, two Kyrgyz-Russian interpreters, and additional typists. And because an estimated 90 percent were illiterate, the consulate asked for permission to simplify the needed paperwork, eliminating the obligatory autobiographical sketch of each repatriate and allowing heads of households to fill in the forms for all members of their families. Roads and transport in Xinjiang were primitive, and 90 percent of the would-be repatriates lived far from Kul'dzha, so the consulate asked for 100 trucks to help bring families and their belongings to Kul'dzha and for thirty forty-seat buses to take them to

Soviet border points (Khorgos and Bakhty) or to Sandakhotsze on the Ili River, from where they would be taken by barge to near Panfilov. They planned to carry out the preparatory paperwork in 1959 at thirteen points throughout the consular region and were beginning to organize appropriate housing and eating facilities at gathering places and reception sites. They also were preparing garages and repair shops for trucks and buses in Kul'dzha and Chuguchak, dormitories for their drivers, and storage sheds for baggage at all the assembly points.

The 1959 repatriation did wind up being considerably larger than those of the previous several years, but it was not accomplished without serious problems. Some of these stemmed from the difficulties encountered in previous years and anticipated by the consulates; others were the result of the attitude of Chinese officialdom toward the would-be émigrés, which continued to worsen. One new problem, or at least one that had not been mentioned earlier, developed from the Kul'dzha Consulate's reliance on local assistance to process all the applications it received. Because Moscow did not send the additional interpreters and typists requested by the consulate, its three-person staff leaned heavily on the help and advice of the nongovernmental Society of Soviet Citizens, which in Kul'dzha was headed by Iakhia Baltiev. When Moscow sent a high-level MID official to the region in May to observe and investigate the repatriation, the Chinese officials complained to him about Baltiev, whom they characterized as "an ardent nationalist, a cheat, speculator, and bribe-taker," who had been selling the *sovgranvidy* of deceased Soviet citizens to other would-be émigrés. This practice was apparently widespread.[40] In a year-end report, Consul E. Shalunov defended the necessity of relying of the Society of Soviet Citizens in the absence of sufficient help at the consulate, reminding Moscow that it was impossible to process the paperwork of more than 40,000 semiliterate, non-Russian-speaking émigrés with a staff of three.[41]

The 1959 repatriation totaled 41,463 people. Shalunov's report provided details about their residence in China, destination in the USSR, citizenship, nationality, age, and occupation. A total of 23,418 possessed *sovgranvidy.* Except for a very few Chinese citizens, who were dependents of the Soviets citizens, the rest were family members who had no citizenship. A total of 30,519 were Kazakh, 6,438 were Uigur, 1,221 were Kyrgyz, and 1,186 were Russian. Uzbeks, Tatars, and Dungans numbered in the hundreds. A total of 38,499 of these repatriates were resettled in the Kazakh SSR, 2,796 were resettled in the Kyrgyz SSR, and the remaining 168 were resettled elsewhere, usually to live with relatives who had agreed to take them in. Of the 23,536 adults, 14,880 were classified as farmers, 1,174 as herders, 1,777 as laborers, 807 as office workers, and 4,898 as other. Most of the last category were housewives.[42]

Shalunov took the opportunity of making his year-end report to defend himself again against the charges of incompetence and corruption that had been leveled during the year. He pointed out that during the 1954–57 period, the Chinese authorities had been glad to assist with the repatriation. Private property had still dominated in Xinjiang, and the Chinese had been glad to see as many foreign property owners as possible depart for the Soviet Union. Local Chinese residents had purchased the property—farms, homes, cattle, and so on—of those who left. But by 1959, social reforms in the cities and collectivization in the countryside had claimed most property and disrupted the repatriation effort. Shalunov claimed that Chinese customs agents had become strict and corrupt; they even employed torture to make sure the repatriates did not take more than permitted, and, because there were no written rules about what items could be taken, they seized goods arbitrarily. In 1954–57, there were still numerous branch offices of the Society of Chinese-Soviet Friendship, which had helped repatriation in a variety of ways; but by early 1959, very few still existed.[43]

Sino-Soviet relations were deteriorating rapidly by this time. Soviet specialists were being expelled by the Chinese or recalled by Moscow. Soviet consulates throughout China were being shut down.[44] As a consequence, very few people, including those who already had Soviet citizenship, repatriated legally from China to the USSR in 1960 or 1961. According to a report filed by Shalunov in January 1961, Soviet citizens who still remained in Xinjiang faced increasing harassment and pressure to take Chinese citizenship. He counted 17,172 adult Soviet citizens, many of whom wanted to repatriate. Those who received permission to emigrate were immediately fired by "our Chinese friends," even though many months remained before they could actually depart. Many were also expelled from their living quarters and deprived of ration coupons, which caused them great hardship.[45] In September 1961, he reported that the Chinese authorities had begun to register all foreign citizens living in the Kul'dzha consular region, and he called their attitude "increasingly unfriendly."[46] Tensions built through 1961 into the spring of 1962. In March, approximately 20,000 Kazakh exiters fled Xinjiang illegally. This led to mutual recriminations between the Chinese and Soviet diplomats. In the aftermath, the Chinese authorities permitted some further legal migration in May. When they changed their minds again and abruptly stopped issuing exit visas, a demonstration broke out in

Kul'dzha that, according to Soviet sources, turned bloody when Chinese soldiers opened fire on the demonstrators. More Kazakhs left illegally in May and June. The migration in 1962, both legal and illegal, totaled approximately 67,000.[47]

Between 1954 and 1962, approximately 200,000 people migrated from Xinjiang to the USSR. It is impossible to know how many of these were exiters, or children of those who had migrated from Soviet territory around 1931, but presumably they made up the bulk. They belonged to ethnic groups that had for centuries moved back and forth over what by that time had become fixed and jealously guarded borders. In the past, many things had caused migrations, including war and drought. In the modern period, interference in their traditional ways of life by increasingly effective governments became a more important factor. When collectivization threatened them in the Soviet Union, they retreated to the more weakly governed region of Xinjiang. When the intrusive policies of the PRC began to push them off their lands and into collectives in the 1950s, they returned to Soviet lands, where they hoped such policies would be less zealously prosecuted.

The process of returning to the Soviet Union was far from simple. Prospective returnees were caught in a complex negotiation process between the Soviet and Chinese governments. China was eager to rid Xinjiang of potentially troublesome minority groups, but at the same time it feared the economic consequences of a mass exodus. The USSR, for its part, wanted to attract migrants to rebuild the labor pool devastated by World War II, but it did not want to antagonize China by encouraging the outmigration of groups that the Chinese government wished to keep in the region. Nevertheless, although the ups and downs of Sino-Soviet relations made the process of return migration much more complex, it did not prevent a large proportion of migrants and their descendants from eventually returning to the USSR.

Notes

1. N. E. Ablova, *Istoriia KVZhD i rossiiskoi emigratsii v Kitae (pervaia polovina xx v.)* (Minsk: BGU, 1999), 32; "Doklad russkogo obshchestva v Man'chzhurii i Mongolii o pravovom i ekonomicheskom polozhenii russkikh v Man'chzhurii," Gosudarstvennyi Arkhiv Khabarovskogo Kraia, f. 830, o. 1, d. 218, l. 3.

2. See G. V. Melikhov, *Man'chzhuriia dalekaia i blizkaia* (Moscow: Nauka, 1991); and G. V. Melikhov, *Rossiiskaia emigratsiia v Kitae, 1917–1924 gg.* (Moscow: Institut, 1997).

3. For information in the preceding two paragraphs, see Linda Benson and Ingvar Svanberg, *China's Last Nomads: The History and Culture of China's Kazaks* (Armonk, N.Y.: M. E. Sharpe, 1998), 42, 59–63; and James A. Millward and Nabijan Tursun, "Political History and Strategies of Control, 1884–1978," in *Xinjian: China's Muslim Borderland,* ed. S. Frederick Starr (Armonk, N.Y.: M. E. Sharpe), 63–65.

4. Benson and Svanberg, *China's Last Nomads,* 185; William Fierman, ed., *Soviet Central Asia: The Failed Transformation* (Boulder, Colo.: Westview Press, 1991), 18; Martha Brill Olcott, *The Kazakhs,* 2nd ed. (Stanford, Calif.: Hoover Institution Press, 1995), 169–70, 183–85; R. W. Davies and S. G. Wheatcroft, *The Years of Hunger: Soviet Agriculture, 1931–1933* (New York: Palgrave Macmillan, 2004), 321–26.

5. Olcott, *The Kazakhs,* 185.

6. Private communication with author, March 8, 2005.

7. Benson and Svanberg, *China's Last Nomads,* 185.

8. Millward and Tursun, "Political History," 75–78; Benson and Svanberg, *China's Last Nomads,* 66–67.

9. Millward and Tursun, "Political History," 75.

10. Benson and Svanberg, *China's Last Nomads,* 78–85; Linda Benson, *The Ili Rebellion: The Moslem Challenge to Chinese Authority in Xinjiang, 1944–1949* (Armonk, N.Y.: M. E. Sharpe, 1990).

11. See, e.g., Georgii Zaitsev, "Shankhai," *Rodina,* no. 2 (1998): 74–80, and no. 3 (1998): 80–85. Numerous articles in the repatriates' newsletters—*Russkie v Kitae,* published in Ekaterinburg, and *Na Sopkakh Man'chzhurii,* published in Novosibirsk—describe aspects of life in Shanghai, émigrés' attitudes, and the repatriation.

12. Arkhiv vneshnei politiki Rossiiskoi Federatsii (hereafter, AVPRF), f. 100, o. 45, d. 53.

13. Ibid., o. 42, d. 15, l. 1.

14. Ibid., d. 79, ll. 1–4.

15. Ibid., o. 43, d. 44, ll. 2–3.

16. Ibid., ll. 3-4. On PRC policy and practice in Xinjiang, see also Benson and Svanberg, *China's Last Nomads,* 88–90, 96–99.

17. AVPRF, f. 100, o. 43, d. 44, ll. 5–10.

18. Ibid., o. 44, d. 53, ll. 26–33.

19. This *spravka,* prepared in the Far Eastern Department (DVO) of the MID, is undated but filed so that appears to have been written between August and November 1953. Ibid., o. 46, d. 52, l. 58.

20. Ibid., o. 47, d. 42, ll. 5–7.

21. Ibid., l. 9.

22. Ibid., l. 15.

23. Ibid., ll. 35–39.

24. Ibid., o. 48, d. 49, l. 210. This *delo* of 221 pages has details of the whole 1955 repatriation. It includes drafts of the complete plan in the Council of Ministers, orders to consulates, ministries, and other agencies about the preparation of the removal, working papers on the numbers of repatriates from each consular area, their transportation, reception at the border, and dispersion and resettlement. It concludes with provisional and final reports from each consulate and a summary report from the MID to the Council of Ministers.

25. Ibid., o. 42, d. 15, ll. 4–13.

26. Ibid., o. 48, d. 49, ll. 58–59.

27. The whole report occupies ibid., ll. 95–136. Most of the discussion that follows comes from there.
28. Ibid., ll. 97–98.
29. The report from Chuguchak occupies ibid., ll. 137–62. The quotations are from ll. 140–41, 143, 148.
30. The report from Kul'dzha occupies ll. 176–206.
31. Ibid., o. 48, d. 49, ll. 156–58.
32. On the Kirei clan see ibid., l. 167. The vice consul's report can be found in ibid., o. 44, d. 19, 11. 1–7. The following paragraphs derive from that report.
33. Ibid. and o. 49, d. 47, ll. 6–7.
34. Ibid., o. 50, d. 34, ll. 1–2.
35. Ibid., ll. 2–3.
36. Ibid., o. 52, d. 30, 1. 3.
37. Benson and Svanberg, *China's Last Nomads,* 103–4.
38. AVPRF, f. 100, o. 52, d. 30, ll. 7–9.
39. Ibid., o. 51, d. 33, 11. 1–2.
40. On the Society of Soviet Citizens in China, see ibid., o. 53, d. 55, papka 460, l. 460, which is a short history of the organization written by an attaché of the Consular Administration in 1960. On Baltiev and the problems of corruption in the repatriation process, see ibid., o. 52, d. 30, papka 446, ll. 42, 61–100 passim.
41. Ibid., ll. 140–41.
42. Ibid., ll. 144–45.
43. Ibid., ll. 145–47.
44. Lorenz Lüthi, "The Sino-Soviet Split, 1956–1966," PhD dissertation, Yale University, 2003, chap. 4; David Wolff, "One Finger's Worth of Historical Events," Working Paper 30, Woodrow Wilson International Center for Scholars, Cold War International History Project, Washington, 2000; Anne-Marie Brady, *Making the Foreign Serve China: Managing Foreigners in the People's Republic* (Lanham, Md.: Rowman & Littlefield, 2003), 122–23.
45. AVPRF, f. 100, o. 53, d. 55, papka 460, ll. 1–13.
46. Ibid., ll. 19–25.
47. Lüthi, "Sino-Soviet Split," chap. 6.

7

The Loss, Retention, and Reacquisition of Social Capital by Special Settlers in the USSR, 1941–1960

J. Otto Pohl

The wealth of national communities lies not only in their physical capital and monetary assets but also in their human capital and social capital.[1] Human capital consists of those individual assets such as education, skills, and knowledge possessed by individuals. Social capital, in contrast, consists of the bonds, networks, and mutual obligations between individuals. These connections provide a social fabric that facilitates political and economic activity. Social capital comes in two forms, "bonding social capital" and "bridging social capital." The bonds within nationalities or ethnic groups that reinforce identification by members with their heritage are bonding social capital, which promotes group cohesion and mobilization. The networks of organizations that span various exclusive groups are bridging social capital. These connections allow the flow of information and other assets across communities. Organizations that represent bridging capital include political parties and veterans groups. Bridging social capital allows communities to tap into external sources of physical capital and human capital. The wholesale displacement of national or ethnically based communities will inevitably seriously disrupt the networks that form both their bonding social capital and bridging social capital. The ability to retain and regenerate or create new networks in the wake of catastrophe is vital to the social health of such communities. The experience of the nationalities deported wholesale from their homelands by Joseph Stalin demonstrates how forced migrants used these networks to mitigate this disruption. In the most successful cases, they organized their return home through these networks.

The Early Years: Deportation, Massive Mortality, and Sociocultural Fragmentation

During World War II, the Stalin regime deported eight nationalities in their virtual entirety from their homelands in the western part of the USSR to restricted areas, known as special settlements, in Kazakhstan, Central Asia, the Urals, and Siberia. In the fall of 1941, the Soviet government forcibly resettled the Russian-Germans. Next, it deported the Karachais and Kalmyks in late 1943. Finally, during 1944, the People's Commissariat of Internal Affairs, known as the NKVD, exiled the Chechens, Ingush, Balkars, Crimean Tatars, and Meskhetian Turks to Kazakhstan and Central Asia. The Stalin regime deported 846,340 Russian-Germans, 69,267 Karachais, 93,139 Kalmyks, 387,229 Chechens, 91,250 Ingush, 37,713 Balkars, 183,155 Crimean Tatars, and 94,955 Meskhetian Turks.[2] It also sent an additional 203,796 Russian-Germans forcibly repatriated from Germany and elsewhere to special settlements in Siberia and Central Asia.[3] In total, the Soviet government banished nearly 2 million people to special settlements during World War II on the basis of their nationality. This forced dispersal greatly disrupted the social capital accumulated by these nationalities. They permanently lost many of their former social networks. Other networks, such as the family and clan connections of the Chechens, could be reconstructed in exile on the basis of surviving social connections. The groups with the greatest amount of social capital before the deportations fared the best in recreating the social networks that were important to their collective well-being.

The government of the USSR targeted specific nationalities for total deportation due to a perceived inability to successfully incorporate them into Soviet society. It deemed certain nationalities as inherently incompatible with a secure and stable Soviet state. The Stalin regime viewed nationalities with ethnic ties to foreign states, such as the Russian-Germans and

Meskhetian Turks, as potential fifth columnists. The decrees ordering their deportation justified their forced removal from their homelands as prophylactic security measures.[4] The Soviet state considered these nationalities to be innately treasonous on the basis of sharing a common ancestry and cultural heritage with the dominant population of these foreign states. This xenophobia rested upon a fear "that these nationalities could not be 'reinvented' as Soviet nations—national in form, but socialist in content—because other states or class enemies had 'control' over the histories and traditions that shaped their national consciousness."[5] The Soviet regime posited this national consciousness to rest upon primordial cultural essences so ingrained as to be innate and immutable.[6] This racialization of nationality explains the Soviet government's deportation of all Russian-Germans and Meskhetian Turks without making any exceptions for loyal Communists.

A similar process occurred regarding Soviet thinking about the other nationalities deported during World War II. The native nationalities of the USSR subjected to deportation during World War II all shared certain traits. They had concentrated populations, adhered to non-Christian religions, and lived on the periphery of the USSR. Most important, they all had a history of resisting Russian and Soviet rule, marking them as "enemy nations" in the eyes of the Soviet state. The Stalin regime came to view these nationalities as innately "anti-Soviet" as a result of this history. They could not be successfully integrated into the USSR as national units. The regime thus resolved to eliminate them as distinct ethnic entities through physical dispersal and cultural deprivation.[7] In doing so, it punished the deported nationalities for past resistance and aimed to prevent all future opposition. The racial logic of viewing all Karachais, Kalmyks, Chechens, Ingush, Balkars, and Crimean Tatars as inherent enemies of the Soviet order regardless of their political beliefs or acts condemned these nationalities to deportation in their entirety.

The Soviet government determined settlement destinations for these condemned nationalities, dispersing them across the expanses of the Urals, Kazakhstan, Uzbekistan, Kygyzstan, and Siberia. The Stalin regime assigned the deportees to already-existing villages and settlements. In many cases, they even housed the "special settlers" in buildings already inhabited by Kazakhs and Russians.[8] The deportees, however, did not have the same rights as the original Kazakh and Russian inhabitants of these settlements. Instead they came under a special legal regime enforced by commandants of the NKVD. These commandants maintained offices in the vicinity of the deportees and had responsibility for their living and labor arrangements, keeping them under surveillance, rooting out "anti-Soviet" and criminal elements, preventing escapes, and maintaining social order.[9] The special settlers could not leave their assigned settlements without special permission from their local commandants. The deportees had no choice in their living arrangements and job assignments. They had to register regularly—usually once a month, but frequently often more—with these commandants and had to carry identification papers that marked them as special settlers.[10] These registrations often devolved into humiliating interrogations for the exiles.[11] Special NKVD boards tried all escape attempts, unauthorized absences, and politically suspect behavior by special settlers.[12] After November 24, 1948, these boards received the mandate to try special settlers for refusing to perform assigned work tasks. This particular violation carried an eight-year sentence in a corrective labor camp.[13] Escape attempts first carried a sentence of eight years, and after November 26, 1948, they garnered a twenty-year sentence of hard labor.[14] NKVD commandants could punish lesser infractions without trial by imposing jail detentions of up to five days and fines of up to 100 rubles.[15] The NKVD strictly controlled the movement and activities of the special settlers. The deported nationalities represented a captive labor force. These restrictions prevented their social integration into the surrounding population.

In being confined to special settlements in Kazakhstan, Central Asia, Siberia, and the Urals, these ethnic deportees shared many of the same misfortunes inflicted upon internally displaced persons today in places like Darfur, Sudan. Having been forcibly relocated within the borders of their own state, these people shared problems common to refugees in other settings and periods. Among these problems are the loss of property, family separation, increased mortality due to poor living conditions in the new areas of settlement, a loss of traditional skills by generations maturing after the displacement, a lack of educational and economic opportunities, emotional trauma, and the breakdown of communal structures.[16] The special settlers suffered from a lack of proper housing, food, clothing, and medicine. Unlike refugees, they could not benefit from outside assistance and remained dependent upon the Soviet state for the necessities of life. The Soviet state, however, considered the material well-being of the special settlers to be a low priority and failed to provide sufficient assistance for their maintenance, even as they provided resources to restrict the mobility of the deportees.

The material deprivations resulting from the conditions in exile resulted in hundreds of thousands of special settlers' deaths from disease, malnutrition, and exposure. The partial documentation available in the NKVD records on this subject gives some indication as to the scale of these deaths. By July 1, 1948, the NKVD had recorded the total number of deaths among the Karachai, Chechen, Ingush, and Balkar special settlers as 144,704, or 23.7 percent of their population.[17] Other deported nationalities suffered only slightly lower overall rates of mortality in the special settlements. The NKVD recorded 44,887 deaths among the Crimean Tatars, Greeks, Armenians, and Bulgarians, or 19.6 percent of their population; 16,594 Kalmyk deaths, or 17.4 percent of their population; and 14,895 deaths among the Turks, Kurds, and Hemshins (Meskhetian Turks), or 14.6 percent of their population. The Karachai demographer D. M. Ediev estimates that there were 228,800 excess deaths due to deportation and exile among the Russian-Germans from 1942 to 1952.[18] These deaths equaled 19.17 percent of the total Russian-German special settler population. His estimates for the other deported nationalities are equally high. He calculates the excess mortality or deaths above what would be expected absent the deportations for each nationality separately. He does this by constructing a model population projection for each individual nationality based upon the available data about their demographic dynamics before the deportations. For the years 1944–52, he estimates the deaths above expected normal mortality at 13,100 Karachais (19 percent of the total deported population), 12,600 Kalmyks (12.87 percent), 125,500 Chechens (30.76 percent), 20,300 Ingush (20.3 percent), 7,600 Balkars (19.82 percent), 34,300 Crimean Tatars (18.01 percent), and 12,859 Meskhetian Turks (13 percent). In total, these people suffered over 450,000 excess deaths out of a population of 2,303,760. Thus nearly 20 percent, or 1 out of 5 people, from these nationalities perished as a result of the deportations. Even during times of war, these are extraordinarily high death rates.

In fact, the mortality rates of the deported peoples exceeded those for the USSR as a whole by a factor of four to five. In 1945, the NKVD recorded 89,659 deaths among the 2,230,500 special settlers counted by the NKVD that year, or 4 percent of the population, versus a death rate of 0.9 percent for the Soviet Union as a whole.[19] During the height of World War II, Soviet mortality peaked at 2.4 percent a year. In contrast, a number of deported nationalities lost more than 10 percent of their population in the first year of exile. The NKVD recorded 569,212 Karachais, Chechens, Ingush, and Balkars arriving in Kazakhstan and Kyrgyzstan in 1944.[20] Its records indicate that 58,387 (10.25 percent) of these exiles perished before 1945.[21] By July 1, 1944, the NKVD recorded 151,424 Crimean Tatars arriving in

Uzbekistan.[22] One NKVD report places the number of these arrivals who died by July 1, 1945, at 22,355 (14.76 percent).[23] This massive loss of life afflicted nearly every family among the deported nationalities. Almost all of them lost members to hunger, cold, and disease in the first years of exile.

The deportations also greatly reduced the birthrates of the special settlers. Until 1948, deaths exceeded births among all the deported nationalities.[24] Exile reduced the birthrates of the special settlers by about half from 1944 to 1952.[25] Ediev estimates the demographic losses of the deported peoples, measured as excess deaths plus the resulting birth deficit, at more than 40 percent of their population before their exile.[26] The deportations represented a demographic disaster of colossal proportions for the victimized nationalities.

In addition to the loss of property and lives suffered during the deportation, the special settlers lost a great deal of social capital as a result of being forcibly uprooted from their homelands and dispersed across the interior of the USSR. The Soviet government dissolved the autonomous state structures of the deported peoples along with the cultural institutions, media, and schools they supported. The dispersal of traditional communities and dissolving of religious congregations during the deportations seriously threatened the cultural continuity of these nationalities. The breakup of these social networks seriously damaged the bonding social capital of the deported nationalities.

Even individual families became divided as their members were separated during the deportations. In many cases, the NKVD loaded mothers and children into different train wagons in their haste to deport the targeted nationalities. The division of families especially afflicted the North Caucasian deportees. More than 14 percent of Chechen, Ingush, and Karachai families sent to Kazakhstan became divided during the deportations.[27] A total of 11,711 Karachai families and 89,901 Chechen and Ingush families arrived in Kazakhstan in 1943 and 1944.[28] Out of this number, 14,460 families had been divided as a result of the deportations.[29] In the Jambul Oblast alone, more than 2,000 Karachai families out of 5,699, more than a third, had been divided during transit from the Caucasus.[30] Only 5,478 of the divided families in Kazakhstan had been reunited by September 5, 1944, leaving 8,982 divided. In Kyrgyzstan, 2,941 Chechen, Ingush, and Karachai families arrived divided. A total of 952 had been reunified by September 5, 1944, leaving 1,982 divided. During the deportation of the Crimean Tatars, 2,444 families out of 47,750, more than 1 in 20, became divided.[31] This shattering of family and communal bonds interfered with the ability of the exiles to pass on skills, traditions, and knowledge to their children. The cultures, traditional ways of life, and social structures of the deported peoples suffered great damage as a result of this uprooting.

Many of the men still remained in the Soviet Army fighting against Nazi Germany when the NKVD exiled their families to special settlements. An unknown number of soldiers from these nationalities perished in helping secure a Soviet victory over Germany during World War II. The Soviet government demobilized those that survived the war and assigned them to special settlements later. On September 8, 1941, the Soviet authorities ordered the removal of all Russian-Germans from the military.[32] The Soviet government organized these men into forced labor battalions collectively known as the labor army (*trudarmiia*) run by Gulag (Main Administration of Camps).[33] Only near the end of 1945 did the Soviet government begin to release these forced laborers from Gulag discipline and place them under special settlement restrictions.[34] This change allowed them to reunite with their families. The release of Russian-Germans from the labor army took place in a slow, piecemeal fashion. The Soviet government did not release the last labor army conscripts from the camps until 1957, more than a year after the complete removal of the Russian-Germans from the special settlement restrictions.[35] By this time deaths, remarriage, and up to sixteen years of separation made family members' reunifications extremely difficult.

The transfer of soldiers from other deported nationalities to special settlements started in 1944. A considerable number of men from these nationalities served in the Red Army during World War II. In total, 7,335 Karachais, 23,540 Kalmyks, 17,037 Chechens, 3,221 Ingush, 5,609 Balkars, and 25,033 Crimean Tatars fought in the Soviet military against Nazi Germany.[36] Altogether, more than 80,000 front-line soldiers came from these nationalities. The Soviet government ordered all Karachais removed from the Red Army and sent to special settlements in Kazakhstan and Kyrgyzstan on March 3, 1944.[37] From 1944 to 1948, the Soviet government demobilized almost all Karachais, Kalmyks, Chechens, Ingush, Balkars, Crimean Tatars, and Meskhetian Turks from the Red Army and placed them under special settlement restrictions.[38] In early 1944, the Soviet government sent the demobilized Kalmyk soldiers to labor army battalions before dispatching the survivors to special settlements.[39] During the next four years, the NKVD gradually filtered these men into the special settlement zones of Siberia. Later in the year, the Stalin regime began the discharge of Chechens, Ingush, Karachais, and Balkars from the military to special settlements in Kazakhstan and Kyrgyzstan. This process also took four years to complete.

After 1945, the Soviet government demobilized the Crimean Tatars and Meskhetian Turks in the Red Army and sent them to special settlements. Many of these soldiers spent years wandering through Kazakhstan and Central Asia trying to find their lost families, in defiance of the special settlement restrictions, only to find that their families had perished in the meantime.[40] Many family members separated in this manner thus remained divided permanently.

The deported peoples sought to reunite their divided families in the special settlements. The Chechens and Ingush in particular strove to reconstruct their divided families. Many Chechens and Ingush volunteers worked in the *khabar,* a network of people who traveled throughout Kazakhstan and Kyrgyzstan in violation of the special settlement restrictions exchanging information on the location of missing family members.[41] By walking clandestinely from settlement to settlement, the *khabar* succeeded in reuniting most of the Chechen and Ingush families separated during the deportations.

The Middle Years: Efforts to Retain and Reacquire Social Capital

The efforts by the deported peoples to retain and reacquire their social capital faced formidable obstacles in the 1940s and early 1950s. Despite these obstacles, they did retain some valuable assets that allowed them to improve their economic, social, and political status. They retained familial and communal bonds that in some cases could be reconstructed, despite being dispersed over a large area. The success of the Chechens and Ingush in reuniting divided families relied upon a conscious reconnection with these networks. They successfully invested their bonding social capital to repair many of the social networks severed by the deportation. The deported peoples also retained skills and cultural assets that helped them collectively survive and improve their lot.

The Soviet government abolished the special settlement regime during the mid-1950s. First, it released the Russian-Germans from the special settlement restrictions on December 13, 1955.[42] Next, it released the Kalmyks on March 17, 1956; the Crimean Tatars, Balkars, and Meskhetian Turks on April 28, 1956; and the Chechens, Ingush, and Karachais on July 16, 1956.[43] These decrees, however, still prohibited the deported nationalities from returning to their homelands or receiving any compensation for property lost during the deportations.

In late 1956, the Soviet regime began the process of restoring the national territories of some of the deported peoples. For almost its entire existence, however, the regime continued to prevent the Russian-Germans, Crimean Tatars, and Meskhetian Turks from returning to their previous places of residence. On November 24, 1956, the central committee of the Communist Party of the Soviet Union passed the resolution titled On Restoring National Autonomy to the Kalmyk, Karachai, Balkar, Chechen, and Ingush Peoples.[44] This resolution subsequently received endorsement by the Presidium of the Supreme Soviet on January 9, 1957, and became enshrined in Soviet law on February 11, 1957.[45] On January 9, 1957, the Soviet government re-created the Karbardian-Balkar Autonomous Soviet Socialist Republic (ASSR), the Karachai-Circassian Autonomous Oblast, the Kalmyk Autonomous Oblast, and the Chechen-Ingush ASSR. This legislation also lifted all restrictions on these nationalities from returning to their native areas. Hundreds of thousands of deportees and their descendants returned to their newly reestablished autonomous territories during the next couple of years.

The initial Soviet decisions on which nationalities to deport had all relied on motives related to strengthening the Soviet state and its Russian core. Moscow sought to remove nationalities deemed treasonous from its borders and other strategic areas. Economics, however, motivated the decisions to prevent the Russian-Germans, Crimean Tatars, and Meskhetian Turks from returning home. The Soviet state had come to rely upon the labor of these groups in Siberia, Kazakhstan, and Central Asia. They constituted a reliable and permanent workforce in regions short of labor. The Soviet government had difficulty attracting voluntary labor to these regions. Other involuntary laborers, such as the deported North Caucasians and Kalmyks, had proven difficult to integrate into the local economies.[46] Violence, flight, and refusal to work all continued to mark these nationalities to a much greater extent than the Russian-Germans, Crimean Tatars, and Meskhetian Turks. In particular, the Chechens demonstrated a propensity for insubordination. The Chechens' resistance to integration in the agricultural economy of Kazakhstan and Kyrgyzstan reached its pinnacle in their mass return to the Caucasus in defiance of the Soviet regime. In the wake of this event, the Soviet government decided to facilitate the return of the North Caucasians and Kalmyks. The costs of maintaining them in exile outweighed the economic benefits. The Russian-Germans, Crimean Tatars, and Meskhetian Turks, in contrast, cost considerably less to keep in the areas of deportation and constituted an irreplaceable workforce there.

The Russian-Germans came to constitute a large, permanent, and reliable workforce on the farms, mines, and forests of Siberia and Kazakhstan. By August 1, 1950, the number of Russian-Germans employed in the Soviet economy in this region had reached 633,378.[47] This skilled workforce, which was roughly divided between agricultural and industrial workers, proved necessary for the development of the USSR's Asian regions in the postwar period. Certain segments of this workforce maintained levels of productivity far ahead of the Soviet average. In particular, the nearly 70,000 Russian-German coal miners had an impressive record in this regard. In the Kuzbass Coal Basin, 2,559 out of 7,577 (33.9 percent) Russian-German miners exceeded their quotas by more than 125 percent during May 1947, whereas only 980 (12.8 percent) failed to meet their quota.[48] Both their large numbers and strong work ethic made the Russian-Germans a valuable workforce in the sparsely populated regions of Kazakhstan and Siberia. No other comparably large number of disciplined workers could be found to replace them in their new areas of settlement.

In the mid-1960s, the Soviet government publicly acknowledged its economic motives in keeping the Russian-Germans confined to Kazakhstan and Siberia. On August 29, 1964, the Supreme Soviet issued a decree annulling the charges of treason against the Russian-Germans.[49] This document, however, did nothing to remove the punishment of exile imposed for these now-rescinded charges. It justified this continued exile by noting that the Russian-Germans had become "rooted" in their new areas of settlement. The same decree stressed that the Russian-Germans had played an important role in the development of the Soviet economy after the end of World War II. In particular, it noted their contributions to developing the industry and agriculture of Kazakhstan, Uzbekistan, and Kyrgyzstan. These areas remained desperately short of skilled native workers in industry and such agricultural occupations as tractor drivers, machine tractor station mechanics, and combine operators.

In the year following the 1964 decree, the Russian-Germans sent two delegations to Moscow to discuss restoring the Volga German ASSR. The chairman of the Presidium of the Supreme Soviet, Anastas Mikoyan, put the Soviet justification for the continued exile of the Russian-Germans in northern Kazakhstan in its most basic terms during a meeting with the second delegation on July 7, 1965:

> I think that enough statements have been made. The Soviet Germans conducted themselves well during the war, after the war, and are now con-

> ducting themselves well. They work well. At present in the Virgin Lands Region, without the Germans it is impossible to run the rural economy.[50]

The northern oblasts of Kazakhstan had grown dependent upon Russian-Germans as their core labor force in growing wheat and raising cattle. The Soviet government could not allow them to return to their homes on the Volga and elsewhere without seriously disrupting Kazakhstan's agriculture.

The Crimean Tatars filled the construction, mining, and factory jobs in Uzbekistan's industrial towns shunned by the Uzbeks. Between May 20, 1944, and July 1, 1948, the proportion of Crimean Tatars working in such occupations in Uzbekistan increased from 15 to 70 percent.[51] The NKVD noted that they had a "positive attitude" toward labor and that many of them overfulfilled their assigned work quotas by substantial margins, thus qualifying them as Stakhanovites.[52] In 1945, the NKVD noted that 50 to 60 percent of Crimean Tatar workers at the Fergana Textile Combine, construction sites in Fergana, Ozakerit mines in Fergana, and silk factories in Margilan had exceeded their assigned quotas by 200 to 300 percent. The same report also commended the work ethic of Crimean Tatar workers in the Samarkand and Namagan oblasts. The Crimean Tatars became prized workers in the undesirable and thus difficult-to-fill jobs in Uzbekistan's underdeveloped industrial economy.

The Soviet authorities had great difficulty finding sufficient numbers of industrial laborers to work in the mines and factories of Uzbekistan. The Uzbeks remained mostly rural and were reluctant to leave their traditional agricultural pursuits. In 1959 only 27 percent of the Uzbek labor force worked in industry.[53] At the same time, only a limited number of Russians were willing to move to Uzbekistan. The Crimean Tatars thus filled an important economic niche in the republic, similar to the role of economic migrants in destination economies across the globe. To better integrate the Crimean Tatars into the industrial economy, the leader of the Uzbek SSR, N.A. Mukhitdinov, requested that they be removed from the special settlement restrictions as early as 1954.[54] The Uzbek authorities also greatly feared that if the Crimean Tatars were allowed to leave that it would significantly disrupt Uzbekistan's industrial production.[55] They thus successfully lobbied Moscow to adopt policies to keep the Crimean Tatars confined to Uzbekistan as an industrial labor force.

The Meskhetian Turks likewise earned a reputation for being hard workers. Unlike the Crimean Tatars, more than 90 percent of Meskhetian Turks worked in the agricultural sector of the economy.[56] Their contributions and achievements on the *kolkhozes* (collective farms) of Kazakhstan attracted official Soviet notice. Here they planted and harvested cotton, potatoes, and vegetables. One team of Meskhetian Turks at the *kolkhoz* named Third International in the Kzyl-Orda Oblast exceeded their assigned production quota by 200 percent.[57] At the Novy Stroi *kolkhoz* in the South Kazakhstan Oblast, a Meskhetian Turk named Valiev completed 1,005 labor days in only nine months. Surpassing even this feat, a Meskhetian Turk named Malkhasan-Ogly fulfilled 2,000 labor days in the same period of time on the Kubishev *kolkhoz*. This feat allowed the farm to harvest a record 164,677 kilograms of potatoes and 75,728 kilograms of vegetables that season. The Meskhetian Turks became a productive and reliable workforce in the agricultural economy of Kazakhstan and Central Asia.

Special settlers with membership in the Communist Party, Komsomol (the party's youth wing), or service in the Soviet Army constituted a particularly valuable form of "bridging social capital" for the deported peoples. These people had above average-levels of education and a familiarity with Soviet law, and they represented a living refutation of the Stalin regime's charges of universal treason. Many of them had occupied leadership roles in their national autonomous territories before the deportations and thus had acquired useful organizational skills. They also had ties through their Communist Party membership with representatives of the Soviet leadership. Party members among the deported peoples could use their personal and ideological connections with the Soviet regime to appeal on behalf of their nationalities. Unsurprisingly, these people formed the core of the early national movements among the deported peoples, agitating for a right to return to their homelands. In the 1950s, they organized petition drives and delegations aimed at convincing the post-Stalinist leadership of the USSR to restore their national rights. They appealed to the Soviet authorities as fellow Communists to return to the Leninist nationality policies that had prevailed before Stalin. The education, skills, and experience of these men and women allowed them to effectively organize political movements seeking this goal within the constraints of the Soviet system.

Organized national movements among the deported peoples working for a right to return to their homelands and a restoration of their autonomous territories began in 1956 after the abolition of the special settlement regime. Communist Party members took the leading role in these movements. The ability of these movements to successfully mobilize grassroots support depended upon their level of bonding social capital. Those nationalities that had the most national cohesion and consciousness before the deportations had the greatest degree of political mobilization in the post-Stalin years. The strongest movements existed among those nationalities with a highly developed sense of being a common people deeply rooted in a defined and contiguous territory.

The Russian-Germans had the weakest sense of national cohesion of all the people deported in their entirety during World War II. Unlike the other deported nationalities, they could trace their migration to the Russian Empire only back to 1763.[58] They continued to settle in the Volga River region, along the Black Sea coast, and in other regions in waves during the next century. These different waves of settlers often spoke different dialects of German and belonged to different religious denominations. They established geographically disparate settlements largely isolated not only from the surrounding Russians and Ukrainians but also from each other. This settlement occurred mostly before the development of German nationalism, and the colonists in the Russian Empire remained largely immune to its advent. Instead, they retained a sense of community and homeland predating nationalism that centered on their individual villages and churches. The German colonists in the Russian Empire never developed a strong sense of themselves as a single people linked by virtue of a shared culture, history, and territory. Only after World War II did the Russian-Germans begin to conceive of themselves as a single nationality. This new self-conception developed primarily as a result of shared persecution at the hands of the Soviet government on the basis of their German descent. The government of West Germany strongly reinforced this identification by projecting itself as the only homeland for the Russian-Germans, regardless of their origins.

During the 1920s and 1930s, the Soviet Union followed a policy of ruling over its large and diverse non-Russian population by creating a system of national territories united by socialist ideology. These territories served to promote the Sovietization of these ethnicities by linking them to specific territories within the USSR and promoting socialist versions of their culture. Known as *korenizatsiia* (literally, to take root), the construction of these national state formations was the core of early Soviet nationality policy.[59] These territorial formations used national languages in administration and education, practiced affirmative action regarding the titular nationality, and provided many of the symbolic trappings and cultural institutions of nation-states. But they lacked any real political or economic autonomy. The success of these national state formations in creating territorially based nationalities out of more amorphous ethnic groups varied. Those territories that fit well with the preexisting settlement patterns and historical conceptions of their titular nationality became internalized to a much greater extent then those that did not.

The attempt to create a territorially rooted Soviet German nationality had limited success. The dispersed and isolated nature of the various Russian-German settlements in the USSR made it impossible to root the majority of the population in a single demarcated and contiguous territory. Instead, the Soviet government created one large national territory for the Russian-Germans in the Volga region and numerous smaller ones in Ukraine and elsewhere. Only the territory in the Volga had the large enough expanse, the sufficiently compact population, and the adequate state infrastructure it needed to have any success. Initially formed as the Volga German Labor Commune on October 19, 1918, the Soviet government upgraded this territory to the Volga German ASSR on February 20, 1924.[60] Even at its peak, only a third of the Russian-German population lived within the borders of the Volga German ASSR.[61] Most Russian-Germans living in the territory continued to maintain a stronger attachment to their individual villages than the newly created state formation. The attempt to create a Soviet German nationality rooted in the Volga German ASSR largely failed.[62] The majority of the population failed to become nationally conscious and territorialized.

The failure of *korenizatsiia* to create a territorialized Soviet German nation accounts in large part for the relative weakness of the Russian-German movement to restore the Volga German ASSR during the 1950s and 1960s. Before 1964, there was no organized movement toward this goal, only the efforts of individual activists. Most of these activists were members of the Communist Party and had been involved as teachers and writers in the official culture of the Volga German ASSR. Two such early activists were Dominik Hollmann and Adolf Bersch, who began writing letters to the Soviet leadership requesting a restoration of their national territory in 1956 and 1957, respectively.[63] The lack of an organized movement by the Russian-Germans for return to their homeland in the USSR during the 1950s contrasted sharply with the mass activity of the other deported peoples.

The Karchais, Kalmyks, Chechens, Ingush, Balkars, Crimean Tatars, and Meskhetian Turks all differed considerably from the Russian-Germans in their historical settlement patterns. They all lived in compact territories in the USSR and identified these specific geographic regions as their people's historic and often even primordial homeland. They considered themselves to be natives of this soil rather than colonists with cultural origins abroad. Unlike the Russian-Germans, each of these nationalities had possessed a common contiguous homeland for centuries. In addition to this geographic concentration, these ethnic groups also possessed a cultural homogeneity lacking among the Russian-Germans. Living in compact areas, these nationalities did not have large internal differences regarding language and religion. Almost all Chechens, Ingush, Karachais, Balkars, Crimean Tatars, and Meskhetian Turks belonged to the Hanafi School of Sunni Islam dominant in the Ottoman Empire. The Kalmyks all shared a common Tibetan form of Buddhism. In contrast, the Russian-Germans remained deeply divided along confessional lines until the deportations. The various Lutheran, Catholic, and Mennonite communities had little contact with each other. The Russian-Germans thus had considerably less bonding social capital than the other deported nationalities before the formation of the USSR.

In the 1920s, as part of *korenizatsiia,* the Soviet government created national administrative territories for the Karachais, Kalmyks, Chechens, Ingush, Balkars, and Crimean Tatars as well as the Volga Germans. The Karachai Autonomous Oblast, Kalmyk ASSR, Chechen-Ingush ASSR, Karbardian-Balkar ASSR, and Crimean ASSR all corresponded to the historic settlement patterns of these nationalities. They all contained the majority of their titular nationalities. These administrative territories served to strengthen the territorialized national identification of these peoples by providing them with national public symbols, education systems, media, and borders specifically delineating their historic lands. Soviet policies also created native elites to lead these newly created territories and their increasingly nationalized populations. This process created a large amount of social capital for the deported peoples. They successfully tapped into it to help reconstruct their shattered communities in the wake of the deportations.

The Crimean Tatars not only had a very well organized movement; they also took care to document it. In September 1956, five Crimean Tatar Communists who had been influential in the Crimean ASSR sent a letter to the Soviet government regarding these issues.[64] This letter secured a meeting between fifty Crimean Tatars with membership in the Communist Party and the central committee of the Uzbek Communist Party. This meeting did nothing to advance the Crimean Tatar cause but did embolden the Crimean Tatar national movement. The Crimean Tatar activists mobilized support for their cause from outside the small group of Communist Party members that constituted the leadership of the movement. They secured 6,000 signatures for a petition to the Soviet leadership in July 1957.[65] This petition succeeded in securing a meeting between a delegation of Crimean Tatar Communist Party members and Anastas Mikoyan on March 17, 1958. The delegation presented Mikoyan with another petition signed by 16,000 Crimean

Tatars. Throughout the 1950s, the leadership of the Crimean Tatar national movement remained dominated by members of the Communist Party. Only in the 1960s did the movement's leadership become dominated by younger individuals born in exile who had not participated in the affairs of the Crimean ASSR. This new generation had grown up in exile under the special settlement restrictions. Their experiences of discrimination and poverty contrasted sharply with the idyllic stories of Crimea told to them by their elders. The younger activists in the movement did not view the deportations as a mistake but rather a crime. In contrast to the earlier activists, they did not ask for rehabilitation as a reward for their loyalty to the USSR. Instead they demanded that their right to return to Crimea be respected in accordance with Soviet and international law.

Another deported nationality that showed a great deal of initiative in organizing a peaceful movement aimed at securing the right to return to their homeland were the Karachais. Like the Crimean Tatars, they organized a petition and letter campaign. Also like the Crimean Tatars, members of the Communist Party, such as B. A. Karaev and A. D. Bauchiev, took a leading role in the national movement.[66] On May 13, 1956, some five hundred Karachais met at Vorontsovke near Frunze (Bishkek) in Kyrgyzstan to formulate a strategy to allow them to return home to the Caucasus.[67] Their letters and petitions succeeded in garnering a one-hour meeting between an eight-person Karachai delegation and Nikita Khrushchev on July 4, 1956.[68] Unlike the Crimean Tatars, the Soviet government did not perpetually ignore the demands of the Karachais. The Soviet government restored their national territory and allowed them to return home in early 1957. More than 80 percent of the remaining exiled Karachais returned to the newly formed Karachai-Cherkess Autonomous Oblast during the next two years.[69] They had achieved their foremost demand, the right to return to their homeland.

The most spectacular organizational effort for return to a homeland during the 1950s occurred among the Chechens. They retained and reconstructed a surprisingly high level of bonding social capital after the deportations. Family and communal networks remained particularly strong among the Chechens and Ingush. They used these networks to organize their mass return to their homelands in the fall of 1956. Starting in October, large numbers of Chechens began collectively buying train passage back to the Caucasus and paying the necessary bribes.[70] They organized the collection of money, purchasing of train tickets, and paying of bribes. Thousand of Chechens and Ingush returned to their homelands in defiance of the Soviet regime. In January 1957, the Soviet government restored the Chechen-Ingush ASSR in response to this mass movement. The surviving social networks among the Chechens allowed them to organize on a mass scale when the opportunity to return manifested itself. Other deported nationalities lacked the ability to mobilize such large sections of their population at this time and remained exiled in Kazakhstan and Central Asia.

Conclusions

The Stalin regime's uprooting of the Russian-Germans, Karachais, Kalmyks, Chechens, Ingush, Balkars, Crimean Tatars, and Meskhetian Turks during World War II represented an attempt to forcibly dissolve these nationalities as collective entities. The Soviet government deprived them of their homelands, cultural institutions, and even basic material possessions. The regime, however, could not permanently sever many of the connections binding these nationalities together. In particular, the government found it difficult to break the deportees' collective emotional ties to their ancestral lands.

Most of the deported nationalities made use of their bonding capital to maintain their national cohesion and psychological connection to their former homelands. Only in the case of the Russian-Germans did the Stalin regime successfully break these bonds. Unlike the other nationalities, the Russian-Germans had a relatively weak sense of national cohesion and territorial roots in the USSR. They lacked sufficient bonding social capital to rebound from the assault on their national existence by the Soviet state. All the other deported nationalities managed to better resist this assault. Most even managed to return to their homelands and to reconstitute national autonomous territories. They made successful use of their bridging capital to pressure the Soviet government to allow them to return home. Only the Crimean Tatars and Meskhetian Turks remained exiled along with the Russian-Germans after 1957. However, they continued to vigorously struggle to return to their homelands. In contrast, the Russian-German movement to return to the Volga River region had largely died out by 1968. The 1941 deportations essentially destroyed them as a viable nationality in the USSR.

Notes

1. R. D. Putnam, *Bowling Alone* (New York: Simon & Schuster, 200), 19–23.
2. N. F. Bugai, ed., *Iosif Stalin: Lavrentiiu Berii—"Ikh nado deportirovat"—Dokumenty, fakty, kommentarii* (Moscow: Druzhba narodov, 1992), doc. 45, 75–76 (Germans), doc. 2, 85–86 (Kalmyks), doc. 13, 105–6 (Chechens and Ingush), doc. 29, 113–14 (Balkars), doc. 20, 144 (Crimean Tatars), doc. 7, 157 (Meskhetian Turks); and N. F.

Bugai, ed., "'Pogruzheny v eshelony I otpravelny k mestam poselenii . . .' L. Beria – I. Stalinu," *Istoriia SSSR* 1 (1991): doc. 4, 145 (Karachais).

3. Bugai, *Iosif Stalin – Lavrentiiu Berii: "Ikh nado deportirovat,'"* doc. 45, 75–76.

4. Ibid., doc. 3, 37–38; and T. S. Kulbaev and A. Iu. Khegai, *Deportatsiia* (Almaty: Deneker, 2000), 186–87.

5. Francine Hirsch, "Race without the Practice of Racial Politics," *Slavic Review* (Spring 2002): 38.

6. Eric D. Weitz, *A Century of Genocide: Utopias of Race and Nation* (Princeton, N.J.: Princeton University Press, 2003), 97–98.

7. Hirsch, "Race," 37–43.

8. O. L. Milova, ed., *Deportatsii narodov SSSR (1930–1950-e-gody): Chast' 2—Deportatsiia nemtsev (Sentiabr' 1941–Fevral' 1942 gg.)* (Moscow: RAN, 1995), doc. 57, 219; and Bugai, *Iosif Stalin,* doc. 13, 92–93.

9. V. I. Bruhl, *Nemtsy v zapadnoi sibiri* (Topchikha: Topchikhinskaia tip., 1995), vol. 2, 107, 109, and doc. 7, 212–13; A. I. Kokurin, "Spetsperselentsy v SSSR v 1944, ili god bol'shogo pereseleniia," *Otechestvennye arkhivy* 5 (1993): doc. 3, 103–7; P. D. Bakaev, ed., *Ssylka kalmykov: Kak eto bylo—Sbornik dokumentov I materialov* (Elitsa: Kalmytskoe knizhnoe izd-vo, 1993), doc. 145, 144–45, doc. 147, 146–49, doc. 189, 182–83; Bugai, *Iosif Stalin,* doc. 10, 231.

10. Nelly Daes, *Gone without a Trace: German-Russian Women in Exile,* trans. Nancy Holland (Lincoln, Neb.: American Historical Society of Germans from Russia, 2001), 66, 137; S. U. Alieva, ed., *Tak eto bylo: Natsional'nye repressi v SSR, 1919–1952* (Moscow: Insan, 1993), vol. 1, 289, vol. 2, 95, and vol. 3, 165; Bruhl, *Nemtsy,* doc. 8, 213; L. Belvokets, "Spetsposelenie nemtsev v Zapadnoi Sibiri (1941–1955 gg)," in *Nakazannyi narod: Repressii protiv rossiiskikh nemtsev,* ed. I. L. Shcherbakova (Moscow: Zve'ia, 1999), 160.

11. Daes, *Gone without a Trace,* 66–67; V. I. Bruhl, "Deportirovannye narody v Sibiri (1935–1965 gg.), Sravnitel'nyi analiz," in *Nakazannyi narod,* ed. Shcherbakova, 104.

12. Bakaev, *Ssylka kalmykov,* doc. 189, 182–83.

13. Document reproduced in Alieva, *Tak eto bylo,* vol. 1, 297.

14. N. F. Bugai and A. M. Gonov, *Kavkaz: Narody v eshelonakh (20–60-e gody)* (Moscow: Insan, 1998), 234; and document reproduced in Alieva, *Tak eto bylo,* vol. 1, 294–95.

15. Bakaev, *Ssylka kalmykov,* doc. 189, 182–83; Bugai, *Iosif Stalin,* doc. 10, 231.

16. Roberta Cohen and Francis Deng, *Masses in Flight: The Global Crises of Internal Displacement* (Washington, D.C.: Brookings Institution Press, 1998), 23–26.

17. Bugai, *Iosif Stalin,* doc. 48, 264–65.

18. D. M. Ediev, *Demograficheskie poteri deportirovannykh narodov SSSR* (Stavropol': Izd-vo stGAU 'Argus', 2003), table 104, 294, 300.

19. Bugai, *Iosif Stalin,* doc. 17, 237, and doc. 18, 231–38; Edwin Bacon, "Glasnost and the Gulag: New Information on Soviet Forced Labor around World War II," *Soviet Studies* 6 (1992): table 5, 1080.

20. Bugai, *Iosif Stalin,* 117–18; V. N. Zemskov, "Spetsposelentsy (po dokumentatsii NKVD-MVD SSSR)," *Sotsiologicheski issledovaniia* 11 (1990): 8. The NKVD records initially recorded 602,193 North Caucasians arriving in Kazakhstan and Kyrgyzstan during February and March 1944. This number, however, included 32,981 special settlers counted twice.

21. N. F. Bugai, "20–50-e gody: Posledstviia deportatsii narodov (svidetel'stvuiut arkhivy NKVD-MVD SSSR)," *Istoriia SSSR* 1 (1992): doc. 35, 142, gives the number

of deaths from 1944 to 1948 at 144,704; doc. 30, 138–40, gives a year-by-year breakdown of deaths from 1945 to 1950. The number of deaths from 1945 to 1948 is given as 86,317; the difference between 144,704 and presumed number of deaths for 1944 is 58,387.

22. The document is reproduced in *Khronika tekushchikh sobytii* 31 (May 17, 1974): 148–49.

23. Gulnara Bekyrova, "No Provision Was Made to Supply the Special Settlers with Clothes and Shoes, and Were Like Destitute Rejects Though Many of Them Wore Orders and Medals," *Krimskii studii,* nos. 3–4 (2002), http://www.cidct.org.ua/en/studii/13-14/7.html, doc. 7, 10.

24. Bugai, "Posledstviia," doc. 30, 138–40.

25. D. M. Ediev, "Demograficheskie poteri deportirovannykh narodov SSSR," Polit.Ru, table 2, 4, found at http://www.polit.ru/research/2004/02/27demoscope147.html.

26. Ibid., table 3, 4–5, and table 6, 12.

27. N. F. Bugai and A. M. Gonov, *"Po resheniiu pravitel'stva soiuza SSSR-" [deportatsiia narodov: dokumenty I materially]* (Nal'chik: El'fa, 2003), doc. 11, 415–16, and doc. 20, 41.

28. Ibid., doc. 11, 415–16.

29. Ibid., doc. 20, 41.

30. Ibid., doc. 4, 405-406.

31. Gulnara Bekyrova, "No Provision Was Made"; Bugai, *Iosif,* doc. 20, 144; *Khronika tekushchikh sobytii* 31 (May 17, 1974): 148–49.

32. The document is partially reproduced in Alieva, *Tak eto bylo,* vol. 1, 148.

33. N. F. Bugai, ed., *"Mobilizovat' nemtsev v robochie kolonny . . . I. Stalin": Sbornik dokumentov (1940-e gody)* (Moscow: Gotika, 1998), doc. 30, 53, doc. 31, 53–55, and doc. 32, 55–56.

34. Alfred Eisfeld and Victor Herdt, eds., *Deportation, Sondersiedlung, Arbeitsarmee: Deutsche in der Sowjetunion 1941 bis 1956* (Cologne: Verlag Wissenschaft und Politik, 1996), doc. 256, 281, and doc. 259, 282.

35. Alfred Eisfeld, *Die Aussiedlung der Deutschen aus der Wolgarepublik 1941–1957* (Munich: Osteuropa-Institut, Mitteilungen nr. 50, 2003), 63.

36. Ediev, "Demograficheskie poteri," table 94, 277.

37. N. F. Bugai, *L. Beria—I. Stalinu: "Soglasno vashemu ukazaniiu . . . "* (Moscow: AIRO XX, 1995), 63.

38. Bugai, *Iosif Stalin,* "Zakliuchenie," 94–59, doc. 18, 108, 47, 126–27, "Zakliuchenie," 126–27, doc. 26, 147–48, doc. 20, 165–69, 29, 247–48, and 30, 248–50.

39. A. Pan'kin and V. Papuev, eds., *Dorogoi pamiati* (Elista: Dzhangar, 1994), 4, 8; Bugai, *L. Beria—I. Stalinu,* 77.

40. See, e.g., the account of Ali Yusupov, a Meskhetian Turk in Alieva, *Tak eto bylo,* vol. 3, 169–73.

41. Valery Tishkov, *Chechnya: Life in a War-Torn Society* (Berkeley: University of California Press, 2004), 28.

42. The document is reproduced by V. A. Auman and V. G. Chebotareva, *Istoriia rossiiskikh nemtsev v dokumentakh, 1763–1992 gg.* (Moscow: MIGUP, 1993), 177.

43. Bugai, *Iosif Stalin,* doc. 55, 270–71, doc. 57, 273, and doc. 59, 274–75.

44. The document is reproduced by Ismail Aliev, *Reabilitatsii narodov I grazhdan, 1954–1994 gody: Dokumenty* (Moscow: RAN, 1994), 44–49.

45. The documents are reproduced by Aliev, *Reabilitatsii narodov I grazhdan,* 49–55.

46. Michaela Pohl, "'It Cannot Be That Our Graves Will Be Here': The Survival of Chechen and Ingush Deportees in Kazakhstan, 1944–1957," *Journal of Genocide Research* 4 (2002): 411–26.

47. Eisfeld and Herdt, *Deportation,* doc. 336, 343–46.

48. Bruhl, *Zapadnoi sibiri,* . 95.

49. The document is reproduced by Auman and Chebotareva, *Istoriia rossiiskikh nemtsev,* 178–79.

50. As quoted by Eric J. Schmaltz, "Reform, 'Rebirth,' and Regret: The Early Autonomy Movement of Ethnic Germans in the USSR, 1955–1989," PhD dissertation, University of Nebraska, 2002, 164.

51. Bugai, *L. Beria – I. Stalinu,* 152; Bugai, *Iosif Stalin,* doc. 48, 264–65.

52. Bekyrova, "No Provision Was Made," doc. 7, 13.

53. Michael Rywkin, *Moscow's Muslim Challenge: Soviet Central Asia* (London: C. Hurst, 1982), 52.

54. Semyon Gitlin, "Crimean Tatars in Uzbekistan: Problems and Developments," *Central Asia and the Caucasus* 1 (2000) at http://www.ca-c.org/journal/eng-012000/10.gitlin.shtml, 5–6.

55. Ibid., 4.

56. Bugai, *Iosif Stalin,* doc. 48, 264–65.

57. Bugai, *L. Beria—I. Stalinu,* 184–85.

58. German colonists first settled the Volga region in response to Empress Catherine II issuing a manifesto on July 22, 1763, inviting Christian foreigners to settle in the Russian Empire. The document is reproduced by Auman and Chebotareva, *Istoriia rossiiskikh nemtsev,* 18–21.

59. Terry Martin, "An Affirmative Action Empire: The Soviet Union as the Highest Form of Imperialism," in *A State of Nations: Empire and Nation-Making in the Age of Lenin and Stalin,* ed. Ronald Grigor Suny and Terry Martin (Oxford: Oxford University Press, 2001), 67–90.

60. The documents are reproduced by Auman and Chebotareva, *Istoriia rossiiskikh nemtsev,* 75–76, 80–82.

61. Bugai, *Iosif Stalin,* doc. 1, 36.

62. Ingeborg Fleischhauer and Benjamin Pinkus, *The Soviet Germans: Past and Present* (London: C. Hurst, 1986), 60.

63. Schmaltz, "Reform," 104–6.

64. Gulnara Bekyrova, "Crimean Tatar National Movement in the 50s–60s: Formation, First Victories and Disappointments," *Krimskii studii,* nos. 3–4 (2002): 6–7; http://www.cidct.org.ua/en/studii/13-14.html.

65. Radio Liberty, *Sobranie dokumentov samizdata (Materialy perepechatay iz Arkhiv Samizdata),* 630, vol. 12, 2–4.

66. The letter is reproduced by I. M. Shamanov, ed., *Karachaevtsy: Vyselenie I Vozrashchenie (1943–1957): Materialy I dokumenty* (Cherkessk: PUL, 1993), 109–13.

67. Ibid., 97–103.

68. The stenograph of the meeting is reproduced in ibid., 120–26.

69. Pavel Polian, *Against Their Will: The History and Geography of Forced Migrations in the USSR* (Budapest: Central European University Press, 2004), table 11, 198.

70. Pohl, "It Cannot Be," 424–25.

Part III

Transnationalism

Many scholars over the past two decades have challenged the long-held conception of migration as a one-time event. The classical understanding of migration, in which individuals leave one country to make their home in another, sooner or later being assimilated into the host society, is not adequate to explain the complex paths that migrants take today. Over the course of their lives, migrants may live in many different countries or divide their time between two or more countries. They may maintain strong interpersonal or business ties with their places of origin, or with relatives and co-ethnics in other countries. As geographic location becomes less important for practical purposes, it may become more important for purposes of identification. Migrants may develop a complex sense of identity that encompasses more than one country, or they may develop strong emotional ties to a place where they no longer live.

All these possibilities are generally classified under the heading of transnationalism. Vertovec defines transnationalism as "a condition in which, despite great distances and notwithstanding the presence of international borders, . . . certain kinds of relationships have been globally intensified and now take place paradoxically in a planet-spanning . . . arena of activity."[1] As an analytical concept, transnationalism can describe both the process of creating and maintaining cross-border social networks[2] and the identities that link migrants to more than one nation.[3] Transnationalism is a complex concept that opens a rich field of questions for investigation. Is transnationalism a new phenomenon in the era of globalization, or an old phenomenon becoming more visible? How can transnationalism be measured? What is the role of the state in creating, controlling, and responding to transnational migration and identities?

The chapters that follow in part III cover a variety of groups that can be classified as transnational migrants. The stories of these groups highlight interesting observations on both transnational networks and transnational identities. The Mongolian-Kazakh *Oralmandar* described by Alexander Diener in chapter 9 and the German and Jewish migrants from Kazakhstan to Germany described by Ruth Mandel in chapter 10 are both examples of migrant communities where members maintain cross-border social networks and often travel beyond their host countries. Many Jewish and German *Aussiedler* in Germany have strong business and personal links not only with the places in Kazakhstan that they left behind but also with Russia and other former Soviet states. Their combination of cultural, linguistic, and legal capital makes them uniquely qualified to function across these particular states.

When the Kazakh government offered members of the Kazakh diaspora the opportunity to settle in newly independent Kazakhstan, Kazakh families and communities in Mongolia sent members to Kazakhstan to scout out the situation and determine whether or not the community would migrate. When life in Kazakhstan turned out to be less than appealing, many Kazakhs returned to Mongolia. Interestingly, as Diener notes, these transnational linkages between Kazakhstan and Mongolia are not a function of the faster and cheaper transportation and communication generally associated with globalization. Rather, for a historically nomadic people such as the Kazakhs, migration in search of the best possible living conditions, regardless of national borders, seems a perfectly natural state of affairs.

Chapter 8, Idil Izmirli's study of Crimean Tatar repatriates in Crimea, demonstrates a different type of transnational linkage. When the entire Crimean Tatar population was forced to leave Crimea and settle in Uzbekistan in 1945, the Crimean Tatars were officially barred from any travel back to their former homes. Though this was an effective means of breaking all practical linkages between the Crimean Tatars and Crimea, the psychological attachment that the Crimean Tatars felt to their homeland remained strong for more than fifty years. Izmirli demonstrates the power of this attachment with examples of Crimean Tatars who gave up homes and jobs in Uzbekistan for unemployment and uncertainty in Crimea.

A changing conception of "home" that is no longer directly tied to a specific geographical location is one of the central theories of transnationalism. According to Glick Schiller, Basch, and Szanton-Blanc, transnational migrants expand their understanding of home by maintaining "multiple relations—familial, economic, social, organizational, religious, and political that span borders."[4] The case of the Crimean Tatars demonstrates that people can remain strongly attached to a geographically defined homeland that they may have never even seen.

Further complicating the issue of multiple and transnational identities are the ways in which transnational migrants are perceived. *Ausseidler* may have multiple identities that link them to Germany, Russia, and Kazakhstan, but in all three countries they are often viewed and treated as outsiders. In spite of an official state policy that welcomed ethnic Germans "back" to Germany, the Kazakh Germans who settled in Germany tended to have more in common with each other than with native Germans, who referred to the newcomers as "Russians." Similarly, the Mongolian Kazakhs who thought of Kazakhstan as their national homeland have not integrated easily into post-Soviet Kazakh society. And the powerful attachment that the Crimean Tatar repatriates feel toward Crimea has not prevented local Russians and Ukrainians from seeing them as invaders.

The chapters that follow demonstrate that migration is neither a simple nor a one-way process. The transnational ties that link migrants with their countries of origin, places of settlement, and third countries are extremely complex and are affected by a wide range of factors—including transportation and communication technology, historical legacies, economic imperatives, family and social networks, language, and social perceptions. How these factors come together and influence the ways in which people behave is a key question in understanding migration processes.

Notes

1. Steven Vertovic, "Conceiving and Researching Transnationalism," *Ethnic and Racial Studies* 22 (1999): 447–62; the quotation is on 447.

2. Nina Glick Schiller and Georges E. Fouron, "Terrains of Blood and Nation: Haitian Transnational Social Fields," *Ethnic and Racial Studies* 22 (1999): 340–66.

3. Nina Glick Schiller, Linda Basch, and Christina Szanton-Blanc, *Towards a Transnational Perspective on Migration: Race, Class, Ethnicity and Nationalism Reconsidered* (New York: New York Academy of Sciences, 1992).

4. Ibid., 1.

8

Return to the Golden Cradle: Postreturn Dynamics and Resettlement Angst among the Crimean Tatars[1]

Idil P. Izmirli

The Crimean Tatars are not simply an ethnic group or an ethnic minority; they are an indigenous population, returning to their historical homeland.

—Lenur Arifiev, member of the Crimean Tatar Mejlis (Parliament), 1992

The demise of the Soviet Union generated both vast population movements and sporadic, often violent, ethnic conflicts among and within the fifteen newly independent states. This chapter examines the potential link between the two processes. Migration alone does not cause conflict, but it can often change the ethnic and religious balance within regions, challenging diverse groups to coexist in close proximity. The resulting interethnic dynamics can foster grievances, especially in cases of group perceptions of relative deprivation[2] or top-down structural violence.[3] In such cases, incentives for ethnopolitical action surface, and may lead to latent or manifest conflict.[4]

To capture the complexity of a postreturn dynamics, this chapter develops a detailed overview of the lives and resettlement angst of the Crimean

Tatars, who, since the demise of the Soviet Union, have been going back to their historical homeland. It utilizes an interdisciplinary approach to return migration, examining the issue from the perspective of conflict analysis. It focuses on the shifting identities, attitudes/behaviors, perceptions, and conflict strategies of the Crimean Tatars against the background of relative deprivation.

The chapter is divided into five sections. First, a summary of the current ethnopolitical dynamics in Crimea is presented to give the context. The second section highlights the history of Crimean Tatar forced migration, first in Imperial and then in Soviet Russia. The third section links the Crimean Tatar case to the literature on migration and conflict resolution. Fourth, in the chapter's main focus, I analyze the resettlement dynamics of self-selected returnees, using data including self-administered questionnaires and face-to-face interviews conducted among urban both and rural Crimean Tatars in 2003.[5] The fifth section provides conclusions and suggestions for further research on the topic.

The Current Ethnopolitical Dynamics in Post-Soviet Crimea

The Crimean Peninsula covers a territory of approximately 26,000 square kilometers, and its current population is nearly 2.5 million. The population distribution in Crimea is unique in postindependence Ukraine, because it is "the only major territorial-administrative unit of Ukraine where the ethnic Russians are the majority."[6] Although exact numbers are not known, according to recent figures, in Crimea ethnic Russians constitute 64 percent of the population; Ukrainians, 23 percent; and Crimean Tatars, 12 percent. Other ethnic groups (including Karaims, Krymchaks, Bulgarians, Germans, Koreans, Jews, and Armenians) constitute the remaining 1 percent of the population.[7]

The ethnopolitical situation in post-Soviet Crimea is complex, reflecting simmering ethnic hostilities and negative peace[8] between the three central actors: the Russians, the returning Islamic Crimean Tatars, and the Ukrainians.[9] "The image of the Crimea as a historically Russian territory is [still] deeply rooted in Russian national consciousness."[10] Although as much as 90 percent of the republic's ethnic Russian population settled in Crimea after World War II (following the deportation of the Crimean Tatars in 1944), many continue to consider Crimea part of the historical Russian *rodina* (homeland), despite its official inclusion in newly independent Ukraine. The majority of the Russophobes believe that Crimea belongs to Russia and that it should never have been given to Ukraine. These ethnic Russians tend to mistrust the Ukrainian government, and they also view Crimean Tatars as untrustworthy. The negative perception of the Crimean Tatars as the natural enemies of Russian statehood is depicted in the official versions of the Soviet history books, native folk tales, proverbs,[11] songs, and Soviet films. Accordingly, resident ethnic Russians have perceived the return of the Crimean Tatars as a threat to their existence and security.

The Crimean Tatars consider themselves as the *indigenous* people of Crimea,[12] viewing their peninsular homeland as an indivisible part of their national-territorial identity. After they were deported from Crimea en masse under Joseph Stalin's orders on May 18, 1944,[13] they were denied basic cultural rights and ethnic identity in their places of exile.[14] "Until the late 1980s, they never appeared as a recognized ethnic group in Soviet population statistics."[15] The Crimean Tatars were not the only deported group of the Stalin era, but they were one of the few who were not allowed to return to their homeland during Nikita Khrushchev's thaw.[16]

The Crimean Tatars were able to go back to Crimea only after the demise of the Soviet Union. At "home," they face dire socioeconomic conditions,[17] a lack of political representation, and ethnic discrimination. Regardless of their circumstances, they continue to remain committed to nonviolence,[18] with their leadership—that is, de facto, the Mejlis (Parliament)[19]—consistently advocating peaceful means.[20] In addition, they have kept a pro-Ukrainian stance. As the years have passed since their return, however, frustrations have increased and fragmentations have emerged. Given continuing, unaddressed grievances, a shift might be seen from orientations stressing nonviolence and seeking power-sharing agreements within the framework of the Ukrainian state to more focused approaches to ethnic secessionism. Specifically, for Crimea, such a shift might be challenging for bringing sustainable peace and security, not only in Crimea but also in Ukraine and in post-Soviet Eurasia.

Ethnogenesis and the Forced Migration History of Crimean Tatars

The current grievances of the the Tatars in Crimea are historically based. Though the interpretation of the historical record remains open for debate, the majority of Soviet scholars depict the Crimean Tatars as the direct descendants of the nomadic Mongol Golden Horde,[21] who arrived in Eurasian plains in about the thirteenth century. However, a number of diverse ethnohistorians trace the origins of Crimean Tatars to much earlier times,[22] thus providing a logical foundation for the Crimean Tatars' claim that they are the "indigenous people" (*korennoi narod*) of the Crimean Peninsula, along with the Karaims[23] and the Krymchaks.[24] Crimean Tatar literature (including poetry) from the ninth and tenth centuries is not written in Mongol but in Crimean Tatar,[25] further supporting this claim. Currently, the most widely accepted version of Crimean Tatar history views them as the end result of intermixing of the native peoples of the peninsula (Tavris, Scythians, Sarmatians, Goths) with the Turkic tribes (Khazars, Pechenegs, Kipchacks) and the Mongols.[26]

The Crimean Tatars' Khanate ruled Crimea for three centuries (1440–1783) until its annexation to the Russian Empire by Catherine II. Thereafter, several waves of mass expulsions changed the Crimean Peninsula's ethnodemographic structures significantly. The first to be deported from the peninsula were the Nogais in 1784.[27] Later, in 1778, 30,000 Crimean Tatars were expelled from Crimea, and some 100,000 were forced to flee to avoid arrests between 1783 and 1791. After the Crimean War (1853–56), in which the Crimean Tatars were accused of collaboration with the Ottoman Turks, 100,000 to 150,000 more Tatars were exiled from the peninsula. Between 1860 and 1862, 192,360 Tatars were forced to leave Crimea and migrate to the Ottoman Empire.[28] Due to the ongoing colonization and resettlement policies of Imperial Russia, the relative size of the Crimean Tatar population sharply decreased as the "imported" Slavic immigration started to increase on the peninsula.[29] Forced migration continued between 1891 and 1902;[30] according to an 1897 census, the Tatar presence in Crimea "declined by at least one-half, and its percentage of the total population fell to 35.1 percent."[31]

The disintegration of the Russian Empire in 1917 led to a brief period of Crimean semi-independence on the peninsula.[32] In November 1917, the first Crimean Tatar Qurultai (Crimean Tatar National Congress) was convened, adopting the first Crimean Constitution. On October 18, 1921, the Nar Komnats[33] of the Russian Soviet Federated Socialist Republic granted the Crimea territorial autonomy within the Russian Federation. Thereafter, this region became the Crimean Autonomous Soviet Socialist Republic (ASSR).[34] The Crimean Tatars were given de facto recognition as the

Crimean ASSR's *indigenous* nationality. During this era, they experienced a cultural revival, with Crimean Tatar and Russian becoming joint official languages. This short-lived revival ended with the rise of Stalin and imposition of forced collectivization, artificially created famines, and the infamous deportations of targeted Soviet nationalities.[35]

On May 18, 1944, Stalin issued GKO (State Defense Committee) decree 5859ss, ordering the mass expulsion of the Crimean Tatars from the Crimean territory to special settlement camps established throughout the Soviet Union.[36] A well-organized deportation of the Crimean Tatars began, supervised by 5,000 armed agents of the Soviet state security services, 20,000 Interior Ministry troops, and thousands of regular army soldiers.[37] Some reports estimated that 86.1 percent of the deportees consisted of the elderly, invalids, women, and children,[38] because most of the able-bodied Crimean Tatar men were in the Red Army fighting the Nazis at the front.[39] Many deportees died due to poor sanitary conditions and a lack of food and water.

On August 14, 1944, the GKO authorized the settlement of 51,000 people, mostly ethnic Russians, in 17,000 emptied collective farms (*kolkhozes*) to replace the deported Crimean Tatars.[40] Imported Russian and Ukrainian settlers (many forcefully settled on the Crimean Peninsula) became Crimean residents, filling the vacuum left by the deported Tatars. The Crimean ASSR was officially abolished with a decree published on June 30, 1945, and it became an oblast within the Russian Soviet Federated Socialist Republic.[41] Tatar monuments, mosques, cemeteries, and cultural facilities were all destroyed. The survivors of the 1944 mass deportations remained confined to highly regimented and strict special settlement camps (*spetsposolonets*) in their various places of exile, unable to visit their relatives or friends—even in case of emergency—without permission from the camp's commander.[42]

During Khrushchev's de-Stalinization campaign, Crimea was the transferred to the Ukrainian SSR by a decree issued on February 19, 1954, by the Presidium of the Supreme Soviet of the USSR. Crimea was a "special gift" to commemorate the three-hundredth anniversary of Ukrainian-Russian fraternal unity on the anniversary of the [January] 1654 Treaty of Pereiaslav, an affirmation of East Slavic union (against the Tatars and Lithuanian/Polish rule) between Kyiv and Moscow.[43]

In a special decree issued on April 28, 1956, numerous deported peoples were finally released from the settlement camps. By the same decree, most of the exiled ethnic groups were granted permission to return to their homelands—with the exception of the Volga Germans, the Meskhetian (Ahiska)

Turks, and the Crimean Tatars.[44] This decree specifically stated that "Crimean Tatar properties confiscated at the time of deportation would not be returned, and [they] did not have the right to return to Crimea."[45]

Despite its limitations, this decree was an important turning point for the Crimean Tatars. Once out of the camps, they established the Crimean Tatar National Movement, which called attention to their continued demands for return through demonstrations, hunger strikes, and organized letter-writing campaigns. They maintained adherence to nonviolent principles, and they were the first ethnic group to stage a sit-in in Moscow's Red Square, demanding justice and repatriation.[46] Despite their continuous attempts, they were not able to return to Crimea until after the dissolution of the Soviet Union. Analyzing how the Crimean Tatars maintained a sense of home during more than a generation of exile highlights the persistence of memory and the limitation of assimilationist approaches in understanding the integration of forced migration flows.

A Review of Some Useful Concepts and Theories

Economists and demographers explain migration through two sets of operational forces: push factors and pull factors.[47] Sociologists and anthropologists study the socioeconomic and political consequences of migrants' presence in host societies, examining integration processes. Earlier sociologists viewed integration as "assimilation" and argued that newcomers would eventually lose their ethnic and cultural distinctiveness vis-à-vis the destination culture (the melting pot phenomenon).[48] The persistence of ethnic identity among second- and third-generation migrants led to increasing attention to the interaction between the migrants and their host society—instead of looking at the migrants as "absorbent sponges."[49]

Within multiethnic societies, conflict and competition over scarce resources can occur along ethnic lines. When members of dominant groups receive unequal access to the society's valued resources—such as land, housing, employment, participatory power, wealth, and prestige—the marginalization of other groups becomes solidified. This can be categorized as the hidden tools of *structural violence.* Structural violence goes hand in hand with *cultural violence.*[50] Through it, newcomers could be denied education in their own native tongue, the chance to practice their own religion, and permission to celebrate their own (religious or national) holidays. These differential treatments and unilateral top-down political policies can create bottom-up reactions that often pave the way for grievances and conflict. As Shanta Hennnayake suggests, conflict spirals often result from state-sponsored resolution strategies, and subsequently shift toward ethnonationalism, because the strategies are perceived by the minority group(s) as tools of the dominant status quo that were formulated by the single "core" group.[51]

The Theory of Relative Deprivation provides insight into the social psychological linkages between feelings of deprivation and grievance formation relative to other individuals or groups.[52] Ted Gurr highlights the importance of expectations in the perception of inequity and characterizes the gap between "is" and "ought," defining relative deprivation as the balance between value expectation and value capabilities.[53] Value expectations (anticipated reality) are the resources to which one feels entitled, and value capabilities (manifest reality) are the resources one feels the desire to acquire and keep.[54] This theory suggests that when groups (or individuals) perceive they are getting less than that to which they feel entitled—that is, if there is a gap between personal expectations and attainment—this perception of inequity produces discomfort and distress, which can motivate protest and rebellion.[55] Hence, relative deprivation is determined both by *perceptions* of inequality (the cognitive element), the state of mind, and also by *feelings* of discontent (the affective element).[56]

Social comparison is fundamental to the relative deprivation approach, linking relative deprivation and approaches to identity, as in Social Identity Theory, which suggests that "social identity is a part of an individual's self-concept which derives from his knowledge of his membership in a social group (or groups) together with the value (evaluative) and emotional significance attached to that membership."[57] Therefore, these "identities are maintained and sustained primarily through social comparisons between in-groups and comparable out-groups."[58] The favorable social comparisons between in-groups and out-groups demonstrate "positive in-group distinctiveness,"[59] whereby individuals are able to achieve positive social identity, which may in turn contribute to positive self-esteem and increased salience of identity. The resulting distinctions support solidarity (cohesion) and out-group antagonism, spurring social protest and social change in reference to "others."[60]

On the basis of these linking notions, this chapter utilizes these theories to analyze and understand the persistence of Crimean Tatar identity and the challenges posed in balancing ideas of separation and autonomy,[61] and of unification and integration,[62] in the multiethnic, multireligious Crimea to which many Crimean Tatars have returned.

The Crimean Tatars in Crimea, 1991 to the Present

The Crimean Tatars identify with Crimea historically, geographically (as their namesake region), and emotionally, stating that they have no homeland other than Crimea, although the majority of were born in exile. This remarkable attachment to their homeland is visible through their personal narratives. A quotation from one returnee captures this strong attachment to the Crimean territory:

> Crimea has a special soil that is powered by a special sunlight. After you eat an apricot, if you throw its seed to the ground by mistake, you will see an apricot tree growing from that seed within the next year. Nowhere in the world is there such land, other than in our homeland Crimea.

Although there is a collective connection to the homeland, the experiences of Crimean Tatar returnees differ. The very first waves of returnees who arrived in Crimea before November 13, 1991, were able to obtain citizenship.[63] When the new Ukrainian Citizenship Law of 1991 was enforced (with the later addition of the 1997 amendment), it granted citizenship for only those who were born or permanently resided on the Ukrainian territory. As a result, until the adoption of the new Ukrainian Citizenship Law in 2001, the majority of the returnees remained as noncitizens, ineligible for employment, social services, and the Ukrainian internal residency permits (*propiska*) needed for housing and basic services, such as electricitiy, gas, and sewage.[64] Even after 2001, citizenship problems continued. Because dual citizenship was not allowed in Ukraine, the returnees had to first renounce their exile citizenship, a lengthy and costly process, and then apply for Ukrainian citizenship.

Today there are approximately 300,000 Crimean Tatars in Crimea, while approximately 150,000 remain in Uzbekistan and in other republics of the former Soviet Union. The exact number of Crimean Tatars in Crimea is difficult to pinpoint, because censuses do not include those people without passports, that is, the unregistered returnees. Currently, the majority of Crimean Tatars are either unemployed or underemployed. The underemployed are unable to find work in their professional specialty and are forced to work in secondary labor markets doing menial jobs, even if they have a high level of education. Since their return to Crimea, they have not been rehabilitated or financially compensated for the trauma they endured and the property they lost during the deportation.

Crimean Tatar returnees identify their major grievances as follows:

- Land and housing deficiencies.
- Unemployment based on ethnic lines.
- A lack of native language schools.
- Political exclusion (the problem of quotas in the Parliament).
- False labeling based on religion.
- The desire for autonomy within the Ukrainian state and the issue of indigenousness.
- Recent constitutional changes that target Crimean Tatars.
- Ethnic clashes with groups like the Cossacks[65] and the skinheads.[66]
- Unresolved sporadic violence against Crimean Tatars.[67]

Research Results on the Resettlement Dynamics of Self-Selected Returnees

For the in-depth analysis of the postreturn dynamics of the Crimean Tatars, multimethod research was conducted in 2003 among Crimean Tatars age eighteen to eighty years living in Crimea and possessing Ukrainian citizenship.[68] The survey respondents were identified through twenty gatekeepers in thirteen cities, nineteen microdistricts (these *mikroraioni* are located on the outskirts of the cities), and seven villages across Crimea. Interviews were conducted by the researcher in Russian and in Crimean Tatar, in seven cities, five microdistricts, and two villages. Due to the lack of infrastructure in Crimea—such as the absence of telephone lines in rural as well as in certain urban areas where Crimean Tatars live in compact settlements—picking names from a telephone book for random sampling is impossible. Moreover, in the majority of the microdistricts, there are no paved roads and no street signs. In some rural as well as urban areas, Crimean Tatars' houses are scattered between those of Russians and Ukrainians; thus, it becomes impossible to utilize any kind of systematic or random sampling strategy. Accordingly, snowball sampling was utilized for the survey design.

A total of 484 questionnaires were completed, supplemented by 62 face-to-face interviews. Respondents consisted of 225 males (46.5 percent) and 259 females (53.5 percent); 31.4 percent of the survey participants were between the ages of eighteen and twenty-nine, 28.3 percent were between the ages of thirty and forty-four, 26.7 percent were between the ages of forty-five and fifty-nine, and the remaining 13.6 percent were sixty or older.

Migration and Identity

The majority (77.2 percent) of the survey respondents were born in Uzbekistan.[69] A total of 13.6 percent said they were born in Crimea, constituting the oldest age group category (sixty years or older). A total of 3.7 percent of the remaining respondents were born in Tajikistan, 1.0 percent were born in the Marii Soviet Socialist Republic (Mariiskii SSR), 1.0 percent were born in Kazakhstan, and 3.5 percent were born in other regions of the USSR. The majority of the respondents (66.9 percent) returned to Crimea between 1989 and 1994,[70] with the most important reason for repatriation to Crimea being the "desire to return to the homeland" (92.9 percent). The importance of Crimea and Crimean Tatar identity was also reflected in participant observation and survey results highlighting distinctively high rates of endogamous marriages among Crimean Tatars.[71] Of the 337 married or engaged respondents to the survey questionnaire, 95 percent indicated that their spouse or fiancé was a Crimean Tatar.

Postrepatriation Locales: Urban versus Rural Dichotomy

During postdeportation resettlement, the Crimean Tatars were concentrated in urban locations. In the 1980s, in Central Asia, 69 to 80 percent of the Crimean Tatars lived in urban areas.[72] In Uzbekistan, 75 percent of the Crimean Tatars lived in cities.[73] Typically, in urban areas, their residences had electricity, gas, water service, a telephone, connection to a sewage system, and other amenities.[74] Upon returning to Crimea, this residential portrait changed drastically. In 2002, 192,000 (73 percent) of the returnees lived in rural areas.[75] Survey results supported the ruralization trend. Though 81.2 percent of the survey respondents indicated that their pre-Crimea locale was a city, only 56.2 percent had lived in an urban location in Crimea. In exile, only 7 percent had lived in villages, and 11 percent indicated that they had lived in other locations, such as a collective farm (again, *kolkhoz*) or a structured city-type village (*poselok gorodskogo typa,* PGT).[76] In Crimea, conversely, 23.3 percent lived in villages and 20.5 percent lived in PGTs. Currently, in Crimea, there are approximately three hundred newly established compact settlements. A total of 89 percent of the houses in these settlements now have electricity. However, only 58 percent of the houses have water, no more than 5 percent have natural gas (for heating and cooking), and none are connected to a sewage system.[77]

There are several reasons behind the ruralization of Crimean Tatars in Crimea. When they first returned to Crimea, the Tatars were only allowed to settle in government-designated areas, compact settlements, and PGTs. Difficulties with Ukrainian citizenship created obstacles for the returnees in both housing and employment. Lacking the financial resources to overcome these obstacles, even the well-educated former urbanites had to move into rural areas, where housing costs are much lower. In addition, village houses are more productive, because they have some land that provides an area for planting produce (fruits and vegetables) for home consumption, for sale, or for both.

Because of forced ruralization, land ownership, especially in agricultural areas, became an important issue for the Crimean Tatars. According to a report in 1999, a series of presidential decrees were able to break up the collective agricultural farm system (again, *kolkhozes*) and bring in privatization laws, which allowed land from the farms to be distributed among all former *kolkhoz* members.[78] Because the Crimean Tatars did not live in Crimea before the demise of the Soviet Union, they were not able to receive land under the new law. Consequently, while Russian and Ukrainian farmers received between 5 and 7 acres each, the vast majority of the Crimean Tatars were denied land shares.

The shortage of spare land is particularly grave in some regions. In 2000 alone, the representative of the president of Ukraine in Crimea has received 46,603 appeals from returnees with the request for a share of land.[79] The majority of these appeals were rejected. Around the big cities, particularly in Simferopol, Crimea's capital, an average plot of reserve land that a Crimean Tatar may receive is about 0.04 hectare (0.09 acre). According to Mustafa Cemilev, head of the Crimean Tatar Mejlis, in most cases, the reserved plots allocated to the Crimean Tatars are inferior lands that cannot be used for planting crops or feeding animals. Around the southern coast of Crimea, the situation is especially grim. The Crimean Tatars are not allowed to apply for land titles, reside, buy, or self-seize land in the coastal areas, whereas Russian and Ukrainian businesspeople, foreign enterprises, and corporations can freely buy and own land and build hotels and casinos.[80]

Housing Deficiencies

Approximately 128,298 returnees have no permanent housing of their own in Crimea. More than 15,000 returnee families are on the waiting list for state-sponsored housing projects.[81] About 25,000 Crimean Tatars live in rented apartments with relatives or in dormitories resembling Soviet communal apartments, where they must share bath facilities and are not allowed to cook. Moreover, 50 percent of the families that have land plots for housing cannot finish building their houses because of financial problems,[82] and they have to live in partially built, unfinished houses.[83] About 15 percent of the land plots on the outskirts of the cities are filled with these unfinished structures constructed of beige limestone blocks with no roofs or windows, making them look like ancient ruins. Some of these houses have only one complete room for the whole family, and they lack basic necessities such as heat, water, and electricity. The survey results indicate that 14 percent of urban respondents and 18 percent of rural respondents live in such unfinished houses.

Education

While they were exiled in Central Asia and the Urals, the Crimean Tatars faced significant ethnic discrimination in the sphere of education. The researchers Mukomel and Pain estimated higher education rates by ethnicity within Uzbekistan as follows: Russians, 153 per 1,000; Uzbeks, 143 per 1,000; and Crimean Tatars, 109 per 1,000.[84] These numbers, based on Soviet data, are likely to underestimate the actual educational disadvantage faced by the Crimean Tatars in exile. After their 1944 deportation, the term "Crimean Tatar" was taken out of the Russo-Soviet lexicon, and all the Crimean Tatar toponyms (i.e., the names of the cities, towns, villages, and mountains) in Crimea were changed into Russian on all the geographical maps.[85] Throughout the Stalin era, no one could even acknowledge that such a nationality group as the Crimean Tatars existed among the Soviet nationalities. As a result, in Soviet censuses (in 1959, 1970, and 1979), many could not identify themselves[86] as Crimean Tatars on the Soviet census nationalities lists. In 1989, the secret ban on the ethnonym "Crimean Tatar" was lifted.

Although there are still no precise statistics about the education rates of the Crimean Tatars in Central Asia and the Urals, according to Brian Williams, the Crimean Tatars excelled in education as a means for overcoming their exile, stating: "They had a culture, which cherished education and in socioeconomic and educational terms surpassed their Uzbek neighbors."[87] According to Fevzi Yakubov, 75 percent of the Crimean Tatars who currently live in Crimea have completed higher education (university and college degrees), an estimate supported by the Maarifci (Association of Crimean Tatar Educators) report on language and education conducted in the Krasnogvardeiskoi Raion (district) of Crimea.[88] This 1992 sociological survey indicates that 39 percent of the Crimean Tatars living in that district had a university education, and 43 percent had a college[89] education.[90] The results of a study by the Russian Academy of Sciences Oriental Institute that was conducted in Crimea from 1994 through 1996 point out that "professional and educational levels of the repatriates [are] fairly high, but the majority of the university-educated returnees cannot find a job [in Crimea] in their own specialty."[91]

According to my survey in 2003, 58.9 percent of the respondents had university degrees, 1.2 percent had postuniversity degrees (candidate of science), and 21.7 percent possessed technical or arts college degrees (a total of 81.8 percent with higher education). A total of 5.8 percent of the respondents also indicated that they were currently university students during the time of the study. The remaining 9.5 percent of the respondents said they had completed high school, 2.3 percent had completed middle school, and only a few of advanced age reported no education at all.

Employment and Unemployment

In 2000, a report by Lord Ponsonby indicated that in Crimea, 60 percent of the Crimean Tatars were unemployed.[92] The results from a 2000 Gallup poll also revealed that only 29.5 percent of the Crimean Tatars were employed and 70.5 percent were unemployed.[93] According to the Crimean Tatar National Mejlis,[94] currently 55 percent of the educated Crimean Tatars in Crimea work in agriculture, 20 percent in construction, and 25 percent in either service industries, such as restaurants or gas stations, or in other types of small businesses.

In terms of government employment, there are indications of overt discrimination against the Crimean Tatars. The percentage of Crimean Tatars working in government offices is three times lower than the population as a whole. There are no Crimean Tatars employed in the customs or security services of Ukraine.[95] Only 1.5 percent of the staff workers on the Republican Committee for Nationalities and Deported Citizens of the Autonomous Republic of Crimea are Crimean Tatars.[96] Similarly, only 1.3 percent of the workers in the Ministry of Internal Affairs are Crimean Tatars. In the health care industry in Crimea, Crimean Tatars make up only 6 percent of the workforce. Among the medical doctors, only 3.5 percent are Crimean Tatars. Moreover, only 18 percent of the Crimean Tatar professors and doctors of sciences have jobs that fit their education.[97]

Among the survey respondents, 63.3 percent of the returnees did not have employment in Crimea. Among those employed, only 19 percent worked in a profession fitting their education. Moreover, approximately

4 percent indicated that they were not registered in Crimea and lacked identity cards and registration (*propiska*). Without documents, they are not eligible for employment, housing, or benefits from health services.

Because the majority of the returnees cannot find jobs in their own specialty, most of them work as city bazaar vendors, get temporary jobs in construction, or become beach vendors during the summer months. With its sandy beaches, reasonable prices, and the "healing" mud locations in the Evpatoria (Kezlev)-Sakhi area, Crimea is very popular for tourists from other parts of the former USSR. Summer tourism provides job opportunities for the returnees, who can earn money either by selling products (from produce to baked food and even alcohol) or by providing services—such as a room in their house, or their entire house while they live with relatives—to the vacationers. However, these jobs are not permanent and do not provide families with steady incomes. Participant observation and interviews reveal that due to unemployment, many Crimean Tatar families live solely on the retirement or disability pension of an elder member of their family, which on average equates to about $15 per month.

Linguistic Angst and the Lack of Native Language Schools

Although 67 percent of Ukrainian citizens indicated that their native tongue is Ukrainian, in Crimea, where Russians constitute 64 percent of the population, Russian is the most common language.[98] In Crimea, the Russian and Ukrainian languages are being used interchangeably in the public spheres,[99] while the Crimean Tatar language is not legally recognized as one of the "official" languages of Crimea.

The Crimean Tatars grew up within the Soviet education system and are highly proficient in Russian. While living in Central Asia, their proficiency in Russian, knowledge of the titular languages of their region, and high levels of education clearly separated them from the natives and provided a certain status and prestige.[100] However, in exile they did not have access to their native language and literary works (or later, visual media production), outside their own homes. The native language abilities of the returnees are limited. To bridge this gap, it is essential for them to have their own native language schools in Crimea, so that their children may grow up learning their native tongue.

In Crimea, the first "four-class" school was opened in 1990, and the first Crimean Tatar elementary school was opened in 1993. Currently, there are only fourteen native language schools in Crimea conducting classes in Crimean Tatar. Yet subjects such as mathematics and natural and social sciences are taught in Russian, due to the lack of books in Crimean Tatar. Similarly, Maarifci reports that of 46,968 Crimean Tatar school-age students, only 5,872 (12.5 percent) can attend schools where Crimean Tatar is a language of instruction.[101] Today, the dominant language among the Crimean Tatars in Crimea is Russian. Although the older Crimean Tatars have tried to preserve their linguistic heritage, their native language[102] underwent severe atrophy (a progressive decline)[103] during the exile years. In the words of Mica Hall, this was "partly the product of Soviet language policy, which paid lip service to preserving the languages of the peoples of the USSR, but in practice did little or nothing to preserve them."[104] As a result, today the spoken Crimean Tatar language among the returnees is a highly Russified hybrid, where they switch back and forth between Russian and Crimean Tatar.

Presently, in Crimea, almost all the newspapers and journals are published in Russian, with a few in Ukrainian. There are seven weekly Crimean Tatar newspapers in Crimea,[105] and all but two—*Yani Dunya* and *Qirim,* in Crimean Tatar—are in Russian.[106] On Crimean radio and television, all the major news and entertainment programs are in Russian and/or Ukrainian. Radio Meydan, which was established in 2006, is the only radio station that broadcasts in Crimean Tatar, in addition to Russian and Ukrainian. Although this is a major step forward, this radio station can only be listened in Simferopol, due to infrastructure problems. Of the ten Crimean television channels,[107] only one, GTRK Krim (Channel 1), has a slot of an hour and forty-five minutes each Wednesday evening in Crimean Tatar, and ten-minute daily evening news show that started to broadcast in 2006.

When asked about the language issue, only 4.8 percent of the respondents said that they believed Crimean Tatars spoke their native language perfectly. A total of 41.5 percent suggested that Crimean Tatars spoke their language adequately, and 53.3 percent claimed that Crimean Tatars spoke their native language "badly." Yet only 0.4 percent suggested that they were working hard to learn their language. Participant observation confirmed the lack of ability to speak and write in Crimean Tatar, creating anxiety among the returnees, who are afraid of linguistic and subsequent cultural assimilation into the Russian majority living in Crimea. During interviews, the majority of the repatriates cited the importance of native language proficiency for the preservation and continuity of their culture and nationhood.[108] They also often expressed embarrassment with regard to their linguistic "disability," and they apologized when they admitted that they speak very little (or no) Crimean Tatar.

Political Exclusions

Mass demonstrations before the 1994 elections led to fourteen Crimean Tatar seats being established in the Crimean Parliament. However, before the March 1998 elections, the Ukrainian Verhovna Rada (Upper Parliament) adopted a new Constitution, stipulating that the Crimean Parliament, unlike the Parliament of Ukraine, would be elected by a pure majority.[109] This decision shattered the possibility of electing Crimean Tatar delegates to the Crimean Parliament, because they did not constitute a majority in any voting district.[110] Moreover, during the March 29, 1998, elections, 90,000 of the repatriates were denied the right to vote, based on their status as noncitizens.[111] Crimean Tatars lost all their 14 seats in the Crimean parliament but did gain 2 seats[112] in the Ukrainian Verkhovna Rada, which consists of 450 deputies. Although symbolically important, 2 among 450 were insignificant, in terms of having an impact on decisionmaking processes.[113]

During the 2002 parliamentary elections, there was some progress for the Crimean Tatars at the local elections level, when seven of their Crimean Tatar candidates were elected to the Upper Parliament of the Autonomous Republic of Crimea,[114] which consists of 100 members.[115] They still lack a voice in decisionmaking processes, because within the Presidium[116] of the Parliament, there is only one Crimean Tatar deputy.[117] Moreover, neither the Crimean Parliament nor the Ukrainian government officially recognizes the Crimean Tatar National Mejlis, claiming that the Crimean Tatars are unconstitutionally attempting to create "parallel structures of power" in both Crimea and Ukraine. The Crimean Tatar leadership denies this accusation. According to Chubarov, "The Mejlis only desires to be included within the government as a consultative body so that [it] could consult on a limited range of policy issues of direct relevance to the Crimean Tatars."[118] The surveyed returnees were hopeful in terms of the Mejlis's recognition within the near future. A total of 51 percent of the participants stated that they believe the Mejlis is going to be recognized by the Ukrainian state within the next five years. Though 38 percent said this was not going to happen, the remaining 11 percent replied with an "I don't know." They were less hopeful about the power-sharing mechanisms. Questionnaires as well as interviews revealed that none of the respondents could foresee a power-sharing system within the next five years.

The Social Construction of the "Other" Based on Religion

One important issue that generates grievances among the returnees is the "negative labeling" by the Russophones and others in Crimea centering on on their Islamic faith. The vast majority of the Crimean Tatars are Sunni Muslims; however, they are also the product of the Soviet system, which forbade all religious practices. Accordingly, the precise meaning of this label is less than clear. Those who have returned to Crimea perceive Islam as a part of their ethnonational identity and are trying to learn and practice their faith. They organize prayer services to commemorate the dead or to celebrate religious holidays. There are no indications of religious radicals or extremists among Crimean Tatars; in fact, the tenets of their faith support just the opposite type of attitudes and behavior.[119]

When questioned on the topic, the majority of the survey participants (87.2 percent) indicated that they were somewhat religious, and only 9.9 percent specified themselves as very religious. Atheists and others were 1.0 percent each, and agnostics were only 0.6 percent of the total population. The survey questionnaires also revealed that 48.1 percent of the Crimean Tatars have never visited a mosque, 38.6 percent visit only sometimes, and only 9.5 percent of the repatriates visit the mosque regularly (once a week). A total of 3.7 percent indicated that they go to a mosque only during religious holidays and funerals.[120] The survey results also indicate a clear division between religious orientation and politics among respondents. The vast majority (82 percent) of the Crimean Tatars surveyed view personal religious faith and politics as two different spheres.

The Crimean Tatar leadership welcomes Turkish-style secular Islam,[121] vehemently opposing and combating the establishment of certain sects—such as Wahabis, Hizb-ut Tahrir, Hambali, and Habashi—in Crimea. Only a small minority of Crimean Tatars who are losing hope in resolving their issues through their de facto Mejlis as well as the Ukrainian state are drawn to these extremist groups, which see an opportunity to expand among such frustrated returnees. The majority of the Crimean Tatars, conversely, by no means support political Islam as a leadership style, for it suggests to them a world caliphate under Islamic (and not national-territorial) leadership. The interviews revealed that this idea was not feasible to the majority of the returnees, because for them the most salient identity is their Crimean Tatar ethnonational identity, which they are not ready to sacrifice for any cause. Regardless, certain anti-Tatar propagandists still employ the Islamic orientation of the returnees for their own agenda. For example, Leonid Grach, a member of the Crimean Parliament, continuously accuses the Crimean Tatars of being political Islamists, labeling them as friendly to Chechens.[122]

Buying into these rumors, on September 7, 2004, the former Ukrainian president, Leonid Kuchma, ordered his law enforcement agencies to investigate the recent appearance of radical and extremist Islamic organizations in Crimea. He based his accusations on an alleged conversation with Mustafa Cemilev, the chair of the Mejlis. Cemilev denied Kuchma's allegations and claimed that he had never discussed this issue with Kuchma and that Kuchma was misinformed.[123] A week later, on September 15, 2004, a memorial stone dedicated to the victims of Crimean Tatar deportation was vandalized and broken into two pieces.[124] Later, a statue of a Crimean Tatar educator in Salgirka Park was also vandalized.

The Questions of Independence and Indigenousness

In spite of difficulties related to economic integration, education, language, and religion, the majority of the returnees opt for Crimean Tatar political and cultural autonomy within the framework of a Ukrainian state. The survey results indicate that 54.3 percent of the returnees would like to achieve both political and cultural autonomy for the betterment of their current situation in Crimea. Though 19.2 percent said political autonomy would be sufficient, only 9.3 percent of the respondents asserted that cultural autonomy would be adequate for them. The remaining 17.1 percent marked "other," and specified "other" as "national-territorial" autonomy.

The autonomy question is very important for the Crimean Tatars returnees and is closely linked to the question of indigenousness.[125] They believe that although they are a "numerical" minority on the Crimean Peninsula, they are nevertheless its indigenous people. Crimea has remained their unique homeland. They also maintain that they are unique among the other ethnic groups of Crimea. One interviewee summarized this idea as follows:

> The other ethnic groups that reside in Crimea today are in fact not the descendants of the deportees of the Stalin era but simply migrants who arrived in Crimea from different parts of the former Soviet Union, fleeing a war or some other catastrophic event.[126] None of them had a three-hundred-year Khanate that ruled Crimea or an autonomous republic that recognized them as the indigenous people of Crimea. We belong here, we are the indigenous people of Crimea, and as our name suggests, we are the *Crimean* Tatars.

Another interviewee added:

> As Crimean Tatar people, first we need to be recognized as the indigenous population of Crimea. Second, we need to have our own autonomy

> with its own laws, Constitution, and security system for our [own] people. Under this autonomy, there needs to be a total cultural revival of Crimean Tatar nation. At the same time, there should be established equal rights for all the other ethnic groups on the peninsula, where they can enjoy freedom of religion and freedom of expression within Crimean Tatar autonomy.

The problem with the indigenousness issue is rooted in the Ukrainian Constitution. Although it recognizes the *difference* between indigenous peoples and national minorities, it does not specify the criteria for the differences between them. Article 11 states that the Ukrainian state should facilitate the growth and the development of the ethnic, cultural, linguistic, and religious aspects of all the indigenous peoples and national minorities of Ukraine.[127] Article 92 states that the rights of the indigenous peoples and national minorities are to be determined by Ukrainian law.[128] Finally, article 119 states that the local state administrators should support certain programs on the national-cultural development of indigenous peoples and national minorities in their areas of compact settlements.[129] Though the term "indigenous" appears, it is not explicitly defined. Each of the three articles is vague, and this ambiguity creates problems in their application.

Recent Constitutional Changes and Their Implications

Even years after forced deportation, the Crimean Tatars returned to their ancestral homeland to have "a home in [their] homeland."[130] Return was not easy, because many came back to find their ancestral land occupied by others.[131] Although the returnees continuously appealed for restitution and possible compensation for their lost property and rights, they were refused land, while it was being allocated to others, as a result of privatization laws.[132] Consequently, the returnees launched a unique protest action for land ownership: the collective self-seizing (*sama-zaxvat*) movement.

The self-seizing movement represents a superb nonviolent collective strategy, in which pockets of returnees self-seize different pieces of land on the outskirts of cities by squatting on them for months or even years, until they are finally allowed to live there legally by the authorities. Interviews revealed that during the self-seizing movement, tent cities were built on the seized lands, and men, women, and even adult children shared the tasks and implemented a division of labor to achieve their common goal.

Today, many families in Crimea have houses on these self-seized lands with their unique individual stories:

> After living in a tent on our self-seized land for a long winter, finally we were able to build the framework of our house and put a roof on top of it. During the first night we were sleeping under that roof, winds started to blow and before we knew it, our roof collapsed. The rain was so heavy that we could not fight it off. The roof totally collapsed. Since we have used all our money for the house, we were penniless and we did not have anyplace to go. We built our tent in the yard of our roofless house and lived there for a long time in humidity, rain water, and cold. My husband got sick with kidney problems, and now he is an invalid. We got the house finished in the end, but my husband's health is gone. Now we live on his [disability] pension. He is an engineer and he just turned forty-seven. It is very hard for him to live like this, but we are grateful. We are finally in our home in our homeland.

Between 1990 and 1995, in the southern regions of Crimea, the returnees squatted on 1,000 land plots, with local authorities only allowing 270 of them (from the reserve) to be officially allocated. A total of 147 of the 270 distributed lands were unlivable, located on hillsides and prone to frequent mudslides.[133] The remaining 123 plots were also on a hillside location called Derekoy, where there were no electric cables, gas pipes, or sewage lines.[134] Land remained a constant grievance, for a new change in the criminal code of Ukraine had created even more anxiety among the returnees. The Soviet version of the Criminal Code of Ukraine, adopted in 1961, did not include strong penalties against self-seizing squatters, because during that time there were no self-seizers. This situation changed when the head of the Crimean Parliament, Boris Deych, appealed to the president of Ukraine in November 2003 to implement a new version of the Criminal Code of Ukraine, retroactively effective as of September 2001. The new code detailed punishments—including fines, two years of forced work, and imprisonment—for squatting on land in Crimea. Moreover, special amendments to the Ukrainian Law on Militia authorized the use of dogs, chemicals, and special arms for the purpose of "preventing" or "liquidating" mass squatting.[135]

In response, the Crimean Tatar Mejlis banned land squatting on land plots and other independent protest actions, to avoid confrontations with the state. Regardless, pockets of returnees, disillusioned with the Ukrainian state and their own leadership, renamed their action from self-seizing (again, *sama-zahvat*) to "field protests" (*polyana protesta*) and continued to squat, especially along the southern coast, where the Crimean Tatars are not allowed to own or buy land.[136] Because no other ethnic group in Ukraine utilized squatting tactics as nonviolent means for political protests, the implementation of the antisquatting laws specifically targeted the Crimean Tatars, as was seen when the militia implemented the law against the self-seizers in Simeiz from March 5 to 7, 2004.

Ethnic Clashes and Conflictual Events

At the beginning of 2004, land distribution issues in coastal Crimea (including the cities of Yalta, Simeiz, Partenit, and Alushta) created major grievances among the returnees, particularly when the local authorities did not deliver the lands previously promised. Consequently, groups of Crimean Tatars occupied the lands, including the area around Aqua Park,[137] which had been sold illegally to Nikolai Leontievich Yanaki,[138] a member of the Crimean Parliament and the son-in-law of the former chair of the Crimean Parliament, Leonid Grach.[139] The Simeiz (greater Yalta) conflict escalated when Yanaki mustered the so-called Crimean Cossacks,[140] a group of mercenaries, to guard his property against the Crimean Tatar squatters near Aqua Park.[141] When the mercenary Cossacks arrived in their full uniforms, they marched through the Crimean Tatar squatter camps displaying their bullwhips and waving their Cossack flags. Thereafter, they started to build a fence around Aqua Park to keep the self-seizers out of the area. The Crimean Tatars continued patiently squatting on the lands. But when the Cossacks began to rally, shouting slogans against the returnees, some of the field protestors attacked the fence and started dismantling it. Shortly afterward, the Cossacks left, but they returned the next day with the special militia Berkut (Black Hawk).[142] The Tatar camp was surrounded, leaving the returnees to watch the progress of events without interfering. The Cossacks first attacked and demolished the Crimean Tatars' temporary houses in the camp area and then rebuilt the fence around Aqua Park.[143] After this event, the leaders of the squatters were thrown in jail and fined for their alleged "criminal" activity, but the Cossacks faced no punishment.

A few weeks after the Simeiz incident, on March 23, 2004, a group of skinheads attacked and stabbed a twenty-year-old Crimean Tatar at the Cotton Bar on Pushkin Street in Simferopol. This confrontation led to further clashes between the Crimean Tatar and Slavic youth. In the end, nine Crimean Tatars were attacked and hospitalized, but their assailants were never found. In the meantime, Kurtseit Abdullaev—a veteran of the Crimean Tatar National Movement, and a member of the working group on the prevention of interethnic conflicts organized by the Council of Ministers of the Autonomous Republic of the Crimea—was arrested along with six other Crimean Tatars for allegedly breaking the camera of a cameraman from the Russian television channel ORT (Channel 1). Abdullaev was sentenced to nine years in jail.[144] The other six arrested were sentenced to between three and eight years in jail. A week later, in the early hours of March 31, 2004, unknown assailants attacked the Mejlis building in Simferopol and tried to burn it by throwing two Molotov cocktails through a window.[145]

On July 19, 2004, then–Ukrainian president Kuchma vetoed the Law on Restoration of the Rights of Persons Deported on an Ethnic Basis because of the alleged objections of the Ukrainian presidential administration.[146] This law was going to classify the people deported from Ukraine specifically based on their ethnic background. Moreover, it was to establish state guarantees on the restoration of rights, including material compensation for losses suffered during deportation.[147] The program was to be funded by a special budget line item. The rejection of this law, in addition to the contentious issues discussed above, led to feelings of frustration and hopelessness among the Crimean Tatar returnees.

The 2004 Ukrainian Presidential Election

The Crimean Tatars supported Viktor Yushchenko (over Kuchma's candidate, Viktor Yanukovych) in the 2004 Ukrainian presidential elections, hoping for improved conditions and a better future for the Crimean Peninsula.[148] However, because they constituted only 0.5 percent of the overall Ukrainian population, the Crimean Tatars could not sway the elections.[149] Regardless, they overwhelmingly voted for Yushchenko, believing that he was better than the alternative. At the end of three rounds of elections in Ukraine, ending with election violations and the consequent "Orange Revolution," Yushchenko became president by a narrow margin. In Crimea, however, where a strong Russian Bloc supported by Moscow was active, Yushchenko received only 12 percent.[150] The Crimean Russians strongly supported Yanukovych, perhaps partially because of his promises about future rapprochement with the Russian Federation, and partially to prevent the Crimean Tatars from achieving their autonomy in Crimea.[151]

Under the new national regime, the Tatar leadership continued to seek resolutions for their grievances. The public apology of Crimean premier Anatoliy Matviyenko (who replaced Sergei Kunytsin) for the 1944 deportation and other crimes committed by the authorities on Crimean land was a major event, as the *first* apology in Soviet/post-Soviet history for what had been done to the Crimean Tatars.[152] In terms of the land problem, although no land allocation mechanism for returnees was prepared, in a meeting with the journalists in Crimea, Yushchenko stated that "the land problem in Crimea emerged as a result of local authorities' behind-the-scenes and often dishonest and unjust policies, and not because of physical shortages of lands."[153] Later, in June 2005, then–Ukrainian prime minister Yulia Tymoshenko echoed these same concerns, suggesting that the local budgets of the Ukrainian cities could be increased so that the "land could be auctioned or sold, and not given away for bribes."[154] The Crimean Tatar Mejlis opposed this statement, reminding Timoshenko of the inequities of the initial land distribution and the problems with excluding returnees from the land market.

On May 5, 2005, Yushchenko met with the representatives of the Crimean Tatar leadership to discuss proactive government action for ensuring adequate Crimean Tatar participation in the legislative and executive branches of the Crimean government.[155] During this meeting, he recommended that the Mejlis reject its stand on national territory autonomy,[156] because it "contradicts the Ukrainian Constitution and causes anxiety among [other] Crimean communities."[157] This suggestion evoked negative reactions among the returnees. On May 12, a power-sharing agreement between Cemilev and then–Crimean prime minister Matviyenko was drawn up,[158] in which the Crimean Tatars were expected to receive two ministry positions as well as the post of deputy prime minister in the local government.[159] On July 7, Ilmi Umerov—one of the Mejlis's top leaders and deputy speaker of the Verhovna Rada of Crimea—was appointed head of the district state administration in Bakhcisaray, where large numbers of returnees reside.[160] This seemed like a step in the right direction; however, the majority of the returnees perceived this as an inclusive "deal between the two leadership elites."

Struggles related to resettlement coincide with the emergence of political cleavages among the Crimean Tatars. Groups of returnees who are not pleased with the progress (or the lack of it) of the Mejlis have formed their own opposition groups. One of these groups is the Coordination Council (consisting of mostly elderly former Crimean Tatar National Movement members), and the other is the Freedom Initiative Azadliq (mostly younger returnees). Moreover, groups of returnees in several regions of Crimea are continuing their self-seizing movement regardless of the Mejlis' ban on land squatting. For example, in Tykha Bukhta (a southern spot near Koktebel/Feodosia), a land conflict arose on July 8, 2005, when a group of Crimean Tatars started to build temporary houses on squatted land without permission.[161] According to a Chernomorka television report, on July 10, the mayor of Koktebel called 2,000 troops (including Special Forces)[162] against these squatters in Tykha Bukhta under the pretense of "maintaining order" in the area. On July 11, Matviyenko criticized the Crimean Tatars who took part in the Tykha Bukhta self-seizing movement on television and reported that "a crime was committed and the law was violated."[163] Regardless, the squatters remained. On July 11, another group of activists (the Partenit Group), which was asking for land allocation in the town of Partenit,[164] held a big protest rally in front of the Crimean government building in Simferopol.

As these sporadic conflicts were taking place between the returnees and the state actors, the Russian Bloc and the Russian Community of Crimea started to get aggravated. Claiming that Crimean Tatar "extremists" were threatening to drive ethnic Russians away from their homes, the Russian Bloc lamented that neither the Ukrainian government nor the Crimean government was taking any action to "protect" them.[165] Their dissatisfaction was deepened by Umerov's appointment to the Bakhcisaray administration and by Matviyenko's appointment.[166]

The Russophones was also unhappy with the refusal of the Crimean authorities to allow the Russian language to be as a means of officially communicating information. They claimed that the refusal to officially distribute information in Russian contradicts the European Charter for Regional or Minority Languages.[167] The language issue has political implications. "According to the most recent Constitution adopted in 1999 [article 10 in chapter 1 of the Constitution], Russian,[168] as the language of the majority and that of interethnic communication, *may* be used in all spheres of public life, while Ukrainian is the official state language."[169] As conflicts begin to spiral between the Ukrainians, the Russians, and the Crimean Tatars, according to the State Statistics Committee, Ukraine's economy[170] has taken a sharp downturn in recent months.[171]

Conclusion

> Die Muhender Gebirge liegen hinter uns
> Vor uns liegen die Muhen der Ebenen.
> (The hardships of the mountains are behind us,
> Before us lie the hardships of the plains.)
>
> —Berthold Brecht

The Crimean Tatars are self-selected returnees, motivated by the transgenerational transmission of their "lost" homeland. The economic, social, and political situation in Crimea is not entirely welcoming. In their places of exile, especially after perestroika, the Crimean Tatars were able to get fairly equal opportunities in education, employment, housing, and health services—yet they did not assimilate into local cultures or lose their notion of Crimean Tatar identity. As chapter 10 in this volume by Ruth Mandel also illustrates, returning to an imagined home is often linked to difficulties of integration.

The Crimean Tatars, after generations in exile, chose to return home as soon as they were able and formed their own leadership within their homeland. Faced with economic exclusion, they developed informal and secondary forms of employment. Marginalized politically, they organized action groups on key issues for their rehabilitation and strove for equal political participation in the Crimean political arena. Regardless of the political challenges and ethnic discrimination, they focused on rebuilding their lives in Crimea. They had simply wanted to come home, and now they *were* home. In fact, when asked, 484 out of 484 questionnaire participants and all the interviewees indicated that they were happy to be in their homeland and that they were not going to leave Crimea under any circumstances.

Referring back to frameworks of assimilation, the return-migration process of the Crimean Tatars clearly illustrates the strength of cultural maintenance. Though some aspects, such as formal language knowledge, diminished during the period of deportation, their collective identity and psychological ties to their homeland remained strong. Endogamous marital patterns, which must have assisted in maintaining such strong cultural ties, continue among Crimean Tatars in Crimea. Once they returned, they were able to instantly assimilate into some levels of the common culture, because the Crimean Tatars, like all the others on the Crimean Peninsula, are also the social products of the former Soviet Union. They speak Russian;[172] their dress patterns are the same their counterparts'; in their homes, in addition to Crimean Tatar national dishes, they often prepare and eat Russian food, such as kasha, blini, pirogi, borscht; and although they are Muslims, they decorate Christmas trees and give each other presents in celebration of the New Year. Physically, it is hard to distinguish them from others—almost half the Crimean Tatars are blond or brunette and have blue or green eyes—unless they have other distinguishing features (e.g., the Nogais).

The interviews and participant observation conducted for this chapter indicate that on the primary group level, the majority of the Crimean Tatars—especially the younger generations—befriend Russians and Ukrainians and develop good relationships. In secondary group relations, such as in neighborhoods and schools, the vast majority also feels comfortable in a multiethnic environment. In spite of clear economic and political grievances, interpersonal relationships with Russians, Ukrainians, and other ethnic groups appear strong.

The structural disadvantages faced by the returning Crimean Tatars can be best understood through the lens of the Theory of Relative Deprivation. In fact, a major part of the survey discussed here aimed to measure the differential effects of cognitive and affective relative deprivation through a series of questions about economic, social, and political group comparisons (cognitive) and the feelings about those comparisons (affective), vis-à-vis other groups on the Crimean Peninsula. Through the responses to the questionnaires and interviews, it becomes clear that returnees perceive themselves at the bottom of the hierarchical pyramids in Crimea, seeing their economic, social, and political situation as worse than that of all the other ethnic groups. The most frequently selected emotions toward ethnic Russians and the Ukrainians were anxiety, frustration, and hopelessness. These collective responses on perceptions and feelings indicate that the returnees have experienced cognitive as well as affective relative deprivation.

When questioned about their present situation, the majority of the Crimean Tatar respondents (84.4 percent) report a worsening of their material situation since returning to Crimea, with 54.1 percent expecting no material improvement in the past five years. More than a third (36.6 percent) are more optimistic, replying that they have hope for an improvement in their collective situation within the next five years.

A common theme emerging from the research is the focus on nonviolence. Regardless of the situation, the majority of the participants did not approve of violence, or violent activities, and always aspired toward peaceful resolutions. This is an important finding, for it displays that *not every relatively deprived, structurally violated "Islamic collective" will choose a violent path for social change.* This finding points out that instead of following the logic of historians like Yaroslav Hrytsak—who stated that "Ukraine's goal must be to create a new Ukrainian nation, which is based *not* on exclusive ethnic, linguistic, religious, or cultural principles, but on the principle of the political, economic, and territorial unity of Ukraine"[173]—it would be better for the "Orange" policymakers of the new Ukrainian government to take a more inclusive and collaborative approach, to provide a space where the people have an opportunity to assert or experience their identity freely and help build a distinct but equal consciousness in all the ethnic groups and nations. I argue that the territorial integrity and unity of Ukraine could be more effectively preserved if key grievances were resolved and a power-sharing/

cooperative framework was established. This type of progress could speed up the integration process, bringing sociopolitical stability and sustainable peace and security not only in Crimea but also in Ukraine overall.

The research presented here attempts to analyze the resettlement dynamics of the returning Crimean Tatars in Crimea. The findings provide clear evidence of the salience of identities that in due course also influence conflict strategies, contingent upon the differential effects of relative deprivation. Further research on the resettlement experiences of forced migrants is warranted. Although going home is often a difficult process, the complexities of being home could be even more challenging. As Alexander Diener suggests in the next chapter, once everyone settles in, the nationalization (and hardening) of social space becomes a key concern for *all* those living in the shared territory. Then the next question prevails: Nationalization of social space for whom? This question also remains the main challenge for Crimea today.

Notes

1. In the chapter title, the name "Golden Cradle" (Altin Besik in Tatar) for the Crimean Tatar homeland comes from a Crimean Tatar proverb about the Tatars' love for their motherland—the motherland is a golden cradle. See http://www.qurultay.org/linkshow.asp?AD=../links/eng/culture/folk/4_2.html.

2. Gurr defines relative deprivation as the *perceived* gap between aspirations and achievements, especially in comparison with other groups. Ted R. Gurr, *Why Men Rebel* (Princeton, N.J.: Princeton University Press, 1970).

3. Various authors define structural violence differently. Galtung defines it as "a structurally based discrepancy between actual and potential states of somatic and mental well-being." Galtung also suggests that structural violence is the "hidden part of the iceberg" imbedded in the social structure. J. Galtung, *Peace by Peaceful Means: Peace and Conflict, Development and Civilization* (Oslo: International Peace Research Institute, 1996), 271. Similarly, Burton argues that *structural violence* is the "damaging deprivations caused by the nature of social institutions and policies." J. W. Burton, *Violence Explained* (Manchester: Manchester University Press, 1997), 32. Sandole explains it as the "situations of unfair access to political, economic, and other resources because of one's *involuntary* membership in certain ethic, religious, racial, and/or other groups." Dennis J. D. Sandole, "A Comprehensive Mapping of Conflict and Conflict Resolution: A Three Pillar Approach," http://www.gmu.edu/academic/pcs/sandole.htm; also see Dennis J. D. Sandole, "Paradigms, Theories, and Metaphors in Conflict and Conflict Resolution: Coherence or Confusion?" in *Conflict Resolution, Theory and Practice-Integration and Application,* ed. Dennis J. D. Sandole and Hugo van der Merwe (Manchester: Manchester University Press, 1993), 11.

4. Gurr defines incentives for ethnopolitical action as "awareness of losses suffered in the past; fear of future losses, and hopes for relative gains—all in relation to other

groups and to the state." R. Tedd Gurr, *Peoples versus States: Minorities at Risk in the New Century* (Washington, D.C.: U.S. Institute of Peace Press, 2000), 5.

5. The initial formulations and pilot studies of the study started during two earlier field trips to Crimea in 2001 and 2002 under the auspices of a grant provided to the Institute for Conflict Analysis and Resolution by the U.S. State Department's Office of Global Educational Programs of the Bureau of Educational and Cultural Affairs.

6. Maria Drohobycky, ed., *Crimea: Dynamics, Challenges, and Prospects* (Lanham, Md.: Rowman & Littlefield, 1995), 5.

7. *Komsomolskaia Pravda,* January 19, 2003.

8. Lund defines *negative* or *unstable* peace as a "situation in which tensions and suspicions among parties run high but violence is either absent or sporadic." Michael S. Lund, *Preventing Deadly Conflict* (Washington, D.C.: U.S. Institute of Peace Press, 1997), 39.

9. The Ukrainians follow Russian Orthodoxy or Greek Catholicism, based on their region (East/West).

10. U.S. Institute of Peace, "Sovereignty after Empire Hopes and Disappointments: Case Studies—Crimea," *Peaceworks* 19, http://www.usip.org/pubs/pworks/pwks19/chap3_19.html, 16.

11. One of the well-known proverbs in the Russian language is: Any unexpected guest is better than an unexpected Tatar.

12. *The Random House Unabridged Webster's Dictionary,* 3rd edition, defines indigenous as "original inhabitant, innate, inherent, and natural." Indigenous people are defined as the natives of a specific location, who have no other homeland or a "kin state" other than that particular territory.

13. In this chapter, although I am using the term "deportation," "genocide" or "ethnocide" could also have been used to describe Crimean Tatars' expulsion from their homeland. In fact, in his orders, Stalin used the term *ochistit* (to cleanse) for the elimination of the Crimean Tatars. Hence, Crimean Tatar returnees themselves have a problem with the semantics of the term "deportation" stemming from the Russian usage of *deportatsiia. The Random House Unabridged Webster's Dictionary* defines "deportation" as "the lawful expulsion of an undesired alien or other person from a state." Conversely, "genocide" is defined as "the deliberate and systematic extermination of a national, racial, political, or cultural group," and "ethnic cleansing (ethnocide)" means "the elimination of an unwanted ethnic group or groups from a society, as by genocide or forced emigration." Moreover, the UN Charter defines "genocide" as "efforts to remove the whole or a part of a people from their natal lands" as genocide, which was certainly what happened to the Crimean Tatars.

14. For more information, see chapter 7 in this volume by Pohl.

15. U.S. Institute of Peace, "Sovereignty after Empire Hopes," 14.

16. After 1956, although the majority of the other deported groups of the Stalin era (Chechens, Ingush, Karachais, Balkars, Kalmyks, Koreans) were granted permission to return to their homelands, the Crimean Tatars, Volga Germans, and Meskhetian Turks were forbidden to repatriate.

17. These conditions include ethnically based high unemployment rates, [forced] land deficiencies and housing crisis, lack of drinking water, electricity, plumbing/sewage system, roads, social services and educational opportunities in their native language.

18. The Crimean Tatars consistently abstained from violence from the beginning of the Crimean Khanate in the fifteenth century through their mobilization years in exile.

After they returned to Crimea, when their second Qurultai convened in June 1991, they declared "nonviolence" as the fundamental principle of the Crimean Tatar movement. Refat Chubarov, "Different Nationalisms: The Case of Crimea," *Uncaptive Minds,* nos. 3–4 (Summer–Fall 1997): 45.

19. The full name of the Mejlis is the Milli Mejlis, which actually means "People's Parliament." Although it is not recognized as an official parliament, since 1991, the Mejlis is the de facto representative body of Crimean Tatars in Crimea. Brian Glyn Williams, *The Crimean Tatars: The Diaspora Experience and the Forging of a Nation* (Boston: Brill, 2001), xvii.

20. Between March 5 and 7, 2004, there were ethnic clashes between the Crimean Tatars and the Cossack mercenaries. (These so-called Crimean Cossacks have nothing to do with the descendants of the Ukrainian Cossacks that settled along Dnieper in the 1400 and 1500s. Mainly, they are retired Soviet army/navy officials in Cossack uniforms who see themselves as the keepers of "the order and security" parallel to the existing legal law-enforcement agencies.) Then, on March 23, 2004, there were clashes with the skinheads after a stabbing incident at the Cotton Club in Simferopol. As a result of these events, on March 30, 2004, the Mejlis suspended all protest actions by the Crimean Tatars to prevent further provocations from "others."

21. Turkic/Eastern sources define these descendants as the Joshi ulus (Joshi was Cingiz Khan's son) or Gok Ordu (Green or Sky Army). Russian sources define them as the Zolotaya Orda, i.e., Golden Horde (Altin Ordu). Ismail Noyan, "Kirimli Filolog-Sair Bekir Cobanzade: Hayati ve Eserleri / Crimean Philologist-Poet Bekir Cobanzade—His Life and His Work," master's thesis, Istanbul Universitesi Basilmamis Yuksek Lisans Tezi / University of Istanbul, 1967, 11.

22. For detailed discussions on the topic, see Vozgrin Yevgenii, *Istoricheskiie Sudbi Kkrimskikh Tatar* (Historical Fate of the Crimean Tatars) (Moscow: Misl Press, 1992); Vladimir Polyakov, *Krim: Sudbi Narodov I Lyudei* (Crimea: Fates of the Nations and the Peoples), International Renaissance Foundation Program for Integration of Formerly Deported Crimean Tatars, Armenians, Bulgarians, Germans, Greeks into Ukrainian Community (Simferopol: International Renaissance Foundation, 1998); Ayder Memetov, *Krymskiie Tatari* (The Crimean Tatars) (Simferopol: Anayurt, 1993); and Williams, *Crimean Tatars.*

23. The Karaims were a reformist Jewish sect that arrived in Crimea in the twelfth century. They speak Karay, a language similar to Crimean Tatar, which belongs to the Kipchak-Turkic group. For more information on the Karaims, see Mehmet Tutuncu, ed., *Turkish-Jewish Encounters: Studies on Turkish-Jewish Relations through the Ages* (Haarlem: Stichting SOTA, 2001); and Neal Ascherson, *Black Sea* (New York: Hill and Wang, 1995), 22.

24. The Krymchaks, or the Crimean Jews, first appeared on the Crimean Peninsula in the thirteenth and fourteenth centuries. They did not know Hebrew and spoke a form of Crimean Tatar, but they knew the Hebrew script. During the German occupation of Crimea, the Nazis exterminated 70 percent of the population. Today in Crimea, there are only 500 Krymchaks. See http://www.eki.ee/books/redbook/crimean_jews.shtml.

25. Noyan, "Kirimli Filolog-Sair Bekir Cobanzade," 11.

26. Memetov, *Krymskiie Tatari,* 19–21.

27. Nogais (Col Tatars) lived in the Northern steps of Crimea, and they spoke the purest form of Tatar, which was uninfluenced by Turkish. In addition to Nogais, there were two other Crimean Tatar subidentities on the peninsula: Bahchesaray Tatars (Orta

Yollak / middle zone) and the Yaliboyu Tatars (Tats), whose home was located on the Black Sea coast. The 1784 deportation is discussed by Noyan, "Kirimli Filolog-Sair Bekir Cobanzade," 22.

28. Amet Ozenbashli, "Rol Tsarskogo Pravitelstva v Emigratsii Krimskikh Tatar" (Role of the Tsarist Government in Emigration of the Crimean Tatars), in *Zabveniiyu ne Podlejit* (It Is Beyond Oblivion) (Kazan: Tatarskoie Knijnoiie Izdatelstvo, 1992), 71.

29. Ibid.

30. Kenan Acar, *Kirimli Bekir Sitki Cobanzade: Dilciligi ve Edebiyat Arastirmaciligi* (Crimean Bekir Sitki Cobanzade: His Research on Linguistics and Literature) (Ankara: Ataturk Kultur Dil ve Tarih Yuksek Kurumu Yayinlari, 2001), 6.

31. Graham Smith, *The Nationalities Question in the Soviet Union* (London: Longman, 1990), 323.

32. U.S. Institute of Peace, "Sovereignty after Empire Hopes," 14.

33. The full name of this body is Narodniy Kommiseriat Natsionalnastei / Commissariat of the Soviet Nationalities.

34. Bolshevik leaders established the Crimean ASSR in the context of their so-called nativization (*korenzatsiia*) policy, which encouraged the expression of minority languages and cultures for non-Russian nationalities while minimizing challenges to centralized Communist rule. U.S. Institute of Peace, "Sovereignty after Empire Hopes."

35. According to Pohl, 90 percent of these deportees were Muslims. The first group of the deportees was the Karachays (November 2, 1943). Next were the Chechens and Ingush (February 23–28, 1944), followed by the Balkars (March 8–9, 2003) and the Crimean Tatars (May 18–20, 1944). The Meskhetian (Ahiska) Turks, Kurds, and Khemshils, who lived in Georgia near the Turkish border, became the last victims of Stalin's policy of ethnic cleansing in November 1944. Otto J. Pohl, *Ethnic Cleansing in the USSR, 1937–1949* (Westport, Conn.: Greenwood Press, 1999), 5.

36. According to a Soviet deportation specialist Nikolai F. Bugai, 151,604 Crimean Tatars were sent to the Uzbek SSR, 8,597 were sent to the Udmurt and Mari autonomous oblasts / districts (Ural Mountains region) to work in the lumber industry, and 10,000 were settled in the Molotov Oblast. Williams, *Crimean Tatars,* 390.

37. Justin Burke et al., *Crimean Tatars: Repatriation and Conflict Prevention* (New York: Forced Migration Project, Open Society Institute, 1996), 12.

38. Noyan, "Kirimli Filolog-Sair Bekir Cobanzade," 7.

39. According to a letter sent to Beria, of the 151,529 Crimean Tatars deported to Uzbekistan, 68,287 were children, 55,684 were women, and only 27,588 were men. Williams, *Crimean Tatars,* 376.

40. Otto J. Pohl, "Timeline: Deportation of Crimean Tatars and Their National Struggle under Soviet Rule," 2004, http://www.iccrimea.org/surgun/timeline.html. Also see Andrew Wilson, *Ukrainians: Unexpected Nation,* 2nd ed. (New Haven, Conn.: Yale University Press, 2002), 151.

41. Alan W. Fisher, *The Crimean Tatars* (Stanford, Calif.: Hoover Institution Press, 1987), 167.

42. The Crimean Tatars recall this period as the "Commander's regime."

43. Wilson, *Ukrainians,* 150–51.

44. For more information, see chapter 7.

45. As cited by Ann Sheehy, *The Crimean Tatars, Volga Germans, and Meskhetians* (London: Minority Rights Group, 1971), 9.

46. Michael Ignatieff, *Blood and Belonging: Journeys into the New Nationalism* (New York: Noonday Press, 1995), 133.

47. Push factors can include religious or ethnic persecution and depressed economic conditions, including minimal job opportunities and low wages, along with low expectations of betterment of such conditions. Pull factors entail favorable economic possibilities/opportunities, better living conditions, friends and relatives who have already emigrated, and freer social environments. Martin Marger, *Race and Ethnic Relations: American and Global Perspectives,* 2nd ed. (Belmont, Calif.: Wadsworth, 1991), 44–45.

48. Caroline B. Brettell and James F. Hollifield, eds., *Migration Theory: Talking across Disciplines* (New York: Routledge, 2000), 77–86.

49. Ibid., 79. For more information on the topic, please see Milton M. Gordon, *Assimilation in American Life* (New York: Oxford University Press, 1964), where he distinguishes seven subprocesses as a part of his Straight Line Assimilation Theory: cultural or behavioral assimilation, structural assimilation, marital assimilation, identificational assimilation, behavioral receptional assimilation, attitude receptional assimilation, and civic assimilation.

50. Galtung defines cultural violence as "those aspects of culture, the symbolic sphere of our existence—exemplified by religion and ideology, language and art, empirical science and formal science (logic, mathematics)—that can be used to *justify* or *legitimize* direct or structural violence. Stars, crosses, and crescents; flags, anthems, and military parades; the ubiquitous portrait of the Leader; inflammatory speeches and posters" are all considered as cultural violence. Galtung, *Peace by Peaceful Means,* 196.

51. S. Hennayake, "Interactive Ethnonationalism: An Alternative Explanation of Minority Ethnonationalism," *Political Geography* 11, no. 6 (1992): 526–49.

52. Caroline Kelly and John Kelly, "Who Gets Involved in Collective Action? Social Psychological Determinants of Individual Participation in Trade Unions," *Human Relations, 1994,* vol. 47, 63–83.

53. Gurr, *Why Men Rebel,* 360–67.

54. Ibid.

55. Walker Iain and Mann Leon, "Unemployment, Relative Deprivation, and Social Protest," *Personality and Social Psychology Bulletin* 13, no. 2 (June 1987): 275. Also see Ans E. M. Appelgryn and Bornman Elirea, "Relative Deprivation in Contemporary South Africa," *Journal of Social Psychology* 136, no. 3 (1996): 381–97.

56. Ans E. M. Appelgryn and Elirea Bornman, "Relative Deprivation in Contemporary South Africa," *Journal of Social Psychology* 36, no. 3 (1996): 381–97.

57. Henri Tajfel, *Social Identity and Intergroup Relations* (Cambridge: Cambridge University Press, 1978), 63.

58. Peter R. Grant and Rupert Brown, "From Ethnocentrism to Collective Protest: Responses to Relative Deprivation and Threats to Social Identity," *Social Psychology Quarterly* 58, no. 3 (1995): 195–212.

59. Kelly and Kelly, "Who Gets Involved," 2.

60. Tajfel, *Social Identity,* 63.

61. Gurr defines "ethnonationalists" as a collective "who want separation or autonomy from the states that rule them." Gurr, *Peoples versus States,* 5.

62. Ibid.

63. The independence of Ukraine was declared on August 24, 1991, and confirmed in a referendum on December 1, 1991.

64. According to the Mejlis, approximately 18,000 returnees remain unregistered because they do not have residences for which to register.

65. Between March 5 and 7, 2004, there were ethnic clashes with so-called Crimean Cossacks in the southern coastal town of Simeiz, during which the Crimean Tatar houses on self-seized land were destroyed.

66. On March 23, 2004, there were some clashes between the Crimean Tatars and the Skinheads at the Cotton Club in Simferopol. According to the ITAR-TASS (March 25, 2004), the events were labeled as the Crimean Tatars' "own doing" and the stories of skinheads' attacks on Tatars were invented by the Tatar leaders.

67. On March 29, 2004, there was a stabbing death of a seventeen-year-old boy, Riza Vadzhapov, in Simeiz. This Ukrainian militia labeled this event as suicide, similar to a past labeling of the death of Niyazi Gaffarov, who was thrown from a window of a building where he was being interrogated. The Crimean Tatar Legal Fund Innitsium proved the latter as murder through a lengthy court process (information was provided by the Innitsium).

68. The research entailed a survey questionnaire with sixty questions, face-to-face in-depth interviews, library/archival data, a survey of Crimean Tatar and Russian newspapers, and participant observations.

69. According to Otto J. Pohl, *The Stalinist Penal System* (Jefferson, N.C.: McFarland, 1997), 112–18, the NKVD (People's Commissariat of Internal Affairs) exiled 151,604 of the Tatars to Uzbekistan and 31,551 to the other areas of the Russian Soviet Federated Socialist Republic. Although these numbers change according to different sources, Uzbekistan still remains to be the area to which the most Crimean Tatars were deported.

70. Only 3.7 percent said that they had returned to Crimea between 1965 and 1976, and 11.8 percent said that they came to Crimea between 1977 and 1988.

71. Family is a societal unit, the main agent of socialization of group norms, through which ethnic and cultural continuity is maintained. Fear of extinction and desire for the survival of the group against the assimilationist threats is displayed through endogenous marriages. In multiethnic societies, one key measure of the degree of integration of an ethnic group is the extent to which its members intermarry with the members of other ethnic groups and of the host society. James A. Crispino, *The Assimilation of Ethnic Groups: The Italian Case* (New York: Center for Migration Studies, 1980), 103.

72. A. P. Vyatkin and E. S. Kulpin, eds., *Krimskie Tatari: Problemi Repatriatsii* (Crimean Tatars: Problems of Repatriation) (Moscow: Institute of Oriental Studies, Russian Academy of Sciences, 1997), 100.

73. Remzi Ilyasov, *Krimskie Tatari: Kratkii Obzor Proshlogo i Analiz Sotsialnogo-Ekonomicheskogo Polojenia Nastoyashego* (Crimean Tatars: Short Survey and the Analysis of the Past and Present Social-Economic Situation) (Simferopol: Fond Isledovannii i Podderjkii Korennih Narodov Krima, 1999), 33–35.

74. Vyatkin and Kulpin, "Krimskie Tatari," 96–97.

75. Ilyasov, *Krimskie Tatari,* 33–35.

76. PGTs are structured, city-type villages that are laid out more like a small town with apartment blocks instead of individual houses, better roads, and possibly natural gas, water, and sewage systems. The population of a PGT does not exceed a couple of thousand people, and it is a step above a village. Nevertheless, the majority of a PGT's population is still employed in agriculture because PGTs are located in rural areas.

77. Ilyasov, *Krymskie Tatari,* 33–35.

78. See http://www.rferl.org/nca/features/2000/04/f.ru.000427132641.html.

79. See http://www.cidct.org.ua/en/studii/4(2000)/6.html.

80. Before the 1944 deportation, the Crimean Tatars constituted 80 to 90 percent of the population of the southern coast.

81. "Crimean Republican Committee on Nationalities Report," Simferopol, 2002.

82. Ibid.

83. Ilyasov, *Krimskie Tatari,* 33–38.

84. Vladimir Mukomel and Emil Pain, "Deported Peoples in Central Asia (a Socio-Demographic Analysis)," in *State, Religion, and Society in Central Asia: A Post-Soviet Critique,* ed. Vitaly Naumkin (Reading, U.K.: Ithaca Press, 1993), 147.

85. Vyatkin and Kulpin, "Krimskie Tatari," 82.

86. During those years, to attend universities, many Crimean Tatars had changed their Tatar names and had adopted other mostly Russian names. An interview with Beiye Abdullaeva, the sister of famous Crimean Tatar poet Fazil Iskender, who passed away in 2003, revealed that Fazil took a Greek name so that he could attend a university in the 1960s.

87. Williams, who conducted research and lived in Uzbekistan and other parts of Central Asia, asserts that the Uzbeks he met in Uzbekistan considered the Crimean Tatars to be intellectuals and white-collar professionals; personal correspondence with Brian Glyn Williams, April 8, 2004.

88. This information was obtained from Yakubov, the founder and the current rector of the Crimean Republican University of Engineering and Education, through personal correspondence.

89. Technical colleges and art colleges (*tehnikumi* and *uchilischa*) are institutions of higher education that train students for technical jobs (mechanics, construction engineers, etc.) and for the arts (music education, music teachers, art education, etc.).

90. *Qirim tatarlar / Krimskie Tatari "Obzor Nationalnogo Obrazovaniya"* (Crimean Tatars: The Summary of National Education), report for the roundtable presentation "Problems of Integration of the Deported Peoples," May 19–21, 2003, Simeiz; http://www.qirimtatar.by.ru/maarif_obzor.htm.

91. Vyatkin and Kulpin, "Krimskie Tatari," 92.

92. Report by Lord Ponsonby, April 5, 2000, http://www.unpo.org/print.php?arg=20&par=1749.

93. Irina Prybitkova, "Resettlement, Adaptation, and Integration of Formerly Deported Crimean Tatars," *Krimskii Studii* (Kyiv, Informational Bulletin) 1–2, nos. 13–14 (2002): 31.

94. Ilyasov, *Krimskie Tatari,* 33.

95. Ibid., 35.

96. Ibid. Its name is Respublikanskoi Komitet po Delam Natsionalnostei I Deportirovannih Grajdan Avtonomnoi Respubliki Krim.

97. Qirim tatarlar; see http://www.qirimtatar.by.ru/maarif_obzor.htm.

98. This is from http://www.vatankirim.net.

99. According to the Constitution adopted in 1999, "Russian, as the language of the majority and that of interethnic communication, *may* be used in all spheres of public life, while Ukrainian is the official state language"; article 10, chapter 1, Ukrainian Constitution. Mica Hall, "Crimean Tatar-Russian as a Reflection of Crimean Tatar National

Identity," paper presented at the Ninth Annual World Convention, Association for the Study of Nationalities, Columbia University, New York, April 17, 2004, 14; this paper is also available at the International Committee for Crimea Web site, http://www.iccrimea.org/scholarly/mhall.html.

100. Ibid.

101. Association of Crimean Tatar Educators, Maarifci (Simferopol), *Newsletter,* 2003.

102. Crimean Tatar is a Turkic language that belongs to Ural-Altai language group, like Turkish, Azeri, Hungarian, Korean, Japanese, and Finnish.

103. According to Campbell and Muntzell's four-conditioned typology, one form of language death situation entails "gradual death, with a gradual shift to the dominant language via extensive contact." This is cited by Suzanne Wertheim, *Language Purity and the De-Russification of Tatar,* Berkeley Program in Soviet and Post-Soviet Studies Working Paper, 3; available at http://socrates.berkeley.edu/~bsp/. The original citation is Lyle Campbell and Martha C. Muntzel, "The Structural Consequences of Language Death," in *Investigating Obsolescence: Studies in Language Contraction and Death* (Cambridge: Cambridge University Press, 1989).

104. Hall, "Crimean Tatar-Russian," 2.

105. *Yani Dunya* (New World) and *Qirim* (Crimea), which are published in Crimean Tatar; *Golos Qirima* (Voice of Crimea), *Poluostrov* (Peninsula), and *Dialog* (Dialogue), which are in Russian, are the four regular weekly newspapers that are currently being printed in Crimea every Friday. Among them, the most-read paper is the *Voice of Crimea* (in Russian). *Avdet* (in Russian), which is printed by the Mejlis. *Halq Sedasi* (in Russian), which is printed by the Mejlis's opposition Coordination Council (Koodinatsionnii Soviet); *Areket* (in Russian), which is also the opposition's newspaper, is not printed regularly. *Suvdaq Sesi* (in Crimean Tatar), which was a regional newspaper from Sudak, *Dumka,* which was a Ukrainian-language newspaper from the BakhciSaray region, and its sequence, *BakhciSarayskii Vesnik,* all went out of circulation sometime in the past.

106. This is because the majority of the Crimean Tatars cannot read or fully understand their native tongue.

107. These channels are Inter, UT-2 (Kanal 1+1), UT-1 (TRK "Era"), GTRK Krim (Channel 1), TRK Chernomorskaya, ITV+TONIS (Krim), Novii Kanal, Jisa, CTB, and ICTV.

108. The majority related these feelings in Russian, because they could not speak Tatar fluently.

109. Julia Tystchenko and Vyacheslav Pikhovshek, *The Repatriation of the Crimean Tatars: A Chronicle of Events* (Kyiv: UICPS, 1999), 343. This is cited by Natalya Belitser, "The Constitutional Process in the Autonomous Republic of Crimea in the Context of Interethnic Relations and Conflict Settlement," http://www.cidct.org.ua/en/studii/22000/3.html.

110. Natalya Belitser, "The Constitutional Process in the Autonomous Republic of Crimea in the Context of Interethnic Relations and Conflict Settlement," http://www.cidct.org.ua/en/studii/2(2000)/3.html.

111. Irena Lasotta, "The Rise of Nationalism in Eastern Europe and the Former Soviet Union—Different Nationalisms: The Case of Crimea," *Uncaptive Minds* 9, nos. 3–4, Special Double Issue (Summer–Fall 1997): 49.

112. These were for the Mejlis's chair, Mustafa Cemilev, and deputy chair, Refat Chubarov.

113. After the September 30, 2007, Ukrainian presidential elections, there was only one Crimean Tatar deputy (Mustafa Cemilev) left in the Verkhovna Rada.

114. The general composition of the Crimean deputies elected in 2002 is as follows: 41 Russians, 35 Ukrainians, 7 Crimean Tatars, 4 Jews, 2 Gagauzians, 1 Czech, 1 Greek, 1 Armenian, and 1 Abkhaz. *RFE/RL Newsline,* April 30, 2002.

115. See http://www.rada.crimea.ua.

116. In the Soviet Union (and other communist countries), the Presidium is or was an administrative committee, usually permanent and governmental, acting when its parent body is in recess. In Crimea, this system is still functional.

117. Currently, this person is Remzi Ilyasov; see http://www.rada.crimea.ua.

118. "Summary of Refat Chubarov's Speech on Crimean Politics," *Crimean Daily News,* May 12, 2003.

119. Through participant observation and my own experiences, it became clear that although the Crimean Tatars are Muslims, the majority drink alcohol daily and/or eat pork sausages without even thinking about it.

120. This finding is similar to the results of a poll conducted in 1995 by the All-Russian Center for the Study of Public Opinion (VTsIOM) in the Russian Republic. According to the poll, taken among 1,650 ethnic Russians, 45 percent of the respondents said they considered themselves believers. However, only 10 percent of the Russian Orthodox believers attend church at least once a month, and 50 percent never read the Bible. Furthermore, the poll revealed that only 3 to 5 percent of the population attended church regularly. Samuel Kliger, "The Jews from the Former Soviet Union: Attitudes towards Religion," paper presented at American Association for the Advancement of the Slavic Studies Conference, Washington, October 1995, 2.

121. The Crimean Tatar leaders (the Mejlis), who keenly aim to keep the affairs of "church" and "state" separate, approach Turkish Islam as a role model.

122. Leonid Grach, the former communist leader of Crimea, often states that Chechen fighters/troops are hiding in Crimea under Tatar protection, and that Tatar organizations are linked to al Qaeda. In fact, the security services of Ukraine has looked into these claims and declared that there has been no evidence for them. Roman Zakaluzny, "Communist Deputy's Comments Spark Outcry," *Kyiv Post,* October 23, 2003.

123. "Crimean Tatar Leader Says Ukrainian President 'Misinformed' about Extremists," *Action Ukraine Report 4,* September 10, 2004.

124. See http://www.qurultay.org/eng/ayrinti.asp?HaberNo=2004091501.

125. The topic of Crimean Tatars' being indigenous people of Crimea first surfaced as an important political issue during the debates in the national legislature of Ukraine on February 12, 1991. Consequently, in March 1991, the Rukh Party's Council of Nationalities issued a special statement about the rights of all nationalities, including of the Crimean Tatars "as the indigenous people having no other Motherland."

126. These events were war in Nagorno-Karabagh, Azerbaijan; Georgia; and Israel.

127. Government of Ukraine, *Konstitutsia Ukrainy, 1997* (Ukrainian Constitution, 1997) (Simferopol: Krymuchpedgiz, 1997), 56.

128. Ibid., 76.

129. Ibid., 87.

130. Ignatieff, *Blood and Belonging,* 136.

131. See http://www.unpo.org/print.php?arg=20&par=1749.

132. Before World War II, 1 million hectares of Crimean land belonged to the Crimean Tatars. Gulnara Abbasova, Foundation for Research and Support of Indigenous

Peoples of Crimea, An Appeal to the Commission on Human Rights, Subcommission for the Promotion and Protection of Human Rights Working Group on Minorities, Tenth Session, 2004, agenda item 3a.

133. Personal interviews with Nadir Bekirov, the head of the Judicial Department of the Mejlis.

134. Ibid.

135. Ibid.

136. Ibid.

137. Aqua Park is located near a Crimean natural reserve, where land sales are illegal.

138. In 2004, Yanaki was a member of the Crimean Parliament. He co-owns Aqua Park with three other partners, one of whom is a Russian citizen from the Russian Federation.

139. He is a deputy of the Ukrainian Verkhovna Rada and the leader of Crimean Communists.

140. This was not the first confrontation between the returnees and the so-called Crimean-Cossaks. On January 15, 2003, 150 to 200 Cossacks showed up in Morskoe, where 300 Crimean Tatars live, and attacked and wounded a group of returnees. From the Department of Strategic Information, Kavkaz Center, January 27, 2003.

141. *Yani Dunya* (Crimean Tatar weekly newspaper), February 7, 2004.

142. According to Niyara Gafarova, the assistant of the Political and Legal Directorate of the Mejlis, the Berkut arrived in the area with five trucks full of their armed special forces.

143. Mykyta Kasyanenko, "Bad Games," *Den* (Kyiv), April 1, 2004.

144. This nine-year prison sentence was based on the Ukrainian Criminal Code 3 (causing bodily harm) and Ukrainian Criminal Code 2 (disrupting the order).

145. Wolodymyr Pritula, "On the Ethno-Political Situation in Crimea," 2004; available at http://www.radiosvoboda.org.

146. "Crimean Tatar Leader Denounces Veto of Rights Restoration Law for Those Who Had Been Deported," *Action Ukraine Report 4,* July 23, 2004.

147. See http://www.crimea.vlasti.net; and the Crimean Aspects Web site, http://aspects.crimeastar.net/english.

148. Viktor Yanukovych was a Kremlin-supported candidate in Ukrainian presidential elections. On the eve of the first round of Ukrainian presidential elections, Vladimir Putin, the president of the Russian Federation, visited Ukraine twice and openly endorsed Yanukovych. Among Yanukovych's promises to the Kremlin were granting the right for double citizenship for Russians living in Ukraine, including in Crimea; acknowledgement of Russian as the second state language; and strong cooperation between Russia, Belarus, Kazakhstan, and Ukraine toward a single unified economic space.

149. Mustafa Cemiloglu's speech from the Fourth Qurultai Meeting, *Kirim Bulteni,* July–September 2004, 14.

150. See http://www.theglobeandmail.com/servlet/ArticleNews/TPStory/LAC/20041206/UKCRIMEA06/TPInternational/Europe.

151. During the elections, the vice speaker, Vasilii Kiselev, spread rumors that Yushchenko was going to create Tatar autonomy in Crimea. This was a false rumor, for it was merely two deputies from the Crimean Tatar Mejlis, including their chairperson, Mustafa Cemilev, from Yushchenko's "Our Ukraine" bloc, who raised the issue of cre-

ating Crimean Tatar autonomy in Crimea, although Yushchenko himself has never supported the idea. See http://aspects.crimeastar.net/english/news.php?action=041204.

152. See http://www.iccrimea.org/news/newsdigest1.html.

153. See http://home.uninet.ee/~embkura/Press-84.htm.

154. *Poluostrov* (Peninsula), June 23, 2005.

155. See http://www.qurultay.org/eng/ayrinti.asp?HaberNo=2005050501 and http://www.iccrimea.org/news/newsdigest1.html.

156. The 1991 declaration by the Crimean Tatar Mejlis at the second Qurultay states that "Crimea is a national territory of the Crimean Tatar people on which they alone have the right of self-determination." See http://www.rferl.org/reports/tb-daily-report/2005/05/0-230505.asp.

157. See http://www.iccrimea.org/news/newsdigest1.html and http://www.rferl.org/reports/tb-daily-report/2005/05/0-230505.asp.

158. This agreement was worked out between Cemilev and Crimean prime minister Matviyenko after a four-month administrative deadlock on the peninsula. Although he was appointed by Yushchenko on the eve of the Orange Revolution, Matviyenko was unable to form a new government until the May 12 agreement, because the Crimean Tatar legislators were boycotting the sessions of the regional parliament. See http://www.rferl.org/reports/pbureport/2005/05/19-170505.asp.

159. See http://www.rferl.org/reports/pbureport/2005/05/19-170505.asp.

160. See http://aspects.crimeastar.net/english/news.php?action=100705.

161. Tykha Bukhta has been a hot spot of interethnic tension over land between ethnic Russians and Crimean Tatars for the past two years since the previous Crimean government failed to keep its promise to resettle Crimean Tatars there. *Krymskaya gazeta,* July 13, 2005.

162. Consequently, the Crimean Prosecutor's Office has launched a criminal case against the returnees (according to article 252, part 1, of the Ukrainian Criminal Code), suggesting that they attempted to destroy natural reserve site protected by the state. The squatters insist that two-thirds of the land around Koktebel is already owned by top officials and businesspeople, and they insist on the review of this recent declaration of the area's reserve status. *Krymskaya gazeta* (Yalta), July 13, 2005.

163. Ibid.

164. Partenit is another coastal region around Alushta and Gurzuf.

165. *Krymskaya Pravda* (Simferopol), July, 12, 2005.

166. See http://en.rian.ru/world/20050601/40454529.html.

167. Ibid.

168. According to RFE/RL, on May 17, 2004, the Constitutional Court rejected a request made by 165 lawmakers that read "citizens have the right to use Ukrainian as the state language and Russian as the official language in the process of managing state matters and in self-government bodies." In its rejection, the court cited the December 1999 ruling, in which the terms "state language" and the "official language" are synonymous. *RFE/RL Newsline,* May 18, 2004.

169. Hall, "Crimean Tatar-Russian as a Reflection of Crimean Tatar National Identity," 14.

170. The Ukrainian economy grew only 4 percent in the first six months of 2005, and the growth of gross domestic product slowed down from 6.5 percent in January to 1.1 percent in June 2005. "Ukraine's Economic Growth Slows Down Dramatically in First Six Months of 2005," available at http://www.artukraine.com.

171. According to Paul Collier, low economic growth, economic decline, and low income or no income in combination with rapid population growth constitute major risk factors for rebellion and violence. Collier is cited by Chester A. Crocker, *Turbulent Peace: The Challenges of Managing International Conflict* (Washington, D.C.: U.S. Institute of Peace Press, 2001), 144–57.

172. Cultural or behavioral assimilation or acculturation refers to the adaptation of cultural patterns to fit those of the surrounding society. These cultural patterns include usage of the host country's language, values, religious observances and belief systems, customs and traditions, norms, food, and dress patterns.

173. Quoted by Alexander J. Motyl, *Dilemmas of Independence: Ukraine after Totalitarianism* (New York: Council on Foreign Relations Press, 1993), 80.

9

The Settlement of the Returning Kazakh Diaspora: Practicality, Choice, and the Nationalization of Social Space

Alexander Diener

Although some argue that the Soviet Union was not an empire in the classical sense of the term, imperial characteristics were most certainly evident during its seventy-year reign.[1] Among the most prominent was the existence of an "imperial diaspora" of ethnic Russians, along with a dispersal of subject peoples from their historic homelands.[2] This dispersal of national communities throughout the titular units of the Soviet Union formed complicated and potentially volatile ethnodemographic landscapes between and within the countries to emerge from the Soviet collapse. Indeed, titular ethnonationalist movements played a significant role in the demise of the Soviet Union. These were symbolized and advanced by the conversion of the ethnic provincial names of the Soviet Republics into ethnic state names (i.e., from the Kazakh Soviet Socialist Republic to the Republic of Kazakhstan). These new "nation-states" problematized the territorialized identities of many nontitular communities. Rising ethnonationalism and persistent territoriality among diasporas—many multigenerational—present serious challenges to the states of the former Soviet Union, more than a decade after independence. Perhaps the most vulnerable is the "Republic of Kazakhstan," where the titular Kazakhs gained majority status only recently (c. 1997–99); see table 9.1.

This chapter examines the long-term legacy of migration and a state's conscious manipulation of the process of settlement in pursuit of legitimacy and a redefinition of "belonging." Both links and tensions between migration, economic development, and political interests are explored within the context of a long-dispersed group's return to a historic homeland. Numeric parity of titular and nontitular populations throughout the first decade of Kazakhstan's independence represent perhaps the most extreme case where the emigration of nontitular groups and immigration of titular peoples combined to alter the sociopolitical landscape of a post-Soviet state. Population processes such as "nationalizing social space" and "diasporic return migration" play powerfully into the societal development of Kazakhstan, as they do other states contending with the challenges of both ethnic and civic nationalisms.

These two processes are intimately linked, often manifesting in a collaborative relationship, wherein titular ethnonationalism catalyzes the emigration of minority populations and creates demographic space (jobs, homes, etc.) to be filled by return migrants of the titular diaspora. It may also be stated that migration to an ethnic kin state is often a consequence of ethnodiasporic nationalization and its commensurate activation of "return myths."[3] Return myths constitute idealized conceptions of a historic homeland that have been produced and reproduced among dispersed populations for generations. With expanded opportunities for migration following the collapse of the Soviet Union, states were much inclined to use these myths as catalysts of reconceptualized ideals of belonging. Often overtly constructed or reified through the export of nationalist rhetoric from a "kin state" or resulting from ethnically exclusive sociopolitical policies of titular ethnonationalists in a given "host state," return migrations have become commonplace throughout Eurasia.[4]

Roughly half of all diasporic Kazakhs descend from those that fled the famines and purges of the early Soviet period. These groups have existed for generations as small minorities in underdeveloped regions of peripheral or semiperipheral states (Mongolia, Afghanistan, China, Iran, Turkey, etc.). The other half of the Kazakh diaspora is comprised of those caught on the wrong side of a political boundary. This group has only recently come to understand the true nature of a "diasporic existence" due to the formation of the interstate borders around, and titular nationalisms within, their for-

Table 9.1. National Composition of Kazakhstan, 1989–99

	1989		1990		1993		1995		1999	
Nationality	Number	Percent	Number	Percent	Number	Percent	Number	Percent	Number	Percent
Kazakhs	6,534,616	39.7	6,700,363	40.3	7,287,635	43.1	7,636,205	46.0	7,985,039	53.4
Russians	6,227,549	37.8	6,241,930	37.6	6,168,740	36.5	5,769,711	34.7	4,479,620	30.0
Ukrainians	896,240	5.4	893,780	5.4	875,434	5.2	820,871	4.9	547,054	3.7
Germans	957,518	5.8	917,485	5.5	696,042	4.1	507,199	3.1	353,441	2.4
Uzbeks	332,017	2.0	340,532	2.0	364,159	2.2	378,811	2.3	370,663	2.5
Tatars	327,982	2.0	333,412	2.0	335,514	2.0	319,592	1.9	248,954	1.7
Uighurs	185,301	1.1	N.A.	N.A.	N.A.	N.A.	N.A.	N.A.	210,365	1.4
Belarusans	182,601	1.1	182,814	1.1	181,486	1.1	171,716	1.0	111,927	0.7
Koreans	103,315	0.6	N.A.	N.A.	N.A.	N.A.	N.A.	N.A.	99,665	0.7
Others	717,325	4.4	1,007,997	6.1	1,004,743	5.9	1,002,986	6.0	546,398	3.7
Total	16,464,464	100.0	16,618,313	100.0	16,913,753	100.0	16,607,091	100.0	14,953,126	100.0

Note: Changes in Kazakhstan's territorial administrative structure have altered some of the population data from 1989 to 1999. N.A. = not available.

Sources: N. Oka, "The Korean Diaspora in Nationalizing Kazakhstan: Strategies for Survival as and Ethnic Minority," in *Koryo Saram: Koreans in the Former USSR,* ed. G. N. Kim and R. King (New Haven, Conn.: East Rock Institute, 2001), 89–113; the citation here is on 94. 1989 USSR Population Census, CD-ROM. Natsionalnoe Statisticheskoe Agentstvo Respubliki Kazakhstan, *Demograficheskii Yezhegodnik Kazakhstana* (Almaty: Natsionalnoe Statisticheskoe Agentstvo Respubliki Kazakhstan, 1996), 56–58. Agenstvo Respubliki Kazkahstana po Statistike, *Natsionalnyi Sostab Naselenia Respubliki Kazakhstana: Itogi Perepisi Naselenia 1999 v Respublike Kazakhstana* (Almaty: Agenstvo Respubliki Kazkahstana po Statistike, 2000), vol.1, 6–8.

mer provincial units of the Soviet Union (i.e., Kazakhs in Russia, Uzbekistan, Tajikistan, etc.).[5] With the emergence of an independent Kazakhstan, the opportunity to exist as members of a titular community within their "historic homeland" and to contribute to the construction of a "Kazakh nation-state" compels "return migration."[6] This return migration is, however, not without its consequences in the formation of Kazakhstan's civil society.

Over the decade of the 1990s, Russian and other minority groups were confronted with an increasing percentage of ethnic-Kazakhs within the governmental structures of Kazakhstan and across the full extent of the state's territory (see figures 9.1 and 9.2, and table 9.2).[7] These represent dramatic changes from previously extant ethnic regionalisms and proportions of ethnic Russians within the political structure. Enhancing the presence of ethnic Kazakhs throughout the country, or "Kazakhization," as it is referred to in many scholarly works, improves sociopolitical penetration and commensurately leads to greater legitimacy of the predominantly ethnic-Kazakh "[Nursultan] Nazarbayev regime."[8] Giving rise to an ethnonational culture that more closely resembles the return myths of dispersed titular peoples affirms the potential advantages of return migrations but also problematizes the homeland conceptions of nontitular groups.

Reactions of nontitular peoples to such efforts have largely involved migration to their ethnic kin states (historical homelands) or an uncertain reconciliation of their ethnic identity with the newly constructed and limitedly actualized Kazakhstani (civic national) identity.[9] Paralleling the forces compelling the return of the Kazakh diaspora, the emigration of minority communities results from both a compulsion to exist within an ethnonational homeland (i.e., a pull factor generating from ethnodiasporic nationalization and reterritorialization to a remote kin state) and a perceived impetus to leave their territory of residence (i.e., a push factor stemming from economic difficulties and the perception of exclusive titular nationalism—deterritorialization within the "host state"). Yet the complexity of the migration process and the role of perceived notions of belonging preclude the explanation of decisionmaking processes in such stark neoclassical terms.

A myriad of factors motivating ethnic Kazakhs to leave regions outside the titular states relate directly to the "nationalization of social space" in pursuit of governmental legitimacy. Even a cursory analysis of the first decade of Kazakhstan's independence reveals that the Nazarbayev regime has existed within a dichotomy of identity paradigms that have affected and continue to affect the Kazakhstani sociopolitical landscape. On the one hand, multinational identity builders endeavor to form an inclusive state,

Figure 9.1. Distribution of Ethnic Kazakhs in Kazakhstan, 1989

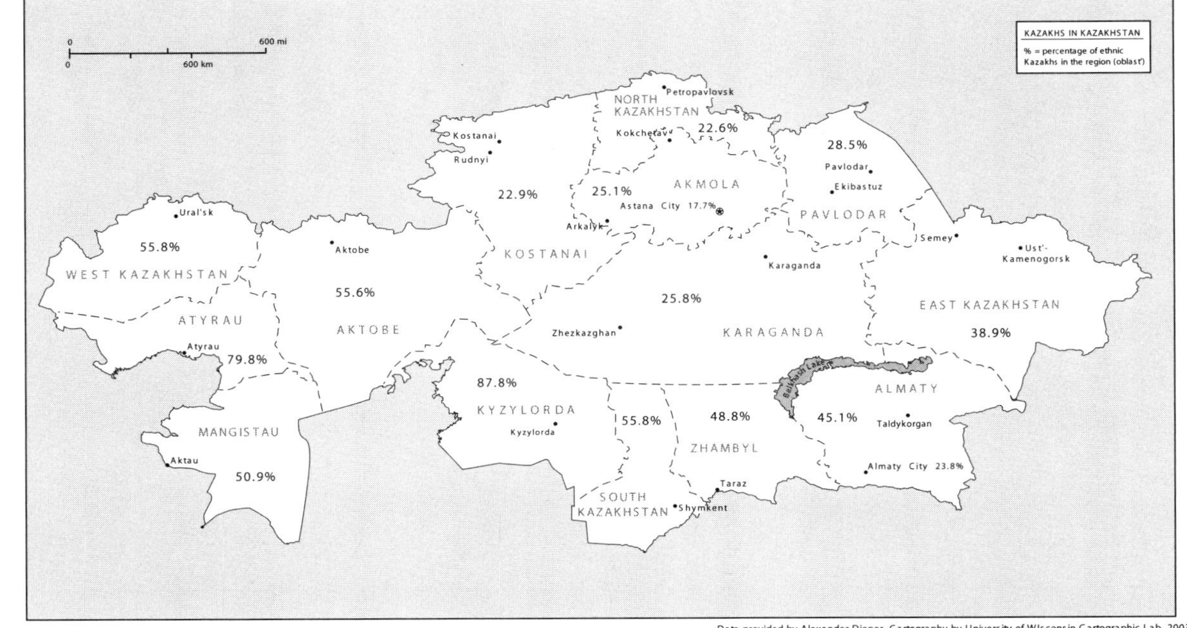

Data provided by Alexander Diener, Cartography by University of Wisconsin Cartographic Lab, 2003

Figure 9.2. Distribution of Ethnic Kazakhs in Kazakhstan, 1999

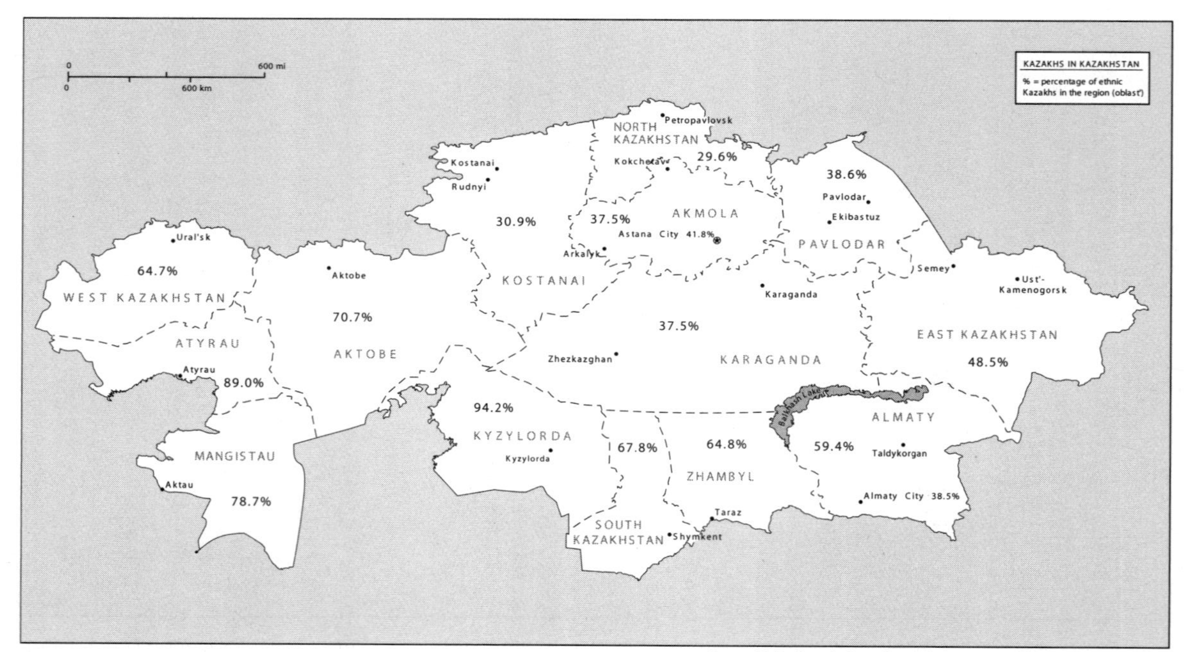

Data provided by Alexander Diener, Cartography by University of Wisconsin Cartographic Lab, 2003

Table 9.2. Shifts in Ethnic-Kazakh Predominance per Oblast, 1989–99

Oblasts	1989		1999		Oblasts: Kazakh Share of Population (percent)		Increase in Number of Kazakhs, 1989–99	Increase in Number of Kazakhs: 1999 as percentage of 1989
	Kazakhs	Non-Kazakhs	Kazakhs	Non-Kazakhs	1989	1999		
Akmola	266,831	797,575	313,488	522,783	25.1[a]	37.5[b]	46,657	17.5
Aktobe	407,222	325,431	482,285	200,273	55.6[b]	70.7[c]	75,063	18.4
Almaty	741,137	901,780	926,137	632,397	45.1[b]	59.4[b]	185,000	24.9
Atyrau	338,998	85,710	391,672	48,614	79.8[c]	89.0[c]	52,674	15.5
East Kazakhstan	687,879	1,079,346	743,098	787,926	38.9[b]	48.5[b]	55,219	08.0
Zhambyl	507,302	531,365	640,346	348,494	48.8[b]	64.8[c]	133,044	26.2
West Kazakhstan	351,123	278,371	399,030	217,770	55.8[b]	64.7[c]	47,907	13.6
Karaganda	449,837	1,295,611	529,478	880,740	25.8[a]	37.5[b]	79,641	17.7
Kostanai	279,787	944,057	314,801	702,928	22.9[a]	30.9[a]	35,014	12.5
Kyzylorda	504,126	70,338	561,630	34,585	87.8[c]	94.2[c]	57,504	11.4
Mangistau	165,043	159,200	247,644	67,025	50.9[b]	78.7[c]	82,601	50.0
Pavlodar	268,512	673,801	311,862	495,121	28.5[a]	38.6[b]	43,350	16.1
North Kazakhstan	206,060	706,005	214,697	511,283	22.6[a]	29.6[a]	8,637	04.2
South Kazakhstan	1,017,470	806,058	1,340,889	637,450	55.8[b]	67.8[c]	323,419	31.2
Astana city[d]	49,798[d]	231,454[d]	133,585[d]	185,739[d]	17.7[a,d]	41.8[b,d]	83,787[d]	168.3[d]
Almaty city[d]	255,133[d]	816,794[d]	434,397[d]	694,959[d]	23.8[a,d]	38.5[b,d]	179,264[d]	70.0[d]

a. Highly non-Kazakh: non-Kazakhs ≥ 70 percent.
b. Moderately non-Kazakh: 70 percent > non-Kazakh > 39 percent.
c. Slightly non-Kazakh: 39 percent ≥ non-Kazakhs.
d. City specific.
Source: Agentstvo Respubliki Kazakhstana po Statistikye, 1999.

wherein all ethnic groups can feel an equal sense of belonging. On the other hand, Kazakh nationalists imagine an ethnic-Kazakh homeland, wherein other ethnonational communities are relegated to a second-class status.[10] The legitimacy of the current government is difficult to build in such a blatantly dichotomous sociopolitical environment. Though the Nazarbayev regime has been successful in providing stability within the state, the future remains unclear. It is, therefore, imperative to understand the ethnodemographic processes affecting the sociopolitical situation in Kazakhstan.

Stark neoclassical approaches to migration fail to provide an accurate picture of contemporary return migrations. To make this case, I posit that the settlement patterns of the returning Kazakh diaspora must be seen as an ongoing negotiation of governmental structure and individual choice. Surveys, interviews, and focus groups have been conducted among members of various repatriated Kazakh communities.[11] Expert interviews, as well as library and archival research, have also been employed to enhance the depth of analysis. In this chapter, I first briefly discuss a theoretical framework for the "nationalization of social space" and its relationship to "return migration." Then I analyze data pertaining to the connections or lack of connections between the settlement patterns of return migrants and the government's quest for legitimacy in Kazakhstan. Finally, I offer conclusions and suggestions for research pertaining to this and related topics.

Theoretical Framework

Researching the Kazakh diaspora and Kazakhstan's sociopolitical situation from abroad has a potential to leave the impression of a direct link between the repatriation process and the emigration of nontitular peoples from Kazakhstan, which is misleading on several levels. The "return" of Kazakhs from abroad began in the early 1990s and coincided with the years of greatest minority emigration (see tables 9.1 and 9.3). Indeed, Peter Finke explicitly states that Kazakhstan's government settled incoming migrants in the northern, mostly Russian, oblasts of the state to "fill the gap left by the massive emigration of Germans . . . and to make this part of the country somewhat more *Kazak*."[12] But was the state so clearly conscious in encouraging out-migration and managing the settlement patterns of the returning diaspora?

Investigations of Kazakh migration throughout the 1990s suggest an active and direct role of the state in managing population processes and mi-

Table 9.3. Quota for Kazakh Diasporic Return throughout the 1990s

Year	Quota of Families	General Estimate of People Based on Number of Families	Percentage of Fulfillment
1993	10,000	60,000	76.5
1994	7,000	42,000	51.5
1995	5,000	30,000	66.6
1996	4,000	24,000	63.6
1997	2,200	13,200	56.0
1998	3,000	18,000	53.4
1999	500	3,000	56.0
2000	500	3,000	91.6
2001	600	3,600	N.A.

Note: N.A. = not available.

Sources: A. C. Diener, "Kazakhstan's Kin-State Diaspora: Settlement Planning and the *Oralman* Dilemma," *Europe Asia Studies* 57, no.2 (2005): 327–48. Compiled from data derived from Z. Kinayatuly, *Mongholiyadaghy Kazakhtar* (Mongolian Kazakhs) (Almaty: Dunizhuzi Kazakhtarynyng Kauymdastyghy, 2001); author interview with Abai Maukarauly, editor of the newspaper *Kow,* Almaty, February 2002; author interview with Zarkikhan Kinayatuly, Kazakhstan Academy of Sciences, Almaty, December 2001; author interview with Didakhmet Ashimkhanuly, journalist, *Habar News,* Almaty, December 2001; author interview with Kaldarbek Naimanbai, director of the World Association of Kazakhs, Almaty, March 2002.

gration specifically. In a 1995 article in the Kazakhstani journal *Sayasat* (Policy), the prominent Kazakh demographer Markash Tatimov asserted that "the government must work out its conception for the republic's demographic evolution, and ensure that population changes best serve the interests of internal and domestic policies."[13] According to Ian Bremmer and Cory Welt, this "conception of demographic evolution" has manifested in attempts to "entice new immigrants [diasporic Kazakhs], along with Kazakhs living in the south of Kazakhstan, to settle in the north of the country with offers of subsidized housing, employment, and Kazakh language schools."[14] Such a policy of government-directed settlement could be interpreted as an attempt to alter the ethnodemographic balance of certain regions and is consistent with the theories of the "nationalization of social space" proposed by Colin Williams and Anthony Smith.[15]

The Nationalization of Social Space

According to Williams and Smith, it is through the national construction of social space that both internal and external legitimacy are most readily cultivated.[16] This process entails the promotion of three broadly defined political-geographic trends: "manipulation of the environment,"[17] "hardening of space," and "abstraction of the land."[18] Gaining momentum since the eighteenth century, these three trends have contributed to the sanctity with which the international system continues to regard the nation-state, and in consequence the sociogeographical and sociopolitical standards to which new states must accede.[19] For the purposes of this chapter, I concentrate on the "hardening of space" as the most relevant to the settlement of Kazakh return migrants.

The Hardening of Space

The "hardening of space" refers to "the *filling-out* of power vacuums and the utilization of all areas for social benefit and communal power."[20] A process that began in Europe under the direction of "absolute monarchs" has since been handed over to nationalist/patriotic elites, who seek to eliminate any vestige of political territorial uncertainty by implanting their own and their community's control over even uninhabited parts of the territory.[21] The nomadic history of the Central Eurasian steppe makes the idea of hardened space with rigid boundaries a relatively new phenomenon. The division of the region into individual ethnic units under the Soviet Union gave rise to this process, which has achieved far greater momentum with the emergence of the post-Soviet independent states. The settlement of ethnic Kazakhs in predominantly nontitular oblasts would certainly fall within this category, as would the transfer of the capital city status from the southern city of Almaty (formerly Alma Ata) to the northern/central city of Astana (formerly Akmola).[22]

External sovereignty is a related component of this process, wherein the state seeks to "present to the world the face of a united and mobilized community securely based throughout a compact territory, which brooks no external interference or internal subversion and which is able to unleash a collective energy for development that can utterly transform its environment and deter aggressors."[23] Transstate/transnational, irredentist, and autonomous territorial identities among minority populations pose challenges to this hardening of space.[24]

The Kazakhstani government's adoption of polices seemingly promoting the hardening of space has been attributed to concerns over the largely nontitular demographic character of the state's northern oblasts (see table 9.2 and figures 9.1 and 9.2), and prior advancement of proposals for autonomous regions within Kazakhstani territory (Cossacks and Germans).[25]

For virtually any state, let alone a newly independent state forming modern political institutions for arguably the first time in the nation's history,[26] such geopolitical conditions could be readily perceived as genuine threats to territorial sovereignty.[27] The resettlement of ethnic Kazakhs in regions wherein populations exhibit divergent conceptions of homeland and alternative definitions of the social space would most certainly enhance the legitimacy of the Nazarbayev regime. This is especially so for diasporic returnees from outside the Commonwealth of Independent States (CIS), given the likelihood of a high degree of nationalistic fervor relating to their fulfillment of "return myths." Pursuing this matter in Kazakhstan, however, provided a radically different story.

Interviews with Kazakhstani scholars and political officials garnered strong statements against the idea that the Kazakhstani government had any intention of demographically diluting non-Kazakh oblasts:

> Kazakhstan has many nationalities. They have lived on this territory for many years and are now citizens of the Republic of Kazakhstan. While it is true certain groups live compactly in certain regions, it is not the policy of our President to push other groups into their regions. We do not need to do this. Kazakhstan is a sovereign country and our borders are not in question.[28]

Officials from Kazakhstan's Agency of Information pointed to a variety of alternative factors affecting the settlement patterns of return migrants:

> Yes, it is true that more Kazakhs live in the north than have in the past decades. But this is a natural occurrence. Russian peoples have moved away and abandoned jobs that must be filled. We have need to develop the north and this requires a population of workers. We have many workers moving to the west for jobs in the oil industry as well—this too is a natural process.[29]

Research conducted among pockets of return migrants supported challenges to the notion of a full-scale state-directed resettlement process. As I demonstrate below, return migrants' responses to questions pertaining to their reasons for settling in particular locations led to a more textured understanding of this process. However, rather than naively asserting that the "nationalization of social space" has not, in any way, been a consideration in the settlement process, I argue instead that this situation constitutes a combination of a state's "natural" inclination to ensure its territorial integrity through the hardening of space, the logical spatial distribution of the returning diaspora along socioeconomic lines, and the exercise of free will within a condition of imperfect information on the part of the return migrants. To make this case, I present these points as distinct perspectives from which the settlement can be viewed.

The Hardening of Kazakh Space

With Kazakhstan's emergence as an independent country, the raison d'être of the state was largely focused on the creation of a Kazakh homeland. The preamble to the 1993 Kazakhstani Constitution makes this point by defining the state as a homeland for the "self-determined Kazakh nation."[30] Even the 1995 Constitution, rewritten to appear more ethnically neutral, contained only slightly more subtle expressions of the underlying centrality of the Kazakh ethnic group in the formation of a Kazakhstani nation. The preamble of this document states: "We, the people of Kazakhstan, united by a common historical destiny, constituting statehood on the native Kazakh land."[31] By defining the territory as "Kazakh land," other groups are furtively characterized as subject to the titular community's hospitality (i.e. the formation of a "host state" structure).

The goal of elevating ethnic Kazakhs to a position of "first among equals" is also evident in the "Concept [Kontsept] for the Formation of the State Identity of the Republic of Kazakhstan." Despite its general theme of civic/territorial nationalism, this document differentiates between Kazakhs and other Kazakhstani citizens by noting that "Kazakhstan is the ethnic center of the Kazakhs. They have no other state entity anywhere in the world that would show concern for the preservation and development of Kazakhs as an ethnic group."[32] Such a statement backhandedly indicates that alternatives exist for Russians, Germans, Uzbeks, and other Kazakhstani citizens who are titular members of actualized kin states. Though the rhetoric and other laws of this period also implied the desire for an inclusive, civic conception of nationhood, an analysis of policies in the early stages of Kazakhstan's independence suggests a de facto focus on the fulfillment of a "nation-state" ideal.[33]

The fact that Kazakhs represented a minority within their own state brought into question the legitimacy of the ethnic Kazakh regime and clearly compelled the enactment of each component of "nationalization of social space." "Manipulation of the environment" was evident in the nationalization of the *Vaikanour Kosmodrom* and its subsequent "lease" to the Russian Federation, the elimination of nuclear weapons on Kazakhstani territory, and the implementation of government control over oil and mineral resources. "Abstraction of the land" was evident in the rewriting of Kazakh history, the renaming of towns and streets, and the promotion of "Kazakh" national iconography throughout the country. The "hardening of space" was, and remains, an active dynamic represented in the above-mentioned transfer of the Kazakhstani capital from the city of Almaty (in the southwest of the country) to the renamed city of Astana (center of the country), as well as in the agreement to uphold the sanctity of the Soviet provincial borders between the states emerging from the Soviet Union's collapse. All this being said, extending the "hardening of space" argument to include ethnodemographic dilution of highly nontitular oblasts through a "state-directed settlement" of the returning diaspora is not so easy. In table 9.2, we are presented with evidence that not every highly non-Kazakh oblast (nontitular equal to or greater than 70 percent) has seen a large-scale increase in the percentage of Kazakhs.

A comparison of 1989 and 1999 census data allows Kazakhstan's oblasts to be divided into three general categories: highly nontitular (with a non-Kazakh population equal to or greater than 70 percent), moderately nontitular (non-Kazakh population between 69.9 and 40 percent), and slightly nontitular (non-Kazakh population equal to or less than 39 percent). With every oblast seeing an increase in the number of Kazakhs since 1989 (with an average increase per oblast of 19.1 percent, excluding the cities of Almaty and Astana),[34] a pattern of demographic Kazakhization is clearly taking form. However, none of the oblasts with a population greater than 70 percent nontitular increased their percentage of ethnic Kazakhs by more than the average. Taking into consideration the change in total population per oblast (emigration and immigration), three oblasts (Akmola, Karaganda, and Pavlodar) shifted into the middle category (non-Kazakh less than 70 percent but greater than 39 percent) of nontitular oblasts. Due to the existence of large urban centers in each of these oblasts, this change could, however, be attributed to the urbanization trend that so dramatically increased the number of Kazakhs in Almaty and Astana (with gains of 70 percent and 168 percent, respectively).[35]

The North Kazakhstan and Kostanai oblasts had the lowest percentages of Kazakhs in 1989, and by 1999 this proportion increased by only by 04.2 and 12.5 percent, respectively. Taking into consideration the change in the total population of these oblasts, the increase was only slightly more substantial (07.0 percent) for North Kazakhstan, and there was actually a decrease (08.0 percent) for Kostanai. This stands in stark contrast to the 50 percent increase from the 1989 titular population figures in the Mangistau Oblast and the 31.2 percent increase in the South Kazakhstan Oblast. Both these oblasts fell within the moderately nontitular (non-Kazakh less than 70 percent but greater than 39 percent) category and received far more Kazakh settlement than any of the "highly nontitular" oblasts. We can, therefore, assert that either the implementation of a dilution policy was inefficient or the strategy was not fully formed. Such a conclusion raises the question: If state-directed settlement in the interests of the "nationalization of social space" has not been the prime determinant in the emplacement of the returning Kazakh diaspora, then what factors have been?

The following sections explore *practicality* and *choice* as two factors simultaneously influencing the settlement of Kazakh return migrants. The mere existence of these factors challenges the centrality of "ethnic dilution" as the prime determinant in the settlement patterns of return migrants that manifested over the course of the 1990s.

"Practicality" in Return-Migrant Settlement

I begin by discussing the "practicality" factors in the settlement of Kazakh return migrants, presenting evidence that establishes a pattern of socioeconomic pragmatism in the state-directed elements of their settlement. The prime determinants of this pattern are the availability of housing, the congruence of occupational specialty and economic region, and the climatic similarity with region of departure (former diasporic residence). The first step in examining these practicality factors, however, is to discuss the policies limiting diasporic in-migration enacted by the Kazakhstani government as an example of socioeconomic considerations running in the face of nationalistic fervor.

Limitations of the Kazakh Diaspora's Migration to Kazakhstan

Invitations for Kazakhs living abroad to join their ethnic kinsmen in the new state bearing their name were issued by President Nazarbayev and his representatives throughout the 1990s.[36] The publication of these invitations in newspapers exported to Kazakhs abroad ironically coincided with the Nazarbayev regime's realization that the state was not ready for the volume of return migration that was being catalyzed. By 1993, it became readily apparent to both Kazakhstani officials and many return migrants that the lack of both a political infrastructure (an organization to mange the settlement and citizenship of the "returnees") and a material/economic infrastructure (housing, jobs, funds to support pensioners, education, etc.) for managing the immigrant settlement could cause serious social problems.[37]

Interviews with recently immigrated Kazakhs and directors of funding institutions established to support the settlement of the "returning diaspora" made clear that while some Kazakhs from the "far abroad," or the Oralmandar, were initially provided adequate housing, jobs, and support in accordance with the terms of their labor contracts, there was a dearth of support for those not arriving via labor contracts, those arriving from former Soviet republics, and those opting to remain after the standard five-year contract expired.[38]

As the provision of labor contracts to facilitate migration to Kazakhstan declined over the course of the 1990s, population figures indicate that many diasporic Kazakhs continued to migrate to Kazakhstan.[39] The state's response to the mounting problems that developed as a result of the return migration was to establish quotas to limit the in-migration.

The effectiveness of these quotas was rather limited, as the first eight years of Kazakhstan's independence (1991–98) saw 176,960 people migrate to the state in accordance with set quotas and 375,623 Kazakhs arrive in excess of these quotas.[40] It is perhaps not so coincidental that the most dramatic scaling down of ethnic Kazakh in-migration coincided with the realization of ethnic Kazakh demographic predominance in Kazakhstan (c. 1997–99).

One interpretation of these data suggests that as the need for more Kazakhs became less pressing, the quota system was employed to ease the burden of settlement on the state. It can be argued that in contrast to the early 1990s, when the position of ethnic Kazakhs in the state was far more questionable and a more aggressive demographic dilution strategy was considered necessary, the latter 1990s saw, and the first decade of the twenty-first century will see, smaller numbers of Kazakhs allowed to migrate to Kazakhstan.[41]

An alternative view of the demographic policies enacted by the Kazakhstani government holds that following the initial wave of nationalistic emotion that swept the Kazakh people following independence in 1991, a more realistic appraisal of the country's economic condition compelled a scaling down of diasporic return migration. Such a perspective would be consistent with the public policy shift toward a multinational homeland ideal embodied in the 1995 rewriting of the Constitution. This revision of the Constitution saw the removal of the clause explicitly portraying Kazakhstan as a national homeland for "the self-determined Kazakh nation" and placed far greater emphasis on "Kazakhstani patriotism" as the ultimate goal of the state.[42]

Given the fact that more than 90 percent of the Oralmandar had not received Kazakhstani citizenship by 2000,[43] it can be further argued that their usefulness as a political tool has been greatly limited. Their lack of citizenship has prevented them from voting and thus relegated this category of return migrant to a cultural force. Kazakhs migrating from former Soviet republics had an easier path to naturalization in that they were able to exchange their Soviet passports for Kazakhstani passports. Both perspectives on the scaling down of diasporic ingathering outlined above have merit. However, as will be discussed throughout the next several subsections, a series of socioeconomic factors and individual choices have had a substantial impact on the determination of return-migrant settlement locations. Such evidence supports the latter perspective without completely negating the former.

Practicality: The Availability of Housing

Following interviews in the homes of the Oralmandar, questions arose as to the effectiveness and even existence of a policy of ethnic dilution. In various urban and rural settings, including large cites (Pavlodar, Astana, Karaganda, Almaty), small cities (Temertau, Aktau, Eikbastuz), and a number of villages within several oblasts, Oralman respondents revealed that many of the houses and apartments where they resided were previously the homes of Germans or other minority group members that had emigrated from Kazakhstan. The "abandonment issue" is quite significant when taken in the context of the limited resources available for the construction of new homes for the return migrants. As demonstrated in table 9.1, the high volume of German, Ukrainian, Belarusan, and Russian migration from the northern oblasts has been significant enough to open up considerable space for new settlers.

The practicality of settling the Oralmandar in the abandoned homes of departing ethnic groups is unambiguous and not necessarily related to an ethnic-dilution policy. President Nazarbayev acknowledged that the process was occurring and even encouraged it in a speech given in 2000, excerpted here:

> About the policy of demography and migration—it was the policy to move the capital to Astana. For example, you know how many Kazakhs were in Akmola in 1996, now the number of Kazakhs is more than half of the inhabitants. From there (Astana) Germans migrated and left their houses and I know that Kazakhs who moved to the Akmola region get these empty houses. This is one process. But, we cannot tell to the Kazakhs who live in the south to move to the north, and yet we have to open institutions of industry and petroleum in these regions by sending graduates to work in the north.[44]

Although this speech acknowledges the difficulty of impelling Kazakhs from the south to move north in the interest of obtaining jobs abandoned by the departing Russians and Germans, it also implies satisfaction with the increase in the number of ethnic Kazakhs in Akmola/Astana.[45]

The matter of language is especially important in the "nationalization of social space," because one of the central precepts for the creation of most nation-states is the establishment of a common language among the peoples of that state. For Kazakhstan, the promotion of the Kazakh language to the position of "official state language" runs counter to a long history of Russification in the region.

As discussed in a series of Kazakh-language newspaper articles impelling the resettlement of Kazakhs from the southern oblasts to the northern oblasts, the lack of Kazakh speakers in these oblasts is seen as a threat to the legitimacy of the state.[46] These publications make a point of the fact that, even among the long-standing ethnic Kazakh population of the northern oblasts, the Kazakh language remains in rather limited use.[47] Proximity to Russian labor markets and greater numbers of non-Kazakhs impede a large-scale embrace of the Kazakh language among the peoples of this region, thus compelling the resettlement of Kazakhs in accordance with "nationalization of social space." As I demonstrate here, however, the settlement of return migrants from non-CIS countries in such circumstances is a double-edged sword.

For those Kazakhs migrating from countries like China, Mongolia, Iran, Turkey, and Afghanistan, their command of Kazakh is most often far superior to their knowledge of Russian; in many cases, they have no knowledge of the Cyrillic alphabet[48] or Russian language at all.[49] Though increasing the "traditional Kazakh" cultural character of these oblasts, the emplacement of these Oralman return migrants within a highly Russified environment impairs their ability to socially integrate and gain employment. Such a condition sets the stage for dissatisfaction with settlement venues and the rupturing of "return myths."

Practicality: The Availability of Jobs

As noted in the Nazarbayev speech excerpted above, the availability of jobs in the aftermath of the large-scale migration of European groups increases the attractiveness of the northern oblasts for the settlement of return migrants. Though it is true that many Germans and Russians functioned in managerial positions in the Soviet Union, many members of these groups also functioned in the "labor/industrial" and "labor/agriculture" sectors. This is especially true in rural regions, where many return migrants are currently working in the cattle-raising industry regardless of the specialty of training they brought with them from their country of diasporic residence.

According to interviews, the vast majority of labor contracts that brought diasporic Kazakhs to Kazakhstan in the early 1990s required five years of service on animal-raising *kolkhozy* or state farms. For many Oralmandar, this was a difficult period because a considerable portion of the initial migrants were elites, who had little experience with raising cattle:

> I was an engineer in Mongolia but here I raise cattle. My sister is a nurse, my brother is a journalist but they also raise cattle. I have requested that I be allowed to work in my specialty but our degrees are not very respected here in Kazakhstan and my Russian is not so good. Many Oralmandar have no jobs at all, so we must work where we can and trust that the future will be better—God willing.[50]

The policy of compelling most Oralmandar, especially those from Mongolia, to work as "cattle raisers" held a sociogeographic component in that, according to economic data, the primary regions of cattle production in Kazakhstan are the northern oblasts of Kostanai, Akmola, Pavlodar, Aktobe, and West Kazakhstan.[51] The pastoral industry in the southern oblasts revolves around sheep and goats, and return migrants from Uzbekistan and states with warmer climates are used to bolster this labor force (see figure 9.3).

Figure 9.3. Pastoral Regions of Kazakhstan

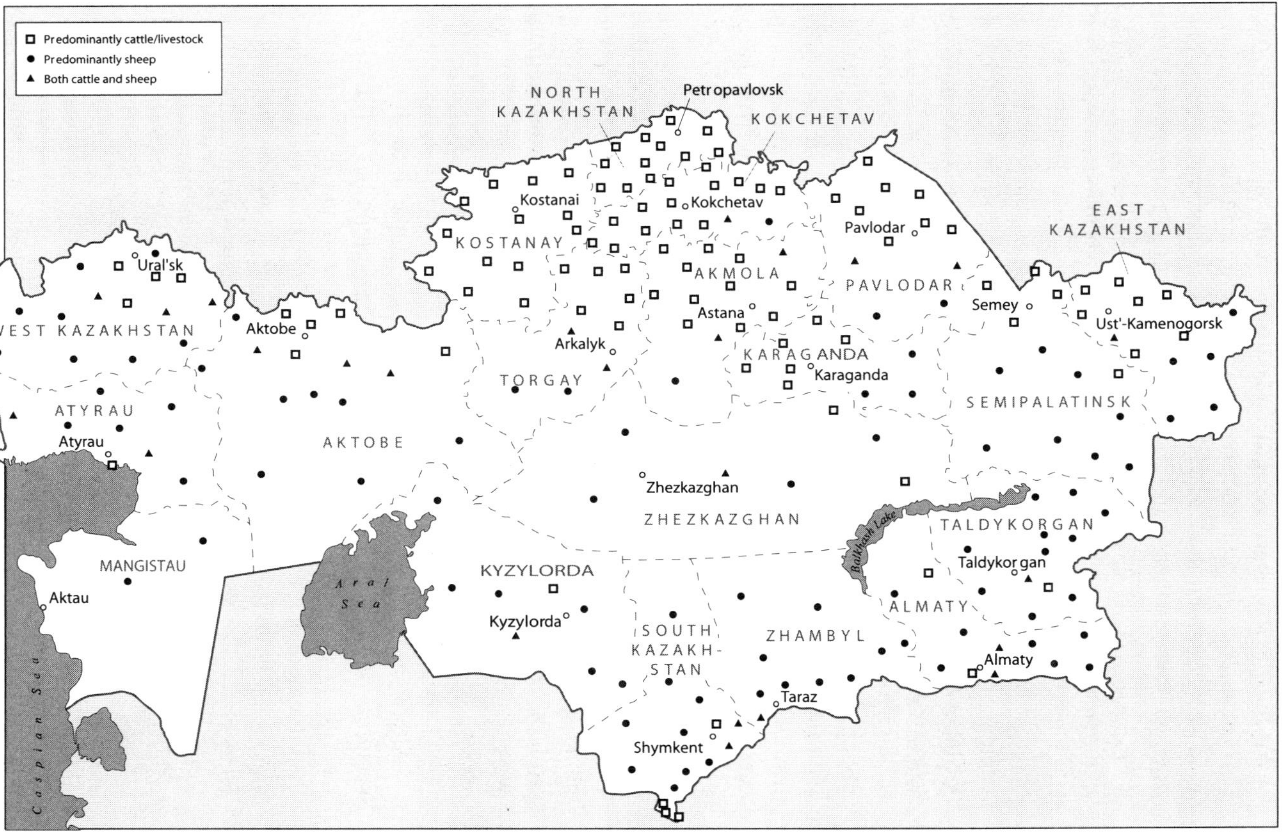

With the agricultural sector of Kazakhstan's economy suffering greatly during the 1990s, improving the economic conditions in these regions would have been commensurate with the "nationalization of social space." High unemployment in these regions raises the specter of "geographies of resistance," wherein various groups could potentially challenge the sovereignty of the state.[52] By improving the economic conditions in the northern oblasts, it is hoped that the nontitular populations will integrate within the economy and find a means of reterritorializing their identities within Kazakhstan. Settlement of ethnic Kazakhs in the regions serves a dual purpose. It bolsters the labor force and enhances the presence of peoples considered more loyal to the regime.

Such a twofold benefit is also regarded by the Nazarbayev regime as applying to the dramatic demographic increase in the number of Kazakhs in the cities of Almaty and Astana over the last sixteen years. In 1989, Almaty was 76.2 percent nontitular and Astana (then called Akmola) was 82.3 percent nontitular; today Almaty stands at 61.5 percent and Astana 58.2 percent nontitular (an increase in Kazakhs of some 70.3 percent for Almaty and 168.3 percent for Astana).[53] Rather than resulting from a government settlement policy, however, this shift may be regarded as a natural process of intrastate migration filling the void left by nontitular emigration. The economic downturn in Kazakhstan's rural regions catalyzes urbanization, particularly among Kazakhs (both Kazakhstani Kazakhs and return migrants), who represent the majority of Kazakhstan's rural population. For those seeking to escape the poverty of the countryside, the employment, educational, and cultural centers of Almaty and Astana serve as magnetic poles.[54]

Although Almaty and Astana are somewhat unique in the Kazakhstani socioeconomic landscape, ethnic Kazakh urbanization has occurred in almost all the regional urban centers of the state. It should also be noted that the settlement of return migrants has not been carried out strictly on the basis of housing and job availability. As noted above, where possible, climatic factors have also been considered in the determination of optimal settlement locations for the various communities of repatriates.

Practicality: Climatic Similarity with the Departed Region

Although not true in every case, a pattern of climatic determinism is evident in the settlements of the return migrants. Iranian, Afghanistani, Uzbekistani, and Karakalpaki returnees have been predominantly settled in southern oblasts. The large numbers of nonquota returnees make this pattern even more pronounced, as they have been inclined to settle in regions of ecological familiarity and where family members preceded them.[55] In contrast, a large percentage of Mongolian, Chinese, and Russian returnees were settled in northern oblasts.[56]

As noted above, much of this pattern can be related to the availability of jobs and housing and to the policy of assigning Mongolian and Chinese Kazakhs to cattle-raising *kolkhozy.* However, on several occasions, communities of return migrants from various venues of former diasporic existence have called for the creation of "areas of compact living" for their specific hyphenated identity group. The regions suggested for these areas of compact living are of relative climatic familiarity for these groups.[57] An example is available in a letter from a Mongolian Kazakh parliamentarian to President Nazarbayev dated April 28, 1992, in which a specific request is made for Mongolian Kazakh Oralmandar to live compactly:

> We, Mongolian Kazakhs want to settle in the East Kazakhstan Oblast and in the Aksuat region of the Semipolitinsk Oblast,[58] because they are comfortable in this setting and the climate is similar to Mongolia. It is also our ancestral land.[59]

The climatic and ecological similarities between northeastern Kazakhstan and the Mongolian Kazakh *aimag* (province) of Bayan Olgi (western Mongolia) are significant, as to similar length of winter and considerable grazing lands. However, due to the higher elevation of Bayan Olgi, the climate is considerably dryer than Kazakhstan's.

Interviews with several return-migrant groups revealed serious health problems among many of the older and younger family members. These problems are quite often attributed to the humidity or temperature of settlement locations in Kazakhstan. Uzbekistani Kazakh return migrants settling in the northern oblasts and Mongolian Kazakh Oralmandar settling in southern oblasts aired comparable complaints. Many eventually engaged in secondary migrations, which are discussed below. Attempts to settle return-migrant communities within regions of greater ecological and climatic familiarity appear to run counter to a strategy of overt demographic dilution, which would logically be unconcerned with such factors.

Having said this, I must admit that the pragmatic approach to settlement discussed above should be viewed with a skeptical eye. Given that housing and jobs were available because European groups emigrated, the question of the impact of the settlement of return migrants on the remaining European groups must be addressed. If this settlement were in fact a causal force in European minority emigration (which has not been concretely established), then the settlement location would be tautologically justified (i.e., settlement causes the emigration of European groups—and the emigration of European groups impels further settlement). Climatic similarity could also be manipulated to rationalize settlement where the government wanted more Kazakhs, in that the government could control the number migrating from each country. If more Kazakhs were needed in the south, then more Iranian, Afghanistani, and Uzbekistani Kazakhs could be added to the quota; whereas, if more Kazakhs were needed in the north, then more Mongolian, Chinese, and Russian Kazakhs could be added.

The fact remains, however, that much of the original settlement pattern of return migrants has become moot, as Kazakhs, often priding themselves on their nomadic traditions, have engaged in secondary migrations once within Kazakhstan. Such secondary migrations problematize efforts to ascertain the centrality of government direction in the settlement of returning Kazakhs by negating whatever governmental influence existed in the initial placement of these groups. The matter of return-migrant "choice" in settlement is, therefore, explored in the following section.

"Choice" in Return-Migrant Settlements

The secondary migration of return migrants is often attributed to the nomadic cultural background of the Kazakh people and, among those migrating from the "far abroad," was regularly cited in interviews as an example of the cultural purity retained among the Kazakhs in "exile." This notion of cultural purity has become a major issue among Oralmandar elites, who relate many of their problems of adaptation in Kazakhstan to the Russification that took place among Kazakhstani and other Kazakhs in the Soviet Union during the communist era.[60] Among the various return-migrant communities, dreams of a "Kazakh" homeland have quite often been unfulfilled. Rather than linking secondary migration to cultural issues alone, however, interviews suggest that secondary migrations were compelled by a variety of problems in locales of initial settlement:[61]

> Internal migrations? Yes, these are very common. In 1991, in Taldikurgan 1,000 Kazakh families were settled. They chose this place after

> scouts had said it was good. After ten months, 600 families moved to another oblast. Fifty families moved back to Mongolia and a large percentage to Karaganda and Pavlodar and the East Kazakhstan Oblast as well, but 100 families then returned from East Kazakhstan because they thought it would be like Mongolia but found it too cold and went back to Taldikurgan, where they thought it was too hot.[62]

As suggested in this quotation and supported by other interviews with return migrants, settlement of the initial migration was not strictly dictated by the state. Rather, a measure of choice of settlement location was evident for many immigrants from the start. The most prominent factors affecting the choice of location for settlement of the Oralmandar were climate, family (social networks), employment opportunities, subcultural heritage, educational opportunities, and cultural purity.

Choice: Scouts and the Settlement of the Initial Return Migrants

According to return migrants in various regions of Kazakhstan, the decision to migrate to their "historical homeland" was undertaken with high hopes of joining the new independent Kazakh nation-state. Nationalistic fervor was high in the aftermath of the Soviet collapse, as diasporic Kazakhs were quick to reify the memories of their community's dispersal and the hardships of their lives "abroad." When overtures were made by the Kazakhstani government or its agents (state farms, etc.) to migrate to Kazakhstan, a list was often provided to community and family leaders from which a settlement destination could be selected. As discussed above, this list was often adjusted for the climatic, occupational, and housing needs of the community, but the element of *choice* remained available. In addition to the listed sites of potential settlement, 70 percent of those interviewed indicated that their families sent a "scout" to ascertain the best venue for the family's settlement.

The choices made by these scouts and by family leaders were often based, however, on imperfect information about the availability of housing, climatic conditions, and the cultural compatibility of diasporic Kazakhs with the social environment of their intended settlement location. Problems arising after initial settlements were commonplace,[63] leading occasionally to return migration to the region/country of departure (i.e., Mongolia or Russia, etc.), but more commonly to secondary migrations to new settlement sites within Kazakhstan. The factors playing into the decision are outlined below.

Choice: Social Networks as Factors in the Settlement Location

Among the more prominent factors compelling return-migrant settlement in particular regions of Kazakhstan is the existence of social networks into which a returnee family can find security and be provided employment opportunities. Culturally, Kazakhs are highly inclined to function within extended family networks. In their sites of diasporic residence, it is not uncommon for Kazakhs to have a vast knowledge of the family history of most of the community. "Degrees of separation" are maintained by patrilineal endogamy taboos (to the seventh historical generation), although intraclan marriages have become more prominent among diasporic Kazakh communities than among Kazakhstani Kazakhs. Among the chief complaints of return migrants, particularly the Oralmandar, is the dispersal of their diasporic community in Kazakhstan (i.e., the distances, both social and physical, from their relatives).

As noted in the previous section, many return migrants have proposed the creation of "areas of compact living" for Kazakhs from particular countries (i.e., a Mongolian Kazakh area of compact living, and an Iranian Kazakh area of compact living, etc.) as a means of addressing the issue of dispersal.[64] Others have strongly opposed such concentrations of returnees on the basis of the need to integrate return migrants into the more broadly defined Kazakhstani society and in the interests of avoiding a precedent for autonomous area construction that could be utilized by "ethnic" minority communities within Kazakhstan.[65]

What is often undervalued in this argument is the fact that proximity to familial social networks is imperative for the integration of return migrants into Kazakhstani society. As discussed by Edward Schatz and Nurbulat Masanov, deep-seated norms impelling familial and ethnic nepotism among Kazakhs are prevalent in contemporary Kazakhstani society.[66] To gain employment, "strings must be pulled." This is especially so for return migrants. Among those from the "far abroad," the lack of Kazakhstani citizenship and Russian language skills often hampers their capacity to function in the job market. Living in proximity to one's relatives not only provides access to the everyday support networks, which are invaluable in the underdeveloped economy of Kazakhstan's rural regions, but also enables employment-seeking return migrants to tap into an "*aga* (Kazakh word for 'brother') network."[67]

As late migrants join early migrants, however, this "pipeline of employment" becomes increasingly crowded, leading to tensions within clans and families. One outlet of this tension, which has been prominently utilized by young Oralmandar, is the opportunity for free higher education provided by the Kazakhstani government to Kazakhs from non-CIS countries. Among 641 Oralmandar surveyed, 57 percent stated that they "strongly agreed" that their children's futures were better in Kazakhstan than in their country of diasporic existence. Another 20.6 percent stated that they "somewhat agreed," with 10 percent providing no response and only 12.3 percent disagreeing. Follow-up interviews revealed that educational opportunities for children were among the more prominent reasons for their decisions to migrate and remain in Kazakhstan. Educational opportunities can also have an effect on the location of settlement, in that family leaders often stated a desire to be near universities for their older children. As time passes, the return migrants that came to Kazakhstan as children grow to become young adults seeking university educations for themselves and the families they have started since their "repatriation."

In accordance with the issues of job and housing availability discussed above, secondary migrations were also catalyzed by a desire to move to regions where greater material benefits were available. Kazakh-language newspapers carried a series of articles wherein the construction of new towns for return migrants,[68] as well as advantages of moving from southern oblasts to northern oblasts, were discussed.[69] These articles served as advertisements, impelling many Kazakhstani Kazakhs, as well as return migrants, to relocate. For a number of return migrants, two additional factors playing into the decision to relocate were the combination of climatic familiarity and subcultural history.

Choice: Subcultural Factors in the Settlement Location

The Kazakh ethnos possesses a number of subethnic categories, including *zhuz, orda,* tribe, and clan. Wheras *ordalar* (*-lar* being the plural ending for the word *orda*) were political configurations that were obliterated by tsarist rule, *zhuzdar* (*-dar* being the plural ending for the word *zhuz*) could not be suppressed and continue to serve as a component of Kazakh identity to this day. In fact, the *zhuzdar* are the largest subdivision of the Kazakh ethnos, representing genealogical configurations to which every Kazakh belongs.

Historically, each *zhuz* occupied a traditional region, within which it would conduct its seasonal migrations. The senior *zhuz* occupied the Semireche and southeastern portions of the steppe, while the junior *zhuz* occupied the northwestern region, with the middle *zhuz* existing between them. The exact date of the division of the Kazakhs into separate *zhuzdar* is unknown, because Islamic sources do not mention the division of the Kazakhs into *zhuzdar* and *ordalar.* In 1616, Russian sources elude to a "big" or "senior" horde, implying that a "little" or "junior" horde must also have existed. It is, however, not until 1731 that all three Kazakh divisions are mentioned.

Many of the tribal groupings composing each *zhuz* can be traced to a pre-Mongol occupation of the Eurasian steppes and are subidentities historically evident in prior political confederations, such as the Kipchak, Pecheneg, and Uzbek. Examples of these tribes include the senior *zhuz*'s Dulat, Kangli, Zhalyir, and Alban; and the middle *zhuz*'s Kipchak, Naiman, Kongrat, and Kereit; whereas the junior *zhuz*'s tribes appear to be unique to the Kazakh confederation. Clan distinctions fall along the lines of smaller-scale genealogical distinctions, usually relating to a particular ancestor (e.g., the Kereit tribe has numerous clan subdivisions, such as Zhadik, Sherushi, Zhantekei, Iteli, Karakas, Molky, Shybaraighyr, and Merkit).

These subethnic divisions are significant in that the Kazakh diasporic communities were often composed predominantly of one *zhuz* and a small number of tribes. A clear example of this is available in the Mongolian Kazakh community, which is almost exclusively *orta* (middle) *zhuz* and comprises predominantly the Kereit, Naiman, Uak, and Arghyn tribes.[70] The geographical histories of these groups are highly localized,[71] and, given that the migrants that formed the Kazakh diaspora left Kazakhstan arguably before Kazakh nationalization, the territorialization of subnational identities could be far stronger than the national.

In an effort to explore this hypothesis, survey responses to questions relating to the desire to settle in the region of one's ancestors (i.e., the ancestors who left or those who preceded those who left Kazakhstan) were sought from 642 Kazakh Oralmandar in various regions of Kazakhstan. These responses revealed 32.4 percent as "very strongly" factoring this region into their settlement plans; 14.5 percent, "somewhat"; 15.2 percent, providing no response; 14.5 percent, "somewhat not"; and 23.4 percent, not considering their ancestor's regions at all. In a follow-up interview, a Mongolian Kazakh Oralman stated:

> I am *orta zhuz* [middle *zhuz*]. My tribe is Naiman. Where would I place my *ui* [*yurta,* home] in Kazakhstan? I must be in the lands of the Naiman, I must feed my horses in the grasses on the shores of the Oz Zaisan [Lake Zaisan]. My fathers [ancestors] were buried there. I cannot live in the desert or the city. I must be in the steppe place of my relatives.[72]

As demonstrated by this quotation, consideration of ancestral land as a factor in family-unit resettlement within Kazakhstan is especially prevalent when viewed in combination with ecological conditions.

Choice: Climate as a Factor Influencing Oralmandar Choice of the Settlement Location

According to survey data, only 6.8 percent of 642 Oralmandar consider climate to be the "biggest problem" facing them in their resettlement in Kazakhstan, but this statistic must be considered in light of the secondary migrations that have resorted not only the Oralmandar but also the broadly defined return-migrant population. Former return migrants interviewed in Bayan Olgi (i.e., those that had returned to Mongolia after an attempted repatriation to Kazakhstan), presented their inability to adapt to the climate of their Kazakhstani settlement venue as a primary factor in their decision to return to Mongolia. Stories of sickness (even to the point of death) among children and the elderly were commonly attributed to greater humidity.

The vast majority of Kazakhs living outside CIS countries, including Mongolia,[73] had little opportunity to visit Kazakhstan before their migration. Scouts for various prospective migrant groups often made their choices based on experience over a short period of time. The seasonal climatic variance between different regions of Kazakhstan is considerable and, when taken in combination with the climatic difference between Kazakhstan and the regions of diasporic residence, return migrants were often confronted with living conditions for which they were unprepared:

> My brother came [to Kazakhstan] first—to find a good place for us. He chose Kyzylorda for our home, but when we settled there, we found it too hot, too humid, and the water was not pure like Bayan Olgi's. After one year we moved to Pavlodar and, here, we are much happier. It is more like our homeland in Mongolia.[74]

Similar patterns of secondary migration are evident in moves south by Uzbekistani, Afghanistani, and Iranian Kazakh return migrants. Interviews with students in Almaty suggested that even young people from these groups have opted for universities in regions of greater climatic familiarity. One Oralman student stated, "My first years after returning to Kazakhstan were spent in Astana, but I was unable to live there. It was so cold and wet or hot and wet. I left law school and now study finance in Almaty. It is better for me, better for my health."[75]

While withholding comment on the validity of these unfavorable climatic comparisons between Kazakhstani regions and the regions/countries of diasporic residence, I am confident in concluding that most Oralmandar and many members of the general return-migrant group were not fully aware of the cultural character or natural environment that awaited them in Kazakhstan. Their migrations were often undertaken amid nationalistic fervor resulting from the emergence of a state bearing the Kazakh ethnonym and within the context of imperfect information that generated grand dreams (return myths), which have, quite often, been unfulfilled.

Conclusion

Although it is not possible to ascertain every motive for the Kazakhstani government's ingathering of diasporic peoples, it would be naive to think that this policy was not intended to provide the human resources necessary to increase the general legitimacy of the ethnic Kazakh regime. Having said this, the data presented in this chapter suggest a dearth of evidence in support of the thesis that the settlement of the returning diaspora overtly targeted regions with a high concentration of nontitular populations. These data also demonstrate that a series of other factors played into the emplacement of Kazakh return migrants. Among these factors were practical issues, such as employment and housing availability and the climatic compatibility of returning groups within settlement regions. Additional factors included personal choice issues, such as the consideration of ancestral history and a desire to reside within existing sociospatial networks as criteria for assessing potential settlement sites by family or community scouts. This study has also hopefully revealed that reality is often far less opaque up close than it appears when studied from afar.

Important facets of this book's broader discussion of migration brought to light in this chapter include state control versus individual choice, the tension between nationalism and economic pragmatism, and the role of memory in dispersed groups' attachments to home and homeland. It seems clear that stark neoclassical terms relating to migration fail to capture the breadth and diversity of migration experiences. A more textured understanding of historical, social, political, and economic factors in shaping attitudes and beliefs about "home" is imperative to understanding migration decisions.

Despite the state's apparent stability, Kazakhstan's raison d'être is among the least securely defined of all the states emerging from the Soviet collapse. The question remains to be answered: Is Kazakhstan a homeland for ethnic Kazakhs, or is it a multinational homeland wherein all peoples have equal access to belonging? Like other postcolonial states, the retention of the provincial ethnic place name in the creation of the Republic of Kazakhstan sent a message to all ethnic Kazakhs living within and outside the new state that "a historical wrong had been righted," as a portion of the Earth's surface would finally serve as the independent homeland for the Kazakh people. Such a declaration is not surprising given the years of repression of Kazakh culture and language, first within the Russian and later Soviet "imperial" structures. However, the cultural revival inspired by this symbolic act has great potential to catalyze interactive ethnonationalism and, ironically, threaten the very existence of the state. The need to find a means to resurrect and celebrate Kazakh-ness within the structure of a *Kazakhstani* civic-national identity has been discussed by Kazakhstan's Nazarbayev regime throughout the independence period. This public discourse has, however, not quelled the passions of Kazakh nationalists or the fears of nontitular citizens.

The Kazakh diaspora, like many diasporas of the titular and nontitular nations of Eurasia, remains sorely understudied. Given varied living conditions of its branch communities, challenges to the integration of those migrating to Kazakhstan are not and will not be uniform. Return migrants from CIS countries are and will be far more capable of functioning within Kazakhstan's Russified environs and familiar with the form and function of post-Soviet society. In contrast, the Oralmandar or migrants from the far abroad must adapt to the continued predominance of the Russian language in Kazakhstani society and adjust their dreams of a "Kazakh" homeland to fit the multinational reality of their settlement locales. Further research is needed to understand these and other challenges, as well as the impact of this diasporic ingathering on the future "nationalization of social space" within an independent Kazakhstan.

Notes

1. For a discussion of contrasting views relating to the Soviet Union's role as colonizer, see A. Stringer, "Soviet Development in Central Asia: The Classic Colonial Syndrome?" in *Central Asia Aspects of Transition,* ed. T. Everett-Heath (London: RoutledgeCurzon, 2003), 146–66.

2. The formation of the "Imperial diaspora" of ethnic Russians and incorporation of the "near abroad" into the Soviet state have their roots in the Russian Empire but were maintained and enhanced within the Soviet Union. See J. Chinn and R. Kaiser, *Russians as the New Minority: Ethnicity and Nationalism in the Soviet Successor States* (Boulder, Colo.: Westview Press, 1996); N. V. Masanov, "Mugratsionnyye Meta'orfozy Kazakhstana" (Migration Metamorphoses of Kazakhstan), in *Dvizhenii Dobrovolnom i Vynuzhdennom* (On the Move: Voluntarily and Involuntarily), ed. A. Vyatikin et al. (Moscow: Natalis Press, 1999), 127–52; N. Melvin, *Russians beyond Russia: The Politics of National Identity* (London: Royal Institute of International Affairs, 1995); and D. Laitin, *Identity in Formation: The Russian-Speaking Populations in the Near Abroad* (Ithaca, N.Y.: Cornell University Press, 1998).

3. W. Safran, "Diasporas in Modern Societies: Myths of Homeland and Return," *Diaspora* 1, no. 1 (1991): 83–92.

4. As noted by Shantha Henneyake, this process may also be covertly or even unintentionally catalyzed through more subtle forms of interactive ethnonational expression. The reconstruction of national histories, various landscape changes (i.e., public iconography, street signs, toponyms), and ethnonepotism are examples of these more subtle forms of ethnonationalism. Both overt and covert manifestations of these processes are readily apparent in the 'repatriation' of ethnic-Kazakhs to an independent Kazakhstan. Shantha Hennayake, "Interactive Ethnonationalism: An Alternative Explanation of Minority Ethnonationalism," *Political Geography* 11, no. 6 (1992): 526–49. Also see A. C. Diener, "One Homeland or Two? Territorialization of Identity and the Repatriation Decision of the Mongolian Kazakh Diaspora," PhD dissertation, Department of Geography, University of Wisconsin–Madison, 2003; and S. N. Cummings, "The Kazakhs: Demographics, Diasporas, and Return," in *Nations Abroad,* ed. C. King and N. Melvin (Boulder, Colo.: Westview Press, 1998), 137–54.

5. Cummings, "The Kazakhs," 136, places these numbers at 1,665,000 within the former Soviet Union and 1,535,000 outside the former Soviet Union. It should be noted that more recent estimates of the size of the Kazakh diaspora have elevated the total to roughly 4.1 million; see S. Zhusupov, *Strategiya Migratsionnoi Programmy "Oralman," Materialy po Stratelicheskomu S'ezbu* (Almaty: Kazakhstan Institue for Social and Economic Information and Forecasting, 2001). One may also note that many Kazakhs in China consider themselves indigenous to Eastern Turkestan and do not trace themselves to the early Soviet era exodus.

6. There is a problem with the terms "return" migrants and "repatriates," in that the multigenerational members of the Kazakh diaspora are not "re-patriating"—they are in fact "patriating" for the first time. The Kazakh term for people migrating from the "far-abroad" is *Oralman-dar* (*dar* being the plural ending). This term derives from the Kazakh verb *oralu* = to return. It should also be noted that the term *Oralman* is legally restricted to Kazakhs coming to Kazakhstan within the structure of the quota system established by the Kazakhstani government in 1993. According to Cummings, "The Kazakhs," 148, this system sought to differentiate between Kazakhs from the former Soviet Union and from the far abroad. In other words, Kazakhs migrating to Kazakhstan outside the quota system or from former Soviet republics were not officially designated as *Oralmandar* or eligible for the benefits of sponsored settlement. Despite this technical distinction, the term has come into popular use in reference to all Kazakhs migrating to Kazakhstan from outside the state's territory.

7. The results of the latest Kazakhstani elections indicate that 80 percent of the rep-

resentatives to the lower chamber of the Kazakhstani legislature (Majlis) are ethnic Kazakhs.

8. It should be noted that the Russophone community of Kazakhstan, made up of virtually all the nontitular peoples and, rather interestingly, a majority of the titular peoples of the state, have demonstrated considerable support of the Nazarbayev regime over the course of the first decade of independence. See J. Holm-Hansen, "Political Integration in Kazakhstan," in *Nation Building and Ethnic Integration in Post Soviet Societies: An Investigation of Latvia and Kazakhstan,* ed. Pol Kolsto (Oxford: Westview Press, 1999), 126–53; Bhavna Dave, "National Revival in Kazakhstan: Language Shift and Identity Change," *Post Soviet Affairs* 12, no. 1 (1996): 51–72; and M. B. Olcott, *Kazakhstan: Unfulfilled Promise* (Washington, D.C.: Carnegie Endowment for International Peace, 2002).

9. See Holm-Hansen, "Political Integration"; Chinn and Kaiser, *Russians as the New Minority;* Olcott, *Kazakhstan;* R. Wofel, "North to Astana: Nationalistic Motives for the Movement of the Kazakh(stani) Capital," *Nationalities Papers* 30, no. 3 (2002): 485–505; Cengiz Surucu, "Modernity, Nationalism, Resistance: Identity Politics in Post Soviet Kazakhstan," *Central Asian Survey* 21, no. 4 (2000): 385–402; A. C. Diener, "National Territory and the Reconstruction of History in Kazakhstan," *Eurasian Geography and Economics,* no.8 (2002): 632–50; and A. C. Diener, *Homeland Conceptions and Ethnic Integration among Kazakhstan's Germans and Koreans* (Lampeter, U.K.: Edwin Mellen Press, 2004).

10. As adroitly noted by Surucu, "Kazakh nationalism is an umbrella term comprising a diverse spectrum of opinions rather than a coherent political position." Surucu, "Modernity, Nationalism, Resistance," n. 27. Nevertheless, it can be fairly stated that a common element binding the various political factions promoting Kazakh nationalism is a belief in the primacy of ethnic Kazakhs within the territory of Kazakhstan. The degree to which this is to be exclusive of other groups varies but the "Kazakhs first" mentality is, by definition, pervasive among these groups.

11. A survey of forty questions was conducted among 600+ Kazakh return migrants in various venues throughout Kazakhstan during 2001 and 2002. These venues included Almaty, Astana, Pavlodar, Karaganda, and a number of smaller towns and villages. Fifty in-depth interviews, ten focus groups, and library/archival research methods were employed in these locales in an effort to triangulate data on this complex and highly subjective topic.

12. P. Finke, "The Kazaks of Western Mongolia," in *Contemporary Kazakhs: Cultural and Social Perspectives,* ed. I. Svanberg (Richmond, U.K.: Curzon Press, 1999), 115; the emphasis is in the original, using quotation marks around the word "Kazak."

13. M. Tatimov, "Etnicheskiye Arealy v Kazakhstane," in *Potentsialynye Etnokonflikty v Kazakhstane i Preventivnaya Etnopolitika* (Potential Ethnoconflict in Kazakhstan and Preventive Ethnopolitics), ed. Y. Kasenov et al. (Almaty: Atamura, 1997), 19–24; the quotation is on 19.

14. Ian Bremmer and Cory Welt, "The Problem with Democracy in Kazakhstan," *Central Asian Survey* 15, no. 2 (1996): 179–99; the quotations are on 184. See also the discussion by Cummings, "The Kazakhs," 141, of the dovetailing of repatriation policy with internal redistribution polices of the Kazakhstani government seeking to increase the ethnic Kazakh population in various border regions. Melvin, *Russians beyond Russia,* 109, also states that "many (returning Kazakhs) are being resettled in the European-Slav areas in order to redress the demographic imbalance." Bremmer states that "the

Kazakh government has also worked to increase the Kazakh population in the north by stimulating migration. This has involved both the channeling of diaspora Kazakhs from Mongolia, Uzbekistan and other countries to northern Kazakhstan, as well as the creation of financial incentives for Kazakhs from densely populated Kazakh areas to resettle." I. Bremmer, "Nazarbayev and the North: State Building and Ethnic Relations in Kazakhstan," *Ethnic and Racial Studies* 17, no. 4 (1994): 619–35; this quotation is on 621.

15. Colin Williams and Anthony Smith, "The National Construction of Social Space," *Progress in Human Geography* 7, no. 4 (1983): 502–19. The settlement of ethnic Kazakh immigrants in the predominantly Russian northern oblasts (see table 9.2 and figures 9.1 and 9.2), is argued to be a deliberate effort by the Kazakhstani government to "Kazakhize" the population in the north; "Kazakhstan: The Question of Dual Citizenship Is Entirely Appropriate," *Current Digest of the Post-Soviet Press* 45, no. 48 (1993): 20.

16. Williams and Smith, "National Construction of Social Space."

17. "Manipulation of the environment" refers to the activation of both the physical and social resources of a given territory for service of the nation. Substate rejection of the state's purview to manipulate the physical environment, such as protests against foreign companies extracting Kazakhstani oil, criticism of the Nazarbayev regime's cession of land to China and Uzbekistan (E. M. Aben, R. K. Zholaman, Y. T. Karin, S. K. Kushkumbaev, and M. U. Spanov, "Potentsialnye Territorialnye Spory i Konflikty v Kontekste bezopasnosti Tsentralno-aziatskovo Regiona" [Potential Territorial Disputes and Conflicts in the Context of the Security of Central Asian Region], *Evraziiskoe Soobshestvo* 4, no. 24 [1998]: 54–84) use of Kazakhstan as a corridor for drug trafficking, and movements to formulate autonomous regions for particular minority communities (M. Maksimov, "Seoul Likely to Seek 'Korean National Enclave'," *Komsomolskaya Pravda,* November 18, 1992; R. Moniac, "Bonn Insists on CIS Area for Ethnic Germans," *Die Welt,* January 31, 1992; P. A. Goble, "Can Republican Borders Be Changed?" *Report on the USSR,* no. 28, 1990, 20–21), threaten the internal territorial sovereignty of the state. As a result, states seek not only to monopolize the legitimate use of violence in order to control the social environment but to exercise control and surveillance over the physical environment as well; M. Foucault, *Discipline and Punish: The Birth of the Prison* (New York: Vintage Books, 1995).

18. "Abstraction of the land" refers to the process by which nationalist exertions confer new meanings upon territory and redefine society's relationship to nature. See D. W. Meinig, *The Interpretation of Ordinary Landscapes* (Oxford: Oxford University Press, 1979); R. Koshar, *From Monuments to Traces: Artifacts of German Memory 1870–1990* (Berkeley: University of California Press, 2000); K. Till, "Staging the Past: Landscape Design, Cultural Ideas, and *Erinnerungspolitik* at Berlin's *Neue Wache,*" *Ecumene* 6, no. 2 (1999): 251–83; R. J. Kaiser, *The Geography of Nationalism in Russia and the USSR* (Princeton, N.J.: Princeton University Press, 1994); and R. J. Kaiser, "Geography and Nationalism," in *Encyclopedia of Nationalism,* ed. A. Motyl (London: Academic Press, 2001). Linguistic revival and historiographic alignment of regional heroes and territorially autochthonous stories with national myths are examples of this trend; see Anthony Smith, "Culture, Community and Territory: The Politics of Ethnicity and Nationalism," *International Affairs* 72, no. 3 (1996): 445–58; and G. Hage, "The Spatial Imaginary of National Practices: Dwelling-Domestication/Being-Exterminating," *Society and Space* 14 (1996): 463–85. Through its provision of "voice" and individual

rights, democracy is hoped to engender territorialized identity within the patriotic (civic-national) framework of modern multinational states; A. O. Hirschman, *Exit, Voice and Loyalty: Responses to Decline in Firms, Organizations, and States* (Cambridge, Mass.: Harvard University Press, 1970). However, in the case of Kazakhstan, as with many burgeoning states of former Soviet Central Asia, its questionable status as a modern "nation" and lack of historical state tradition brings these three trends to the fore. See Bremmer, "Nazarbayev and the North"; Bremmer and Welt, "Problem with Democracy"; Melvin, *Russians beyond Russia;* Olcott, *Kazakhstan;* and Diener, "National Territory."

19. Of note here is the current literature challenging the centrality of the state in international relations. See K. Ohmae, *The End of the Nation-State* (New York: Free Press, 1995); A. Appadurai, "Sovereignty without Territoriality: Notes for a Post-National Geography," in *The Geography of Identity,* ed. P. Yaeger (Ann Arbor, Mich.: Ratio, 1996), 41–58; and M. Castells, *The Power of Identity* (Oxford: Blackwell, 1997).

20. Williams and Smith, "National Construction of Social Space," 513.

21. Ibid.

22. See Wofel, "North to Astana"; E. A. D. Schatz, *Modern Clan Politics: The Power of Blood in Kazakhstan and Beyond* (Seattle: University of Washington Press, 2004).

23. Williams and Smith, "National Construction of Social Space," 513.

24. Irredentist sentiment targeting the northern Oblasts of Kazakhstan has periodically emanated from Russia. See Melvin, *Russians beyond Russia;* Bremmer, "Nazarbayev and the North"; Bremmer and Welt, "Problem with Democracy"; Olcott, *Kazakhstan;* Holm-Hansen, "Political Integration"; Chinn and Kaiser, *Russians as the New Minority;* and Aben et al., "Potentsialnye Territorialnye Spory."

25. For discussions of these autonomy discourses and Kazakhstan's reaction to them, see Olcott, *Kazakhstan,* 77; Melvin, *Russians beyond Russia,* 112–23; Holm-Hansen, "Political Integration," 206–10; and Diener, *Homeland Conceptions.* As noted by Bremmer, "Nazarbayev and the North," n. 4, it is virtually impossible to distinguish between Russians and Ukrainians in the northern oblasts due to the high levels of Russification in the region. One should also note that concentrated groups of Cossacks are included in the designation of Russian in this region. The Cossacks have been among the most aggressive of Kazakhstan's minority communities resisting ethnic Kazakh nationalization of social space, as is noted by Olcott, *Kazakhstan,* 77; Bremmer, "Nazarbayev and the North"; and Melvin, *Russians beyond Russia,* 213–19.

26. Some argue that the Alash Orda of the early twentieth century constituted the first modern Kazakh state.

27. It should be noted that some scholars regard concerns over the legitimacy of the Kazakhstani regime in the northern oblasts as a rationalization for the steady disempowerment of the Russian minority. The regime is seen as "inventing" and subsequently defusing the so-called secessionist threat in an effort to secure its dominion through the marginalization of Russian and Cossack claims in border regions.

28. Author interview with Kazakh Parliamentarian, Astana, October 2001.

29. Author interview with official at the Agency of Information, Astana, October 2001.

30. Konstitutsia Respubliki Kazakhstana, 1993.

31. Ibid.

32. "Natsionalnyi sovet po gosudarstvennoi politike pri Prezidente Respubliki Kazakhstana," 1996, 3.

33. A. M. Khazanov, *After the USSR: Ethnicity, Nationalism, and Politics in the Commonwealth of Independent States* (Madison: University of Wisconsin Press, 1995); Holm-Hansen, "Political Integration"; Olcott, *Kazakhstan;* Diener, "National Territory."

34. The cities of Almaty and Astana are excluded from this calculation because as the major occupational, cultural, and educational centers for the country, they have been the target destination of a large-scale urbanization trend, occurring throughout the 1990s.

35. Olcott, *Kazakhstan,* 76, 174, notes that the "rationalization program" of 1997 gerrymandered oblast borders in an effort to enhance the percentage of Kazakhs in various northern oblasts. North Kazakhstan oblast and East Kazakhstan oblast were expanded to include "neighboring territories," thus providing an additional example of the "hardening of Kazakhstani national space." For a detailed discussion of the changes made to the Kazakhstani territorial administrative structure, see N. N. Galikhin, "Administrativno-Territorialnoe Ustroistvo Kazakhstana: Istoricheskiy Opyt Sovremennosti" (The Administrative Territorial Structure of Kazakhstan: Historical Experience and the Present Situation), *Kazkahstan Spekter,* no. 1–2 (1997): 5–14. Table 9.2 represents an attempt to reconfigure 1989 population figures at the *raion* scale to match the oblast data of the 1999 population figures for a better comparative format.

36. See "Reprint of Speech by President Nazarbayev," *Kazakhstanskaya Pravda,* November 23, 1991; B. Bamishuly, "Aghaiynyng Aghyldy Atazhurtka . . ." (Kinsmen Return to the Homeland), *Egemen Kazakhstan,* July 29, 1992; Z. Tursbekov, "Elinge Kait Aghaiyn' (Come Back to the Homeland Kinsmen), *Egemen Kazakhstan,* October 1, 1998; Z. Zhaparuly, "Kazaktar Kshan Atazhurtta Toptasady?!" (When Kazakhs Will Gather at their Fatherland?), *Kazakh El,* September 19, 1997; O. Omirbek, "Kosh Kolik ti Bolsyn, Ortamyz Tola Bersin" (Migration Must Be Continued, All Kazakhs Must Come to Kazakhstan Soon), *Egemen Kazakhstan,* December 16, 1996; and Zh. Shaluly, "Kosh Koshke Uliasty" (Let the Migration Be Continued), *Kazakh Eli,* September 20, 1996.

37. A. C. Diener, "Kazakhstan's Kin-State Diaspora: Settlement Planning and the *Oralman* Dilemma," *Europe Asia Studies* 57, no.2 (2005): 327–48.

38. An interview with an official from an Oralman Support Institution in Astana (October 2001) stated, "It is important to realize that many of the *Oralmandar* came to Kazakhstan from socialist countries soon after the collapse of socialism. They expected to be taken care of—but Kazakhstan was changing—economically. They were not able to sit and let the government pay them; instead, they were required to pay registration fees, most were not granted citizenship, there were many problems for the *Oralmandar.* Kazakhstan was not ready for so many of our relatives to return." Most Kazakhs interviewed indicated that they had no intention of returning to their countries of diasporic existence when they accepted the labor contract. The migration was intended to be permanent, and the labor contract was simply a means of facilitating the migration.

39. S. Zhusupov, *Immigration Policy in Kazakhstan: Case of Repatriates,* Kazakhstan Institute of Social and Economic Information and Forecast (Almaty: Soros Foundation–Kazakhstan, 2000); Zhusupov, *Strategiya Migratsionnoi Programmy "Oralman";* M. Sarsenbayev, *Proposal for the Legislative Components of the Oralman Projects* (Almaty: Soros Foundation–Kazakhstan, 2001).

40. Zhusupov, *Immigration Policy in Kazakhstan,* 2–3.

41. Concern over depopulation of Kazakhstan has prompted the government to reaffirm its commitment to repatriating ethnic Kazakhs (see *Panorama,* January 9, 1998). This commitment has even taken the form of a target figure of 500,000 diasporic Ka-

zakhs to be brought back to Kazakhstan by 2005; see Zhusupov, *Strategiya Migratsionnoi Programmy "Oralman,"* 3; and http://www.bureau.kz/articles/review15040.stml.

42. Article 1 of the 1995 Constitution declares "Kazakhstani patriotism" to be one of the guiding principles of the Republic of Kazakhstan; Konstutsia Respubliki Kazakhstana ot 30 avgusta 1995. See also N. Nazarbayev, *A Strategy for the Development of Kazakhstan as a Sovereign State* (Almaty: Ministry of Foreign Affairs, 1994); N. Nazarbayev, *V Potoke Istorii* (In the Flow of History) (Almaty: Atamura, 1999); and T. Sarsenbayev, *Kultura Mzhnatsionalnovo Obsheniya* (Culture of International Relations) (Almaty: Ana Tili, 1998).

43. According to Zhusupov, only 27,044 of the over 500,000 Oralmandar had received citizenship; Zhusupov, *Immigration Policy in Kazakhstan.* See also B. Sarsembina, "*Oralmandar* Ushinshi Sortty Kazakh Siyakty" (*Oralmandar* Seem Like People of Third Class Quality), *Zhas Alash,* January 22, 2002.

44. This is excerpted by Zh. Beiisuly, "Kostanaigha Nege Barmaidy Byl Kazakh?!" (Why Kazakh Don't Go to Kostanai), *Zhas Alash,* June 3, 2000.

45. Kostanai is cited as having a low proportion (30 percent) of Kazakh speakers and serves as a prime example of an oblast in which little progress is being made in the adoption of Kazakh as the "official state language."

46. Beiisuly, "Kostanaigha Nege Barmaidy Byl Kazakh?!"; E. Kydyr, "Otanymiyz Tek Ongtustik Kana Ma?" (Is Homeland Only South), *Egemen Kazakhstan,* January 5, 1994.

47. See also Dave, "National Revival."

48. Mongolian Kazakhs, particularly elites, are quite familiar with the Cyrillic script, but Kazakhs from most of the other far-abroad diasporic venues have never been exposed to this alphabet.

49. Dave, "National Revival," provides a discussion of language issues and identity among Kazakhs in Kazakhstan. The assertion that Russian speaking Kazakhs are not "Kazakh" is part of what Kazakh nationalists call the *Mankurt* syndrome but as Dave points out is not necessarily reflected in the identity structures of many Russian-speaking Kazakhs, who consider themselves true Kazakhs despite their continued embrace of the Russian language.

50. Author interview, Pavlodar, October 2001.

51. Institut Geografi, *Atlas Kazakhskoi SSR tom 2* (Moscow: Glavnoe Upravlenie eodezii I Kartografii Pri Sovete Ministrov SSSR, 1985), 60. The data for this were taken from the 1985 almanac of Kazakhstan but were supplemented by census data from 2000, which indicated that the location of agricultural industry is climatically dictated, so little has changed in the last twenty years.

52. Tatimov, "Etnicheskiye Arealy v Kazakhstane," 23.

53. This change is even more pronounced when examining data from previous censuses. See *The Almanac of Maps of Kazakhstan,* vol. 2, *Socioeconomic Conditions and History* (Moscow: USSR Ministry of Geography and Cartography, 1982), 13. Herein Almaty (then called Alma Ata) was reported to be 88 percent non-Kazakh and only 12 percent Kazakh.

54. S. Kasymbekkuly, "Auyl Kazaghy Nege Kalagha Aghyldy?" (Why Do Kazakhs from Villages Move to Cities?) *Ana Tili,* January 7, 1999.

55. M. Mukhanov, "Koshting Basyn Soltustikke Buraiyk" (Let Us Turn the Migration to the North), *Egemen Kazakhstan,* August 16, 2001; "Oralmandar Maselesi Koterildi" (Oralman's Issues Were Discussed), *Egemen Kazakhstan,* September 18, 2001;

Kydyr, "Otanymiyz Tek Ongtustik Kana Ma?"; Beiisuly, "Kostanaigha Nege Barmaidy Byl Kazakh?!"; A. Balta, "Koshting Basyn Kaskelengge Burghan Bauyrlarymyzdyng Zhai-Kuii Kalai Zhane Olardy Audan Basshylary Kalai Karsy Aluda" (How Is the Situation for Our Relatives Who Moved to Kazakhstan and How Did the Head of the Region Meet Them?) *Egemen Kazakhstan,* February 10, 1994; A. Mukai, "Otany On Bes Ui Berdy" (Their Homeland Gave 15 Houses), *Zhas Alash,* January 18, 2000.

56. Z. Kinayatuly, *Mongoliaya Kazakhstary* (Mongolian Kazakhs) (Almaty: Duniezhuzi Kazakhtarynyng Kauymdastyghy, 2000).

57. Kydyr, "Otanymiyz Tek Ongtustik Kana Ma?"; Bek Kala, "Zher Turaly Zang Zhobasynda Oralmandar Nege Umyt Kalghan?"; Sarsembina, "*Oralmandar* Ushinshi Sortty Kazakh Siyakty."

58. This was incorporated into other oblasts during the latter half of the 1990s; see Galikhin, "Administrativno-Territorialnoe Ustroistvo Kazakhstana."

59. K. M. Karzhowbai, "Kazakhstan Respublikasynyhg Elteresi Prezidenti Nursultan Abiwuly NazarbayevkaMongholiyaghy Kazakh Zhurtynyhg Otinish Khat" (Letter: Request to the President of the Republic of Kazakhstan N.A. Nazarbayev from the Mongolian Kazakh People), April 28, 1992, 4.

60. Diener, "Kazakhstan's Kin-State Diaspora."

61. Of the forty-five *Oralmandar* (each from separate families) interviewed, thirty-three indicated they or their families had engaged in a secondary migration once in Kazakhstan. Expert interviews with International Organization for Migration officials, Akimat officials, and directors of various return-migrant support foundations confirmed this process.

62. Author interview with Abai Maukarauly, editor of *Kosh* (Migration) newspaper.

63. See O. Urimkhanuly, "Oralmandargha Ortak Mung" (Common Problems of *Oralmandar*), *Kazakh Eli,* February 18, 1998; T. Zakenuly, "Kytaidan Koshuding Kiynshyldyghy" (Difficulties of Migration from China), *Kazakh Eli,* February 28, 1997; B. Sharip, *Zamanai,* a film was made in 1998 by a Kazakh filmmaker in the independent Republic of Kazakhstan and dedicated to the Year of National Accord and the victims of political repression; A. Maukaruly, "Kazakh Repatrianttarynyng Bugim taghdyry Kandai?!" (How Is the Destiny of Kazakh Repatriates at Present?!), *Kazakh Eli,* January 31, 1997; T. Ramberdi, B. Amalbek, C. Beiisbai, B. Iliyas, T. Ilimzhan, A. Nesipabi, and M. Kosymbai, "Koshi-Kon Maselesi Kongilge Kona ma?" (Are We Satisfied by the Migration Issue?), *Egemen Kazakhstan,* July 22, 1998; S. Amiz, "Aghaiyndar Azamattyk Aludy Angsaidy" (Kinsmen Want to Get Citizenship), *Egemen Kazakhstan,* April 27, 2001; A. Bek Kala, "Zher Turaly Zang Zhobasynda Oralmandar Nege Umyt Kalghan?" (Why in Law about Land Is There Nothing about Oralmandar), *Zhas Alash,* April 4, 2000; B. Bitan, "Kosi-Koning Kokeikesti Maselelri" (Migration Situation Discussed), *Egemen Kazakhstan,* October 22, 1993; B. Ilias, "Oralmandardyng Mungy Bir–Endigi Zherde Olar Omip Taukymetin Birlesip Sheshpekshi" (*Oralmandar* Have Common Problems and They Will Try to Solve Them Together), *Egemen Kazakhstan,* November 2, 2000; and A. Kalibai, "Koshting Kidirgeni: Kongilge Shirkeu Tuskeni" (Why Has Migration Decreased), *Egemen Kazakhstan,* July 30, 1994.

64. Karzhowbai, "Kazakhstan Respublikasynyhg Elteresi Prezidenti."

65. The overt rejection of federalism in the Kazakhstani state-building process is discussed by Holm-Hansen, "Political Integration," 163–74; Bremmer and Welt, "Problem with Democracy," 182–87; Melvin, *Russians beyond Russia,* 108–12; and Diener, *Homeland Conceptions.*

66. Schatz, *Modern Clan Politics;* Masanov, "Mugratsionnyye Meta'orfozy Kazakhstana."

67. The term "aga" is utilized in reference to this phenomenon because Kazakhs often address each other as "brother" when seeking a favor.

68. A number of these towns are being built or are planned with the assistance of multinationals such as Phillip Morris, Inc., which is reported to be interested in cultivating tobacco in Kazakhstan. A. Beiisbay, "Nurlydaghy 'Aghaiyn' Kauymdastyghy: Wetelden Kelip Konystanghan Kandas Bauyrlargha Kamkorlyk Korsetetin Bolady" (The Association "Agaiyn" in Nurly Will Help Our Relatives Who Moved from Foreign Countries), *Egemen Kazakhstan,* February 7, 1998.

69. Mukhanov, "Koshting Basyn Soltustikke Buraiyk"; "Oralmandar Maselesi Koterildi"; Kydyr, "Otanymiyz Tek Ongtustik Kana Ma?"; Beiisuly, "Kostanaigha Nege Barmaidy Byl Kazakh?!"; Balta, "Koshting Basyn Kaskelengge Burghan Bauyrlarymyzdyng . . ."; Mukai, "Otany On Bes Ui Berdy."

70. S. Rakhmetuly, *Mongoliya Kazakhtarynyng Ata-Tek Shezhiresi* (The Mongolian Kazakhs Patrilineal Genealogy) (Olgii: Baspager, 1997).

71. "Localized" should be understood here in a regional sense, given the nomadic history of Kazakh peoples.

72. Author interview, Pavlodar, October 2001.

73. Mongolia is noted as a special case because even though it was often referred to as the sixteenth republic of the USSR, Mongolia-Kazakhs had very few opportunities to travel to Kazakhstan or maintain contacts with Kazakhstani Kazakhs.

74. Author interview, Pavlodar, October 2001.

75. Author interview, Almaty, February 2001.

10

Germans, Jews, or Russians? Diaspora and the Post-Soviet Transnational Experience

Ruth Mandel

The changing global conditions brought about by the end of the Cold War have seen an unprecedented movement of peoples, borders, nationalities, and identifications. The national identities and affiliations of peoples who once felt part of the Soviet Union—by definition, an international amalgam of what were termed "nationalities," linked through a state-sponsored cosmopolitanist project—have been fundamentally challenged and even transformed. Some find themselves part of de facto diasporas; others are now titular nationals of new nation-states. Still others—Chechens, Tatars, Meskhetian Turks—have found themselves unwitting minorities without an external nation-state to which they might migrate.[1]

Memories of past identifications often clash with present circumstances. Soviet identities have given way to a diverse set of strategies and options. The discussion here examines how these strategies and options translate into patterns and practices of migration, transnationalism, citizenship, and ethnonationalist ideologies in the context of the collapse of the Soviet state. Through the study of two migrant populations—the "ethnic Germans" (also known as Volga Germans or Russian-Germans)[2] and the Russian Jews who have migrated from Kazakhstan to Germany—I attempt to describe the processes whereby some minority groups have or have not been able to stake a claim within majority society in light of structures of exclusion experienced in Kazakhstan and Germany.[3]

This chapter draws from research on migration and ethnicity in Kazakhstan in the years since its independence in 1991, a period that has seen an escalation of ethnonationalism toward a "Kazakhs first" agenda. Though Kazakhstan's president, Nursultan Nazarbayev, pays lip service to the "multinational" character of Kazakhstan, behind the scenes the "Kazakhification" agenda dominates, in this country where just 50 percent of the population can claim to be titular nationals. This ethnonationalist trend makes itself felt in new language laws, in naming laws, in employment opportunities in both the state and private sectors, in admissions policies to educational institutions (from kindergarten to university), in marriage preferences, in official support for diasporic ingathering, and more generally in informal public life.[4]

Along with the near-total collapse of the social welfare state and its Soviet-era benefits, an inhospitable, ethnicized environment has provided the impetus for nonethnic Kazakhs to emigrate. Not only have most Jews emigrated (many have gone to Israel, and large numbers to the United States), along with Germans, but so have Russians (the next-largest population after Kazakhs), Poles, Ukrainians, Crimean Tatars, Meskhetian Turks, Greeks, Chechens, and dozens of other groups residing in Kazakhstan. Yet many never will have the means to leave; they lack a sufficient combination of political or ethnic ties, or economic or social capital. Thus, in an era when the future of the nation-state is being questioned in the West, and its demise has been identified on the horizon in favor of postnational identities (e.g., in the ascendancy of the European Union's identities and legal protection), Kazakhstan, like other Soviet successor states (as well as some breakaway regions), has been moving in the opposite direction.

The two groups discussed in this chapter have been recruited, targeted, and privileged by Germany, itself paradoxically a self-avowed "nonimmigration country."[5] The research was carried out in various locations within Kazakhstan, where I conducted interviews with those who have not emigrated, many of whom were waiting to leave. I also interviewed consular officials, who serve as emigration/immigration gatekeepers. In addition, I carried out research among these two groups in Germany (primarily in Berlin) after they arrive from Kazakhstan, where they meet up with their "co-nationals" from throughout the former Soviet Union.

Migration to Germany: Theories and Practices

Theories of migration often address the root causes either from the perspective of the individual agent—the migrant—or from the standpoint of larger forces of political economy. The most extreme example of the former, privileging the individual, might be the neoclassical microeconomic approach, analyzing the migrant's rational decisions, based on his or her potential earning power at home and abroad over *X* number of years, minus the costs migration might entail, and so on. Anthropologists and other social scientists have criticized such approaches as insufficient, neglecting the social, cultural, political, and even historical motivations for migration. Related to this, gender often plays a role in migration decisions, due to any number of causes, from ease at obtaining visas to child-care considerations to earning power.[6]

Crosscutting these approaches, migration conventionally has been seen in terms of push and pull factors, working either independently or in tandem. For example, a migrant-importing country has a particular sort of labor shortage it advertises to a country with a labor surplus and widespread unemployment. In the case of postwar Germany, the labor shortage was acute, due first to the recently lost generation of working men and second to the boom economy, thanks in part to the Marshall Plan, animated by the Cold War. Thus, beginning in the middle to late 1950s, Germans began to look for a new, flexible labor force to import. They located this labor in unemployed and underemployed Turks.[7] In terms of the push/pull model, Turks were seen to have been pushed out for economic reasons, and pulled, or attracted, by what they presumed would be more lucrative economic options in Germany. In this example of migration, as well as the simple "push/pull" description, some analysts have understood it from the point of view of the individual's rational decisionmaking powers, whereas others have addressed it as an example of *Konjungtur*—that is, a moment where the advantageous elements of Germany's economic situation came together to produce the particular set of conditions necessary for the so-called economic miracle. The migrants then entered the equation as part of new center-peripheral relations, bringing workers to the industrial core to service advanced capitalist economies.[8]

Boom economies eventually decline, and the recessions of the late 1960s and early 1970s meant an economic slowdown and subsequent halt in the recruitment of new labor. As is well documented, over the following several decades, the desired guest workers, *Gastarbeiter,* increasingly came to be thought of as undesirable foreigners, *Ausländer.* They were seen to encroach on the German economy and to disrupt the perceived homogeneity of the social order, and they served as convenient scapegoats for the country's social and economic ills. In short, they became guests who had outstayed their welcome. Various schemes were introduced to entice this population to repatriate home to Turkey; legal strictures severely restricted free movement and other rights, and few managed to acquire German citizenship and enfranchisement. Though disenfranchised and subject to discrimination, they have also been blamed for not integrating or assimilating and have been characterized as incapable of integration, as they are marginalized as inassimilable Muslim outsiders with too high a birthrate and are blamed for being a drain on the economic and social welfare system.[9]

By 1990, some thirty years after the first Turks arrived as welcomed "guest workers," when the numbers had ballooned to over 2 million, one might have assumed that Germany was in no position to open itself to still another group of migrants. Yet that is precisely what happened—and in a sense, twice. First, with German unification, Germany essentially took responsibility for the population of five new eastern states. With widespread factory closures and the end of the socialist government's economic and employment subsidies and buffers, unemployment soared, prompting many people to emigrate from the former East Germany to the considerably wealthier and more stable western German states. Formerly, emigration from East Germany had been statistically insignificant. The term *Übersiedler* had been coined to refer to Germans who had come "over" to settle in the West. With one bold stroke, Helmut Kohl had incorporated the whole of this potential *Übersiedler* population into the unified, western-dominated German body politic. However, it would be many years before the significant social and economic divisions receded; ultimately, after the jubilation faded of having "won" the Cold War, Germans living in the western states found themselves increasingly resentful as they were taxed for the exorbitant costs of this unification.

Compounding these social and economic problems, a second group began to arrive in a Germany that already felt itself overwhelmed with foreigners and the social and economic problems of integrating the former East Germans. These newcomers were called *Aussiedler,* resettlers (also known as Volga Germans, Russian-Germans, or ethnic Germans). With the collapse of the Soviet state, swelling numbers of these Russian-Germans flowed into Germany, in accordance with German constitutional law, which essentially considered them German nationals returning from an extended exile of two centuries. After being initially welcomed as persecuted refugees, they were granted numerous privileges, including citizenship, German language courses, financial stipends, and free housing for two years, along with other social services.

Further complicating the situation, the Russian (or post-Soviet) Jews again have not been counted as official immigrants. Instead, they have been gerrymandered into an obscure category of "quota/contingent refugees," *Kontingentfluchtlinge,* to avoid the contentious stigma in Germany of "immigrant," despite the hope that they will, in fact, put down roots.

Finally, in terms of the problematic discourse surrounding immigration, it is significant to recall that the 2.5-million-strong community of Turkish *Ausländer,* foreigners living in Germany, have also never been known officially as immigrants. Consistent with the pervasive ideology that "Germany is not an immigration country," they technically are "foreign employees." Colloquially, they have been called guest workers, Turks, outsiders, foreigners, migrants, and sometimes "Turkish co-citizens" (a term that stresses their *lack* of citizenship) but—crucially—not immigrants.

Citizenship and Diaspora, Homeland and Territory

In concluding an article surveying definitions and conditions of diaspora, William Safran asks whether diasporas present particular public policy problems for their host countries. Should countries be concerned about potential political disloyalty, or should they encourage such ties as "socially useful" and eventually regard such diversity as normal? It is possible, he writes, and this is of specific relevance to our regional focus, "that diaspora communities pose a more serious challenge to host societies than do other minority communities."[10] Perhaps nowhere is this truer than in the states that once lay within the Soviet sphere.

It is partly the movement of populations, migrations—forced or voluntary—that creates diasporas. But a specific diasporic consciousness is not a given, and diasporas do not arise with every instance of migration. The ethos and legal framework of the host state, as well as the social and cultural space into which newcomers are welcomed—or not—together determine what sort of a diaspora community, if any, forms. Moreover, the motivations for the emigration shape its contours. Expulsion and genocide stand at one extreme; individually motivated movement, at the other. The former might create a situation where émigrés seek one another out, live in collectivities, and politically organize; the latter, not at all.

Often, a central concern of migrants is that of citizenship and how to negotiate its permutations in the new context. The range of citizenship options has significant effects across generations. In some cases, inherited feelings of exile and diasporic sensibilities might be predominant, whereas in others an environment conducive to intermarriage and other mechanisms of social integration might preclude such diasporic consciousness. Citizenship offered freely in an inclusive society can create far different potential for expressions of selfhood than a society where exclusivity and civic identities are held at bay.

Citizenship may be framed in an aura of permanency and exclusivity, a relationship of responsibility and rights between an individual and a state. But diaspora and transnational experiences are clearly neither exclusive nor fixed. What makes diaspora peoples imagine they belong together, wherever they may currently be living? How do their changing views of a homeland (and return) affect their adjustments to life in the host country? Is it, as Gilroy suggests, simply a question of learning to live in a different culture on one's own terms? Or is it, as Safran implies, more implicitly a threat to one's own stability?[11] An examination of identification processes at individual, group, and state levels traces different modes of belonging and reveals how diaspora and postdiasporic peoples balance lives rooted in a particular territory, however temporary, while also sharing a very different "social space."[12]

In the case of the movements from the former Soviet Union to Germany, several types of migrations have occurred side by side. The two parallel streams discussed here are in many senses state initiated, and for very different ends. Though overt advertising has not been carried out, explicit information about the possibilities of emigration from Kazakhstan has been disseminated to the relevant organizations and networks of individuals. So successful has this been that 750,000 ethnic Germans from Kazakhstan, out of an original population of 1 million, already have settled in Germany. Of those remaining in Kazakhstan, some are awaiting their visas while others either may not or do not wish to move to Germany.[13]

The post-Soviet Jews, a much smaller group than the ethnic Germans, fall into an unusual legal category. Shortly after the collapse of the USSR, the leader of Germany's officially recognized Jewish Community sought and received agreement from the Interior Ministry to permit 100,000 Jews from the former Soviet Union to immigrate to Germany.[14] The new presence of imported Jews belatedly acknowledges and attempts to rectify the absence of a once-dynamic and very present German Jewish community. In Germany these Jews perform a particular task, assuaging a lingering national guilty conscience. The psychological fallout of the minimal Jewish presence over the past half century has never been resolved at national-political, discursive, or, for many Germans, personal levels.

These two migration movements represent a perplexing attempt by Germany to, on the one hand, repatriate centuries-old diaspora Germans[15] and, on the other hand, create a new diaspora population in their midst—of "ethnic Jews" from the former Soviet Union. At once these represent diasporas replaced, as well as nominal repatriation, and all in a transnational context. The peoples involved continually move between countries; many of the Jews and Germans, for example, maintain their original passports and addresses for business and financial reasons, though the government of Kazakhstan may not allow this indefinitely. Furthermore, depending on their citizenship status, should they remain in Kazakhstan for more than six months on a return visit, they may lose the right to return to Germany. In this way diasporas inherently challenge conventional notions of citizenship, allowing for multiple citizen identities as new modes of citizenship are being refined and redefined by transnational agents carving out new economic and social spaces for themselves.

This points to the importance of state policies, as postunification Germany has been forced to rethink its positions toward foreigners. More particularly, Germany has had to confront the definitions of what constitute foreign and national populations. Not only has no consensus emerged in Germany on this issue, but it has remained in the forefront of domestic policy debate as one of the most sensitive and highly controversial national issues. New notions of citizen have begun to be entertained, as under the post-Kohl Social Democratic–Green coalition government, Germany saw significant changes in its citizenship laws (albeit seemingly minor, when viewed from elsewhere, because the new legislation stops short of acknowledging dual nationality). Since 2000, for the first time, children born in Germany to non-German citizens have the option, when reaching majority, of retaining their German citizenship if they relinquish that of their parents. Previously, several generations of *Ausländer* born in Germany had no automatic right to citizenship. Rather, it was understood as a privilege to be granted on an exceptional basis (see the discussion of jus solis and jus sanguinis below).

As indicated above, complicating this nexus of population movements, both these migrations must be seen in the light of a backdrop of a close-to-half-century-old migration of Turks to Germany.[16] Former Soviet Jews and Germans from Kazakhstan, arriving as recruited newcomers in Germany, are welcomed and cosseted by generous state social welfare coffers. However, they find themselves structurally and socially at odds with the much more established community of 2.5 million Turkish "*Gastarbeiter,*"[17] the "guest workers," most of whom, unlike the Russian-speaking newcomers, still have been unable to change their status from migrant *Ausländer* to enfranchised citizen. Due to German constitutional laws regarding citizenship, birth, and ethnicity, a civil definition of "German"—as opposed to an ethnic definition—has only recently begun to be imagined.

Related to these official ambiguities regarding citizenship and belonging, the question of homeland emerges as a negotiable idea, ideologically motivated, which may be delimited according to political expediency or historical revision. Though "place" as a concrete, geographical referent recedes in significance for some, for others its return and reestablishment or reconsolidation on soil claimed by the group becomes central to their purpose. Thus, diaspora violates contemporary political categories and what is popularly understood as the "naturalness" of the nation-state. Whether in terms of the establishment of a homeland, its protection and recognition, or other politically charged issues, the quest for legitimacy is derived in large part from the Other in whose midst diasporas live.

This points to an essential paradox: Diaspora can be understood as the quintessential "Other" of the nation-state;[18] the enduring, perennial outsider role of many minority diaspora peoples—such as Jews and Gypsies—attests to this, just as the diaspora state reinforces suspicion of divided if not diluted loyalties to the nation-state. Malkki observes that because more and more of the world lives in a "generalized condition of homelessness," there is truly an intellectual need for a new "sociology of displacement" a new "nomadology."[19] But this is not to deny the importance of place in the practices of identification, for reterritorialization and deterritorialization and identity are intimately linked. With the acceleration and preponderance of populations being displaced and replaced, the notion of homeland might just transcend territory, one territory, and assume transnational dimensions; "home" and "homeland" can shift along with citizenship and alternating belongings. In the description of the case of the Volga Germans below, we can identify just such a shift in orientation.

Volga Germans In and Out of Russia

This section provides an overview of the history and population movements of the Volga Germans.[20] The initial settlers arrived in Russia in the eighteenth century, when Empress Catherine II initiated the large-scale movement of Germans to Russia. For Catherine, the combination of, first, having observed the economic benefits that had accrued to England, the Netherlands, and Prussia from accepting Huguenots, and, second, her belief in the current demographic theory of the day—whereby a country's well-being and economic progress were believed to be correlated with population increase—led her to issue manifestos in 1762 and 1763 intended to attract Christian settlers to Russia. The incentives she held out were free religious practice, exemption from military conscription and taxes (for up to thirty years), self-administration, and financial assistance from the Russian government for moving costs. The new settlers were obliged to swear a loyalty oath to the Russian ruler, but in contrast to neighboring Russian serfs, they had more freedoms. The German speakers who responded to these manifestos came from the south and west of what today is Germany, areas that had been affected by the Seven Years' War (1756–63).

In the early years, close to 30,000 migrated. Most founded colonies in the Volga River region. Despite the promises, the first generations suffered great hardships while trying to cultivate difficult virgin land. About these early years, a saying went that "the first generation found death, the second found poverty, and the third found bread." Somewhat later, toward the end of the eighteenth century, Prussian Mennonites responded to a new Imperial edict inviting foreigners to settle in Russia. They had come under increasing pressure from Friedrich Wilhelm II to serve in the military, from which they would be exempt in Russia. Still more German speakers followed in the early years of the nineteenth century, a result of the Napoleonic wars, crop failures, and religious schisms. In the first half of the nineteenth century, approximately 55,000 settlers moved to Russia and settled in the northern Black Sea region as well as the Volga area.

By 1897 (the first Russian census), approximately 1.8 million claimed German as their mother tongue (1.4 percent of the Russian Empire). Religiously, they were divided between Lutherans, Catholics, Mennonites, and Baptists. However, their situation deteriorated in light of growing Slavophila, the abolition of serfdom, and Russia's defeat in the Crimean War, along with the establishment of the German Reich in 1871 and the worsening of

Russian-German relations after the 1878 Berlin Congress. The German settlements in the border regions increasingly were seen as security risks, and the German-speaking minority in Russia began to face legal restrictions. Interestingly, back "home," they were equally unwanted. Otto von Bismarck's policy of nonintervention until World War I meant that he was unwilling to help them. Moreover, he perceived this population as lost to Germany.

For their part, this Russian-German population was loyal to the Russian state and carried out military duties during the Crimean, Russian-Turkish, and Russo-Japanese wars. But with World War I, the German settlements near the border were seen as a potential liability; it was only then that the fate of the Russian-Germans became inextricably linked to Germany. The Duma, in 1915, implemented the "liquidation law," whereby German settlers from a 150-kilometer-wide zone along the border of the European part of Russia were forced to sell their property. Some Mennonites claimed Dutch descent and were exempt from these measures. In Volynia, some 200,000 Germans had to dispose of property within fourteen days and then were subjected to deportation. In Moscow as well, Germans were targets of violence—on May 27, 1915, close to eight hundred homes and businesses owned by Russian-Germans were ransacked. Despite this, about a quarter million Germans served in Russia's army at the time.

Russia's Germans welcomed the 1917 Revolution, hoping for an improvement in their situation. During the early years of the USSR, the Germans did prosper, and the Volga region was elevated to the status of an autonomous Soviet German Republic. In addition, numerous other smaller German autonomous regions were established—eight in Ukraine, and one each in Georgia, Azerbaijan, Crimea, and the Altai. In these regions, German was permitted to be used in schools, theaters, newspapers, and the like. In some areas, however, Germans suffered disproportionately during collectivization. Many of those deemed to be kulaks were repressed or deported to Siberia. Others tried to immigrate to Germany but found the doors tightly shut. Only some five thousand managed to gain admittance, and then just as a transit country. Finally, tainted by their association with the fascist government in Germany in the 1930s, Russian-Germans were liable to be labeled "enemies of the people," resulting in arrests and killings. This was, of course, the period of the worst of Joseph Stalin's terrors, and the Germans certainly were not the only ones who suffered such outrages.

At the start of World War II, after the German attack on the Soviet Union, Stalin feared that an incipient fifth column among the Russian-Germans might arise. He ordered their deportation to Siberia and the Central Asian republics (primarily Kazakhstan). The Volga Autonomous Republic was dissolved in August 1941. By the end of the war, close to 1 million Russian-Germans had been deported to the east.

Initially, the old German Settlements in the Ukrainian Black Sea region were spared the deportations. Their fate was governed instead by the German army's advance in this area, transforming the region into a German occupation zone. Many of these Germans welcomed the occupiers, hoping their distant kinship would liberate them from the recent Stalinist terrors they had suffered, but those Soviet-Germans who were thought to be loyal communists were summarily executed. From 1943, the German Army forced 350,000 of these Ukrainian-Germans to move westward, into the territory of the German Reich and to the occupied eastern territories, particularly the Wartegau (part of what today is western Poland). During this time, these Russian-Germans became naturalized citizens of the Third Reich. This single act would prove critical forty years later when they began applying en masse to settle in Germany, because Germany a half century later still recognized their Nazi-era-bestowed citizenship as valid proof of identity. At the very end of World War II, with the advance of the Soviet Army into some of these regions, many of these newly naturalized Germans formed the final wave of deportees to the Soviet East.

By the postwar period, the once fairly homogeneous German-speaking communities had been disrupted and scattered over many thousands of miles, though certain regions—for example, the Akmolinsk Oblast in Kazakhstan, and the Altai Kray—did have some concentrations. With the stigma attached to all things German, along with the population dispersal, use of the German language began to wane. Many lived under virtual house arrest, continuing into the 1960s. Unable to move, the once-powerful social and linguistic ties that for nearly two hundred years had united this population were severed. One critical component in the social disruption was a change in marriage patterns. Before the war, the Russian-Germans had practiced endogamy; not only did they choose other Germans as marriage partners, but sectarian endogamy was practiced as well within their religious sects, including Catholics, Lutherans, Mennonites, and Baptists. However, after the massive disruptions of the war, such endogamous practices became less important; the salient identity no longer was based on religious sect but instead on ethnicity (*natsionalnost'*). Increasingly, this also lost its salience, and by the late 1980s, 65 percent of the Russian-Germans in Kazakhstan had intermarried with non-Germans, primarily with Poles and Russians, but also with Kazakhs, Koreans, and others.

Dashed Hopes for *Heimat*

In the postwar period, although Germany had its eye on increasing its population by importing "ethnic Germans" from the former Soviet Union, these same "Germans" were focused on a different homeland. In the immediate postwar years, these deportees from the Volga River region hoped for its rehabilitation as an autonomous region and for the restoration of their prewar property and status. To them, the Volga region, and *not* Germany, represented *Heimat*—homeland.[21]

Unlike the Volga Germans, the deportees from the Black Sea region had experienced life under a German government (albeit a fascist one), and many now had relatives in Germany. Their orientation was, therefore, different from that of the Volga Germans, and they were the initiators of the *Aussiedler* resettler movement, setting the chain migration in motion. Thus, in the 1950s, 1960s, and 1970s, long before the collapse of the Soviet regime and the unification of Germany, there was a steady trickle of Russian-German settlers into West Germany. This small stream increased in the 1980s, predominantly from Polish Germans. These were the Germans who had remained there in the postwar period but had been naturalized as Germans under the Nazi regime. After glasnost and perestroika, this changed, and Russia and Kazakhstan became the main points of emigration.

In the late 1980s, Mikhail Gorbachev held out hope for total rehabilitation. This would have meant that Russian-Germans no longer would be considered guilty collaborators and would be able to repatriate to their Volga villages, fulfilling their long-held dream of return. This move was resisted, however, by the Russians in the formerly Volga German areas, particularly the local Communist Party leaders, who organized and lobbied against this repatriation of the former residents, and who had no wish to be displaced. The feeling was so strong, indeed, that a phrase circulated among Russians in this region: "Better AIDS than a German Republic."

A few years later, Boris Yeltsin reassured these Russians that the region would never again be a German area. Instead, he offered the Germans an ecological disaster area in the Siberian Altai region, on the Kazakhstan/Russian border. Indeed, in 1991–92 several small autonomous regions were created, but these were far from the *Heimat* the Germans had envisioned. Memories of the Volga homeland receded, as the Russian-Germans came to realize that they would have no viable future in Russia or Kazakhstan. Their notion of homeland, *Heimat,* began to be redefined and reoriented westward, toward Germany.

The Russian-Germans in their politics and discourse regularly have used the term *Heimat.* This is not an unproblematic term, because it was appropriated as well by the Nazis, along with the term *Volk*—meaning "the people," "the nation," "the folk." It bore a stigma and was rarely heard in postwar West Germany. Critically, however, the Volga Germans' history shows how the referent of *Heimat* is not necessarily fixed—they switched their *Heimat*s in midstream, from their Volga orientation until the early to middle 1990s, only to be replaced by Germany as the new *Heimat* of choice afterward. The timing was fortuitous, because Germany at the time was welcoming them with open arms.

The newcomers readily were incorporated into German ideologies of citizenship, belonging, and racial and ethnic identity, and, moreover, the widespread concern about the negative birthrate among native Germans in Germany. Memories of World War II, memories of German suffering, and specifically memories of a population of *Volksdeutsch* (folk/ethnic-Germans) who had suffered under the Soviets for their Germanness—all coalesced in a generous policy of integration. However, the initial warm welcome cooled considerably, once the early trickle of these *Volksdeutsch* into Germany became a deluge by the mid-1990s.

The early widespread enthusiasm wore off after not only the high economic costs but also the cultural costs became clear. Increasingly, this population of "Germans" became known as "Russki"—Russians—much to their dismay. Having been discriminated against in the Soviet Union for being Germans, once in the "homeland" they found themselves ridiculed and resented by the native population. (Small numbers, in fact, have returned to Kazakhstan and Russia.)

For their part, echoing the disappointment their compatriots feel when sensing that they have imported an enormous population of "Russians" instead of "Germans," the Volga Germans often express extreme dissatisfaction with what they find in Germany. In the Soviet Union, they generally were rural people, farmers, unaccustomed to urban life. Their expectation, after having suffered discrimination for their Germanness at the hands of the Soviets, was to enter what they imagined to be a purely German environment. Instead, they confront what they see as a distinctly non-German social, cultural, and commercial milieu. Rubbing up against pervasive American and global influence in popular culture, and the ubiquity of pornography and of seemingly non-German residents living, working, driving cars, and owning businesses, proves off-putting and offensive to many *Aussiedler.* After the monotonal Kazakh steppe, the collective farm, a paucity of consumer goods, and a culture of Soviet puritanism, they find little in common with their new, putative compatriots.

Given that they often occupy socially and physically marginalized positions in German society, in many cases the Volga Germans prefer to associate with others from the former Soviet Union. In a metropolis such as Berlin, this is unproblematic, and in Berlin several Russian-language newspapers along with numerous shops and services all cater to this community. Entrepreneurial producers sponsor Russian performers, bookstores stock Russian-language magazines and books, and elaborate mass transport networks facilitate the movement of people and goods. All these service the memories of past livelihoods, facilitate past and current associations, and in the process construct a new and viable diasporic space.

Identifications: German, Jewish, Russian

In the post-Soviet context, identity and identifications have taken on new meanings and permutations. To make a case to emigrate, the applicants must meet nationality criteria that are far from simple. Applicants find troubling questions of identity and identification entering the picture, when determining who is and is not a German and a Jew, for purposes of German consular authorities abroad. For example, many in the postwar generations of "ethnic Germans," having been deported to Kazakhstan (and elsewhere) during World War II, consequently no longer speak their grandparents' vernacular Swabian dialect. Yet thanks to Soviet nationality laws, stipulating that all Soviet citizens must have their "nationality" written in their internal passport, many of the applicants still can be documented as "German."

This type of ethnic categorization, derived from an essentialist view of identity and personhood, sits easily with Germany's laws governing citizenship and nationality, which in part still adhere to a jus sanguinis, as opposed to jus soli, definition. (The former, the "law of the blood," permits citizenship on the basis of heritage; the latter, on the basis of place of birth.) According to this law and logic, when making claims to citizenship, the place of one's birth is of secondary importance to one's "blood," cultural heritage, or loosely ascribed ethnicity. Reflecting this ideology, that one must be *born into* an "inalienable Germanness," in the early years of this population movement in the 1990s, applicants needed only to be able to utter *Guten Morgen* (good morning) to be issued visas to Germany.

Given their earlier deportation and decades of discrimination in the Soviet Union, welcoming this population initially was seen as a mercy mission, liberating Germany's long-lost co-nationals from years of repression. Eventually, however, the policy was deemed too liberal and costly in financial, political, and social arenas. Several years and many millions of deutsche marks later, the German government reined in this wave of "ethnic Germans" and introduced stricter criteria. The considerable social problems this population faced once in Germany proved financially and politically expensive and embarrassing to the government. Though intending to import Germans, they increasingly faced a population that looked, acted, and sounded Russian.

To reduce the flow, a number of measures were taken, focusing on issues of identity, nationality, and authenticity. One way the government restricted what was increasingly seen as an onslaught was to examine any changes in nationality more carefully. The default position in the Soviet Union had been to assume the nationality of one's father. The children of a Russian father and German mother would more or less automatically be recorded as having Russian nationality. However, adults did have the right to change their nationalities, and some Germans of mixed marriages opted to become officially Russian, hoping to avoid anti-German sentiment and discrimination. In the post-Soviet situation, this has backfired, and German consular authorities look askance at such past nationality conversions. For such cases, these people and their descendants have forfeited their right to become *Aussiedler.* A key criterion to qualify was to have suffered for one's ethnicity —thus, someone who had prospered and thrived in Soviet times as a German or a (converted) Russian could no longer make this claim.[22] The trope of suffering has become central to the interpretation of the German Constitution's guarantee of the right of return.

The diplomatic, consular mechanics of the effort to displace and replace these populations have been considerable. In the endeavor to identify the right candidates for immigrant visas, "ethnicity" tests have been administered to those applying, to ascertain "authentic Germanness." In these oral interviews, applicants are quizzed on their religious observance, knowledge of customs and folklore, food preferences, and the like to determine "authentic" Germanness.

Currently, of approximately 2 million Kazakhstani Germans, 1.5 million have settled in—*not* "immigrated to"—Germany. It is fundamental that this verbal difference is indicated in the German terminology deployed, for once in Germany they are *Aussiedler* or *Spätaussiedler* ("late resettlers"), not "immigrants." Discursively, this implies a claim to "natural," ethnic belongingness to the German *Volk,* or "the ethnic nation." Because Germany is a self-declared nonimmigration country, it has become politically challenging to permit such large numbers of newcomers. This is particularly so, given the 2.5-million-strong resident ethnic Turkish community, stretching back nearly a half-century. Though most of the Turks are not German citizens, growing numbers have been naturalized.[23]

Unlike the "ethnic Germans," the Jews in the former Soviet Union have no claims to authentic Germanness. As with the Germans, the Jews have been subjected to their own variant of "ethnicity tests" by German consular personnel, to determine the extent of their Jewishness. I conducted interviews at the German Consulate in Almaty, where the obvious historical ironies were glaringly clear to all concerned. Because this is an extremely sensitive area, the Jews in many cases have found it easier to "pass" the German exam than the Israeli immigration interview. The historical ironies of German diplomats issuing examinations to ascertain who is German and Jewish enough to qualify are rich indeed.

Whereas ethnic Germans must prove that they belong to the German "nation" or "folk community," the Jewish applicants need not perform a conscious identification with an imagined German *Volk.* Instead, they must project an ideal of Jewishness, imagined and desired by German consular officials staffing the consulates throughout the former Soviet Union. The Soviet Jews, though commonly known as "Russian," in fact come from throughout the former Soviet Union and not solely Russia. Their large-scale move to Germany was made possible via the legal status of "*Kontingentflüchtlinge,*" quota/contingent refugees, a complicated status shared by certain categories of non-Jewish refugees.[24] In a country closed to "immigrants," it was deemed necessary to create a gerrymandered legal space for this group. In this case, the exceptional de facto but carefully not de jure immigration status granted to these Jews can be read as part of as generalized *Wiedergutmachungspolitik,* the policy of postwar goodwill reparations paid to Jewish victims of Nazism.

Many Jews come to Germany as an active decision *not* to go to Israel. Some have already been to Israel and for a number of reasons do not wish to immigrate there. Most Soviet Jews rarely were observant practitioners of religion, so the religious basis of a "Jewish state" generally is not a motivating factor in their decision. Likewise, the sense of Jewish "national" identity for many is so attenuated that Zionist sentiments do not figure strongly.[25] Some find Israel "too oriental, too Arab, and Middle Eastern, too hot, too socialist." The region's perpetual state of war has also been a disincentive. Furthermore, unlike an Israeli passport, a German passport, which many hope to acquire eventually, is more highly valued, because it is valued as a ticket to nearly anywhere. In addition, for some Jews it can be easier to immigrate to Germany than to Israel. In order to make *aliya,* to immigrate to Israel, one needs to prove one's Jewishness. Though not halachically exacting—according to a strict interpretation of Jewish law (e.g., one can have a Jewish father and Christian mother and still be permitted to immigrate to Israel)—nevertheless, meeting the conditions for *aliya* is not always straightforward. Like the Russian-Germans, some Jews had changed their Soviet-based nationality/identity from "Jewish" to "Russian" and no longer possess the necessary documents proving their Jewish heritage. Thus, unable to satisfy Israeli conditions, some apply to go to Germany. Not unlike the ethnicity exam administered to the Russian-Germans, in which the applicants must exhibit explicit knowledge of and familiarity with a specific Russian-German linguistic and cultural vocabulary, German consular officials in Kazakhstan who vet potential Jewish immigrants query the Jewish applicants about the extent of their Jewishness.

The German consular officials I interviewed at the Almaty Embassy who dealt with this area compared it to treading on eggshells. When speaking of the interviews held with the applicants, one consular officer explained to me, "History does not allow us to ask much about their state of mind—how Jewish they feel, or are. The Israelis can be much more intense in their questioning." However, some of the German consuls do have images of the sort of Jews they seek. One described to me a family to whom she had happily issued a visa the previous week. They were well-educated intellectuals; the woman was a doctor and her husband was a professor. They were very well spoken, well read, they even knew Yiddish; she explained: "They were the perfect sort of Jews—the kind of Jews who we want." The other sort, the unwanted type, were the ones who forged documents (officials estimated that 80 percent of all submitted documents were forgeries) and were not educated professionals; types who might become involved with unsavory activity once in Germany, rather than helping to build the lively, highly cultured Germanized Jewish community that was sought. I was told about a wide range of forgeries, including a case where, to prove his Jewishness, an applicant had produced a photograph of a specially commissioned, artificially aged tombstone with Hebrew writing, claiming that it marked his grandparent's grave. Unfortunately for this person, the German—and

Israeli—consulates had had the foresight to photograph the Jewish cemetery several years earlier, so they could easily verify any new additions to the dead already buried there. In many cases, the German and Israeli consulates work in tandem and with the local police services as well, sharing such findings and other information. Though cooperating in some spheres, in private, Israeli officials expressed resentment toward the German initiative to attract Jews, seeing it as undermining their own Zionist mission of recruiting Jews in the diaspora to make *aliya* to Israel. In fact, in 2004 for the first time, the numbers of Jews from the former Soviet Union moving to Germany exceeded those moving to Israel.

The numbers of Jewish emigrants are small, even insignificant, compared with the number of *Aussiedler,* the ethnic German resettlers. Yet the symbolic significance of the Jewish community in Germany cannot be overestimated, because Jews in Germany undertake to do the ideological work of the state for the state.[26] However, unlike the native German-born Turkish population, who are called "foreign," *Ausländer,* for the purposes of administration and whose interests have been seen to by the Commission for Foreigners, the largely Soviet-born population of Jews is administratively deemed German—its needs are seen to by the Ministry of Culture, which oversees Germans.[27] In a sense, then, the Soviet Jews are transformed into symbolic Germans for administrative and ideological purposes. The financial commitment of the federal government to the Jewish community is enormous relative to their population. The state pays a huge subsidy to Jewish organizations; in a single year, the €23 million subsidy came to approximately €1,500 per Jew; by contrast, the Foreigner Commission's budget amounted to €5 per Turk.

In Berlin, there are some 12,000 registered members of the Jüdische Gemeinde zu Berlin (the officially recognized corporate organization representing the Jewish Community), 8,000 of whom are Russian (Soviet) born. The actual number of Berlin's Jews probably is closer to 25,000, including several thousand in the former East Berlin who have never openly expressed a Jewish affiliation. In comparison, Berlin's Turkish population is close to a quarter million. One observer has commented that the treatment of Jews is a "constant search to create loopholes in the Constitution" to ensure their presence in Germany; this contrasts to the treatment of Turks, which reflects a perception that Turks exercise an "exploitation of loopholes," taking undue advantage of their situation in Germany. An official from the Berlin Ministry of Culture put it this way: "[Our treatment of the Jewish Community] is a form of gratefulness. It is not self-evident that Jews would stay in Germany, organize themselves, or want to stay any longer. We thankfully recognize the fact [that they do]."[28]

The Russian Jews and the *Aussiedler,* then, are each forced to mimic and assume an ascribed identity, to conform to a fixed, projected stereotype set by their German sponsors. The Russian Jews are encouraged to resemble past representations, adapting themselves to projected German memories of Germany's prewar Jews. *Aussiedler* are meant to conform to representations of authentic Germans. Ultimately, the shock of dissimilarity, of difference, is repressed, as the state attempts to mold these groups into the ideal Jew and German, in the attempt to achieve the desired identities. That the groups offer various modes of resistance to these identity projects highlights some of the contradictions in Germany's political and cultural definitions of self and other. Moreover, it calls into question the attempts to legislate identity through techniques of inclusion and exclusion.[29]

Final Thoughts: At Home with Transnationalism

An unexpected by-product of these two migrations—the Volga Germans and the Russian Jews, from Kazakhstan to Germany—has been an increase in transnational movements of people, capital, and commodities. Many in these populations retain their original passports and travel freely back and forth, investing in Kazakhstan (or Russia, etc.), carrying on lively import-export businesses and cultivating local contacts and partners. With the Jews, Israel for some is an additional link in their transnational chain of social and professional activities. For the Germans, the hundreds of thousands of ethnic Germans still in Kazakhstan and in Russia provide a natural connection, exploited by both sides. With increasingly stringent controls on numbers permitted to enter the country, Germany instead has begun to invest in the regions where Germans are living, building infrastructure and health facilities, supporting new enterprises, and the like. As a specific sort of ethnically targeted international development aid, this also offers links between and employment for both the émigrés and those who remain behind.

Returning to the synoptic discussion of migration theory above, we can see how the push/pull model, for example, does not apply here. After all, it is only selective potential migrants to whom the doors were opened, and there were no obvious economic benefits for the host country. Thus, an alternative explanation must be sought, one that takes into account the complexities of this historical and political moment, ethnonationalist ideologies, and the layers of legal rulings permitting such exceptional circumstances. One way that the German government has managed this very sensitive situation is by avoiding the term "immigration" altogether. By shifting the rhetoric away from immigration, with all its attendant stigmatizing associations, and toward one of "resettlement," "return," and contingency—and thus the general discourse surrounding this enormous population not of "foreigners" but of fellow Germans or desired Jews—the government has been able to claim legitimacy and to gain support for the projects.

The range and layering of motivations for migration also need to be addressed, particularly when they operate at cross purposes. Here, the "attracting" factors include ideologies of postwar reparation, on the one hand, and nationalist repatriation, on the other. At the same time, using legalistic means, the German government avoids the immigration contradictions through the conveniently created categories of *Aussiedler* and *Kontingentflüchtlinge.* We can see, therefore, that motivations and conceptualizations for the international movement of populations can be manipulated to avoid any taint of, or association with, immigration. This phenomenon also begs obvious questions about equality, racialization, historical reparations, national responsibilities, and the ethics of reverse discrimination.

Interestingly, though the Soviet successor states are reinventing their own forms of nationalism, ethnicized or otherwise, the emigrants who are excluded are often unconcerned by such identities. The many Jews I spoke with in Berlin, for example have multiple passports. Not wishing to foreclose on any potential options, given their experience and aspirations, collecting passports is seen as a prudent measure. For many in this population, "nationality" recalls years of Soviet-imposed institutional discrimination, when "Jew" was "elevated" to the taxonomic and bureaucratic equivalent of Ukrainian, Pole, Kazakh, or Russian nationalities. But unlike these latter national identities, to be marked as a Jew was to experience discrimination and exclusion. Memories of such identifications, which usually are inescapable, motivate the seeking out of new modes of identity and ways of transnational, cosmopolitan, even diasporic living. Not unlike the Russian-Germans, the memory of Jewish suffering and annihilation facilitates these new nonnational or transnational ways of being. The painful absence of choice of identity and nationality in the Soviet context thus animates the desire for new options, new homes, and perhaps even new homelands. However, the envisioned homelands may not coincide with the ambitions of the German government.

Many Russian Jews defy Germany's ideologically motivated design for them and instead see Germany as a convenient stepping-stone to the United States or other European destinations, despite Germany's alleged desire to reestablish a once-thriving but since-decimated Jewish community. Likewise, significant portions of the ethnic Germans, for their part, see settling in Germany as only second best to a return to the Volga River region, where their ancestral kin had lived for centuries. Both groups, beneficiaries of reverse discrimination, have nevertheless maintained transnational ties with people and places in the former Soviet Union, and, increasingly, in Europe, the Middle East, and North America.

These examples raise a number of questions: Where is "home"? How can transnational identities be accommodated by states with exclusivist citizenship laws? How long can the differentiated legal and political statuses of both citizen and noncitizen residents remain determined by the logic of exception, where the unproblematic acceptance of minorities into the wider society is still considered an exception to the rule? In attempting to formulate answers to such seemingly intractable questions, Germany will need to attend to its policies governing the inclusion of different kinds of outsiders.

Notes

1. See chapter 8 in this volume by Izmirli.
2. I have found no consistently appropriate term for this population; thus, most of the time I refer to them as "Russian-Germans," though occasionally I employ different labels. None is completely satisfactory.
3. The research began as part of a three-part project, comparing three very different situations, all of which emerged as a consequence of the collapse of the former Soviet Union and its Eastern European satellites. It was funded by the Economic and Social Research Council's Transnational Communities Programme (U.K.). The two other projects concerned, first, Susan Pattie's research on the relationship of specific segments of the Armenian diaspora to the newly independent Republic of Armenia; the Armenians appear to continually seek means of redefining themselves as diasporic even when finally "at home" in a newly independent homeland. The second study, undertaken by Michael Stewart, investigated the Hungarian populations living outside Hungary, in Slovakia, Vojvodina, and Transylvania. These can be seen as diasporas created at the end of World War I as a result of the redrawing of the Austro-Hapsburg boundaries. These Hungarians of Slovakia, Romania, and the former Republic of Yugoslavia live on what they consider to be ancestral Magyar land, yet due to geopolitical contingencies they have been redefined into a diaspora-like existence.
4. On ingathering, see chapter 9 in this volume by Diener.
5. This is despite the 7.5 million resident foreigners—known commonly as *Auslän-*

der, foreigners, and not immigrants, despite many having been there for close to a half century. Recent changes in the citizenship law have begun to rectify this situation.

6. See Caroline Brettell and James Hollifield, eds., *Migration Theory: Talking across Disciplines* (New York: Routledge, 2000).

7. Italians, Greeks, Yugoslavs, Spanish, and Portuguese workers were recruited as well. However, the numbers of Turks far outweighed the other nationalities for the purposes of generalization and this discussion.

8. E.g., see S. Castles and G. Kosack, *Immigrant Workers and Class Structure in Western Europe* (Oxford: Oxford University Press, 1973).

9. For an in-depth analysis of the history and cultural implications of the Turkish migration to Germany, see Ruth Mandel, *Cosmopolitan Anxieties: Turkish Challenges to Citizenship and Belonging in Germany* (Durham, N.C.: Duke University Press, 2008).

10. William Safran, "Diasporas in Modern Societies: Myths of Homeland and Return," *Diaspora* 1 (1991): 83–99; the quotation is on 97.

11. Paul Gilroy, *There Ain't No Black in the Union Jack* (New York: Routledge, 1987); Safran, "Diasporas."

12. Roger Rouse, "Mexican Migration and the Social Space of Postmodernism," *Diaspora* 1, no. 1 (1991): 8–23; the quotation is on 8.

13. Germany now has more stringent criteria for deciding who may and may not settle, as discussed below.

14. Closer to 200,000 eventually came to Germany from the former Soviet Union.

15. The ancestors of many of these Volksdeutsch had immigrated to Russia under the protection of Catherine the Great. They were deported en masse to Kazakhstan by Stalin during World War II, as discussed below.

16. "Turks" here is the shorthand for "people from Turkey," Türkiyeli; this term includes citizens of Turkey who do not identify with the ethnic moniker of "Turk."

17. *Gastarbeiter,* literally "guest worker," was the initial epithet common to these migrants. For complex historical reasons, it later assumed derogatory connotations and has been replaced by other terms, most notably *Ausländer*—foreigner, stranger, outsider. Other terms have been used as well, such as *ausländische Mitburger,* foreign co-citizen. Today the preferred, politically correct term is *Migranten,* migrant. Also used are "German-Turks," or "German-with-Turkish-background," but almost never "Turkish-Germans." For fuller discussion, see Mandel, *Cosmopolitan Anxieties.*

18. K. Tölölyan, "The Nation State and Its Others: In Lieu of a Preface," *Diaspora* 1 (1991): 3–7.

19. Liisa Malkki, "National Geographic: The Rooting of Peoples and the Territorialization of National Identity among Scholars and Refugees," *Cultural Anthropology* 7 (1992): 22–44; the quotations are on 37–38.

20. Much of the information in this section relies on the work of U. Kleinknecht-Strähle, "Three Phases of Post–World War II Russian-German Migration from the Former Soviet Union to Germany," DPhil thesis, University of Oxford, 1998.

21. Numerous small-scale protests by Russian-Germans wanting to emigrate occurred throughout the USSR during this period, including one public protest at Red Square.

22. As of January 1, 1993, they became known as *Spätaussiedler,* late-*Aussiedler;* more restrictive criteria applied to persons in this category.

23. See note 17 above.

24. This category generally has applied to populations such as Vietnamese boat

people, Bosnians, and Kosovars, and people from other crisis regions who are expected to return home once the crisis has passed.

25. By this I do not mean to imply that Jewish identity is always linked to Zionism—this is far from the case.

26. A growing literature addresses the situation of Jews in postwar Germany; see, e.g., Y. Michal Bodemann, ed., *Jews, Germans, Memory: Reconstructions of Jewish Life in Germany* (Ann Arbor: University of Michigan Press, 1996); Y. Michal Bodemann, "Between Fürth and Tel Aviv," in *German Cultures, Foreign Cultures: The Politics of Belonging,* ed. Jeffrey Peck (Washington, D.C.: American Institute for Contemporary German Studies, 1997); Michael Brenner, *After the Holocaust: Rebuilding Jewish Lives in Postwar Germany* (Princeton, N.J.: Princeton University Press, 1995); Sander Gilman and K. Remmler, eds., *Reemerging Jewish Culture in Germany* (New York: New York University Press, 1994); Robin Ostow, *Jews in Contemporary East Germany: The Children of Moses in the Land of Marx* (New York: St. Martin's Press, 1989); Jeffrey Peck, ed., *German Cultures, Foreign Cultures: The Politics of Belonging* (Washington, D.C.: American Institute for Contemporary German Studies, 1998), and M. Tress, "Foreigners or Jews? The Soviet Jewish Refugee Populations in Germany and the United States," *East European Jewish Affairs* 27, no. 2 (1997): 21–38.

27. Many now are called "migrants commissioner" or "foreigner and migrants commissioner."

28. J. Laurence, "(Re)constructing Community: Turks, Jews, and German Responsibility," *German Politics and Society* 19, no. 2 (Summer 2001): 22–61; the quotation is on 40.

29. For an insightful analysis of *Aussiedler* and mimesis, see S. Senders, "Coming Home: *Aussiedler* Repatriation, History, and Justice in Post–Cold War Berlin," PhD thesis, Cornell University, 1999.

Conclusion: Godot Is Already Here

Blair A. Ruble

In November 2005, just as protests by second-generation Muslim residents of the Paris suburbs were turning into more general public disturbances, the mayor of a major postcommunist city expressed surprise at the absence of a "rigorous" response by the French authorities. Noting in a private conversation that his administration would have responded with greater force, the mayor observed that such civil disturbances were unthinkable in his city. After all, he continued, his town's population was ethnically, racially, and culturally homogeneous, and would remain so for the next twenty or thirty years.

In fact, his particular city was becoming increasingly heterogeneous. As in many communities throughout the formerly communist world, a diverse collection of peoples moved into and out of his city every day, and the number of nonindigenous residents was growing constantly. The fall of various walls—symbolic and legal as well as physical—has meant that the space between Berlin and Beijing has become a newly open territory for an increasingly free and rapid flow of capital, goods, and people. As the preceding chapters have demonstrated, transnational migration throughout Eurasia is becoming the norm for a region once thought to be bound in place.

The disconnectedness of perceptions—both those of the mayor mentioned above and of researchers who have largely failed to explore the Eurasian region's growing population movements—and the realities on the ground suggest a fertile arena for further research and public discussion. The work presented in this volume highlights at least four dimensions along which transnational migration in Central Eurasia demands additional academic and policy consideration.

First, the movement of people around, into, and out of the region is already significant. Second, this movement is the norm for the region, and it has been so for a surprisingly long period of time. Third, policy responses at the regional, national, and municipal levels have been inadequate to the challenges posed by migration. Fourth, the experience of migrants throughout the region is strikingly similar to that of migrants elsewhere on the planet.

The Future Is Now

Timothy Heleniak's overview of migration in the post-Soviet space illustrates the first observation, namely, that the number of people on the move in the former Soviet Union is substantial. The direction and motivation of this ebb and flow of human beings is complex and multifaceted. Any discussion of migration in the former Soviet Union, for example, must include voluntary along with forced migration; movement within large states such as Russia, Ukraine, and Kazakhstan along with movement across international borders; emigration out of the region along with immigration into it; and economic migrants seeking seasonal employment along with refugees fleeing communal violence.

Heleniak rightly cautions that measuring migration movements is an elusive assignment even in countries with more fulsome statistical systems than Russia. He nonetheless demonstrates that Russia serves as a primary migration magnet in the broader post-Soviet region, having gained about 3.7 million new residents since 1989. Though Russia's migrant population generally remains a relatively modest proportion of its total population (approximately 2.5 percent), regional concentration as well as population movements within Russia magnify the policy challenges for the country's leaders.

Heleniak's most important finding could well be that temporary, at times illegal, and often circular population movements flow throughout the region. The appearance of migrants following the push and pull of labor supply and demand (as opposed to permanent migrants, who must be integrated into local institutions and communities) may, in fact, present the largest challenge to policymakers. This reality poses particularly acute challenges to communities that are failing to attract sufficient replacement migration to sustain their shrinking labor forces. Thus, as Heleniak concludes, even low levels of migration will require very careful political and social balancing acts in Russia, the other northern countries of the former Soviet Union, and other major migration destinations. Policies must be designed to accommodate these new migration realities in destinations, in origins, and, most important, between the two.

Andrei Korobkov amplifies the economic and public policy challenges generated by post-Soviet migration to communities throughout the region. He identifies five discernible stages in the evolution of post-Soviet migration patterns. Following an initial period (1991–92) during which migration flows essentially remained at the same level as in the late Soviet era (with the important exception of the first large-scale movement of refugees), former Soviet citizens began to repatriate themselves to their heritage states during a period of unidirectional, permanent relocation (1993–95). This resorting of the Soviet population largely had run its course by the middle of the decade, when, Korobkov argues, a new set of migration patterns emerged, dominated by temporary labor migration. From 1996 to 1999, the Russian government did not respond to this new phenomenon, but beginning in 2000 and continuing until 2005, Vladimir Putin's regime attempted to increase state regulation of migration. The government's anti-immigrant position began to soften in 2005, and Korobkov argues that Putin now appears to recognize the importance of immigration for Russia, but the effectiveness of a liberalized migration regime remains to be seen.

The current period is characterized by a general contraction of intraregional migration, an increase in the importance of external emigration, and a growing role for socioeconomic factors in determining the character and intensity of migration flows. Korobkov thus describes a migration regime within the former Soviet Union that begins to resemble more established patterns of permanent and temporary labor migration in the Americas, in Europe, as well as in the Persian Gulf region. Migration has become essential for the functioning of the region's increasingly marketized economies and, therefore, is likely to remain a significant and permanent feature of economic life. Migration has become the norm, which means that it must be incorporated into scholarly social scientific analysis focused on the region as well as into policy and political calculations about how best to govern communities throughout the region.

Andrew Robarts amplifies Korobkov's discussion of contemporary Russian state migration policies. Robarts carefully charts an increasingly restrictive policy toward refugees that is driven by broader shifts in discussions among Russian politicians, journalists, and scholars concerning the nature and meaning of "Russia" and the "Russian Federation." Nationalist media and intellectuals increasingly argue that the influx of nonethnic Russians into the Russian Federation has become destabilizing and unhealthy.

As under previous Russian regimes, various state agencies are staking out positions that are more or less alarmist in tone as well as more or less anti-immigrant in their policy recommendations. Efforts to create a comprehensive legislative framework concerning migration policy are set against regional and local approaches that often contradict national policy as well as increasingly strident nationalist rhetoric proclaimed by national politicians.

Robarts argues that the Russian case—like so many other studies in this volume—cautions against reading the state out of theoretical discussions about migration. In the Russian and other cases, state policies define who can move where, when, and how. The state can neither control nor suspend migration that is driven by economic forces. Nonetheless, state policies—and the concepts upon which those policies rest—powerfully shape the choices that are available to migrants and their host communities. If migrants do not exist in the minds of policymakers who prefer to see their communities as inevitably homogeneous for at least a generation ahead, the life chances for those migrants and their children will necessarily become limited.

Seema Iyer redirects attention away from the federal policies examined by Korobkov and Robarts and toward regional responses to the arrival of migrants. By analyzing migrant self-selectivity in a single region—the Irkutsk Oblast—she highlights the extent to which migrants are already shaping how communities throughout the former Soviet Union thrive, stagnate, or die as a consequence of population movement.

Iyer begins by noting that the increasingly unfettered movement of people throughout the former Soviet Union is slowly reordering what many analysts have considered to be a "'misallocation' of labor, capital, and infrastructure" by Soviet economic planners. The dramatic out-migration from remote regions in the Far North and Far East began during the 1990s, and continues. Significantly, people are choosing not to leave the macro regions in which they live. Instead, they are resettling in larger cities within their general region of residency.

Iyer supports her argument through an examination of migration into the Siberian city of Irkutsk—one of a limited number of smaller, regional capital cities throughout the former Soviet Union that are sustaining renewed population growth—as well as into other cities of the Irkutsk Oblast. Drawing on data compiled from residency registration (*propiska*) records, she reports that migration choices among destinations remain dynamic. Where and when people move is determined by a confluence of various historical, social, and economic factors. The precise contours of individual migration decisions may be shaped by considered policy responses as well as by economic development. Understanding the precise outcomes of these decisions demands additional investigation of a wider assortment of communities. Thus, Iyer tells readers how complex migration systems have already become throughout the Soviet Union, while simultaneously revealing how much additional research remains to be done before that complexity can be better appreciated.

Thus, Heleniak, at the level of the entire former Soviet Union, Korobkov and Robarts, at the level of the Russian Federation, and Iyer, at the level of a single region, all demonstrate from a variety of disciplinary and methodological perspectives the degree to which the movement of populations into, out of, and around the territory of the Soviet Union is significant both in scale and in its impact on local communities. They each describe a world rich in new agendas for social science research, in possibilities for paradigmatic shifts concerning how the region is conceptualized, and in policy choices for communities and politicians alike. In different ways, Heleniak, Korobkov, Robarts, and Iyer describe a world where big city mayors do not have a quarter century before they need to begin to ponder the challenges and opportunities presented by diversity. Insofar as migration is concerned, the post-Soviet future is now.

Back to the Future?

Several contributors to this volume reveal that migration may have been more a part of the Soviet and pre-Soviet past than conventional analysis has suggested. Heleniak, for example, reports that 5.5 percent of the Soviet population moved in 1989. This level of population movement, though modest in comparison with levels in mobile societies like the United States, appears strikingly robust, in contradiction to widely accepted notions that Soviet citizens did not move. Lay and specialist analysts have both long suggested that people in the Soviet Union stayed where they lived, either because of cultural predilection (they were rooted in a place) or because of administrative fiat (they were prohibited from moving due to a powerfully restrictive internal passport regime and the *propiska* permit system). The contributions to this volume by Eric Lohr, Bruce Adams, and Otto Pohl indicate some of the ways in which reality may have been far more labyrinthine.

Lohr's review of population and emigration policy during the late Imperial period reminds readers that the issue of emigration and immigration is not new to the region. Unlike in other parts of the world, in Central Eurasia people are scarce rather than land. Population and migration policies have thus become the subjects of intense discussion and frequent revision, as was the case before the collapse of the Imperial regime in 1917. Most important for consideration of future migration regimes in the region, the efforts of Russian government officials to restrict Jewish residence in certain areas of the empire demonstrate the limits of calculated state migration controls. International and economic factors powerfully influenced when, where, and how people moved, even as the state explicitly sought to control human mobility.

Lohr's historical perspective underscores both how unstable migration policies can be and how much controversy they can incite among governmental and social groups. There has long been tension between a desire to extend state power, on the one hand, and the pressures of economic and social reality, on the other. The impulse to seek greater control over population movements that is evident in Soviet-era administrative restrictions on population movements existed long before commissars came to power, and it will likely continue to exist well into the future.

Lohr notes that Russia's relations with its immediate neighbors played a critical role in shaping Imperial migration policies. Not surprisingly, neighboring states remained important factors in determining migration policies throughout much of the Soviet era as well. For example, Adams tells a remarkable and largely unknown story of population movements across the Soviet and Chinese borders for much of the twentieth century. His examination of roughly 300,000 Soviet émigrés in Xinjiang—a community from which about 200,000 people returned to the Soviet Union between 1954 and 1962—demonstrates both the power and the limits of state policy in shaping migration patterns.

Beyond the human drama of such large-scale migration, Adams provides a powerful reminder of how tightly migration policies can become intertwined with international relations. The repatriation of Soviet citizens in Xinjiang—like the expulsion of Jews from Imperial Russia explored by Lohr—ebbed and flowed in step with the larger state-to-state relationship between the Soviet Union and the People's Republic of China. Governmental policies—together with the preferences of the state agencies determining the rules and regulations implementing those policies—literally determine when, where, and how people can move. As Adams concludes, the intervention of the Soviet and Chinese governments disrupted migration patterns that had existed for centuries. Research on the migration history of Central Eurasia thus opens up an opportunity to explore the extent and conditions under which government policy plays a central role in shaping the movement of peoples, as well as those under which the state becomes largely irrelevant to individual and group decisions to move in response to other factors, such as labor markets.

Any consideration of population movements in Central Eurasia must come to terms with a bleak past of tragic forced migrations, particularly during the middle decades of the twentieth century. Pohl's assessment of the relative human and social capital of the peoples deported by the Soviet government during World War II reminds readers of the barbarous lengths to which the Stalinist regime was prepared to pursue its own brand of ethnic cleansing. As the Chechen wars of the post-Soviet period reveal, the legacies of resettlement policies based on nationalities remain painfully present. When, how, and where people move in Central Eurasia is often a response to the region's brutal history as much as it is a reaction to economic forces and labor markets.

Pohl's chapter is a compelling reminder of the vitality of human dignity and motivation in the face of ambitious government policies. Forced deportations constitute a movement of population that is the furthest removed from migration driven by market factors. As Pohl records, it is particularly important that the deported peoples of the Soviet Union retained "some valuable assets that allowed them to improve their economic, social, and political status. They retained familial and communal bonds that in some cases could be reconstructed, despite being dispersed over a large area. . . . They successfully invested their bonding social capital to repair many of the social networks severed by the deportation."

Such "bonding social capital" constitutes a powerful resource for many migrants in today's voluntary Eurasian migration systems. Individual migrants carry the social capital accumulated over their own lifetimes and the history of their communities. Migrant behavior, success, and failure depend to a considerable degree on the stock of social capital embedded in each migrant before his or her departure. Much more research is required before the depth and extent of such capital is fully understood among Central Eurasian migrants. Pohl identifies an area in which future investigation can both expand an appreciation of the realities of the present-day territory that once constituted the Soviet Union and a possible connection to broader research questions about migration evident in scholarship examining other regions.

Lohr, Pohl, and Adams briefly cast light on very disparate aspects of Soviet and Russian Imperial population and migration policies. Their chapters serve as reminders of the constancy of migration issues for policymakers throughout the region under a variety of regimes. Their work similarly amplifies the prospects for a rich research agenda that seeks to reexamine the Eurasian past in light of migration issues.

In each of the stories told by Lohr, Pohl, and Adams, we see national and local officials—like the mayor mentioned at the outset of this chapter—approaching migration issues with a set of perceptions and impulses that often promotes actions on the ground that are antithetical to policy goals. The policies whereby Jews left the Russian Empire, deported peoples reestablished a productive role within post-Stalinist society, and Soviet citizens returned from China could well have had more positive results for the Russian Imperial and Soviet regimes if the architects of these policies had thought differently about the role of the state in society. The consequences of these policies—prejudice and inadequate social knowledge—continue to cast destructive shadows across Central Eurasia. The experiences and legacies described by Lohr, Pohl, and Adams suggest that analysts should look beyond economic factors to consider the vocabulary and conceptual constructs of policymakers when analyzing future migration patterns and their effects.

Outmoded Futures

If the chapters by Lohr, Pohl, and Adams emphasize the peculiarities of the region's past and present migrations, the chapters by Ruth Mandel and Idil Iizmirli remind readers of some of the ways in which that history has been formed and shaped by the attitudes and policy preferences of local and national leaders, such as the mayor mentioned at the outset of this chapter. Their contributions also highlight the extent to which present challenges are partially a consequence of inadequate past policies.

Mandel's examination of the emigration of "ethnic Germans" and Russian Jews from Kazakhstan to Germany focuses the reader's attention on some of the ways in which the sequencing of migrant arrivals in a given community can influence the chance for successful adaptation among different migrant groups. The layering of Turkish, "Soviet," and East German migrants in Germany constrained the opportunities available to later migrants as German economic performance began to falter under the strains of reunification. Once again, more than economic factors were at play. As Mandel writes, several migration regimes coexisted side by side, constituting different efforts to "repatriate centuries-old diaspora Germans and . . . to create a new diaspora population in their midst." These policies, in turn, were predicated on the notions of nationality and citizenship that informed Germany policies. The "ethnicity" tests administered by German diplomats would have appeared to be nonsensical within the context of civic-based immigration policies along the lines of those of Canada or the United States. Significantly, the inclusion of Soviet and post-Soviet diaspora migrants in a broader "German" community placed them at an advantage in important ways in relation to decades-old Turkish communities that had stronger ties to everyday life in the Germany of the late twentieth century.

Ethnic-driven migration policies interacted with the self-identity of migrants even as they delineated life choices in Germany. At what point and how did the descendants of ethnic Germans deported to Kazakhstan during World War II begin to think of themselves as "German?" At what point did a Soviet Jew become "Jewish?" To what extent did migration and nationality policies driven by a jus sanguinis definition of citizenship foster resentment among the children of Turks who were born and raised in Germany? Mandel writes that "the Russian Jews and the *Aussiedler,* then, are each forced to mimic and assume an ascribed identity, to conform to a fixed, projected stereotype set by their German sponsors." The results for migrant and host society alike are often perniciously contradictory. Mandel thus demonstrates with clarity how the concepts held by policymakers can, in certain circumstances, outweigh economic push and pull factors in shaping both migration flows and migrant-host relations.

Izmirli explores some of the intricacies of repatriation policies within the context of Crimea. Large numbers of Crimean Tatars—one of the deported peoples at the center of Pohl's chapter—have been able to return to independent Ukraine (approximately 300,000 at present). Once in Ukraine, the Crimean Tatars confront a range of challenges that include constrained economic opportunity, political exclusion, limited opportunity for education in their native language, and harsh clashes with Cossacks and other groups. By exploring the very real travails of returning Crimean Tatars, Izmirli examines some of the ways in which social space had congealed following their deportation so that as returning migrants they must once again expand the social definition of place so that it can become a shared territory for all. This process is inherently prone to conflict and violence, resting, as it does, on contrasting conceptions of Crimea that are held by returning Cossacks and long-resident Slavs. As in the case of the returning "ethnic Germans" who stand at the center of Mandel's chapter, the ideas and concepts that inform public policy have a direct impact on the life chances of the people who must redefine social, economic, and cultural space on the ground.

Izmirli and Mandel write from the opposite perspective of the mayor mentioned above. "Ethnic Germans" and Crimean Tatars become part of a heterogeneity that remains invisible to policymakers. Such attitudes created situations in which conflict becomes inevitable because confrontation is the only means at the disposal of the invisible to break open a social space that had congealed before they arrived.

The chapters by Mandel and Ismirli examine very different migration contexts. In doing so, they elegantly reveal how policy conceptions and intellectual constructs determine who can move, when they can do so, where they can move to, and, once having moved, what sorts of opportunities exist for success. Their work places the migration of people into a political context that is shaped as much by what is in peoples' minds as by state-to-state relations or economic prospects. Their work highlights the extent to which research on migration in Central Eurasia opens up possibilities for exploring the significance of conceptual models for how and why people move.

A Future Like Elsewhere?

Ethnic Germans and Crimean Tatars exist within the territory once controlled by the Soviet government and have ties outside that region. Mandel and Ismirli thus naturally relate their findings to larger migration systems and contexts than those of the Soviet Union alone. Increasingly, the reader comes to understand that, over time, a large migration system has emerged in Central Eurasia that is beginning to resemble migration systems elsewhere. This is so despite the seeming peculiarities of history, thought, and place identified by many of the contributors mentioned thus far.

For example, as in other regions, the movement of people in response to opportunity is shaped (rather than limited) by a variety of historical and mental factors. Moreover, the relationships and migratory behavior seen in other regions are becoming increasingly apparent in Central Eurasia. Thus, patterns of seasonal migration and remittances between relatively poorer states in southern Central Asia with relatively more economically robust regions in Kazakhstan and Siberia increasingly resemble migration and remittance patterns between Central and North America.

Alexander Diener's chapter examining the long-term impact of previous migration by ethnic Kazakhs reveals some of the ways in which research on migration in Central Asia can inform broader discussions of migration elsewhere. As he demonstrates, the experience of "diasporic Kazakhs" is both rooted in the specifics of the Kazakh experience and shaped by the decisions made by migrants in ways that resemble the choices made by migrants everywhere.

Like Ismirli, Diener describes a "hardening" of social space throughout the 1990s in a manner that excludes others. Even so, climate, family, social networks, employment opportunities, and educational opportunities exert powerful pulls over migration and life choices. As everywhere, migrants must make life-altering decisions based on imperfect information; as everywhere, social networks become critical to those choices that are made.

The peculiarities of Kazakh experience, history, and culture are important for any appreciation of the processes under way. They alone do not define the Kazakh migrant experience. The reader can only interrogate Diener's study though a lens that incorporates more universal theories of migration and migrant behavior.

Understanding how migration works at the global level is vital for anyone who hopes to understand population movements in Eurasia. At the same time, an understanding of the specifics of Eurasian migration can inform more universal theories. The millions of people who move across Eurasia each year are motivated by economic incentives, social networks, and political realities similar to those of migrants the world over. Nevertheless, specific aspects of Eurasian history have shaped, and are continuing to shape, migration processes in the region. The strong regional identity, dense social and economic networks, and close political ties that developed during the Soviet period have facilitated temporary and circular (and often undocumented) migration throughout the region. The legacies of state-ascribed national identity, official national homelands, and ethnic cleansing and deportation have demonstrated the very strong attachments that people can feel toward specific places, even in an era of transnationalism.

The contributors to this volume powerfully demonstrate the importance of migration for understanding the future of Central Eurasia as well as the potential significance of the experience of the region's migrants for migration theory more universally defined. The contributors write about a search for home in a region where far too many homes have been destroyed during the past century. More than most regions of the world, the territory under examination in this volume has been the site of history's most appalling outbreaks of ethnic cleansing. Collectively, the contributors reveal opportunities for migration and diversity to become a positive norm for the region, as well as potential obstacles that can only sour the migration reality for all.

The hundreds of thousands of people moving across the Central Eurasian landmass at this moment can only go home if the region's societies and leaders define a place in their own homes for people other than themselves. This book leaves open the question of the future of the region's communities. The answer hinges on whether that future will be defined by those who falsely believe that their communities are homogeneous or by the heterogeneous populations that are already in place. Which group exerts the larger influence will have a lot to say about the region's prospects in the years ahead. Godot has already arrived.

Contributors

Bruce F. Adams teaches Russian history at the University of Louisville. He has been researching the emigration of Russians to China in the twentieth century and the reemigration of some of those émigrés and refugees to the Soviet Union later in the century. His article "Repatrianty iz Kitaia v SSSR: Problemy integratsii v sovetskoe obshchestvo, 1934–1960-e gg," coauthored with Natasha Ablazhei, appeared in *Sotsial'no-demograficheskoe razvitie Sibiri v XX stoletii* in Novosibirsk in 2003. He recently presented a paper on another aspect of the reemigration at the Australasian Association for European History Conference in Melbourne. His most recent book is *Tiny Revolutions in Russia: Twentieth-Century Soviet and Russian History in Anecdotes* (Routledge, 2005). He is also editor of the *Supplement* to the *Modern Encyclopedia of Russian, Soviet, and Eurasian History* (Academic International Press).

Cynthia J. Buckley is associate professor in the Department of Sociology at the University of Texas, Austin. She received her MA and PhD in sociology from the University of Michigan, where she also received an MA in Russian and East European studies and a BA in economics. She has published numerous articles on health, migration, and citizenship in Eurasia and other regions in journals such as *Studies in Family Planning, International Migration Review, International Migration,* and *Slavic Review.* Her chapter "The Ties That Bind: Citizenship and Regionalism in the Russian Federation," appeared in *Fragmented Space in the Russian Federation,* edited by Blair A. Ruble, Jodi Koehn, and Nancy E. Poson (Woodrow Wilson Center Press and Johns Hopkins University Press, 2001). From 2004 to 2005, she served as an expert consultant for the Flanders/UNESCO/UNAIDS Project on Sociocultural Coordinates of HIV/AIDS in the Caucasus.

Alexander Diener is an assistant professor of geography in the International Studies and Languages Division of Pepperdine University. He received his PhD from the University of Wisconsin–Madison in 2003. He is the author of *Homeland Conceptions and Ethnic Integration among Kazakhstan's Germans and Koreans* (Edwin Mellen Press, 2004). During 2003 and 2004, he was a research scholar at the Kennan Institute of the Woodrow Wilson International Center for Scholars. His interests range from political/cultural geography to security studies. He has published in journals such as *Europe-Asia Studies, Eurasian Geography and Economics, Nationalities Papers,* and *Central Eurasian Studies Review.*

Timothy Heleniak is a faculty research assistant in the Department of Geography at the University of Maryland. He has researched and written extensively on migration, demographic change, regional development, and Siberian/Arctic development in the countries of the former Soviet Union and Eastern Europe. Before coming to the University of Maryland, he worked at the U.S. Census Bureau, the World Bank, and the United Nations Children's Fund. He also taught courses on the demography and geography of the former Soviet Union as an adjunct faculty member at Georgetown University. He is on the editorial board of the journal *Eurasian Geography and Economics.*

Erin Trouth Hofmann is currently a PhD student in the Department of Sociology and a graduate trainee in the Population Research Center at the University of Texas, Austin. Her research interests are in demography and the former Soviet Union. From 2003 to 2006, she worked as a program assistant at the Kennan Institute of the Woodrow Wilson International Center for

Scholars. She holds a BA in international studies from American University and an MA in Russian and East European studies from Georgetown University.

Seema Iyer received her PhD in urban and regional planning in 2003 from the University of Michigan and has written about comprehensive plans and planning processes in post-Soviet Russia. She was a faculty lecturer in city and regional planning at the University of Pennsylvania until 2005, where she taught a graduate seminar on planning in postsocialist cities. She is currently chief of research and strategic planning for Baltimore City's Department of Planning.

Idil P. Izmirli is a doctoral candidate at the Institute for Conflict Analysis and Resolution, George Mason University. She holds a BS in physics from Istanbul University and an MA in sociology from George Mason University. Currently, she works as an adjunct faculty member at George Mason University and Strayer University. She is a recent recipient of the International Research and Exchanges Board's Individual Advanced Research Opportunities grant for 2005–6. In 2001 and 2002, she received grants from the U.S. State Department to teach undergraduate and graduate courses in conflict resolution and to conduct mediation and facilitation training at the National Taurida University in Simferopol, Crimea. Her research interests are international immigration, emigration, forced migrations, and refugees; cross-cultural adaptation and integration; conflict analysis and transformation; ethnopsychological aspects of identity and their implications for conflict behavior; ethnoreligious conflicts; the root causes of violence; nonviolence and strategic nonviolence; and early warning signs, preventive diplomacy, and multitrack diplomacy.

Andrei V. Korobkov is associate professor of political science at Middle Tennessee State University. He also serves as chair of the Post Communist States in International Relations section of the International Studies Association. He holds a PhD in political science from the University of Alabama and a PhD in economics from the Institute of Economics of World Socialist Systems of the USSR Academy of Sciences. His research interests include comparative migration policy, nationalism, interethnic relations, and economic development. He has published articles on post-Soviet migration in *Communist and Post-Communist Studies, Mediterranean Quarterly,* and *The Carl Beck Papers in Russian and East European Studies,* as well as in numerous journals in Russia, Portugal, Turkey, and Croatia. He is currently working on a monograph titled *Migration Aspects of the Post-Soviet Transition.*

Eric Lohr is an assistant professor of history at American University. He is founder and chair of the Washington Russian and East European History Workshop, held monthly at Georgetown University. He is the author of *Nationalizing the Russian Empire: The Campaign against Enemy Aliens during World War I* (Harvard University Press, 2003), coeditor with Marshall Poe of *Military and Society in Russian History, 1450–1917* (Brill, 2002), and editor of *The Papers of Grigorii N. Trubetskoi* (Hoover Institution Web site, 2006). His current book projects include a study of citizenship in Imperial Russia and revolutionary Russia and another on World War I and the end of the Russian Empire.

Ruth Mandel teaches anthropology at University College London. On the basis of her long-term research with the Turkish community in Germany, she has published numerous articles as well as a book, *Cosmopolitan Anxieties: Turkish Challenges to Citizenship and Belonging in Germany* (Duke University Press, 2007). She has also carried out research in Kazakhstan, on issues ranging from ethnicity and migration to international development. She is the coeditor, with Caroline Humphrey, of *Markets and Moralities: Ethnographies of Postsocialism* (Berg Press, 2002). She has been a Berlin Prize Fellow at the American Academy in Berlin and a Title VIII–supported research scholar at the Kennan Institute of the Woodrow Wilson International Center for Scholars.

J. Otto Pohl is associate professor of international and comparative politics at American University of Central Asia in Bishkek, Kyrgystan. He is the author of two books, *The Stalinist Penal System* (McFarland, 1997) and *Ethnic Cleansing in the USSR, 1937–1949* (Greenwood Press, 1999). For more than a decade, he has been researching and writing on the topic of Joseph Stalin's national deportations. He received his PhD in history from the School of Oriental and African Studies at the University of London in 2004.

Andrew Robarts is a PhD candidate in history at Georgetown University. He is a graduate of Bowdoin College and holds an MA in international relations from Georgetown University. His research interests include migration to and from Russia in both the Imperial and post-Soviet periods and the state regulation of population movements. From 1997 to 2003, he worked in the refugee and immigration fields in a variety of capacities, including at the International Rescue Committee and the Office of the United Nations High Commissioner for Refugees, with a professional focus on refugee relief and resettlement.

Blair A. Ruble is currently director of the Kennan Institute of the Woodrow Wilson International Center for Scholars in Washington. He also serves as director of comparative urban studies at the Woodrow Wilson Center. He received his MA and PhD in political science from the University of Toronto (1973, 1977), and an AB in political science, with highest honors, from the University of North Carolina at Chapel Hill (1971). He has edited more than a dozen volumes. His book-length works include a trilogy examining the fate of Russian provincial cities during the twentieth century: *Leningrad: Shaping a Soviet City* (University of California Press, 1990); *Money Sings! The Changing Politics of Urban Space in Post-Soviet Yaroslavl* (Woodrow Wilson Center Press and Cambridge University Press, 1995); and *Second Metropolis: Pragmatic Pluralism in Gilded Age Chicago, Silver Age Moscow, and Meiji Osaka* (Woodrow Wilson Center Press and Johns Hopkins University Press, 2001). His latest book is *Creating Diversity Capital: Transnational Migrants in Montreal, Washington, and Kyiv* (Woodrow Wilson Center Press and Johns Hopkins University Press, 2005).

Index